1sc : ch 2, 8-11

2nd : ch 1-2, 7 - 19

Saal Ansai

Rethinking the Western Tradition

The volumes in this series
seek to address the present debate
over the Western tradition
by reprinting key works of
that tradition along with essays
that evaluate each text from
different perspectives.

Two Treatises of Government

and

A Letter Concerning Toleration

JOHN LOCKE

Edited and with an Introduction by

Ian Shapiro

with essays by

John Dunn

Ruth W. Grant

Ian Shapiro

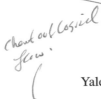

Yale University Press

New Haven and London

Published with assistance from the Annie Burr Lewis Fund.

Set in Times Roman type by Keystone Typesetting, Inc.
Printed in the United States of America by Vail-Ballou Press, Binghamton, New York.

ISBNs: 0-300-10017-5 (cl.)
0-300-10018-3 (pbk.)

A catalogue record for this book is available from
the Library of Congress and the British Library.
The paper in this book meets the guidelines
for permanence and durability of the Committee on
Production Guidelines for Book Longevity of the
Council on Library Resources.

10 9 8 7 6 5 4

Contributors

John Dunn is Fellow of King's College and Professor of Political Theory at the
University of Cambridge.
Ruth W. Grant is Professor of Political Science at Duke University.
Ian Shapiro is William R. Kenan, Jr., Professor and Chair of the Department of
Political Science at Yale University.

Contents

Introduction:
Reading Locke Today

IAN SHAPIRO

Old books are read for many reasons. Intrinsic enjoyment is one. Coming to
grips with the past is another. Understanding the origins of the world we
live in is a third. Additional purposes become relevant when old books are
part of a received canon. Canonized texts may be heralded as repositories of
important truths. They might codify ideologies, whether dominant or subversive. They might be objects of controversy as to their true meaning.
When canonized texts are works of political theory, it is usually because
they are thought to illuminate enduring fundamentals of political association. Sometimes they gain additional notoriety when they move people,
individually or collectively, to political action.

John Locke's mature writings about politics, collected here, are worth
reading for all these reasons at least. They have stood the test of time as
captivating works, in print more or less continuously for well over three
centuries and translated into all of the world's major languages. They are
remarkable historical documents addressed to the turbulent political conflicts of Locke's day, yet at the same time they transcend that and many
another particular context to which they have been deemed relevant. In
them Locke develops arguments about freedom of conscience and belief,
the relations between religion and politics, the nature of property, the family, consent, majority rule, resistance, and the foundations of political legitimacy that have become perennials of political argument in the modern
West. Locke's views on all these subjects are taken up in the interpretive
essays that follow the texts in this volume. Here I will limit myself to some
general remarks about his life and political writings.

As is frequently true with canonized texts—indeed this often facilitates
canonization—Locke's central arguments are sufficiently complex that
they invite disputations about their true meaning. Similar controversy attends the question whether Locke's political writings stand independently
of, are derived from, or live in tension with, his voluminous writings on
philosophy and theology, and the degree to which his views evolved over
the course of his lifetime. He was born in 1632 and died in 1704, so that his

life spanned one of the most tumultuous periods of English history. He was ten years old when England became divided by civil war and still at Westminster School when Charles I was executed nearby in 1649. He lived through the subsequent interregnum when various governments of the Commonwealth and Cromwell's Protectorate were in power, the subsequent Restoration of Charles II in 1660, and the radicalization of English politics in which he was sufficiently implicated so that he was forced into exile for most of the 1680s — returning only after the Glorious Revolution of 1688.

For a long time it was believed that the *Two Treatises,* first published in 1690, had been written as a justification for the Revolution. Locke had sympathized with Parliament's actions in forcing James II from the throne in response to his attempts to Catholicize the army, pack Parliament with his supporters, and suspend restrictions on his fellow Catholics. Following these and other provocations, the birth of James's son in 1688 made the possibility of a Catholic dynasty in England real, leading Parliament to act by replacing James with William and Mary and instituting significant constitutional constraints on the monarchy. The supremacy of Parliament, thus established, fit hand in glove with the concluding arguments of the *Second Treatise,* and seemed to be validated by the right to resist that lay at the heart of Locke's argument.

The received view of Locke as the philosopher of the Revolution and the *Two Treatises* as his manifesto has been conclusively debunked by Peter Laslett and Richard Ashcraft who established that the bulk of it had in fact been written almost a decade earlier, so that, whatever its purposes, justifying the Glorious Revolution was not among them.[1] The debate on dating the *Two Treatises* has not been resolved definitively, and quite possibly it never will be.[2] However, it now seems clear that most of it was written some time between 1679 and 1681 in the wake of the Exclusion Crisis during which Protestant nobles led by the Earl of Shaftesbury sought to exclude Charles II's Catholic brother James from the succession. It seems likely that initially much of it was written as an Exclusion tract, though Locke may well have revised and added extensively to it in the early 1680s when various plots were afoot to rid England of its monarch because of his pro-Catholic policies — plots in which certainly Shaftesbury, and probably Locke, were deeply implicated. It also seems clear that much of the material in the *First Treatise* — the entire document, if Laslett is to be believed — was written after the *Second Treatise* had been completed in response to the growing influence of Sir Robert Filmer's absolutist views after 1680.

Given this history, it is not surprising that the meaning and significance of Locke's political texts are continuing sources of scholarly controversy, as are the political implications people draw from them. In our own generation Locke's texts have been seen as repositories of the core ideas of bourgeois individualism, but also as providing the intellectual resources and ideological ballast for a radical critique of capitalism and a democratic assault on the liberal constitutionalism.[3] We are not special in this regard. Every generation has bred its Locke controversies, often — as is the case with ours — in ways that reflect and embody the great ideological contests of the day. Locke's standing in the ideological lexicon is sufficient to ensure that fighting over his corpse is one of the forms political argument takes.

Just as the exact role of Locke's ideas in English politics of the 1680s continues to be debated by historians, so does the nature and extent of his influence in subsequent political conflicts, most notably on eighteenth- and nineteenth-century English radicalism and on the architects of the American Revolution.[4] But it is beyond debate that what people have taken to be Locke's arguments have often been sources of political inspiration and activism to a greater degree than the historical Locke could ever have imagined. Although his influence on English high politics grew substantially in the last decade and a half of his life following 1688, he was an unlikely political champion. He lived most of his life before this in the shadows — first in a successful though not especially distinguished academic career at Oxford focused on medicine and philosophy that he began as a student in 1652; then, increasingly, in Shaftesbury's household as a physician, confidant, and tutor of children; and finally in exile in Holland and France after Shaftesbury's death in 1683.

Locke's long association with Shaftesbury, which had begun in the late 1660s when Locke deployed his skill as a physician (most likely supplemented by amazing luck) to plan and direct lifesaving surgery for Shaftesbury, lasted for the rest of Shaftesbury's life.[5] This relationship was the source of Locke's political influence, and, indeed, arguably of his intellectual maturity as well. But even in his last years, when Locke had become a figure of considerable eminence partly due to his changed political fortunes after the Revolution and partly due to the publication of his major philosophical work the *Essay Concerning Human Understanding* in his own name in 1689, he continued to keep his political writings anonymous. This was perhaps out of fear of the possibility that James II, who had fled to France in 1688, might reclaim the throne that Parliament had given William and Mary, or perhaps for other reasons. In any event, it was not until his

Sky - via Prvedsnyva

very last years that he began to allow the political writings to be attributed
to him, and then only among a small group of close acquaintances. The *Two
Treatises* were unambiguously acknowledged as his only in his will.

Locke's political views evolved considerably over the course of his
lifetime. Indeed, what is most remarkable about the young Locke given the
tenor of his mature political writings is how little interested he seems to
have been in politics or political theory. In the 1650s his principal interest
was in medicine, partly as a result of his interactions with Robert Boyle
(1627–1691) and others at the Oxford Experimental Philosophy Club. His
early work with Boyle was on the human blood, then a revolutionary field
following Harvey's discovery of the heart's circulatory function some decades earlier. Locke's medical researches with Boyle and later with the
major physician of his age, Thomas Sydenham (1624–1689), seem first to
have brought him to prominence — leading to his election as a Fellow of the
Royal Society in 1668. In philosophy the major formative influence on him
seems to have been Descartes, though from the beginning Locke's philosophical reflections took a more empirical bent. In his *Essays on the Law of
Nature,* probably prepared as lectures in his capacity as Censor of Moral
Philosophy at Christ Church in 1663 or 1664, we find Locke struggling —
less than altogether successfully — to render arguments from nature, reason, and Scripture mutually compatible. This concern would preoccupy
him for the rest of his life, with decisive implications for his moral and
political philosophy.[6]

To the extent that the young Locke had political views, they were conservative, or at any rate apolitical. His embrace of authoritarian arrangements seems largely to have been unreflective, and his early writing on
toleration gave no clue of the radical tolerationist stand in the *Letter Concerning Toleration* that was first published anonymously in Latin in 1689
(though probably written while he was in exile in 1685) and translated into
English more or less immediately by William Popple. Some scholars have
argued for greater continuity between his earlier and later writings, some
for less; this is not a controversy we will attempt to settle here.[7] It does seem
clear that despite some underlying conceptual continuities, he was radi-
calized politically during and after his association with Shaftesbury — even
if historians continue to debate the extent to which the radicalization of
Shaftesbury's circle reflected tactical maneuvering against the possibility of
a Catholic monarchy as distinct from genuine radical conviction. How
much the changes in Locke's views were accounted for by the association
between the two men and how much by other factors, such as the drift of
political events, no one can say. In any event, the *Letter* is an intensely

political document, geared to expanding toleration for Protestant nonconformists while denying it to Catholics — scarcely a surprising move in light
of not only the English political situation but also developments in France.
In 1685 Louis XIV had revoked the Edict of Nantes that had ensured some
toleration for Protestants for almost half a century. His brutal repression of
the Huguenots must surely have concentrated minds about what would
likely ensue across the Channel were Catholicism to become entrenched in
the English monarchy.

If Locke's *Letter* speaks directly to these concerns by arguing against
toleration for Catholics (along with atheists and "Mahometans") at the
same time as it presses for unusually broad toleration of Protestant nonconformists, his stance is not an unprincipled one. His reasons are political, not
religious: atheists cannot be trusted to keep their promises, and Catholics
and Mahometans are suspect because they owe allegiance to an alien
earthly power.[8] Moreover, commingling earthly religious authority with
political absolutism creates the danger that civil authority will try to tyran-
nize over the soul, which can never be justified or even, ultimately, successful because authentic religious belief requires "inward persuasion of the
mind." Herein lies the link between the *Letter* and Locke's broader political
theory developed in the *Two Treatises:* his doctrine that all legitimate political authority is rooted in the consent of the governed.

It has been clear since John Dunn's seminal study of the religious foundations of Lockean political theory that Locke was not embracing atomistic
individualism by taking this stand. Rather he was committed to a particular
view of the nature of religious belief and the relationship between the
individual and his creator that had to be rooted in authentic individual
commitment.[9] This led to his view that religious convictions of all sorts
should be tolerated so long as they do not threaten the integrity of the state,
but this was a view he affirmed, ultimately, for religious reasons. The goal
was to protect religion by freeing it as much as possible from state interference. In this pursuit, his impulse was comparable to that of the American
founders who would argue a century later for disestablishment of the
church in order to strengthen religion, not, as critics of the First Amendment
to the United States Constitution often seem to assume, to weaken it.

One cannot help but be struck by the affinities between Locke's argument in the *Letter* and John Stuart Mill's argument in *On Liberty,* even if
Mill's principle is more capacious in extending the realm of what must be
tolerated beyond religion and including all types of belief — even atheism
— within it. But there are important underlying differences.[10] Both writers
define the limits to toleration in political terms by reference to when beliefs

or actions become threatening to others, not by reference to any claim about the validity of the beliefs themselves. And, even though Locke was profoundly religious while Mill could scarcely conceal his hostility to religion in general and Christianity in particular, both saw freedom of conscience and belief as the surest path to discovery of the truth in human affairs. But at the end of the day, Mill's commitment to freedom was for its own sake — in this he was a true child of the Enlightenment. He saw individual freedom as the greatest good. For Locke, by contrast, freedom of conscience was valuable for the more Lutheran reason that he thought it essential to spiritual salvation. In this reasoning, as in many other matters taken up in our interpretive essays, Locke is something of a hybrid figure. He makes arguments that endure as defining features of political argument in the modern West, yet he does so in ways that reflect and embody premodern concerns. Reading Locke reveals that we have more complex links to our past than we might otherwise perceive.

NOTES

1. See the introduction to John Locke, *Two Treatises of Government,* Peter Laslett, ed. (Cambridge: Cambridge University Press, 1988), pp. 61, 123–26, and Richard Ashcraft, *Locke's Two Treatises of Government* (London: Allen & Unwin, 1987).

2. For the current state of the debate, see the introduction to Locke, *Political Writings of John Locke,* David Wootton, ed. (New York: Penguin Books, 1993), pp. 49–94.

3. Different variants of the bourgeois individualism charge were leveled by C. B. Macpherson, in *The Political Theory of Possessive Individualism: Hobbes to Locke* (Oxford: Oxford University Press, 1962), pp. 194–257, and Leo Strauss, *Natural Right and History* (Chicago: University of Chicago Press, 1971 [1953]), pp. 202–51. The case for Locke's political radicalism has been most trenchantly made by Richard Ashcraft in *Revolutionary Politics and Locke's Two Treatises of Government* (Princeton: Princeton University Press, 1986).

4. On the use of Locke's arguments by eighteenth- and nineteenth-century arguments over poor relief, see Richard Ashcraft, "Lockean Ideas, Poverty, and the Development of Liberal Political Theory," in John Brewer and Susan Staves, eds., *Early Modern Conceptions of Property* (London: Routledge, 1995), pp. 43–61. On the much debated subject of the relative influence of Lockean versus civic republican and other influences on the

American Revolution, see Bernard Bailyn, *The Ideological Origins of the American Revolution* (Cambridge, Mass.: Harvard University Press, 1967), and Gordon Wood, *The Creation of the American Republic* (New York: W. W. Norton, 1969).

5. See Peter Laslett's introduction in Locke, *Two Treatises of Government*, pp. 25–37.

6. On the relations among Locke's arguments from nature, reason, and Scripture as they affected his political philosophy, see Ian Shapiro, *The Evolution of Rights in Liberal Theory* (Cambridge: Cambridge University Press, 1986), pp. 80–148.

7. See J. W. Gough, "The Development of Locke's Belief in Toleration," and Paul J. Kelly, "John Locke: Authority, Conscience, and Religious Toleration," in Susan Mendus and John Horton, eds., *A Letter Concerning Toleration in Focus* (London: Routledge, 1991), pp. 57–77 and pp. 125–146, for the argument that his later views are reconcilable with his earlier writings. For the contrary view that there is a disjunction between his early authoritarian phase and his later radical one, see Maurice Cranston, "John Locke and the Case for Toleration," ibid., pp. 78–97.

8. This subject is explored at some length in my contribution to the present volume.

9. John Dunn, *The Political Thought of John Locke* (Cambridge: Cambridge University Press, 1969). The religious foundations of Lockean political theory were further explored by James Tully in *A Discourse Concerning Property: John Locke and His Adversaries* (Cambridge: Cambridge University Press, 1980). Perhaps the definitive treatment of Locke's religious views, particularly as they shape his attitude toward toleration, is John Marshall's *John Locke: Resistance, Religion and Responsibility* (Cambridge: Cambridge University Press, 1994).

10. See John Stuart Mill, *On Liberty* (Indianapolis: Hackett, 1978 [1859]).

Note on the Texts

The texts of Locke's *Two Treatises of Government* and *A Letter Concerning Toleration* used here are taken from volumes 5 and 6 of *The Works of John Locke* (10 vols.; London: Thomas Tegg, W. Sharpe and Son, G. Offor, G. and J. Robinson, J. Evans and Co., also R. Griffin and Co, Glasglow, and J. Cumming, Dublin, 1823). Obvious errors have been corrected.

Two
Treatises
of
Government.

IN THE FORMER,

THE FALSE PRINCIPLES AND

FOUNDATION OF SIR ROBERT FILMER,

AND HIS FOLLOWERS, ARE DETECTED

AND OVERTHROWN:

THE LATTER,

IS AN ESSAY CONCERNING THE TRUE

ORIGINAL, EXTENT, AND END, OF CIVIL

GOVERNMENT.

The Preface.

READER,

Thou hast here the beginning and end of a discourse concerning government; what fate has otherwise disposed of the papers that should have filled up the middle, and were more than all the rest, it is not worth while to tell thee. These which remain I hope are sufficient to establish the throne of our great restorer, our present king William; to make good his title in the consent of the people; which being the only one of all lawful governments, he has more fully and clearly than any prince in Christendom; and to justify to the world the people of England, whose love of their just and natural rights, with their resolution to preserve them, saved the nation when it was on the very brink of slavery and ruin. If these papers have that evidence I flatter myself is to be found in them, there will be no great miss of those which are lost, and my reader may be satisfied without them. For I imagine I shall have neither the time nor inclination to repeat my pains, and fill up the wanting part of my answer, by tracing sir Robert again through all the windings and obscurities which are to be met with in the several branches of his wonderful system. The king, and body of the nation, have since so thoroughly confuted his hypothesis, that I suppose nobody hereafter will have either the confidence to appear against our common safety, and be again an advocate for slavery; or the weakness to be deceived with contradictions dressed up in a popular style and well turned periods. For if any one will be at the pains himself, in those parts which are here untouched, to strip sir Robert's discourses of the flourish of doubtful expressions, and endeavour to reduce his words to direct, positive, intelligible propositions, and then compare them one with another, he will quickly be satisfied there was never so much glib nonsense put together in well sounding English. If he think it not worth while to examine his works all through, let him make an experiment in that part where he treats of usurpation; and let him try whether he can, with all his skill, make sir Robert intelligible and consistent with himself, or common sense. I should not speak so plainly of a gentleman, long since past answering, had not the pulpit, of late years, publicly owned his doctrine, and made it the current divinity of the times. It is necessary those men who, taking on them to be teachers, have so dangerously misled others, should be openly showed of what authority this their patriarch is, whom they have so blindly followed; that so they may either retract what upon so ill grounds they have vented, and cannot be maintained; or else justify those principles which they have preached up for Gospel, though they had no better an author than an English courtier. For I should not have writ against sir Robert, or taken the pains to show his mistakes, inconsistencies, and want of (what he so much boasts of, and pretends wholly to build on) Scripture-proofs, were there not men amongst us who, by crying up his books, and espousing his doctrine, save me from the reproach of writing against a dead adversary. They have been so zealous in this point, that if I have done him any wrong, I cannot hope they should spare me. I wish, where they have done the truth and the public wrong, they would be as ready to redress it, and allow its just weight to this reflection, viz. that there cannot be done a greater mischief to prince and people, than the propagating wrong notions concerning government; that so at last all times might not have reason to complain of the "drum ecclesiastic." If any one really concerned for truth undertake the confutation of my hypothesis, I promise him either to recant my mistake, upon fair conviction, or to answer his difficulties. But he must remember two things,

First, That cavilling here and there at some expression or little incident of my discourse, is not an answer to my book.

Secondly, That I shall not take railing for arguments, nor think either of these worth my notice: though I shall always look on myself as bound to give satisfaction to any one who shall appear to be conscientiously scrupulous in the point, and shall show any just grounds for his scruples.

I have nothing more but to advertise the reader, that A. stands for our author, O. for his Observations on Hobbes, Milton, &c. And that a bare quotation of pages always means pages of his Patriarcha, edit. 1680.

Contents

OF THE TWO
TREATISES OF GOVERNMENT.

Of
Government.

BOOK I: FIRST TREATISE

CHAPTER I.

§ 1. Slavery is so vile and miserable an estate of man, and so directly opposite to the generous temper and courage of our nation, that it is hardly to be conceived that an Englishman, much less a gentleman, should plead for it. And truly I should have taken sir Robert Filmer's Patriarcha, as any other treatise, which would persuade all men that they are slaves, and ought to be so, for such another exercise of wit as was his who writ the encomium of Nero; rather than for a serious discourse, meant in earnest: had not the gravity of the title and epistle, the picture in the front of the book, and the applause that followed it, required me to believe that the author and publisher were both in earnest. I therefore took it into my hands with all the expectation, and read it through with all the attention due to a treatise that made such a noise at its coming abroad; and cannot but confess myself mightily surprised that in a book, which was to provide chains for all mankind, I should find nothing but a rope of sand; useful perhaps to such whose skill and business it is to raise a dust, and would blind the people, the better to mislead them; but in truth not of any force to draw those into bondage who have their eyes open, and so much sense about them, as to consider that chains are but an ill wearing, how much care soever hath been taken to file and polish them.

§ 2. If any one think I take too much liberty in speaking so freely of a man who is the great champion of absolute power, and the idol of those who worship it; I beseech him to make this small allowance for once, to one who, even after the reading of sir Robert's book, cannot but think himself, as the laws allow him, a free man: and I know no fault it is to do so, unless any one, better skilled in the fate of it than I, should have it revealed to him that this treatise, which has lain dormant so long, was, when it appeared in the world, to carry, by strength of its arguments, all liberty out of it; and that, from thenceforth, our author's short model was to be the pattern in the mount, and the perfect standard of politics for the future. His system lies in a little compass; it is no more but this,

"That all government is absolute monarchy."

And the ground he builds on is this,

"That no man is born free."

§ 3. In this last age a generation of men has sprung up amongst us, that would flatter princes with an opinion, that they have a divine right to absolute power, let the laws by which they are constituted and are to govern, and the conditions under which they enter upon their authority, be what they will; and their engagements to observe them ever so well ratified by solemn oaths and promises. To make way for this doctrine, they have denied mankind a right to natural freedom; whereby they have not only, as much as in them lies, exposed all subjects to the utmost misery of tyranny and oppression, but have also unsettled the titles and shaken the thrones of princes: (for they too, by these men's system, except only one, are all born slaves, and by divine right are subjects to Adam's right heir); as if they had designed to make war upon all government, and subvert the very foundations of human society, to serve their present turn.

§ 4. However we must believe them upon their own bare words, when they tell us, "We are all born slaves, and we must continue so;" there is no remedy for it; life and thraldom we entered into together, and can never be quit of the one till we part with the other. Scripture or reason, I am sure, do not any where say so, notwithstanding the noise of divine right, as if divine authority hath subjected us to the unlimited will of another. An admirable state of mankind, and that which they have not had wit enough to find out till this latter age ! For however sir Robert Filmer seems to condemn the novelty of the contrary opinion, Patr. p. 3, yet I believe it will be hard for him to find any other age, or country of the world, but this, which has asserted monarchy to be *jure divino.* And he confesses, Patr. p. 4, that "Heyward, Blackwood, Barclay, and others, that have bravely vindicated the right of kings in most points, never thought of this; but, with one consent, admitted the natural liberty and equality of mankind."

§ 5. By whom this doctrine came at first to be broached, and brought in fashion amongst us, and what sad effects it gave rise to, I leave to historians to relate, or to the memory of those who were contemporaries with Sibthorp and Manwaring to recollect. My business at present is only to consider what sir Robert Filmer, who is allowed to have carried this argument farthest, and is supposed to have brought it to perfection, has said in it: for from him every one, who would be as fashionable as French was at court, has learned and runs away with this short system of politics, viz. "Men are not born free, and therefore could never have the liberty to choose either governors, or forms of government. "Princes have their power absolute, and by divine right; for slaves could never have a right to compact or consent. Adam was an absolute monarch, and so are all princes ever since.

CHAPTER II.

Of paternal and regal Power.

§ 6. Sir Robert Filmer's great position is, that "men are not naturally free." This is the foundation on which his absolute monarchy stands, and from which it erects itself to an height, that its power is above every power: *caput inter nubila,* so high above all earthly and human things, that thought can scarce reach it; that promises and oaths, which tie the infinite Deity, cannot confine it. But if this foundation fails, all his fabric falls with it, and governments must be left again to the old way of being made by contrivance and the consent of men (*'ANYRVPÍNH XTÍSIW*) making use of their reason to unite together into society. To prove this grand position of his, he tells us, p. 12, "Men are born in subjection to their parents," and therefore cannot be free. And this authority of parents he calls "royal authority," p. 12, 14, "fatherly authority, right of fatherhood," p. 12, 20. One would have thought he would, in the beginning of such a work as this, on which was to depend the authority of princes, and the obedience of subjects, have told us expressly what that fatherly authority is, have defined it, though not limited it, because in some other treatises of his he tells us, it is unlimited, and unlimitable *; he should at least have given us such an account of it, that we might have had an entire notion of this fatherhood, or fatherly authority,

---

* " In grants and gifts that have their original from God or nature, as the power of the father hath, no inferior power of man can limit, nor shake any law of prescription against them." Obs. 158.

"The Scripture teaches that supreme power was originally in the father, without any limitation." Obs. 245.

whenever it came in our way, in his writings: this I expected to have found in the first chapter of his Patriarcha. But instead thereof, having, 1. *En passant,* made his obeisance to the *arcana imperii,* p. 5; 2. Made his compliment to the "rights and liberties of this or any other nation," p. 6, which he is going presently to null and destroy; and 3. Made his leg to those learned men who did not see so far into the matter as himself, p. 7: he comes to fall on Bellarmine, p. 8, and by a victory over him establishes his fatherly authority beyond any question. Bellarmine being routed by his own confession, p. 11, the day is clear got, and there is no more need of any forces: for having done that, I observe not that he states the question, or rallies up any arguments to make good his opinion, but rather tells us the story as he thinks fit of this strange kind of domineering phantom called the fatherhood, which whoever could catch presently got empire, and unlimited absolute power. He acquaints us how this fatherhood began in Adam, continued its course, and kept the world in order all the time of the patriarchs till the flood; got out of the ark with Noah and his sons, made and supported all the kings of the earth till the captivity of the Israelites in Egypt; and then the poor fatherhood was under hatches, till "God, by giving the Israelites kings, re-established the ancient and prime right of the lineal succession in paternal government." This is his business from p. 12 to 19. And then, obviating an objection, and clearing a difficulty or two with one-half reason, p. 23, "to confirm the natural right of regal power," he ends the first chapter. I hope it is no injury to call an half quotation an half reason; for God says, "Honour thy father and mother;" but our author contents himself with half, leaves out "thy mother" quite, as little serviceable to his purpose. But of that more in another place.

§ 7. I do not think our author so little skilled in the way of writing discourses of this nature, nor so careless of the point in hand, that he by oversight commits the fault that he himself, in his "anarchy of a mixed monarchy," p. 239, objects to Mr. Hunton in these words: "Where first I charge the A. that he hath not given us any definition or description of monarchy in general; for by the rules of method he should have first defined." And by the like rule of method, sir Robert should have told us what his fatherhood, or fatherly authority is, before he had told us in whom it was to be found, and talked so much of it. But, perhaps, sir Robert found, that this fatherly authority, this power of fathers, and of kings, for he makes them both the same, p. 24, would make a very odd and frightful figure, and very disagreeing with what either children imagine of their parents, or subjects of their kings, if he should have given us the whole draught together, in that gigantic form he had painted it in his own fancy; and therefore, like a wary physician, when he would have his patient swallow some harsh or corrosive liquor, he mingles it with a large quantity of that which may dilute it, that the scattered parts may go down with less feeling, and cause less aversion.

§ 8. Let us then endeavour to find what account he gives us of this fatherly authority, as it lies scattered in the several parts of his writings. And first, as it was vested in Adam, he says, " Not only Adam, but the succeeding patriarchs, had, by right of fatherhood, royal authority over their children, p. 12. This lordship, which Adam by command had over the whole world, and by right descending from him the patriarchs did enjoy, was as large and ample as the absolute dominion of any monarch which hath been since the creation, p. 13. Dominion of life and death, making war, and concluding peace, p. 13. Adam and the patriarchs had absolute power of life and death, p. 35. Kings, in the right of parents, succeed to the exercise of supreme jurisdiction, p. 19. As kingly power is by the law of God, so it hath no inferior law to limit it; Adam was lord of all, p. 40. The father of a family governs by no other law than by his own will, p. 78. The superiority of princes is above laws, p. 79. The unlimited jurisdiction of kings is so amply described by Samuel, p. 80. Kings are above the laws," p. 93. And to this purpose see a great deal more, which our A. delivers in Bodin's words: " It is certain, that all laws, privileges, and grants of princes, have no force but during their life, if they be not ratified by the express consent, or by sufferance of the prince following, especially privileges, O. p. 279. The reason why laws have been also made by kings, was this: when kings were either busied with wars, or distracted with public cares, so that every private man could not have access to their persons, to learn their wills and pleasure, then were laws of necessity invented, that so every particular subject might find his prince's pleasure deciphered unto him in the tables of his laws, p. 92. In a monarchy, the king must by necessity be above the laws, p. 100. A perfect kingdom is that, wherein the king rules all things, according to his own will, p. 100. Neither common nor statute laws are, or can be, any diminution of that general power, which kings have over their people, by right of fatherhood, p. 115. Adam was the father, king, and lord over his family; a son, a subject, and a servant or slave, were one and the same thing at first. The father had power to dispose or sell his children or servants; whence we find, that, in the first reckoning up of goods in Scripture, the man-servant and the maid-servant are numbered among the possessions and substance of the owner, as other goods were, O. pref. God also hath given to the father a right or liberty to alien his power over his children to any other; whence we find the sale and gift of children to have been much in use in the beginning of the world, when men had their servants for a possession and an inheritance, as well as other goods; whereupon we find the power of castrating and making eunuchs much in use in old times, O. p. 155. Law is nothing else but the will of him that hath the power of the supreme father, O. p. 223. It was God's ordinance that the supremacy should be unlimited in Adam, and as large as all the acts of his will; and as in him, so in all others that have supreme power," O. p. 245.

§ 9. I have been fain to trouble my reader with these several quotations in our A.'s own words, that in them might be seen his own description of his fatherly authority, as it lies scattered up and down in his writings, which he supposes was first vested in Adam, and by right belongs to all princes ever since. This fatherly authority then, or right of fatherhood, in our A.'s sense, is a divine unalterable right of sovereignty, whereby a father or a prince hath an absolute, arbitrary, unlimited, and unlimitable power over the lives, liberties, and estates of his children and subjects; so that he may take or alienate their estates, sell, castrate, or use their persons as he pleases, they being all his slaves, and he lord or proprietor of every thing, and his unbounded will their law.

§ 10. Our A. having placed such a mighty power in Adam, and upon that supposition founded all government and all power of princes, it is reasonable to expect that he should have proved this with arguments clear and evident, suitable to the weightiness of the cause. That since men had nothing else left them, they might in slavery have such undeniable proofs of its necessity, that their consciences might be convinced, and oblige them to submit peaceably to that absolute dominion, which their governors had a right to exercise over them. Without this, what good could our A. do, or pretend to do, by erecting such an unlimited power, but flatter the natural vanity and ambition of men, too apt of itself to grow and increase with the possession of any power? And by persuading those, who, by the consent of their fellow-men, are advanced to great but limited degrees of it, that by that part which is given them, they have a right to all that was not so; and therefore may do what they please, because they have authority to do more than others, and so tempt them to do what is neither for their own, nor the good of those under their care; whereby great mischiefs cannot but follow.

§ 11. The sovereignty of Adam being that on which, as a sure basis, our A. builds his mighty absolute monarchy, I expected, that, in his Patriarcha, this his main supposition would have been proved and established with all that evidence of arguments that such a fundamental tenet required; and that this, on which the great stress of the business depends, would have been made out, with reasons sufficient to justify the confidence with which it was assumed. But, in all that treatise, I could find very little tending that way; the thing is there so taken for granted, without proof, that I could scarce believe myself, when, upon attentive reading that treatise, I found there so mighty a structure raised upon the bare supposition of this foundation. For it is scarce credible, that in a discourse, where he pretends to confute the erroneous principle of man's natural freedom, he should do it by a bare supposition of Adam's authority, without offering any proof for that authority. Indeed, he confidently says, that Adam had "royal authority, p. 12 and 13. Absolute lordship and dominion of life and death, p. 13. An universal monarchy, p. 33. Absolute power of life and death," p. 35. He is very frequent in such assertions; but, what is strange, in all his whole Patriarcha, I find not one pretence of a reason to establish this his great foundation of government; not any thing that looks like an argument, but these words: "To confirm this natural right of regal power, we find in the decalogue, that the law which enjoins obedience to kings, is delivered in the terms, Honour thy father; as if all power were originally in the father." And why may I not add as well, that in the decalogue the law that enjoins obedience to queens, is delivered in the terms of "Honour thy mother," as if all power were originally in the mother? The argument, as sir Robert puts it, will hold as well for one as the other; but of this more in its due place.

§ 12. All that I take notice of here is, that this is all our A. says, in this first, or any of the following chapters, to prove the absolute power of Adam, which is his great principle: and yet, as if he had there settled it upon sure demonstration, he begins his second chapter with these words, "By conferring these proofs and reasons, drawn from the authority of the Scripture." Where those proofs and reasons for Adam's sovereignty are, bating that of Honour thy father, above-mentioned, I confess, I cannot find; unless what he says, p. 11, "In these words we have an evident confession," viz. of Bellarmine, "that creation made man prince of his posterity," must be taken for proofs and reasons drawn from Scripture, or for any sort of proof at all: though from thence, by a new way of inference, in the words immediately following, he concludes the royal authority of Adam sufficiently settled in him.

§ 13. If he has in that chapter, or any where in the whole treatise, given any other proofs of Adam's royal authority, other than by often repeating it, which, among some men, goes for argument, I desire any body for him to show me the place and page, that I may be convinced of my mistake, and acknowledge my oversight. If no such arguments are to be found, I beseech those men, who have so much cried up this book, to consider, whether they do not give the world cause to suspect, that it is not the force of reason and argument that makes them for absolute monarchy, but some other by interest, and therefore are resolved to applaud any author that writes in favour of this doctrine, whether he support it with reason or no. But I hope they do not expect, that rational and indifferent men should be brought over to their opinion, because this their great doctor of it, in a discourse made on purpose to set up the absolute monarchical power of Adam, in opposition to the natural freedom of mankind, has said so little to prove it, from whence it is rather naturally to be concluded, that there is little to be said.

§ 14. But that I might omit no care to inform myself in our author's full sense, I consulted his Observations on Aristotle, Hobbes, &c. to see whether in disputing with others he made use of any arguments for this his darling tenet of Adam's sovereignty; since in his treatise of the Natural Power of Kings; he hath been so sparing of them. In his Observations on Mr. Hobbes's Leviathan, I think he has put, in short, all those arguments for it together, which in his writings I find him any where to make use of: his words are these: "If God created only Adam, and of a piece of him made the woman, and if by generation from them two, as parts of them, all mankind be propagated: if also God gave to Adam not only the dominion over the woman and the children that should issue from them, but also over all the earth to subdue it, and over all the creatures on it, so that, as long as Adam lived, no man could claim or enjoy any thing but by donation, assignation, or permission from him, I wonder," &c. Obs. 165. Here we have the sum of all his arguments, for Adam's sovereignty, and against natural freedom, which I find up and down in his other treatises: and they are these following; "God's creation of Adam, the dominion he gave him over Eve, and the dominion he had as father over his children;" all which I shall particularly consider.

CHAPTER III.

Of Adam's Title to Sovereignty by Creation.

§ 15. Sir Robert, in his preface to his Observations on Aristotle's Politics, tells us, "A natural freedom of mankind cannot be supposed, without the denial of the creation of Adam:" but how Adam's being created, which was nothing but his receiving a being, immediately from Omnipotency, and the hand of God, gave Adam a sovereignty over any thing, I cannot see; nor consequently understand, how a supposition of natural freedom is a denial of Adam's creation; and would be glad any body else (since our A. did not vouchsafe us the favour) would make it out for him. For I find no difficulty to suppose the freedom of mankind, though I have always believed the creation of Adam. He was created, or began to exist, by God's immediate power, without the intervention of parents, or the pre-existence of any of the same species to beget him, when it pleased God he should; and so did the lion, the king of beasts, before him, by the same creating power of God: and if bare existence by that power, and in that way, will give dominion, without any more ado, our A. by this argument, will make the lion have as good a title to it as he, and certainly the ancienter. No; for Adam had his title "by the appointment of God," says our A. in another place. Then bare creation gave him not dominion, and one might have supposed mankind free, without the denying the creation of Adam, since it was God's appointment made him monarch.

§ 16. But let us see how he puts his creation and this appointment together. "By the appointment of God, says sir Robert, as soon as Adam was created, he was monarch of the world, though he had no subjects; for though there could not be actual government till there were subjects, yet by the right of nature it was due to Adam to be governor of his posterity: though not in act, yet at least in habit, Adam was a king from his creation." I wish he had told us here, what he meant by God's appointment. For whatsoever providence orders, or the law of nature directs, or positive revelation declares, may be said to be by God's appointment: but I suppose it cannot be meant here in the first sense, *i.e.* by providence; because that would be to say no more, but that as soon as Adam was created, he was *de facto* monarch, because by right of nature it was due to Adam to be governor of his posterity. But he could not, *de facto,* be by providence constituted the governor of the world, at a time when there was actually no government, no subjects to be governed, which our A. here confesses. Monarch of the world is also differently used by our A., for sometimes he means by it a proprietor of all the world, exclusive of the rest of mankind, and thus he does in the same page of his preface before cited: "Adam, says he, being commanded to multiply and people the earth, and subdue it, and having dominion given him over all creatures, was thereby the monarch of the whole world; none of his posterity had any right to possess any thing but by his grant or permission, or by succession from him." 2. Let us understand then, by monarch, proprietor of the world, and, by appointment, God's actual donation, and revealed positive grant made to Adam, Gen. i. 28, as we see sir Robert himself does in this parallel place; and then his argument will stand thus: "by the positive grant of God: as soon as Adam was created, he was proprietor of the world, because by the right of nature it was due to Adam to be governor of his posterity." In which way of arguing there are two manifest falsehoods. First, it is false, that God made that grant to Adam, as soon as he was created, since, though it stands in the text immediately after his creation, yet it is plain it could not be spoken to Adam till after Eve was made and brought to him; and how then could he be monarch by appointment as soon as created, especially since he calls, if I mistake not, that which God says to Eve, Gen. iii. 16, the original grant of government, which not being till after the fall, when Adam was somewhat, at least in time, and very much distant in condition, from his creation, I cannot see, how our A. can say in this sense, that, "by God's appointment, as soon as Adam was created, he was monarch of the world." Secondly, were it true, that God's actual donation "appointed Adam monarch of the world, as soon as he was created," yet the reason here given for it would not prove it; but it would always be a false inference that God, by a positive donation, "appointed Adam monarch of the world, because by right of nature it was due to Adam to be governor of his posterity:" for having given him the right of government by nature, there was no need of a positive donation; at least it will never be a proof of such a donation.

§ 17. On the other side, the matter will not be much mended, if we understand by God's appointment the law of nature, (though it be a pretty harsh expression for it in this place) and by monarch of the world, sovereign ruler of mankind: for then the sentence under consideration must run thus: "By the law of nature, as soon as Adam was created he was governor of mankind, for by right of nature it was due to Adam to be governor of his posterity;" which amounts to this, he was governor by right of nature, because he was governor by right of nature. But supposing we should grant, that a man is by nature governor of his children, Adam could not hereby be monarch as soon as created: for this right of nature being founded in his being their father, how Adam could have a natural right to be governor, before he was a father, when by being a father only he had that right, is, methinks, hard to conceive, unless he would have him to be a father before he was a father, and have a title before he had it.

§ 18. To this foreseen objection, our A. answers very logically, "He was governor in habit, and not in act:" a very pretty way of being a governor without government, a father without children, and a king without subjects. And thus sir Robert was an author before he writ his book; not in act, it is true, but in habit; for when he had once published it, it was due to him, by the right of nature, to be an author, as much as it was to Adam to be governor of his children, when he had begot them; and if to be such a monarch of the world, an absolute monarch in habit, but not in act, will serve the turn, I should not much envy it to any of sir Robert's friends, that he thought fit graciously to bestow it upon; though even this of act and habit, if it signified any thing but our A.'s skill in distinctions, be not to his purpose in this place. For the question is not here about Adam's actual exercise of government, but actually having a title to be governor. Government, says our A. was "due to Adam by the right of nature:" what is this right of nature? A right fathers have over their children by begetting them; *generatione jus acquiritur parentibus in liberos,* says our A. out of Grotius, de J. B. P. L. 2. C. 5. S. 1. The right then follows the begetting as arising from it; so that, according to this way of reasoning or distinguishing of our A. Adam, as soon as he was created, had a title only in habit, and not in act, which in plain English is, he had actually no title at all.

§ 19. To speak less learnedly, and more intelligibly, one may say of Adam, he was in a possibility of being governor, since it was possible he might beget children, and thereby acquire that right of nature, be it what it will, to govern them, that accrues from thence: but what connexion has this with Adam's creation, to make him say, that "as soon as he was created, he was monarch of the world?" For it may as well be said of Noah, that as soon as he was born he was monarch of the world, since he was in possibility (which in our A.'s sense is enough to make a monarch, "a monarch in habit,") to outlive all mankind but his own posterity. What such necessary connexion there is betwixt Adam's creation and his right to government, so that a "natural freedom of mankind cannot be supposed without the denial of the creation of Adam," I confess for my part I do not see; nor how those words, "by the appointment," &c. Obs. 254, however explained, can be put together, to make any tolerable sense, at least to establish this position, with which they end, viz. "Adam was a king from his creation;" a king, says our author, "not in act, but in habit," *i. e.* actually no king at all.

§ 20. I fear I have tired my reader's patience, by dwelling longer on this passage than the weightiness of any argument in it seems to require: but I have unavoidably been engaged in it by our author's way of writing, who, huddling several suppositions together, and that in doubtful and general terms, makes such a medley and confusion, that it is impossible to show his mistakes, without examining the several senses wherein his words may be taken, and without seeing how, in any of these various meanings, they will consist together, and have any truth in them: for in this present passage before us, how can any one argue against this position of his, "that Adam was a king from his creation," unless one examine, whether the words,

"from his creation," be to be taken, as they may, for the time of the com-
mencement of his government, as the foregoing words import, "as soon as
he was created he was monarch;" or, for the cause of it, as he says, p. 11,
"creation made man prince of his posterity?" How farther can one judge of
the truth of his being thus king, till one has examined whether king be to be
taken, as the words in the beginning of this passage would persuade, on
supposition of his private dominion, which was, by God's positive grant,
"monarch of the world by appointment;" or king on supposition of his
fatherly power over his offspring, which was by nature, "due by the right of
nature;" whether, I say, king be to be taken in both, or one only of these two
senses, or in neither of them, but only this, that creation made him prince, in
a way different from both the other? For though this assertion, that "Adam
was king from his creation," be true in no sense, yet it stands here as an
evident conclusion drawn from the preceding words, though in truth it be
but a bare assertion joined to other assertions of the same kind, which
confidently put together in words of undetermined and dubious meaning,
look like a sort of arguing, when there is indeed neither proof nor connexion; a way very familiar with our author; of which having given the
reader a taste here, I shall, as much as the argument will permit me, avoid
touching on hereafter; and should not have done it here, were it not to let the
world see, how incoherences in matter, and suppositions without proofs,
put handsomely together in good words and a plausible style, are apt to pass
for strong reason and good sense, till they come to be looked into with
attention.

CHAPTER IV.

Of Adam's Title to Sovereignty, by Donation, Gen. i. 28.

§ 21. Having at last got through the foregoing passage, where we have
been so long detained, not by the force of arguments and opposition, but by
the intricacy of the words, and the doubtfulness of the meaning; let us go on
to his next argument, for Adam's sovereignty. Our author tells us in the
words of Mr. Selden, that "Adam by donation from God, Gen. i. 28, was
made the general lord of all things, not without such a private dominion to
himself, as without his grant did exclude his children. This determination of
Mr. Selden, says our author, is consonant to the history of the Bible, and

natural reason," Obs. 210. And in his Pref. to his Observations on Aristotle, he says thus, "The first government in the world was monarchical in the father of all flesh, Adam being commanded to multiply and people the earth, and to subdue it, and having dominion given him over all creatures, was thereby the monarch of the whole world. None of his posterity had any right to possess any thing, but by his grant or permission, or by succession from him. The earth, saith the Psalmist, hath he given to the children of men, which shows the title comes from fatherhood."

§ 22. Before I examine this argument, and the text on which it is founded, it is necessary to desire the reader to observe, that our author, according to his usual method, begins in one sense, and concludes in another; he begins here with Adam's propriety, or private dominion, by donation; and his conclusion is, "which shows the title comes from fatherhood."

§ 23. But let us see the argument. The words of the text are these: "And God blessed them, and God said unto them, Be fruitful and multiply, and replenish the earth and subdue it, and have dominion over the fish of the sea, and over the fowl of the air, and over every living thing that moveth upon the earth," Gen. i. 28; from whence our author concludes, "that Adam, having here dominion given him over all creatures, was thereby the monarch of the whole world:" whereby must be meant, that either this grant of God gave Adam property, or, as our author calls it, private dominion over the earth, and all inferior or irrational creatures, and so consequently that he was thereby monarch; or, 2dly, that it gave him rule and dominion over all earthly creatures whatsoever, and thereby over his children; and so he was monarch: for, as Mr. Selden has properly worded it, "Adam was made general lord of all things," one may very clearly understand him, that he means nothing to be granted to Adam here but property, and therefore he says not one word of Adam's monarchy. But our author says, "Adam was hereby monarch of the world," which, properly speaking, signifies sovereign ruler of all the men in the world; and so Adam, by this grant, must be constituted such a ruler. If our author means otherwise, he might with much clearness have said, that "Adam was hereby proprietor of the whole world." But he begs your pardon in that point: clear distinct speaking not serving every where to his purpose, you must not expect it in him, as in Mr. Selden, or other such writers.

§ 24. In opposition, therefore, to our author's doctrine, that "Adam was monarch of the whole world," founded on this place, I shall show,

1. That by this grant, Gen. i. 28, God gave no immediate power to Adam over men, over his children, over those of his own species; and so he was not made ruler, or monarch, by this charter.

2. That by this grant God gave him not private dominion over the inferior creatures, but right in common with all mankind; so neither was he monarch upon the account of the property here given him.

§ 25. 1. That this donation, Gen. i. 28, gave Adam no power over men, will appear if we consider the words of it: for since all positive grants convey no more than the express words they are made in will carry, let us see which of them here will comprehend mankind, or Adam's posterity; and those I imagine, if any, must be these, "every living thing that moveth:" the words in Hebrew are רמשת חיה הרמשת, *i. e. bestiam reptantem*, of which words the Scripture itself is the best interpreter: God having created the fishes and fowls the 5th day, the beginning of the 6th, he creates the irrational inhabitants of the dry land, which, ver. 24, are described in these words, "Let the earth bring forth the living creature after his kind; cattle and creeping things, and beasts of the earth, after his kind; and ver. 2, and God made the beasts of the earth after his kind, and cattle after their kind, and every thing that creepeth on the earth after his kind:" here, in the creation of the brute inhabitants of the earth, he first speaks of them all under one general name, of living creatures, and then afterwards divides them into three ranks, 1. Cattle, or such creatures as were or might be tame, and so be the private possession of particular men; 2. חיה which, ver. 24, 25, in our Bible, is translated beasts, and by the Septuagint θηρία, wild beasts, and is the same word, that here in our text, ver. 28, where we have this great charter to Adam, is translated living thing, and is also the same word used, Gen. ix. 2, where this grant is renewed to Noah, and there likewise translated beast. 3. The third rank were the creeping animals, which, ver. 24, 25, are comprised under the word, חרמשת, the same that is used here, ver. 28, and is translated moving, but in the former verses creeping, and by the Septuagint in all these places, ἑρπετὰ, or reptiles; from whence it appears, that the words which we translate here in God's donation, ver. 28, "living creatures moving," are the same, which in the history of the creation, ver. 24, 25, signify two ranks of terrestrial creatures, viz. wild beasts and reptiles, and are so understood by the Septuagint.

§ 26. When God had made the irrational animals of the world, divided into three kinds, from the places of their habitation, viz. fishes of the sea, fowls of the air, and living creatures of the earth, and these again into cattle, wild beasts, and reptiles; he considers of making man, and the dominion he should have over the terrestrial world, ver. 26, and then he reckons up the inhabitants of these three kingdoms, but in the terrestrial leaves out the second rank חיה or wild beasts: but here, ver. 28, where he actually exercises this design, and gives him this dominion, the text mentions the fishes

of the sea, and fowls of the air, and the terrestrial creatures in the words
that signify the wild beasts and reptiles, though translated living thing that
moveth, leaving out cattle. In both which places, though the word that
signifies wild beasts be omitted in one, and that which signifies cattle in the
other, yet, since God certainly executed in one place, what he declares he
designed in the other, we cannot but understand the same in both places,
and have here only an account how the terrestrial irrational animals, which
were already created and reckoned up at their creation, in three distinct
ranks of cattle, wild beasts, and reptiles, were here, ver. 28, actually put
under the dominion of man, as they were designed, ver. 26; nor do these
words contain in them the least appearance of any thing that can be wrested
to signify God's giving to one man dominion over another, to Adam over
his posterity.

§ 27. And this further appears from Gen. ix. 2, where God renewing this
charter to Noah and his sons, he gives them dominion over the fowls of the
air, and the fishes of the sea, and the terrestrial creatures, expressed by חיה
דרמש wild beasts and reptiles, the same words that in the text before us, Gen.
i. 28, are translated every moving thing that moveth on the earth, which by
no means can comprehend man, the grant being made to Noah and his sons,
all the men then living, and not to one part of men over another; which is yet
more evident from the very next words, ver. 3, where God gives every רמש
"every moving thing," the very words used ch. i. 28, to them for food. By
all which it is plain that God's donation to Adam, ch. i. 28, and his designation, ver. 26, and his grant again to Noah and his sons; refer to, and contain
in them, neither more nor less than the works of the creation the fifth day,
and the beginning of the sixth, as they are set down from the 20th to 26th
ver. inclusively of the 1st ch. and so comprehend all the species of irrational
animals of the terraqueous globe; though all the words, whereby they are
expressed in the history of their creation, are nowhere used in any of the
following grants, but some of them omitted in one, and some in another.
From whence I think it is past all doubt that man cannot be comprehended
in this grant, nor any dominion over those of his own species be conveyed
to Adam. All the terrestrial irrational creatures are enumerated at their
creation, ver. 25, under the names, "beasts of the earth, cattle, and creeping
things;" but man, being not then created, was not contained under any of
those names; and therefore, whether we understand the Hebrew words right
or no, they cannot be supposed to comprehend man, in the very same
history, and the very next verses following, especially since that Hebrew
word רמש which, if any in this donation to Adam, ch. i. 28, must comprehend man, is so plainly used in contradistinction to him, as Gen. vi. 20. vii.

14, 21, 23. Gen. viii. 17, 19. And if God made all mankind slaves to Adam and his heirs, by giving Adam dominion over "every living thing that moveth on the earth," ch. i. 28, as our author would have it; methinks sir Robert should have carried his monarchical power one step higher, and satisfied the world that princes might eat their subjects too, since God gave as full power to Noah and his heirs, ch. ix. 2, to eat "every living thing that moveth," as he did to Adam to have dominion over them; the Hebrew word in both places being the same.

§ 28. David, who might be supposed to understand the donation of God in this text, and the right of kings too, as well as our author, in his comment on this place, as the learned and judicious Ainsworth calls it, in the 8th Psalm, finds here no such charter of monarchical power: his words are, "Thou has made him, *i. e.* man, the son of man, a little lower than the angels; thou madest him to have dominion over the works of thy hands; thou hast put all things under his feet, all sheep and oxen, and the beasts of the field, and fowls of the air, and fish of the sea, and whatsoever passeth through the paths of the sea." In which words, if any one can find out, that there is meant any monarchical power of one man over another, but only the dominion of the whole species of mankind over the inferior species of creatures, he may, for aught I know, deserve to be one of sir Robert's monarchs in habit, for the rareness of the discovery. And by this time, I hope it is evident, that he that gave "dominion over every living thing that moveth on the earth," gave Adam no monarchical power over those of his own species, which will yet appear more fully in the next thing I am to show.

§ 29. 2. Whatever God gave by the words of this grant, Gen. i. 28, it was not to Adam in particular, exclusive of all other men: whatever dominion he had thereby, it was not a private dominion, but a dominion in common with the rest of mankind. That this donation was not made in particular to Adam, appears evidently from the words of the text, it being made to more than one; for it was spoken in the plural number, God blessed them, and said unto them, have dominion. God says unto Adam and Eve, have dominion; thereby, says our author, "Adam was monarch of the world:" but the grant being to them, *i. e.* spoken to Eve also, as many interpreters think with reason, that these words were not spoken till Adam had his wife, must not she thereby be lady, as well as he lord of the world? If it be said that Eve was subjected to Adam, it seems she was not so subjected to him as to hinder her dominion over the creatures, or property in them: for shall we say that God ever made a joint grant to two, and one only was to have the benefit of it?

§ 30. But perhaps it will be said Eve was not made till afterward: grant it so, what advantage will our author get by it? The text will be only the more directly against him, and show that God, in this donation, gave the world to mankind in common, and not to Adam in particular. The word them in the text must include the species of man, for it is certain *them* can by no means signify Adam alone. In the 26th verse, where God declares his intention to give this dominion, it is plain he meant that he would make a species of creatures that should have dominion over the other species of this terrestrial globe. The words are, "And God said, let us make man in our image, after our likeness, and let them have dominion over the fish," &c. They then were to have dominion. Who? even those who were to have the image of God, the individuals of that species of man that he was going to make; for that *them* should signify Adam singly, exclusive of the rest that should be in the world with him, is against both Scripture and all reason: and it cannot possibly be made sense, if man in the former part of the verse do not signify the same with *them* in the latter; only man there, as is usual, is taken for the species, and *them* the individuals of that species: and we have a reason in the very text. God makes him "in his own image, after his own likeness; makes him an intellectual creature, and so capable of dominion:" for whereinsoever else the image of God consisted, the intellectual nature was certainly a part of it, and belonged to the whole species, and enabled them to have dominion over the inferior creatures; and therefore David says, in the 8th Psalm above cited, "Thou hast made him little lower than the angels; thou hast made him to have dominion." It is not of Adam king David speaks here; for, verse 4, it is plain it is of man, and the son of man, of the species of mankind.

§ 31. And that this grant spoken to Adam was made to him, and the whole species of man, is clear from our author's own proof out of the Psalmist. "The earth, saith the Psalmist, hath he given to the children of men, which shows the title comes from fatherhood." These are sir Robert's words in the preface before cited, and a strange inference it is he makes: "God hath given the earth to the children of men, *ergo* the title comes from fatherhood." It is pity the propriety of the Hebrew tongue had not used fathers of men, instead of children of men, to express mankind: then indeed our author might have had the countenance of the sounds of the words to have placed the title in the fatherhood. But to conclude, that the fatherhood had the right to the earth, because God gave it to the children of men, is a way of arguing peculiar to our author: and a man must have a great mind to go contrary to the sound as well as sense of the words before he could light on it. But the sense is yet harder, and more remote from our author's purpose: for as it stands in his preface it is to prove Adam's being monarch, and his reasoning is thus, "God gave the earth to the children of men, *ergo* Adam was monarch of the world." I defy any man to make a more pleasant conclusion than this, which cannot be excused from the most obvious absurdity, till it can be shown that by children of men, he who had no father, Adam alone is signified; but whatever our author does, the Scripture speaks not nonsense.

§ 32. To maintain this property and private dominion of Adam, our author labours in the following page to destroy the community granted to Noah and his sons, in that parallel place, Gen. ix. 1, 2, 3; and he endeavours to do it two ways.

1. Sir Robert would persuade us, against the express words of the Scripture, that what was here granted to Noah, was not granted to his sons in common with him. His words are, "As for the general community between Noah and his sons, which Mr. Selden will have to be granted to them, Gen. ix. 2, the text doth not warrant it." What warrant our author would have, when the plain express words of Scripture, not capable of another meaning, will not satisfy him, who pretends to build wholly on Scripture, is not easy to imagine. The text says, "God blessed Noah and his sons, and said unto them, *i. e.* as our author would have it, unto him: for, saith he, although the sons are there mentioned with Noah in the blessing, yet it may best be understood, with a subordination or benediction in succession," O. 211. That indeed is best for our author to be understood, which best serves to his purpose; but that truly may best be understood by any body else, which best agrees with the plain construction of the words, and arises from the obvious meaning of the place; and then with subordination and in succession will not be best understood in a grant of God, where he himself put them not, nor mentions any such limitation. But yet our author has reasons why it may best be understood so. "The blessing," says he in the following words, "might truly be fulfilled, if the sons, either under or after their father, enjoyed a private dominion," O. 211; which is to say, that a grant, whose express words give a joint title in present (for the text says, into your hands they are delivered) may best be understood with a subordination, or in succession; because it is possible that in subordination, or in succession, it may be enjoyed. Which is all one as to say, that a grant of any thing in present possession may best be understood of reversion; because it is possible one may live to enjoy it in reversion. If the grant be indeed to a father and to his sons after him, who is so kind as to let his children enjoy it presently in common with him, one may truly say, as to the event one will be as good as the other; but it can never be true that what the express words grant in possession, and in common, may best be understood to be in

reversion. The sum of all his reasoning amounts to this: God did not give to the sons of Noah the world in common with their father, because it was possible they might enjoy it under or after him. A very good sort of argument against an express text of Scripture: but God must not be believed, though he speaks it himself, when he says he does any thing which will not consist with sir Robert's hypothesis.

§ 33. For it is plain, however he would exclude them, that part of this benediction, as he would have it in succession, must needs be meant to the sons, and not to Noah himself at all: "Be fruitful and multiple, and replenish the earth," says God in this blessing. This part of the benediction, as appears by the sequel, concerned not Noah himself at all: for we read not of any children he had after the flood; and in the following chapter, where his posterity is reckoned up, there is no mention of any; and so this benediction in succession was not to take place till 350 years after: and to save our author's imaginary monarchy, the peopling of the world must be deferred 350 years; for this part of the benediction cannot be understood with subordination, unless our author will say that they must ask leave of their father Noah to lie with their wives. But in this one point our author is constant to himself in all his discourses; he takes care there should be monarchs in the world, but very little that there should be people; and indeed his way of government is not the way to people the world: for how much absolute monarchy helps to fulfil this great and primary blessing of God Almighty, "Be fruitful and multiply, and replenish the earth," which contains in it the improvement too of arts and sciences, and the conveniences of life; may be seen in those large and rich countries which are happy under the Turkish government, where are not now to be found one-third, nay in many, if not most parts of them, one-thirtieth, perhaps I might say not one-hundredth of the people, that were formerly, as will easily appear to any one, who will compare the accounts we have of it at this time with ancient history. But this by the by.

§ 34. The other parts of this benediction or grant are so expressed, that they must needs be understood to belong equally to them all; as much to Noah's sons as to Noah himself, and not to his sons with a subordination, or in succession. "The fear of you, and the dread of you, says God, shall be upon every beast," &c. Will any body but our author say that the creatures feared and stood in awe of Noah only, and not of his sons without his leave, or till after his death? And the following words, "into your hands they are delivered," are they to be understood as our author says, if your father please, or they shall be delivered into your hands hereafter? If this be to argue from Scripture, I know not what may not be proved by it; and I can scarce see how much this differs from that fiction and fancy, or how much a surer foundation it will prove than the opinions of philosophers and poets, which our author so much condemns in his preface.

§ 35. But our author goes on to prove, that "it may best be understood with a subordination, or a benediction in succession; for, says he, it is not probable that the private dominion which God gave to Adam, and by his donation, assignation, or cession to his children, was abrogated, and a community of all things instituted between Noah and his sons — Noah was left the sole heir of the world; why should it be thought that God would disinherit him of his birth right, and make him of all men in the world the only tenant in common with his children?" O. 211.

§ 36. The prejudices of our own ill-grounded opinions, however by us called probable, cannot authorize us to understand Scripture contrary to the direct and plain meaning of the words. I grant it is not probable that Adam's private dominion was here abrogated; because it is more than improbable (for it will never be proved) that Adam had any such private dominion: and since parallel places of Scripture are most probable to make us know how they may be best understood, there needs but the comparing this blessing here to Noah and his sons, after the flood, with that to Adam after the creation, Gen. i. 28, to assure any one that God gave Adam no such private dominion. It is probable, I confess, that Noah should have the same title, the same property and dominion after the flood, that Adam had before it: but since private dominion cannot consist with the blessing and grant God gave to him and his sons in common, it is a sufficient reason to conclude that Adam had none, especially since, in the donation made to him, there are no words that express it, or do in the least favour it; and then let my reader judge whether it may best be understood, when in the one place there is not one word for it, not to say what has been above proved, that the text itself proves the contrary; and in the other, the words and sense are directly against it.

§ 37. But our author says, "Noah was the sole heir of the world; why should it be thought that God would disinherit him of his birth right?" Heir indeed, in England, signifies the eldest son, who is by the law of England to have all his father's land; but where God ever appointed any such heir of the world, our author would have done well to have showed us; and how God disinherited him of his birth right, or what harm was done him if God gave his sons a right to make use of a part of the earth for support of themselves and families, when the whole was not only more than Noah himself, but infinitely more than they all could make use of, and the possessions of one could not at all prejudice, or, as to any use, straiten that of the other.

§ 38. Our author probably foreseeing he might not be very successful in persuading people out of their senses, and, say what he could, men would be apt to believe the plain words of Scripture, and think, as they saw, that the grant was spoken to Noah and his sons jointly; he endeavours to insinuate, as if this grant to Noah conveyed no property, no dominion; because "subduing the earth and dominion over the creatures are therein omitted, nor the earth once named." And therefore, says he, "there is a considerable difference between these two texts; the first blessing gave Adam a dominion over the earth and all creatures; the latter allows Noah liberty to use the living creatures for food: here is no alteration or diminishing of his title to a property of all things, but an enlargement only of his commons," O. 211. So that, in our author's sense, all that was said here to Noah and his sons, gave them no dominion, no property, but only enlarged the commons; their commons, I should say, since God says, "to you are they given;" though our author says *his ;* for as to Noah's sons, they, it seems, by sir Robert's appointment, during their father's lifetime, were to keep fasting-days.

§ 39. Any one but our author would be mightily suspected to be blinded with prejudice, that in all this blessing to Noah and his sons, could see nothing but only an enlargement of commons: for as to dominion, which our author thinks omitted, "the fear of you, and the dread of you, says God, shall be upon every beast," which I suppose expresses the dominion, or superiority, was designed man over the living creatures, as fully as may be; for in that fear and dread seems chiefly to consist what was given to Adam over the inferior animals, who, as absolute a monarch as he was, could not make bold with a lark or rabbit to satisfy his hunger, and had the herbs but in common with the beasts, as is plain from Gen. i. 2, 9, and 30. In the next place, it is manifest that in this blessing to Noah and his sons, property is not only given in clear words, but in a larger extent than it was to Adam. "Into your hands they are given," says God to Noah and his sons; which words, if they give not property, nay, property in possession, it will be hard to find words that can; since there is not a way to express a man's being possessed of any thing more natural, nor more certain, than to say, it is delivered into his hands. And ver. 3, to show, that they had then given them the utmost property man is capable of, which is to have a right to destroy any thing by using it: "Every moving thing that liveth, saith God, shall be meat for you;" which was not allowed to Adam in his charter. This our author calls "a liberty of using them for food, and also an enlargement of commons, but no alteration of property," O. 211. What other property man can have in the creatures, but the "liberty of using them," is hard to be understood: so that if the first blessing, as our author says, gave Adam "dominion over the creatures, and the blessing to Noah and his sons gave them "such a liberty to use them" as Adam had not; it must needs give them something that Adam with all his sovereignty wanted, something that one would be apt to take for a greater property; for certainly he has no absolute dominion over even the brutal part of the creatures, and the property he has in them is very narrow and scanty, who cannot make that use of them which is permitted to another. Should any one, who is absolute lord of a country, have bidden our author subdue the earth, and given him dominion over the creatures in it, but not have permitted him to have taken a kid or a lamb out of the flock to satisfy his hunger, I guess he would scarce have thought himself lord or proprietor of that land, or the cattle on it; but would have found the difference between "having dominion," which a shepherd may have, and having full property as an owner. So that, had it been his own case, sir Robert, I believe, would have thought here was an alteration, nay an enlarging of property; and that Noah and his children had by this grant not only property given them, but such a property given them in the creatures, as Adam had not: for however, in respect of one another, men may be allowed to have propriety in their distinct portions of the creatures; yet in respect of God the maker of heaven and earth, who is sole lord and proprietor of the whole world, man's propriety in the creatures is nothing but that "liberty to use them," which God has permitted; and so man's property may be altered and enlarged, as we see it here, after the flood, when other uses of them are allowed, which before were not. From all which I suppose it is clear, that neither Adam, nor Noah, had any "private dominion," any property in the creatures, exclusive of his posterity, as they should successively grow up into need of them, and come to be able to make use of them.

§ 40. Thus we have examined our author's argument for Adam's monarchy, founded on the blessing pronounced, Gen. i. 28. Wherein I think it is impossible for any sober reader to find any other but the setting of mankind above the other kinds of creatures in this habitable earth of ours. It is nothing but the giving to man, the whole species of man, as the chief inhabitant, who is the image of his Maker, the dominion over the other creatures. This lies so obvious in the plain words, that any one but our author would have thought it necessary to have shown, how these words, that seemed to say the quite contrary, gave "Adam monarchical absolute power" over other men, or the sole property in all the creatures; and methinks in a business of this moment, and that whereon he builds all that follows, he should have done something more than barely cite words, which apparently make against him; for I confess, I cannot see any thing in them tending to Adam's monarchy, or private dominion, but quite the contrary.

And I the less deplore the dulness of my apprehension herein, since I find the apostle seems to have as little notion of any such "private dominion of Adam" as I, when he says, "God give us all things richly to enjoy;" which he could not do, if it were all given away already to monarch Adam, and the monarchs his heirs and successors. To conclude, this text is so far from proving Adam sole proprietor, that, on the contrary, it is a confirmation of the original community of all things amongst the sons of men, which appearing from this donation of God, as well as other places of Scripture, the sovereignty of Adam, built upon his "private dominion," must fall, not having any foundation to support it.

§ 41. But yet, if after all any one will needs have it so, that by this donation of God Adam was made sole proprietor of the whole earth, what will this be to his sovereignty? and how will it appear, that propriety in land gives a man power over the life of another? or how will the possession even of the whole earth give any one a sovereign arbitrary authority over the persons of men? The most specious thing to be said is, that he that is proprietor of the whole world, may deny all the rest of mankind food, and so at his pleasure starve them, if they will not acknowledge his sovereignty, and obey his will. If this were true, it would be a good argument to prove, that there never was any such property, that God never gave any such private dominion; since it is more reasonable to think, that God, who bid mankind increase and multiply, should rather himself give them all a right to make use of the food and raiment, and other conveniences of life, the materials whereof he had so plentifully provided for them; than to make them depend upon the will of a man for their subsistence, who should have power to destroy them all when he pleased, and who, being no better than other men, was in succession likelier, by want and the dependence of a scanty fortune, to tie them to hard service, than by liberal allowance of the conveniencies of life to promote the great design of God, "increase and multiply:" he that doubts this, let him look into the absolute monarchies of the world, and see what becomes of the conveniencies of life, and the multitudes of people.

§ 42. But we know God hath not left one man so to the mercy of another, that he may starve him if he please: God, the Lord and Father of all, has given no one of his children such a property in his peculiar portion of the things of this world, but that he has given his needy brother a right to the surplusage of his goods; so that it cannot justly be denied him, when his pressing wants call for it: and therefore no man could ever have a just power over the life of another by right of property in land or possessions; since it would always be a sin, in any man of estate, to let his brother perish for want of affording him relief out of his plenty. As justice gives every man a title to the product of his honest industry, and the fair acquisitions of his ancestors descended to him; so charity gives every man a title to so much out of another's plenty as will keep him from extreme want, where he has no means to subsist otherwise: and a man can no more justly make use of another's necessity to force him to become his vassal, by withholding that relief God requires him to afford to the wants of his brother, than he that has more strength can seize upon a weaker, master him to his obedience, and with a dagger at his throat offer him death or slavery.

§ 43. Should any one make so perverse an use of God's blessings poured on him with a liberal hand; should any one be cruel and uncharitable to that extremity; yet all this would not prove that propriety in land, even in this case, gave any authority over the persons of men, but only that compact might; since the authority of the rich proprietor, and the subjection of the needy beggar, began not from the possession of the lord, but the consent of the poor man, who preferred being his subject to starving. And the man he thus submits to, can pretend to no more power over him than he has con-sented to, upon compact. Upon this ground a man's having his stores filled in a time of scarcity, having money in his pocket, being in a vessel at sea, being able to swim, &c. may as well be the foundation of rule and domin-ion, as being possessor of all the land in the world: any of these being sufficient to enable me to save a man's life, who would perish, if such assistance were denied him; and any thing, by this rule, that may be an occasion of working upon another's necessity to save his life, or any thing dear to him, at the rate of his freedom, may be made a foundation of sovereignty, as well as property. From all which it is clear, that though God should have given Adam private dominion, yet that private dominion could give him no sovereignty: but we have already sufficiently proved that God gave him no "private dominion."

CHAPTER V.

Of Adam's Title to Sovereignty, by the Subjection of Eve.

§ 44. The next place of Scripture we find our author builds his monarchy of Adam on, is Gen. iii. 26. "And thy desire shall be to thy husband, and he shall rule over thee. Here we have (says he) the original grant of government," from whence he concludes, in the following part of the page, O. 244, "That the supreme power is settled in the fatherhood, and limited to one kind of government, that is, to monarchy." For let his premises be what they will, this is always the conclusion; let rule, in any text, be but once named, and presently absolute monarchy is by divine right established. If any one will but carefully read our author's own reasoning from these words, O. 244, and consider, among other things, "the line and posterity of Adam," as he there brings them in, he will find some difficulty to make sense of what he says; but we will allow this at present to his peculiar way of writing, and consider the force of the text in hand. The words are the curse of God upon the woman for having been the first and forwardest in the disobedience; and if we will consider the occasion of what God says here to our first parents, that he was denouncing judgment, and declaring his wrath against them both for their disobedience, we cannot suppose that this was the time wherein God was granting Adam prerogatives and privileges, investing him with dignity and authority, elevating him to dominion and monarchy: for though, as a helper in the temptation, Eve was laid below him, and so he had accidentally a superiority over her, for her greater punishment; yet he too had his share in the fall, as well as in the sin, and was laid lower, as may be seen in the following verses: and it would be hard to imagine, that God, in the same breath, should make him universal monarch over all mankind, and a day-labourer for his life; turn him out of "paradise to till the ground," ver. 23, and at the same time advance him to a throne, and all the privileges and ease of absolute power.

§ 45. This was not a time when Adam could expect any favours, any grant of privileges, from his offended Maker. If this be "the original grant of government," as our author tells us, and Adam was now made monarch, whatever sir Robert would have him, it is plain, God made him but a very poor monarch, such an one as our author himself would have counted it no great privilege to be. God set him to work for his living, and seems rather to give him a spade into his hand to subdue the earth, than a sceptre to rule over its inhabitants. "In the sweat of thy face thou shalt eat thy bread," says God to him, ver. 19. This was unavoidable, may it perhaps be answered, because he was yet without subjects, and had nobody to work for him; but afterwards, living as he did above 900 years, he might have people enough, whom he might command to work for him: no, says God, not only whilst thou art without other help, save thy wife, but as long as thou livest, shalt thou live by thy labour, "In the sweat of thy face shalt thou eat thy bread, till thou return unto the ground, for out of it wast thou taken; for dust thou art, and unto dust shalt thou return," ver. 19. It will perhaps be answered again in favour of our author, that these words are not spoken personally to Adam, but in him, as their representative, to all mankind, this being a curse upon mankind, because of the fall.

§ 46. God, I believe, speaks differently from men, because he speaks with more truth, more certainty: but when he vouchsafes to speak to men, I do not think he speaks differently from them, in crossing the rules of language in use amongst them: this would not be to condescend to their capacities, when he humbles himself to speak to them, but to lose his design in speaking what, thus spoken, they could not understand. And yet thus must we think of God, if the interpretations of Scripture, necessary to maintain our author's doctrine, must be received for good: for by the ordinary rules of language, it will be very hard to understand what God says, if what he speaks here, in the singular number, to Adam, must be understood to be spoken to all mankind; and what he says in the plural number, Gen. i. 26 and 28, must be understood of Adam alone, exclusive of all others; and what he says to Noah and his sons jointly, must be understood to be meant to Noah alone, Gen. ix.

§ 47. Farther it is to be noted, that these words here of Gen. iii. 16, which our author calls "the original grant of government," were not spoken to Adam, neither indeed was there any grant in them made to Adam, but a punishment laid upon Eve: and if we will take them as they were directed in particular to her, or in her, as their representative, to all other women, they will at most concern the female sex only, and import no more, but that subjection they should ordinarily be in to their husbands: but there is here no more law to oblige a woman to such subjection, if the circumstances either of her condition, or contract with her husband, should exempt her from it, than there is, that she should bring forth her children in sorrow and pain, if there could be found a remedy for it, which is also a part of the same curse upon her: for the whole verse runs thus, "Unto the woman he said, I will greatly multiply thy sorrow and thy conception; in sorrow thou shalt bring forth children, and thy desire shall be to thy husband, and he shall rule over thee." It would, I think, have been a hard matter for any body, but our author, to have found out a grant of "monarchical government to Adam" in these words, which were neither spoken to, nor of him: neither will any one, I suppose, by these words, think the weaker sex, as by a law, so subjected to the curse contained in them, that it is their duty not to endeavour to avoid it. And will any one say that Eve, or any other woman, sinned, if she were brought to bed without those multiplied pains God threatens her here with? or that either of our queens, Mary or Elizabeth, had they married any of their subjects, had been by this text put into a political subjection to him? or that he should thereby have had monarchical rule over her? God, in this text, gives not, that I see, any authority to Adam over Eve, or to men over their wives, but only foretels what should be the woman's lot; how by his providence he would order it so, that she should be subject to her husband, as we see that generally the laws of mankind and customs of nations have ordered it so: and there is, I grant, a foundation in nature for it.

§ 48. Thus when God says of Jacob and Esau, "that the elder should serve the younger," Gen. xxv. 23, nobody supposes that God hereby made Jacob Esau's sovereign, but foretold what should *de facto* come to pass.

But if these words here spoken to Eve must needs be understood as a law to bind her and all other women to subjection, it can be no other subjection than what every wife owes her husband; and then if this be the "original grant of government, and the foundation of monarchical power," there will be as many monarchs as there are husbands: if therefore these words give any power to Adam, it can be only a conjugal power, not political; the power that every husband hath to order the things of private concernment in his family, as proprietory of the goods and land there, and to have his will take place before that of his wife in all things of their common concernment; but not a political power of life and death over her, much less over any body else.

§ 49. This I am sure: if our author will have this text to be a "grant, the original grant of government," political government, he ought to have proved it by some better arguments than by barely saying, that "thy desire shall be unto thy husband," was a law whereby Eve, and "all that should come of her," were subjected to the absolute monarchical power of Adam and his heirs. "Thy desire shall be to thy husband," is too doubtful an expression, of whose signification interpreters are not agreed, to build so confidently on, and in a matter of such moment, and so great and general concernment: but our author, according to his way of writing, having once named the text, concludes presently, without any more ado, that the meaning is as he would have it. Let the words rule and subject be but found in the text or margin, and it immediately signifies the duty of a subject to his prince; the relation is changed, and though God says husband, sir Robert will have it king; Adam has presently absolute monarchical power over Eve, and not only over Eve, but "all that should come of her," though the Scripture says not a word of it, nor our author a word to prove it. But Adam must for all that be an absolute monarch, and so down to the end of the chapter. And here I leave my reader to consider whether my bare saying, without offering any reasons to evince it, that this text gave not Adam that absolute monarchical power, our author supposes, be not as sufficient to destroy that power, as his bare assertion is to establish it, since the text mentions neither prince nor people, speaks nothing of absolute or monarchical power, but the subjection of Eve to Adam, a wife to her husband. And he that would trace our author so all through, would make a short and sufficient answer to the greatest part of the grounds he proceeds on, and abundantly confute them by barely denying; it being a sufficient answer to assertions without proof, to deny them without giving a reason. And therefore should I have said nothing, but barely denied that by this text "the supreme power was settled and founded by God himself, in the fatherhood, limited to monarchy, and that to Adam's person and heirs," all which our author notably concludes from these words, as may be seen in the same page, O. 244, it had been a sufficient answer: should I have desired any sober man only to have read the text, and considered to whom and on what occasion it was spoken, he would no doubt have wondered how our author found out monarchical absolute power in it, had he not had an exceeding good faculty to find it himself, where he could not show it others. And thus we have examined the two places of Scripture, all that I remember our author brings to prove Adam's sovereignty, that supremacy which he says "it was God's ordinance should be unlimited in Adam, and as large as all the acts of his will," O. 254, viz. Gen. i. 28, and Gen. iii. 16; one whereof signifies only the subjection of the inferior ranks of creatures to mankind, and the other the subjection that is due from a wife to her husband; both far enough from that which subjects owe the governors of political societies.

CHAPTER VI.

Of Adam's Title to Sovereignty by Fatherhood.

§ 50. There is one thing more, and then I think I have given you all that our author brings for proof of Adam's sovereignty, and that is a supposition of a natural right of dominion over his children, by being their father: and this title of fatherhood he is so pleased with, that you will find it brought in almost in every page; particularly he says, "not only Adam, but the succeeding patriarchs had, by right of fatherhood, royal authority over their children," p. 12. And in the same page, "this subjection of children being the fountain of all regal authority," &c. This being, as one would think by his so frequent mentioning it, the main basis of all his frame, we may well expect clear and evident reason for it, since he lays it down as a position necessary to his purpose, that "every man that is born is so far from being free, that by his very birth he becomes a subject of him that begets him," O. 156. So that Adam being the only man created, and all ever since being begotten, nobody has been born free. If we ask how Adam comes by this power over his children, he tells us here it is by begetting them: and so again, O. 223, "This natural dominion of Adam," says he, "may be proved out of Grotius himself, who teacheth that 'generatione jus acquiritur parentibus in liberos.'" And indeed the act of begetting being that which makes a man a father, his right of a father over his children can naturally arise from nothing else.

§ 51. Grotius tells us not here how far this "jus in liberos," this power of parents over their children extends; but our author, always very clear in the point, assures us it is supreme power, and like that of absolute monarchs over their slaves, absolute power of life and death. He that should demand of him how, or for what reason it is, that begetting a child gives the father such an absolute power over him, will find him answer nothing: we are to take his word for this, as well as several other things, and by that the laws of nature and the constitutions of government must stand or fall. Had he been an absolute monarch, this way of talking might have suited well enough; "pro ratione voluntas," might have been of force in his mouth; but in the way of proof or argument is very unbecoming, and will little advantage his plea for absolute monarchy. Sir Robert has too much lessened a subject's authority to leave himself the hopes of establishing any thing by his bare saying it; one slave's opinion without proof, is not of weight enough to dispose of the liberty and fortunes of all mankind. If all men are not, as I think they are, naturally equal, I am sure all slaves are; and then I may without presumption oppose my single opinion to his; and be confident that my saying, "that begetting of children makes them not slaves to their fathers," as certainly sets all mankind free, as his affirming the contrary makes them all slaves. But that this position, which is the foundation of all their doctrine, who would have monarchy to be "jure divino," may have all fair play, let us hear what reasons others give for it, since our author offers none.

§ 52. The argument I have heard others make use of to prove that fathers, by begetting them, come by an absolute power over their children, is this; that "fathers have a power over the lives of their children, because they give them life and being," which is the only proof it is capable of: since there can be no reason why naturally one man should have any claim or pretence of right over that in another, which was never his, which he bestowed not, but was received from the bounty of another. 1. I answer, that every one who gives another any thing, has not always thereby a right to take it away again. But, 2. They who say the father gives life to children, are so dazzled with the thoughts of monarchy, that they do not, as they ought, remember God, who is "the author and giver of life: it is in him alone we live, move, and have our being." How can he be thought to give life to another, that knows not wherein his own life consists? Philosophers are at a loss about it, after their most diligent inquiries; and anatomists, after their whole lives and studies spent in dissections, and diligent examining the bodies of men, confess their ignorance in the structure and use of many parts of man's body, and in that operation wherein life consists in the whole. And doth the rude ploughman, or the more ignorant voluptuary, frame or fashion such an admirable engine as this is, and then put life and sense into it? Can any man say he formed the parts that are necessary to the life of his child? or can he suppose himself to give the life, and yet not know what subject is fit to receive it, nor what actions or organs are necessary for its reception or preservation?

§ 53. To give life to that which has yet no being, is to frame and make a living creature, fashion the parts, and mould and suit them to their uses; and having proportioned and fitted them together, to put into them a living soul. He that could do this, might indeed have some pretence to destroy his own workmanship. But is there any one so bold that dares thus far arrogate to himself the incomprehensible works of the Almighty? Who alone did at first, and continues still to make a living soul, he alone can breathe in the breath of life. If any one thinks himself an artist at this, let him number up the parts of his child's body which he hath made, tell me their uses and operations, and when the living and rational soul began to inhabit this curious structure, when sense began, and how this engine, which he has framed, thinks and reasons: if he made it, let him, when it is out of order, mend it, at least tell wherein the defects lie. "Shall he that made the eye not see?" says the Psalmist, Psalm xciv. 9. See these men's vanities; the structure of that one part is sufficient to convince us of an all-wise Contriver, and he has so visible a claim to us as his workmanship, that one of the ordinary appellations of God in Scripture is, "God our maker," and "the Lord our maker." And therefore though our author, for the magnifying his fatherhood, be pleased to say, O. 159, "That even the power which God himself exerciseth over mankind is by right of fatherhood," yet this fatherhood is such an one as utterly excludes all pretence of title in earthly parents; for he is king, because he is indeed maker of us all, which no parents can pretend to be of their children.

§ 54. But had men skill and power to make their children, it is not so slight a piece of workmanship, that it can be imagined they could make them without designing it. What father of a thousand, when he begets a child, thinks farther than the satisfying his present appetite? God in his infinite wisdom has put strong desires of copulation into the constitution of men, thereby to continue the race of mankind, which he doth most commonly without the intention, and often against the consent and will of the begetter. And indeed those who desire and design children, are but the occasions of their being, and, when they design and wish to beget them, do little more towards their making than Deucalion and his wife in the fable did towards the making of mankind, by throwing pebbles over their heads.

§ 55. But grant that the parents made their children, gave them life and being, and that hence there followed an absolute power. This would give the father but a joint dominion with the mother over them: for nobody can deny but that the woman hath an equal share, if not the greater, as nourishing the child a long time in her own body out of her own substance: there it is fashioned, and from her it receives the materials and principles of its constitution: and it is so hard to imagine the rational soul should presently inhabit the yet unformed embryo, as soon as the father has done his part in the act of generation, that if it must be supposed to derive any thing from the parents, it must certainly owe most to the mother. But be that as it will, the mother cannot be denied an equal share in begetting of the child, and so the absolute authority of the father will not arise from hence. Our author indeed is of another mind; for he says, "we know that God at the creation gave the sovereignty to the man over the woman, as being the nobler and principal agent in generation," O. 172. I remember not this in my Bible; and when the place is brought where God at the creation gave the sovereignty to man over the woman, and that for this reason, because "he is the nobler and principal agent in generation," it will be time enough to consider, and answer it. But it is no new thing for our author to tell us his own fancies for certain and divine truths, though there be often a great deal of difference between his and divine revelations; for God in the Scripture says, "his father and his mother that begot him."

§ 56. They who allege the practice of mankind, for exposing or selling their children, as a proof of their power over them, are with sir Robert happy arguers; and cannot but recommend their opinion, by founding it on the most shameful action, and most unnatural murder human nature is capable of. The dens of lions and nurseries of wolves know no such cruelty as this: these savage inhabitants of the desert obey God and nature in being tender and careful of their offspring: they will hunt, watch, fight, and almost starve for the preservation of their young; never part with them; never forsake them, till they are able to shift for themselves. And is it the privilege of man alone to act more contrary to nature than the wild and most untamed part of the creation? doth God forbid us under the severest penalty, that of death, to take away the life of any man, a stranger, and upon provocation? and does he permit us to destroy those he has given us the charge and care of; and by the dictates of nature and reason, as well as his revealed command, requires us to preserve? He has in all the parts of creation taken a peculiar care to propagate and continue the several species of creatures, and makes the individuals act so strongly to this end, that they sometimes neglect their own private good for it, and seem to forget that general rule, which nature teaches all things, of self-preservation; and the preservation of their young, as the strongest principle in them, over-rules the constitution of their particular natures. Thus we see, when their young stand in need of it, the timorous become valiant, the fierce and savage kind, and the ravenous, tender and liberal.

§ 57. But if the example of what hath been done be the rule of what ought to be, history would have furnished our author with instances of this absolute fatherly power in its height and perfection, and he might have showed us in Peru people that begot children on purpose to fatten and eat them. The story is so remarkable, that I cannot but set it down in the author's words: "In some provinces, says he, they were so liquorish after man's flesh, that they would not have the patience to stay till the breath was out of the body, but would suck the blood as it ran from the wounds of the dying man; they had public shambles of man's flesh, and their madness herein was to that degree, that they spared not their own children, which they had begot on strangers taken in war: for they made their captives their mistresses, and choicely nourished the children they had by them, till about thirteen years old they butchered and eat them; and they served the mothers after the same fashion, when they grew past child-bearing, and ceased to bring them any more roasters." Garcilasso de la Vega Hist. des Yncas de Peru, l. i. c. 12.

§ 58. Thus far can the busy mind of man carry him to a brutality below the level of beasts, when he quits his reason, which places him almost equal to angels. Nor can it be otherwise in a creature, whose thoughts are more than the sands, and wider than the ocean, where fancy and passion must needs run him into strange courses, if reason, which is his only star and compass, be not that he steers by. The imagination is always restless, and suggests variety of thoughts, and the will, reason being laid aside, is ready for every extravagant project; and in this state he that goes farthest out of the way, is thought fittest to lead, and is sure of most followers: and when fashion hath once established what folly or craft began, custom makes it sacred, and it will be thought impudence, or madness, to contradict or question it. He that will impartially survey the nations of the world, will find so much of their religions, governments, and manners, brought in and continued amongst them by these means, that he will have but little reverence for the practices which are in use and credit amongst men; and will have reason to think, that the woods and forests, where the irrational untaught inhabitants keep right by following nature, are fitter to give us rules, than cities and palaces, where those that call themselves civil and rational, go out of their way, by the authority of example. If precedents are sufficient to establish a rule in this case, our author might have found in holy writ children sacrificed by their parents, and this amongst the people of God themselves: the Psalmist tells us, Psalm cvi. 38, "They shed innocent blood, even the blood of their sons and of their daughters, whom they sacrificed unto the idols of Canaan." But God judged not of this by our author's rule, nor allowed of the authority of practice against his righteous law; but, as it follows there, "the land was polluted with blood; therefore was the wrath of the Lord kindled against his people, insomuch that he abhorred his own inheritance." The killing of their children, though it were fashionable, was charged on them as innocent blood, and so had in the account of God the guilt of murder, as the offering them to idols had the guilt of idolatry.

§ 59. Be it then, as sir Robert says, that anciently it was usual for men "to sell and castrate their children," O. 155. Let it be, that they exposed them; add to it, if you please, for this is still greater power, that they begat them for their tables, to fat and eat them: if this proves a right to do so, we may, by the same argument, justify adultery, incest, and sodomy, for there are examples of these too, both ancient and modern; sins, which I suppose have their principal aggravation from this, that they cross the main intention of nature, which willeth the increase of mankind, and the continuation of the species in the highest perfection, and the distinction of families, with the security of the marriage-bed, as necessary thereunto.

§ 60. In confirmation of this natural authority of the father, our author brings a lame proof from the positive command of God in Scripture: his words are, "To confirm the natural right of regal power, we find in the decalogue, that the law which enjoins obedience to kings, is delivered in the terms, Honour thy father, p. 23. Whereas many confess, that government only in the abstract, is the ordinance of God, they are not able to prove any such ordinance in the Scripture, but only in the fatherly power; and therefore we find the commandment, that enjoins obedience to superiors, given in the terms, Honour thy father; so that not only the power and right of government, but the form of the power governing, and the person having the power, are all the ordinances of God. The first father had not only simply power, but power monarchical, as he was father immediately from God," O. 254. To the same purpose, the same law is cited by our author in several other places, and just after the same fashion; that is, "and mother," as apocryphal words, are always left out; a great argument of our author's ingenuity, and the goodness of his cause, which required in its defender zeal to a degree of warmth, able to warp the sacred rule of the word of God, to make it comply with his present occasion; a way of proceeding not unusual to those who embrace not truths because reason and revelation offer them, but espouse tenets and parties for ends different from truth, and then resolve at any rate to defend them; and so do with the words and sense of authors, they would fit to their purpose, just as Procrustes did with his guests, lop or stretch them, as may best fit them to the size of their notions; and they always prove, like those so served, deformed, lame, and useless.

§ 61. For had our author set down this command without garbling as God gave it, and joined mother to father, every reader would have seen, that it had made directly against him, and that it was so far from establishing the "monarchical power of the father," that it set up the mother equal with him, and enjoined nothing but was due in common to both father and mother: for that is the constant tenour of the Scripture, "Honour thy father and thy mother," Exod. xx. "He that smiteth his father or mother, shall surely be put to death," xxi. 15. "He that curseth his father or mother, shall surely be put to death," ver. 17. repeated Lev. xx. 9, and by our Saviour, Matth. xv. 4. "Ye shall fear every man his mother and his father," Lev. xix. 3. "If any man have a rebellious son, which will not obey the voice of his father or the voice of his mother; then shall his father and his mother lay hold on him, and say, This our son is stubborn and rebellious, he will not obey our voice," Deut. xxi. 18, 19, 20, 21. "Cursed be he that setteth light by his father or his mother," xxvii. 16. "My son, hear the instructions of thy father, and forsake not the law of thy mother" are the words of Solomon, a king who was not ignorant of what belonged to him as a father or a king; and yet he joins father and mother together, in all the instructions he gives children quite through his book of Proverbs. "Woe unto him, that saith unto his father, What begettest thou? or to the woman, What has thou brought forth?" Isa. xlv. 10. "In thee have they set light by father and mother," Ezek. xxii. 7. "And it shall come to pass, that when any shall yet prophesy, then his father and his mother that begat him shall say unto him, Thou shalt not live; and his father and his mother that begat him shall thrust him through when he prophesieth." Zech. xiii. 3. Here not the father only, but the father and mother jointly, had power in this case of life and death. Thus ran the law of the Old Testament, and in the New they are likewise joined, in the obedience of their children, Eph. vi. 1. The rule is, "Children, obey your parents;" and I do not remember, that I any where read, "Children, obey your father," and no more: the Scripture joins mother too in that homage which is due from children; and had there been any text, where the honour or obedience of children had been directed to the father alone, it is not likely that our author, who pretends to build all upon Scripture, would have omitted it: nay, the Scripture makes the authority of father and mother, in respect of those they have begot, so equal, that in some places it neglects even the priority of order, which is thought due to the father, and the mother is put first, as Lev. xix. 3. From which so constantly joining father and mother together, as is found quite through Scripture, we may conclude that the honour they have a title to from their children is one common right belonging so equally to them both, that neither can claim it wholly, neither can be excluded.

§ 62. One would wonder then how our author infers from the fifth commandment, that all "power was originally in the father;" how he finds "monarchical power of government settled and fixed by the commandment, Honour thy father and thy mother." If all the honour due by the commandment, be it what it will, be the only right of the father, because he, as our author says, "has the sovereignty over the woman, as being the nobler and principal agent in generation," why did God afterwards all along join the mother with him, to share in his honour? Can the father, by this sovereignty of his, discharge the child from paying this honour to his mother? The Scripture gave no such license to the Jews, and yet there were often breaches wide enough betwixt husband and wife, even to divorce and separation: and, I think, nobody will say a child may withhold honour from his mother, or, as the Scripture terms it, "set light by her," though his father should command him to do so; no more than the mother could dispense with him for neglecting to honour his father: whereby it is plain, that this command of God gives the father no sovereignty, no supremacy.

§ 63. I agree with our author that the title to this honour is vested in the parents by nature, and is a right which accrues to them by their having begotten their children, and God by many positive declarations has confirmed it to them: I also allow our author's rule, "that in grants and gifts, that have their original from God and nature, as the power of the father," (let me add "and mother," for whom God hath joined together let no man put asunder) "no inferior power of men can limit, not make any law of prescription against them," O. 158: so that the mother having, by this law of God, a right to honour from her children, which is not subject to the will of her husband, we see this "absolute monarchical power of the father" can neither be founded on it, nor consist with it; and he has a power very far from monarchical, very far from that absoluteness our author contends for, when another has over his subjects the same power he hath, and by the same title: and therefore he cannot forbear saying himself that "he cannot see how any man's children can be free from subjection to their parents," p. 12, which, in common speech, I think, signifies mother as well as father, or if parents here signifies only father, it is the first time I ever yet knew it to do so, and by such an use of words one may say any thing.

§ 64. By our author's doctrine, the father having absolute jurisdiction over his children, has also the same over their issue; and the consequence is good, were it true that the father had such a power: and yet I ask our author whether the grandfather, by his sovereignty, could discharge the grandchild from paying to his father the honour due to him by the fifth commandment. If the grandfather hath, by "right of fatherhood," sole sovereign power in him, and that obedience which is due to the supreme magistrate be commanded in these words, "Honour thy father," it is certain the grandfather might dispense with the grandson's honouring his father, which since it is evident in common sense he cannot, it follows from hence, that "honour thy father and mother" cannot mean an absolute subjection to a sovereign power, but something else. The right therefore which parents have by nature, and which is confirmed to them by the fifth commandment, cannot be that political dominion which our author would derive from it: for that being in every civil society supreme somewhere, can discharge any subject from any political obedience to any one of his fellow-subjects. But what law of the magistrate can give a child liberty not to "honour his father and mother?" It is an eternal law, annexed purely to the relation of parents and children, and so contains nothing of the magistrate's power in it, nor is subjected to it.

§ 65. Our author says, "God hath given to a father a right or liberty to alien his power over his children to any other," O. 155. I doubt whether he can alien wholly the right of honour that is due from them; but be that as it will, this I am sure, he cannot alien and retain the same power. If therefore the magistrate's sovereignty be, as our author would have it, "nothing but the authority of a supreme father," p. 23, it is unavoidable, that if the magistrate hath all this paternal right, as he must have if fatherhood be the fountain of all authority; then the subjects, though fathers, can have no power over their children, no right to honour from them: for it cannot be all in another's hands, and a part remain with the parents. So that, according to our author's own doctrine, "Honour thy father and mother" cannot possibly be understood of political subjection and obedience: since the laws both in the Old and New Testament, that commanded children to "honour and obey their parents," were given to such, whose fathers were under civil government, and fellow-subjects with them in political societies; and to have bid them "honour and obey their parents," in our author's sense, had been to bid them be subjects to those who had no title to it: the right to obedience from subjects being all vested in another; and instead of teaching obedience, this had been to foment sedition, by setting up powers that were not. If therefore this command, "Honour thy father and mother," concern political dominion, it directly overthrows our author's monarchy: since it being to be paid by every child to his father, even in society, every father must necessarily have political dominion, and there will be as many sovereigns as there are fathers: besides that the mother too hath her title, which destroys the sovereignty of one supreme monarch. But if "Honour thy father and mother" mean something distinct from political power, as necessarily it must, it is besides our author's business, and serves nothing to his purpose.

§ 66. "The law that enjoins obedience to kings is delivered," says our author, "in the terms, Honour thy father, as if all power were originally in the father," O. 254: and that law is also delivered, say I, in the terms, "Honour thy mother," as if all power were originally in the mother. I appeal whether the argument be not as good on one side as the other, father and mother being joined all along in the Old and New Testament wherever honour or obedience is enjoined children. Again, our author tells us, O. 254, "that this command, Honour thy father, gives the right to govern, and makes the form of government monarchical." To which I answer, that if by "Honour thy father" be meant obedience to the political power of the magistrate, it concerns not any duty we owe to our natural fathers, who are subjects; because they, by our author's doctrine, are divested of all that power, it being placed wholly in the prince, and so being equally subjects and slaves with their children, can have no right, by that title, to any such honour or obedience as contains in it political subjection: if "Honour thy father and mother" signifies the duty we owe our natural parents, as by our Saviour's interpretation, Matth. xv. 4, and all the other mentioned places, it is plain it does: then it cannot concern political obedience, but a duty that is owing to persons who have no title to sovereignty, nor any political authority as magistrates over subjects. For the person of a private father, and title to obedience, due to the supreme magistrate, are things inconsistent; and therefore this command, which must necessarily comprehend the persons of natural fathers, must mean a duty we owe them distinct from our obedience to the magistrate, and from which the most absolute power of princes cannot absolve us. What this duty is, we shall in its due place examine.

§ 67. And thus we have at last got through all, that in our author looks like an argument for that absolute unlimited sovereignty described, sect. 8, which he supposes in Adam; so that mankind have ever since been all born slaves, without any title to freedom. But if creation, which gave nothing but a being, made not Adam prince of his posterity: if Adam, Gen. i. 28, was not constituted lord of mankind, nor had a private dominion given him exclusive of his children, but only a right and power over the earth and inferior creatures in common with the children of men: if also, Gen. iii. 16, God gave not any particular power to Adam over his wife and children, but only subjected Eve to Adam, as a punishment, or foretold the subjection of the weaker sex, in the ordering the common concernments of their families, but gave not thereby to Adam, as to the husband, power of life and death, which necessarily belongs to the magistrate: if fathers by begetting their children acquire no such power over them; and if the command, "Honour thy father and mother," give it not, but only enjoins a duty owing to parents equally, whether subjects or not, and to the mother as well as the father: if all this be so, as I think by what has been said is very evident; then man has a natural freedom, notwithstanding all our author confidently says to the contrary; since all that share in the same common nature, faculties, and powers, are in nature equal, and ought to partake in the same common rights and privileges, till the manifest appointment of God, who is "Lord over all, blessed for ever," can be produced to show any particular person's supremacy; or a man's own consent subjects him to a superior. This is so plain, that our author confesses that sir John Hayward, Blackwood, and Barclay, "the great vindicators of the right of kings," could not deny it, "but admit with one consent the natural liberty and equality of mankind," for a truth unquestionable. And our author hath been so far from producing any thing that may make good his great position, "that Adam was absolute monarch," and so "men are not naturally free," that even his own proofs make against him; so that, to use his own way of arguing, "the first erroneous principle failing, the whole fabric of this vast engine of absolute power and tyranny drops down of itself," and there needs no more to be said in answer to all that he builds upon so false and frail a foundation.

§ 68. But to save others the pains, were there any need, he is not sparing himself to show, by his own contradictions, the weakness of his own doctrine. Adam's absolute and sole dominion is that which he is every where full of, and along builds on, and yet he tells us, p. 12, "that as Adam was lord of his children, so his children under him had a command and power over their own children." The unlimited and undivided sovereignty of Adam's fatherhood, by our author's computation, stood but a little while, only during the first generation; but as soon as he had grandchildren, sir Robert could give but a very ill account of it. "Adam, as father of his children," saith he, "hath an absolute, unlimited, royal power over them, and by virtue thereof over those that they begot, and so to all generations;" and yet his children, viz. Cain and Seth, have a paternal power over their children at the same time; so that they are at the same time absolute lords, and yet vassals and slaves; Adam has all the authority, as "grandfather of the people," and they have a part of it as fathers of a part of them: he is absolute over them and their posterity, by having begotten them, and yet they are absolute over their children by the same title. "No," says our author, "Adam's children under him had power over their own children, but still with subordination to the first parent." A good distinction, that sounds well; and it is pity it signifies nothing, nor can be reconciled with our author's words. I readily grant, that supposing Adam's absolute power over his posterity, any of his children might have from him a delegated, and so a subordinate power over a part, or all the rest: but that cannot be the power our author speaks of here; it is not a power by grant and commission, but the natural paternal power he supposes a father to have over his children. For, 1. he says, "As Adam was lord of his children, so his children under him had a power over their own children:" they were then lords over their own children after the same manner, and by the same title, that Adam was; *i. e.* by right of generation, by right of fatherhood. 2. It is plain he means the natural power of fathers, because he limits it to be only "over their own children;" a delegated power has no such limitation as only over their own children; it might be over others, as well as their own children. 3. If it were a delegated power, it must appear in Scripture; but there is no ground in Scripture to affirm, that Adam's children had any other power over theirs than what they naturally had as fathers.

§ 69. But that he means here paternal power, and no other, is past doubt, from the inference he makes in these words immediately following, "I see not then how the children of Adam, or of any man else, can be free from subjection to their parents." Whereby it appears that the power on one side, and the subjection on the other, our author here speaks of, is that natural power and subjection between parents and children: for that which every-man's children owed could be no other; and that our author always affirms to be absolute and unlimited. This natural power of parents over their children Adam had over his posterity, says our author; and this power of parents over their children, his children had over theirs in his lifetime, says our author also; so that Adam, by a natural right of father, had an absolute, unlimited power over all his posterity, and at the same time his children had by the same right absolute, unlimited power over theirs. Here then are two absolute, unlimited powers existing together, which I would have any body reconcile one to another, or to common sense. For the salvo he has put in of subordination makes it more absurd: to have one absolute, unlimited, nay unlimitable power in subordination to another, is so manifest a contradiction, that nothing can be more. "Adam is absolute prince, with the unlimited authority of fatherhood over all his posteriority;" all his posterity are then absolutely his subjects; and, as our author says, his slaves, children, and grandchildren, are equally in this state of subjection and slavery; and yet, says our author, "the children of Adam have paternal, *i. e.* absolute, unlimited power over their own children:" which in plain English is, they are slaves and absolute princes at the same time, and in the same government; and one part of the subjects have an absolute, unlimited power over the other by the natural right of parentage.

§ 70. If any one will suppose in favour of our author, that he here meant that parents, who are in subjection themselves to the absolute authority of their father, have yet some power over their children; I confess he is something nearer the truth: but he will not at all hereby help our author: for he nowhere speaking of the paternal power, but as an absolute, unlimited authority, cannot be supposed to understand any thing else here, unless he himself had limited it, and showed how far it reached; and that he means here paternal authority in that large extent, is plain from the immediately following words: "This subjection of children being," says he, "the foundation of all regal authority," p. 12. The subjection then that in the former line, he says, "every man is in to his parents," and consequently what Adam's grandchildren were in to their parents, was that which was the fountain of all regal authority, *i. e.* according to our author, absolute, unlimitable authority. And thus Adam's children had regal authority over their children, whilst they themselves were subjects to their father, and fellow-subjects with their children. But let him mean as he pleases, it is plain he allows "Adam's children to have paternal power," p. 12, as also all other fathers to have "paternal power over their children." O. 156. From whence one of these two things will necessarily follow, that either Adam's children, even in his life time, had, and so all other fathers have, as he phrases it, p. 12, "by right of fatherhood, royal authority over their children," or else that Adam, "by right of fatherhood, had not royal authority." For it cannot be but that paternal power does, or does not, give royal authority to them that have it: if it does not, then Adam could not be sovereign by this title, nor any body else; and then there is an end of all our author's politics at once: if it does give royal authority, then every one that has paternal power has royal authority; and then, by our author's patriarchal government, there will be as many kings as there are fathers.

§ 71. And thus what a monarchy he hath set up, let him and his disciples consider. Princes certainly will have great reason to thank him for these new politics, which set up as many absolute kings in every country as there are fathers of children. And yet who can blame our author for it, it lying unavoidably in the way of one discoursing upon our author's principles? For having placed an "absolute power in fathers by right of begetting," he could not easily resolve how much of this power belonged to a son over the children he had begotten; and so it fell out to be a very hard matter to give all the power, as he does, to Adam, and yet allow a part in his life time to his children when they were parents, and which he knew not well how to deny them. This makes him so doubtful in his expressions, and so uncertain where to place this absolute natural power which he calls fatherhood. Sometimes Adam alone has it all, as p. 13, O. 244, 245, and Pref.

Sometimes parents have it, which word scarce signifies the father alone, p. 12, 19.

Sometimes children during their father's lifetime, as p. 12.

Sometimes fathers of families, as p. 78, 79.

Sometimes fathers indefinitely, O. 155.

Sometimes the heir to Adam, O. 253.

Sometimes the posterity of Adam, 244, 246.

Sometimes prime fathers, all sons of grandchildren of Noah, O. 244.

Sometimes the eldest parents, p. 12.

Sometimes all kings, p. 19.

Sometimes all that have supreme power, O. 245.

Sometimes heirs to those first progenitors who were at first the natural parents of the whole people, p. 19.

Sometimes an elective king, p. 23.

Sometimes those, whether a few or a multitude, that govern the commonweath, p. 23.

Sometimes he that can catch it, an usurper, p. 23. O. 155.

§ 72. Thus this new nothing, that is to carry with it all power, authority, and government; this fatherhood, which is to design the person, and establish the throne of monarchs, whom the people are to obey; may, according to sir Robert, come into any hands, any how, and so by his politics give to democracy royal authority, and make an usurper a lawful prince. And if it will do all these fine feats, much good do our author and all his followers with their omnipotent fatherhood, which can serve for nothing but to unsettle and destroy all the lawful governments in the world, and to establish in their room disorder, tyranny, and usurpation.

CHAPTER VII.

Of Fatherhood and Property considered together as Fountains of Sovereignty.

§ 73. In the foregoing chapters we have seen what Adam's monarchy was in our author's opinion, and upon what titles he founded it. The foundations which he lays the chief stress on, as those from which he thinks he may best derive monarchical power to future princes, are two, viz. "fatherhood and property:" and therefore the way he proposes to "remove the absurdities and inconveniencies of the doctrine of natural freedom is, to maintain the natural and private dominion of Adam," O. 222. Conformable hereunto, he tell us, "the grounds and principles of government necessarily depend upon the original of property," O. 108. "The subjection of children to their parents is the fountain of all regal authority," p. 12. "And all power on earth is either derived or usurped from the fatherly power, there being no other original to be found of any power whatsoever," O. 158. I will not stand here to examine how it can be said without a contradiction, that the "first grounds and principles of government necessarily depend upon the original of property," and yet, "that there is no other original of any power whatsoever but that of the father:" it being hard to understand how there can be "no other original but fatherhood," and yet that the "grounds and principles of government depend upon the original of property;" property and fatherhood being as far different as lord of a manor and father of children. Nor do I see how they will either of them agree with what our author says, O. 244, of God's sentence against Eve, Gen. iii. 16, "that it is the original grant of government:" so that if that were the original, government had not its original, by our author's own confession, either from property or fatherhood; and this text, which he brings as a proof of Adam's power over Eve, necessarily contradicts what he says of the fatherhood, that it is the "sole fountain of all power:" for if Adam had any such regal power over Eve as our author contends for, it must be by some other title than that of begetting.

§ 74. But I leave him to reconcile these contradictions, as well as many others, which may plentifully be found in him by any one, who will but read him with a little attention; and shall come now to consider, how these two originals of government, "Adam's natural and private dominion," will consist and serve to make out and establish the titles of succeeding monarchs, who, as our author obliges them, must all derive their power from these fountains. Let us then suppose Adam made, "by God's donation," lord and sole proprietor of the whole earth, in as large and ample a manner as sir Robert could wish; let us suppose him also, "by right of fatherhood," absolute ruler over his children with an unlimited supremacy; I ask then, upon Adam's death, what becomes of both his natural and private dominion? and I doubt not it will be answered, that they descended to his next heir, as our author tells us in several places. But this way, it is plain, cannot possibly convey both his natural and private dominion to the same person: for should we allow that all the property, all the estate of the father, ought to descend to the eldest son, (which will need some proof to establish it) and so he has by that title all the private dominion of the father, yet the father's natural dominion, the paternal power, cannot descend to him by inheritance: for it being a right that accrues to a man only by begetting, no man can have this natural dominion over any one he does not beget; unless it can be supposed that a man can have a right to any thing, without doing that upon which that right is solely founded: for if a father by begetting, and no other title, has natural dominion over his children, he that does not beget them cannot have this natural dominion over them; and therefore be it true or false, that our author says, O. 156, That "every man that is born, by his very birth, becomes a subject to him that begets him," this necessarily follows, viz. That a man by his birth cannot become a subject to his brother, who did not beget him; unless it can be supposed that a man by the very same title can come to be under the "natural and absolute dominion" of two different men at once; or it be sense to say, that a man by birth is under the natural dominion of his father, only because he begat him, and a man by birth also is under the natural dominion of his eldest brother, though he did not beget him.

§ 75. If then the private dominion of Adam, i. e. his property in the creatures, descended at his death all entirely to his eldest son, his heir; (for, if it did not, there is presently an end of all sir Robert's monarchy) and his natural dominion, the dominion a father has over his children by begetting them, belonged, immediately upon Adam's decease, equally to all his sons who had children, by the same title their father had it, the sovereignty founded upon property, and the sovereignty founded upon fatherhood, come to be divided; since Cain, as heir, had that of property alone; Seth, and the other sons, that of fatherhood equally with him. This is the best can be made of our author's doctrine, and of the two titles of sovereignty he sets up in Adam: one of them will either signify nothing; or, if they both must stand, they can serve only to confound the rights of princes, and disorder government in his posterity: for by building upon two titles to dominion, which cannot descend together, and which he allows may be separated, (for he yields that "Adam's children had their distinct territories by right of private dominion," O. 210, p. 40) he makes it perpetually a doubt upon his principles where the sovereignty is, or to whom we owe our obedience; since fatherhood and property are distinct titles, and began presently upon Adam's death to be in distinct persons. And which then was to give way to the other?

§ 76. Let us take the account of it, as he himself gives it us. He tells us out of Grotius, that "Adam's children, by donation, assignation, or some kind of cession before he was dead, had their distinct territories by right of private dominion; Abel had his flocks, and pastures for them: Cain had his fields for corn, and the land of Nod, where he built him a city," O. 210. Here it is obvious to demand, which of these two after Adam's death was sovereign? Cain, says our author, p. 19. By what title? "As heir; for heirs to progenitors, who were natural parents of their people, are not only lords of their own children, but also of their brethren," says our author, p. 19. What was Cain heir to? Not the entire possessions, not all that which Adam had private dominion in; for our author allows that Abel, by a title derived from his father, "had his distinct territory for pasture by right of private dominion." What then Abel had by private dominion, was exempt from Cain's dominion: for he could not have private dominion over that which was under the private dominion of another; and therefore his sovereignty over his brother is gone with this private dominion, and so there are presently two sovereigns, and his imaginary title of fatherhood is out of doors, and Cain is no prince over his brother: or else, if Cain retain his sovereignty over Abel, notwithstanding his private dominion, it will follow, that the "first grounds and principles of government" have nothing to do with property, whatever our author says to the contrary. It is true, Abel did not outlive his father Adam; but that makes nothing to the argument, which will hold good against sir Robert in Abel's issue, or in Seth, or any of the posterity of Adam, not descended from Cain.

§ 77. The same inconvenience he runs into about the three sons of Noah, who as he says, p. 13, "had the whole world divided amongst them by their father." I ask then, in which of the three we shall find "the establishment of regal power" after Noah's death? If in all three, as our author there seems to say, then it will follow, that regal power is founded in property of land, and follows private dominion, and not in paternal power or natural dominion; and so there is an end of paternal power as the fountain of regal authority, and the so much magnified fatherhood quite vanishes. If the regal power descended to Shem as eldest, and heir to his father, then "Noah's division of the world by lot to his sons, or his ten years' sailing about the Mediterranean to appoint each son his part," which our author tells of, p.14, was labour lost; his division of the world to them, was to ill, or to no purpose: for his grant to Cham and Japhet was little worth, if Shem, notwithstanding this grant, as soon as Noah was dead, was to be lord over them. Or, if this grant of private dominion to them, over their assigned territories' were good, here were set up two distinct sorts of power, not subordinate one to the other, with all those inconveniencies which he musters up against the "power of the people," O. 158, which I shall set down in his own words, only changing property for people: "All power on earth is either derived or usurped from the fatherly power, there being no other original to be found of any power whatsoever: for if there should be granted two sorts of power, without any subordination of one to the other, they would be in perpetual strife which should be supreme, for two supremes cannot agree: if the fatherly power be supreme, then the power grounded on private dominion must be subordinate, and depend on it; and if the power grounded on property be supreme, then the fatherly power must submit to it, and cannot be exercised without the licence of the proprietors, which must quite destroy the frame and course of nature." This is his own arguing against two distinct independent powers, which I have set down in his own words, only putting power rising from property, for power of the people; and when he has answered what he himself has urged here against two distinct powers, we shall be better able to see how, with any tolerable sense, he can derive all regal authority "from the natural and private dominion of Adam," from fatherhood and property together, which are distinct titles, that do not always meet in the same persons; and it is plain, by his own confession, presently separated as soon both as Adam's and Noah's death made way for succession: though our author frequently in his writings jumbles them together, and omits not to make use of either, where he thinks it will sound best to his purpose. But the absurdities of this will more fully appear in the next chapter, where we shall examine the ways of conveyance of the sovereignty of Adam to princes that were to reign after him.

CHAPTER VIII.

Of the Conveyance of Adam's sovereign monarchical Power.

§ 78. Sir Robert, having not been very happy in any proof he brings for the sovereignty of Adam, is not much more fortunate in conveying it to future princes; who, if his politics be true, must all derive their titles from that first monarch. The ways he has assigned, as they lie scattered up and down in his writings, I will set down in his own words: in his preface he tells us, that "Adam being monarch of the whole world, none of his posterity had any right to possess any thing, but by his grant or permission, or by succession from him." Here he makes two ways of conveyance of any thing Adam stood possessed of; and those are grants, or succession. Again he says, "All kings either are, or are to be reputed, the next heirs to those first progenitors, who were at first the natural parents of the whole people," p. 19 — "There cannot be any multitude of men whatsoever, but that in it, considered by itself, there is one man amongst them, that in nature hath a right to be the king of all the rest, as being the next heir to Adam," O. 253. Here in these places inheritance is the only way he allows of conveying monarchical power to princes. In other places he tells us, O. 155, "All power on earth is either derived or usurped from the fatherly power," O. 158. "All kings that now are, or ever were, are or were either fathers of their people, or heirs of such fathers, or usurpers of the right of such fathers," O. 253. And here he makes inheritance or usurpation the only way whereby kings come by this original power: but yet he tells us, "this fatherly empire, as it was of itself hereditary, so it was alienable by patent, and seizable by an usurper," O. 190. So then here inheritance, grant, or usurpation, will convey it. And last of all, which is most admirable, he tells us, p. 100, "It skills not which way kings come by their power, whether by election, donation, succession, or by any other means; for it is still the manner of the government by supreme power that makes them properly kings, and not the means of obtaining their crowns." Which I think is a full answer to all his whole hypothesis and discourse about Adam's royal authority, as the fountain from which all princes were to derive theirs: and he might have spared the trouble of speaking so much as he does, up and down, of heirs and inheritance, if to make any one properly a king needs no more but "governing by supreme power, and it matters not by what means he came by it."

§ 79. By this notable way, our author may make Oliver as properly king as any one else he could think of: and had he had the happiness to live under Massaniello's government, he could not by this his own rule have forborne to have done homage to him, with "O king live for ever," since the manner of his government by supreme power made him properly king, who was but the day before properly a fisherman. And if Don Quixote had taught his squire to govern with supreme authority, our author no doubt could have made a most loyal subject in Sancho Pancha's island; he must needs have deserved some preferment in such governments, since I think he is the first politician who, pretending to settle government upon its true basis, and to establish the thrones of lawful princes, ever told the world, that he was "properly a king, whose manner of government was by supreme power, by what means soever he obtained it;" which in plain English is to say, that regal and supreme power is properly and truly his, who can by any means seize upon it: and if this be to be properly a king, I wonder how he came to think of, or where he will find, an usurper.

§ 80. This is so strange a doctrine, that the surprise of it hath made me pass by, without their due reflection, the contradictions he runs into, by making sometimes inheritance alone, sometimes only grant or inheritance, sometimes only inheritance or usurpation, sometimes all these three, and at last election, or any other means, added to them, the ways whereby Adam's royal authority, that is, his right to supreme rule, could be conveyed down to future kings and governors, so as to give them a title to the obedience and subjection of the people. But these contradictions lie so open, that the very reading of our author's own words will discover them to any ordinary understanding; and though what I have quoted out of him (with abundance more of the same strain and coherence, which might be found in him) might well excuse me from any farther trouble in this argument, yet having proposed to myself to examine the main parts of his doctrine, I shall a little more particularly consider how inheritance, grant, usurpation, or election, can any way make out government in the world upon his principles; or derive to any one a right of empire, from this regal authority of Adam, had it been ever so well proved that he had been absolute monarch, and lord of the whole world.

CHAPTER IX.

Of Monarchy by Inheritance from Adam.

§ 81. Though it be ever so plain, that there ought to be government in the world, nay, should all men be of our author's mind, that divine appointment had ordained it to be monarchical; yet, since men cannot obey any thing that cannot command; and ideas of government in the fancy, though ever so perfect, though ever so right, cannot give laws, nor prescribe rules to the actions of men; it would be of no behoof for the settling of order, and establishment of government in its exercise and use amongst men, unless there were a way also taught how to know the person, to whom it belonged to have this power, and exercise this dominion over others. It is in vain then to talk of subjection and obedience without telling us whom we are to obey: for were I ever so fully persuaded that there ought to be magistracy and rule in the world; yet I am nevertheless at liberty still, till it appears who is the person that hath right to my obedience; since, if there be no marks to know him by, and distinguish him that hath right to rule from other men, it may be myself, as well as any other; and therefore, though submission to government be every one's duty, yet since that signifies nothing but submitting to the direction and laws of such men as have authority to command, it is not enough to make a man a subject, to convince him that there is regal power in the world; but there must be ways of designing, and knowing the person to whom this regal power of right belongs; and a man can never be obliged in conscience to submit to any power, unless he can be satisfied who is the person who has a right to exercise that power over him. If this were not so, there would be no distinction between pirates and lawful princes; he that has force is without any more ado to be obeyed, and crowns and sceptres would become the inheritance only of violence and rapine. Men too might as often and as innocently change their governors, as they do their physicians, if the person cannot be known who has a right to direct me, and whose prescriptions I am bound to follow. To settle therefore men's consciences, under an obligation to obedience, it is necessary that they know not only that there is a power somewhere in the world, but the person who by right is vested with this power over them.

§ 82. How successful our author has been in his attempts to set up a monarchical absolute power in Adam, the reader may judge by what has been already said; but were that absolute monarchy as clear as our author would desire it, as I presume it is the contrary, yet it could be of no use to the government of mankind now in the world, unless he also make out these two things.

First, that this power of Adam was not to end with him, but was upon his decease conveyed entire to some other person, and so on to posterity.

Secondly, that the princes and rulers now on earth are possessed of this power of Adam, by a right way of conveyance derived to them.

§ 83. If the first of these fail, the power of Adam, were it ever so great, ever so certain, will signify nothing to the present government and societies in the world; but we must seek out some other original of power for the government of polities than this of Adam, or else there will be none at all in the world. If the latter fail, it will destroy the authority of the present governors, and absolve the people from subjection to them, since they, having no better claim than others to that power, which is alone the fountain of all authority, can have no title to rule over them.

§ 84. Our author, having fancied an absolute sovereignty in Adam, mentions several ways of its conveyance to princes, that were to be his successors; but that which he chiefly insists on is that of inheritance, which occurs so often in his several discourses; and I having in the foregoing chapter quoted several of these passages, I shall not need here again to repeat them. This sovereignty he erects, as has been said, upon a double foundation, viz. that of property, and that of fatherhood. One was the right he was supposed to have in all creatures, a right to possess the earth with the beasts, and other inferior ranks of things in it, for his private use, exclusive of all other men. The other was the right he was supposed to have to rule and govern men, all the rest of mankind.

§ 85. In both these rights, there being supposed an exclusion of all other men, it must be upon some reason peculiar to Adam, that they must both be founded.

That of his property our author supposes to rise from God's immediate donation, Gen. i. 28, and that of fatherhood from the act of begetting. Now in all inheritance, if the heir succeed not to the reason upon which his father's right was founded, he cannot succeed to the right which followeth from it. For example, Adam had a right of property in the creatures upon the donation and grant of God Almighty, who was lord and proprietor of them all: let this be so as our author tells us, yet upon his death his heir can have no title to them, no such right of property in them, unless the same reason, viz. God's donation, vested a right in the heir too: for if Adam could have had no property in, nor use of the creatures, without this positive donation from God, and this donation were only personally to Adam, his heir could have no right by it; but upon his death it must revert to God, the lord and owner again; for positive grants give no title farther than the express words convey it, and by which only it is held. And thus, if, as our author himself contends, that donation, Gen. i. 28, were made only to Adam personally, his heir could not succeed to his property in the creatures: and if it were a donation to any but Adam, let it be shown that it was to his heir in our author's sense, *i. e.* to one of his children, exclusive of all the rest.

§ 86. But not to follow our author too far out of the way, the plain of the case is this: God having made man, and planted in him, as in all other animals, a strong desire of self-preservation, and furnished the world with things fit for food and raiment, and other necessaries of life, subservient to his design, that man should live and abide for some time upon the face of the earth, and not that so curious and wonderful a piece of workmanship, by his own negligence, or want of necessaries, should perish again, presently after a few moments continuance; God, I say, having made man and the world thus, spoke to him, (that is) directed him by his senses and reason, as he did the inferior animals by their sense and instinct, which were serviceable for his subsistence, and given him as the means of his preservation; and therefore I doubt not, but before these words were pronounced, Gen. i. 28, 29, (if they must be understood literally to have been spoken) and without any such verbal donation, man had a right to an use of the creatures, by the will and grant of God: for the desire, strong desire, of preserving his life and being, having been planted in him as a principle of action by God himself, reason, "which was the voice of God in him," could not but teach him and assure him that pursuing that natural inclination he had to preserve his being, he followed the will of his Maker, and therefore had a right to make use of those creatures which by his reason or senses he could discover would be serviceable thereunto. And thus man's property in the creatures was founded upon the right he had to make use of those things that were necessary or useful to his being.

§ 87. This being the reason and foundation of Adam's property, gave the same title on the same ground to all his children, not only after his death, but in his lifetime: so that here was no privilege of his heir above his other children, which could exclude them from an equal right to the use of the inferior creatures, for the comfortable preservation of their beings, which is all the property man hath in them; and so Adam's sovereignty built on property, or, as our author calls it, private dominion, comes to nothing. Every man had a right to the creatures by the same title Adam had, viz. by the right every one had to take care of and provide for their subsistence: and thus men had a right in common, Adam's children in common with him. But if any one had begun, and made himself a property in any particular thing, (which how he, or any one else, could do, shall be shown in another place) that thing, that possession, if he disposed not otherwise of it by his positive grant, descended naturally to his children, and they had a right to succeed to it and possess it.

§ 88. It might reasonably be asked here, how come children by this right of possessing, before any other, the properties of their parent's upon their decease? for it being personally the parents, when they die, without actually transferring their right to another, why does it not return again to the common stock of mankind? It will perhaps be answered, that common consent hath disposed of it to their children. Common practice, we see indeed, does so dispose of it; but we cannot say that it is the common consent of mankind; for that hath never been asked, nor actually given; and if common tacit consent hath established it, it would make but a positive, and not a natural right of children to inherit the goods of their parents: but where the practice is universal, it is reasonable to think the cause is natural. The ground then I think to be this: the first and strongest desire God planted in men, and wrought into the very principles of their nature, being that of self-preservation, that is the foundation of a right to the creatures for the particular support and use of each individual person himself. But, next to this, God planted in men a strong desire also of propagating their kind, and continuing themselves in their posterity; and this gives children a title to share in the property of their parents, and a right to inherit their possessions. Men are not proprietors of what they have, merely for themselves; their children have a title to part of it, and have their kind of right joined with their parents in the possession, which comes to be wholly theirs, when death, having put an end to their parents' use of it, hath taken them from their possessions; and this we call inheritance: men being by a like obligation bound to preserve what they have begotten, as to preserve themselves, their issue come to have a right in the goods they are possessed of. That children have such a right is plain from the laws of God; and that men are convinced that children have such a right is evident from the law of the land; both which laws require parents to provide for their children.

§ 89. For children being by the course of nature born weak, and unable to provide for themselves, they have by the appointment of God himself, who hath thus ordered the course of nature, a right to be nourished and maintained by their parents; nay, a right not only to a bare subsistence, but to the conveniencies and comforts of life, as far as the conditions of their parents can afford it. Hence it comes, that when their parents leave the world, and so the care due to their children ceases, the effects of it are to extend as far as possibly they can, and the provisions they have made in their lifetime are understood to be intended, as nature requires they should, for their children, whom, after themselves, they are bound to provide for: though the dying parents, by express words, declare nothing about them, nature appoints the descent of their property to their children, who thus come to have a title, and natural right of inheritance to their fathers' goods, which the rest of mankind cannot pretend to.

§ 90. Were it not for this right of being nourished and maintained by their parents, which God and nature has given to children, and obliged parents to as a duty, it would be reasonable that the father should inherit the estate of his son, and be preferred in the inheritance before his grandchild: for to the grandfather there is due a long score of care and expenses laid out upon the breeding and education of his son, which one would think in justice ought to be paid. But that having been done in obedience to the same law, whereby he received nourishment and education from his own parents; this score of education, received from a man's father, is paid by taking care and providing for his own children; is paid, I say, as much as is required of payment by alteration of property, unless present necessity of the parents require a return of goods for their necessary support and subsistence: for we are not now speaking of that reverence, acknowledgment, respect, and honour, that is always due from children to their parents; but of possessions and commodities of life valuable by money. But though it be incumbent on parents to bring up and provide for their children, yet this debt to their children does not quite cancel the score to their parents; but only is made by nature preferable to it: for the debt a man owes his father takes place, and gives the father a right to inherit the son's goods, where, for want of issue, the right of issue doth not exclude that title; and therefore a man having a right to be maintained by his children, where he needs it, and to enjoy also the comforts of life from them, when the necessary provision due to them and their children will afford it; if his son die without issue, the father has a right in nature to possess his goods and inherit his estate, (whatever the municipal laws of some countries may absurdly direct otherwise); and so again his children and their issue from him; or, for want of such, his father and his issue. But where no such are to be found, i. e. no kindred, there we see the possessions of a private man revert to the community, and so in politic societies come into the hands of the public magistrate; but in the state of nature become again perfectly common, nobody having a right to inherit them: nor can any one have a property in them, otherwise than in any other things common by nature; of which I shall speak in its due place.

§ 91. I have been the larger, in showing upon what ground children have a right to succeed to the possession of their fathers' properties, not only because by it, it will appear, that if Adam had a property (a titular, insignificant, useless property; for it could be no better, for he was bound to nourish and maintain his children and posterity out of it) in the whole earth and its product; yet all his children coming to have, by the law of nature, and right of inheritance, a joint title, and a right of property in it after his death, it could convey no right of sovereignty to any one of his posterity over the rest; since every one having a right of inheritance to his portion, they might enjoy their inheritance, or any part of it, in common, or share it, or some parts of it, by division, as it best liked them. But no one could pretend to the whole inheritance, or any sovereignty supposed to accompany it; since a right of inheritance gave every one of the rest, as well as any one, a title to share in the goods of his father. Not only upon this account, I say, have I been so particular in examining the reason of children's inheriting the property of their fathers, but also because it will give us farther light in the inheritance of rule and power, which in countries where their particular municipal laws give the whole possession of land entirely to the first-born, and descent of power has gone so to men by this custom, that some have been apt to be deceived into an opinion, that there was a natural or divine right of primogeniture to both estate and power; and that the inheritance of both rule over men, and property in things, sprang from the same original, and were to descend by the same rules.

§ 92. Property, whose original is from the right a man has to use any of the inferior creatures, for the subsistence and comfort of his life, is for the benefit and sole advantage of the proprietor, so that he may even destroy the thing, that he has property in by his use of it, where need requires: but government being for the preservation of every man's right and property, by preserving him from the violence or injury of others, is for the good of the governed: for the magistrate's sword being for a "terror to evil doers," and by that terror to enforce men to observe the positive laws of the society, made conformable to the laws of nature, for the public good, *i. e.* the good of every particular member of that society, as far as by common rules it can be provided for; the sword is not given the magistrate for his own good alone.

§ 93. Children, therefore, as has been showed, by the dependence they have on their parents for subsistence, have a right of inheritance to their fathers' property, as that which belongs to them for their proper good and behoof, and therefore are fitly termed goods, wherein the first-born has not a sole or peculiar right by any law of God and nature, the younger children having an equal title with him, founded on that right they all have to maintenance, support, and comfort from their parents, and on nothing else.

But government being for the benefit of the governed, and not the sole advantage of the governors, (but only for theirs with the rest, as they make a part of that politic body, each of whose parts and members are taken care of, and directed in its peculiar functions for the good of the whole, by the laws of society) cannot be inherited by the same title that children have to the goods of their father. The right of a son has to be maintained and provided with the necessaries and conveniencies of life out of his father's stock, gives him a right to succeed to his father's property for his own good; but this can give him no right to succeed also to the rule which his father had over other men. All that a child has right to claim from his father is nourishment and education, and the things nature furnishes for the support of life: but he has no right to demand rule or dominion from him: he can subsist and receive from him the portion of good things and advantages of education naturally due to him, without empire and dominion. That (if his father hath any) was vested in him, for the good and behoof of others: and therefore the son cannot claim or inherit it by a title, which is founded wholly on his own private good and advantage.

§ 94. We must know how the first ruler, from whom any one claims, came by his authority, upon what ground any one has empire, what his title is to it, before we can know who has a right to succeed him in it, and inherit it from him: if the agreement and consent of men first gave a sceptre into any one's hand, or put a crown on his head, that also must direct its descent and conveyance; for the same authority, that made the first a lawful ruler, must make the second too, and so give right of succession: in this case inheritance, or primogeniture, can in itself have no right, no pretence to it, any farther than that consent, which established the form of the government, hath so settled the succession. And thus we see the succession of crowns, in several countries, places it on different heads, and he comes by right of succession to be a prince in one place, who would be a subject in another.

§ 95. If God, by his positive grant and revealed declaration, first gave rule and dominion to any man, he that will claim by that title, must have the same positive grant of God for his succession: for if that has not directed the course of its descent and conveyance down to others, nobody can succeed to this title of the first ruler. Children have no right of inheritance to this; and primogeniture can lay no claim to it, unless God, the Author of this constitution, hath so ordained it. Thus we see the pretensions of Saul's family, who received his crown from the immediate appointment of God, ended with his reign; and David, by the same title that Saul reigned, viz. God's appointment, succeeded in his throne, to the exclusion of Jonathan, and all pretensions of paternal inheritance: and if Solomon had a right to succeed his father, it must be by some other title than that of primogeniture. A cadet, or sister's son, must have the preference in succession, if he has the same title the first lawful prince had: and in dominion that has its foundation only in the positive appointment of God himself, Benjamin, the youngest, must have the inheritance of the crown, if God so direct, as well as one of that tribe had the first possession.

§ 96. If paternal right, the act of begetting, give a man rule and dominion, inheritance or primogeniture can give no title; for he that cannot succeed to his father's title, which was begetting, cannot succeed to that power over his brethren, which his father had by paternal right over them. But of this I shall have occasion to say more in another place. This is plain in the meantime, that any government, whether supposed to be at first founded in paternal right, consent of the people, or the positive appointment of God himself, which can supersede either of the other, and so begin a new government upon a new foundation; I say, any government began upon either of these, can by right of succession come to those only, who have the title of him they succeed to: power founded on contract can descend only to him who has right by that contract: power founded on begetting, he only can have that begets; and power founded on the positive grant or donation of God, he only can have by right of succession to whom that grant directs it.

§ 97. From what I have said, I think this is clear, that a right to the use of the creatures, being founded originally in the right a man has to subsist and enjoy the conveniencies of life; and the natural right children have to inherit the goods of their parents being founded in the right they have to the same subsistence and commodities of life, out of the stock of their parents, who are therefore taught by natural love and tenderness to provide for them, as a part of themselves; and all this being only for the good of the proprietor or heir; it can be no reason for children's inheriting of rule and dominion, which has another original and a different end. Nor can primogeniture have any pretence to a right of solely inheriting either property or power, as we shall, in its due place, see more fully. It is enough to have showed here, that Adam's property or private dominion could not convey any sovereignty or rule to his heir, who not having a right to inherit all his father's possessions, could not thereby come to have any sovereignty over his brethren: and therefore, if any sovereignty on account of his property had been vested in Adam, which in truth there was not, yet it would have died with him.

§ 98. As Adam's sovereignty, if, by virtue of being proprietor of the world, he had any authority over men, could not have been inherited by any of his children over the rest, because they had the same title to divide the inheritance, and every one had a right to a portion of his father's possessions: so neither could Adam's sovereignty by right of fatherhood, if any such he had, descend to any one of his children: for it being, in our author's account, a right acquired by begetting, to rule over those he had begotten, it was not a power possible to be inherited, because the right being consequent to, and built on, an act perfectly personal, made that power so too, and impossible to be inherited: for paternal power, being a natural right rising only from the relation of father and son, is as impossible to be inherited as the relation itself; and a man may pretend as well to inherit the conjugal power of the husband, whose heir he is, had over his wife, as he can to inherit the paternal power a father over his children: for the power of the husband being founded on contract, and the power of the father on begetting, he may as well inherit the power obtained by the conjugal contract, which was only personal, as he may the power obtained by begetting, which could reach no farther than the person of the begetter, unless begetting can be a title to power in him that does not beget.

§ 99. Which makes it a reasonable question to ask, Whether Adam, dying before Eve, his heir, (suppose Cain or Seth) should have by right of inheriting Adam's fatherhood, sovereign power over Eve his mother? for Adam's fatherhood being nothing but a right he had to govern his children, because he begot them, he that inherits Adam's fatherhood, inherits nothing, even in our author's sense, but the right Adam had to govern his children, because he begot them: so that the monarchy of the heir would not have taken in Eve; or if it did, it being nothing but the fatherhood of Adam descended by inheritance, the heir must have right to govern Eve, because Adam begot her; for fatherhood is nothing else.

§ 100. Perhaps it will be said with our author, that a man can alien his power over his child; and what may be transferred by compact, may be possessed by inheritance. I answer, a father cannot alien the power he has over his child: he may perhaps to some degrees forfeit it, but cannot transfer it; and if any other man acquire it, it is not by the father's grant, but by some act of his own. For example, a father, unnaturally careless of his child, sells or gives him to another man; and he again exposes him; a third man finding him, breeds him up, cherishes, and provides for him as his own: I think in this case, nobody will doubt, but that the greatest part of filial duty and subjection was here owing, and to be paid to this foster-father; and if any thing could be demanded from the child by either of the other, it could be only due to his natural father, who perhaps might have forfeited his right to much of that duty comprehended in the command, "Honour your parents," but could transfer none of it to another. He that purchased and neglected the child, got by his purchase and grant of the father no title to duty or honour from the child; but only he acquired it, who by his own authority, performing the office and care of a father to the forlorn and perishing infant, made himself, by paternal care, a title to proportionable degrees of paternal power. This will be more easily admitted, upon consideration of the nature of paternal power, for which I refer my reader to the second book.

§ 101. To return to the argument in hand; this is evident, That paternal power arising only from begetting, for in that our author places it alone, can neither be transferred nor inherited: and he that does not beget, can no more have paternal power, which arises from thence, than he can have a right to any thing, who performs not the condition, to which only it is annexed. If one should ask, by what law has a father power over his children? it will be answered, no doubt, by the law of nature, which gives such a power over them to him that begets them. If one should ask likewise, by what law does our author's heir come by a right to inherit? I think it would be answered, by the law of nature too: for I find not that our author brings one word of Scripture to prove the right of such an heir he speaks of. Why then the law of nature gives fathers paternal power over their children, because they did beget them: and the same law of nature gives the paternal power to the heir over his brethren who did not beget them: whence it follows, that either the father has not his paternal power by begetting, or else that the heir has it not at all; for it is hard to understand how the law of nature, which is the law of reason, can give the paternal power to the father over his children, for the only reason of begetting; and to the first-born over his brethren without this only reason, i. e. for no reason at all: and if the eldest, by the law of nature, can inherit this paternal power, without the only reason that gives a title to it, so may the youngest as well as he, and a stranger as well as either; for where there is no reason for any one, as there is not, but for him that begets, all have an equal title. I am sure our author offers no reason; and when any body does, we shall see whether it will hold or no.

§ 102. In the mean time it is as good sense to say, that by the law of nature a man has right to inherit the property of another, because he is of kin to him, and is known to be of his blood; and therefore, by the same law of nature, an utter stranger to his blood has right to inherit his estate; as to say that, by the law of nature, he that begets them has paternal power over his children, and therefore, by the law of nature, the heir that begets them not, has this paternal power over them: or supposing the law of the land gave absolute power over their children, to such only who nursed them, and fed their children themselves, could any body pretend that this law gave any one, who did no such thing, absolute power over those who were not his children?

§ 103. When therefore it can be showed that conjugal power can belong to him that is ńot an husband, it will also I believe be proved, that our author's paternal power, acquired by begetting, may be inherited by a son; and that a brother, as heir to his father's power, may have paternal power over his brethren, and by the same rule conjugal power too: but till then I think we may rest satisfied that the paternal power of Adam, this sovereign authority of fatherhood, were there any such, could not descend to, nor be inherited by his next heir. Fatherly power, I easily grant our author, if it will do him any good, can never be lost, because it will be as long in the world as there are fathers: but none of them will have Adam's paternal power, or derive theirs from him; but every one will have his own by the same title Adam had his, viz. by begetting, but not by inheritance or succession, no more than husbands have their conjugal power by inheritance from Adam. And thus we see, as Adam had no such property, no such paternal power, as gave him sovereign jurisdiction over mankind; so likewise his sovereignty built upon either of these titles, if he had any such, could not have descended to his heir, but must have ended with him. Adam therefore, as has been proved, being neither monarch, nor his imaginary monarchy hereditable, the power which is now in the world is not that which was Adam's; since all that Adam could have, upon our author's grounds, either of property or fatherhood, necessarily died with him, and could not be conveyed to posterity by inheritance. In the next place we will consider whether Adam had any such heir to inherit his power as our author talks of.

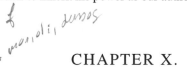

CHAPTER X.

Of the Heir to Adam's monarchical Power.

§ 104. Our author tells us, O. 253, "That it is a truth undeniable, that there cannot be any multitude of men whatsoever, either great or small, though gathered together from the several corners and remotest regions of the world, but that in the same multitude, considered by itself, there is one man amongst them that in nature hath a right to be king of all the rest, as being the next heir to Adam, and all the other subjects to him: every man by nature is a king or a subject." And again, p. 20, "If Adam himself were still living, and now ready to die, it is certain that there is one man, and but one in the world, who is next heir." Let this multitude of men be, if our author pleases, all the princes upon the earth, there will then be, by our author's rule, "one amongst them that in nature hath a right to be king of all the rest, as being the right heir to Adam;" an excellent way to establish the thrones of princes, and settle the obedience of their subjects, by setting up an hundred, or perhaps a thousand titles (if there be so many princes in the world) against any king now reigning, each as good, upon our author's grounds, as his who wears the crown. If this right of heir carry any weight with it, if it be the ordinance of God, as our author seems to tell us, O. 244, must not all be subject to it, from the highest to the lowest? Can those who wear the name of princes, without having the right of being heirs to Adam, demand obedience from their subjects by this title, and not be bound to pay it by the same law? Either governments in the world are not to be claimed, and held by this title of Adam's heir; and then the starting of it is to no purpose, the being or not being Adam's heir signifies nothing as to the title of dominion: or if it really be, as our author says, the true title to government and sovereignty; the first thing to be done is to find out this true heir of Adam, seat him in his throne, and then all the kings and princes of the world ought to come and resign up their crowns and sceptres to him, as things that belong no more to them than to any of their subjects.

§ 105. For either this right in nature of Adam's heir to be king over all the race of men, (for all together they make one multitude) is a right not necessary to the making of a lawful king, and so there may be lawful kings without it, and then kings' titles and power depend not on it; or else all the kings in the world but one are not lawful kings, and so have no right to obedience: either this title of heir to Adam is that whereby kings hold their crowns, and have a right to subjection from their subjects, and then one only can have it, and the rest being subjects can require no obedience from other men who are but their fellow-subjects; or else it is not the title whereby kings rule, and have a right to obedience from their subjects, and then kings are kings without it, and this dream of the natural sovereignty of Adam's heir is of no use to obedience and government: for if kings have a right to dominion and the obedience of their subjects who are not, nor can possibly be, heirs to Adam, what use is there of such a title, when we are obliged to obey without it? If kings, who are not heirs to Adam, have no right to sovereignty, we are all free, till our author, or any body for him, will show us Adam's right heir. If there be but one heir of Adam, there can be but one lawful king in the world, and nobody in conscience can be obliged to obedience till it be resolved who that is; for it may be any one, who is not known to be of a younger house, and all others have equal titles. If there be more than one heir of Adam, every one is his heir, and so every one has regal power: for if two sons can be heirs together, then all the sons equally are heirs, and so all are heirs, being all sons, or sons' sons of Adam. Betwixt these two the right of heir cannot stand; for by it either but one only man, or all men are kings. Take which you please, it dissolves the bonds of government and obedience; since if all men are heirs, they can owe obedience to nobody; if only one, nobody can be obliged to pay obedience to him till he be known, and his title made out.

CHAPTER XI.

Who Heir?

§ 106. The great question which in all ages has disturbed mankind, and brought on them the greatest part of those mischiefs which have ruined cities, depopulated countries, and disordered the peace of the world, has been, not whether there be power in the world, nor whence it came, but who should have it. The settling of this point being of no smaller moment than the security of princes, and the peace and welfare of their estates and kingdoms, a reformer of politics, one would think, should lay this sure, and be very clear in it: for if this remain disputable, all the rest will be to very little purpose; and the skill used in dressing up power with all the splendor and temptation absoluteness can add to it, without showing who has a right to have it, will serve only to give a greater edge to man's natural ambition, which of itself is but too keen. What can this do but set men on the more eagerly to scramble, and so lay a sure and lasting foundation of endless contention and disorder, instead of that peace and tranquillity, which is the business of government, and the end of human society?

§ 107. This designation of the person our author is more than ordinary obliged to take care of, because he affirming that "the assignment of civil power is by divine institution," hath made the conveyance as well as the power itself sacred: so that no consideration, no act or art of man, can divert it from that person to whom, by this divine right, it is assigned; no necessity or contrivance can substitute another person in his room. For if the "assignment of civil power be by divine institution," and Adam's heir be he to whom it is thus assigned, as in the foregoing chapter our author tells us, it would be as much sacrilege for any one to be king, who was not Adam's heir, as it would have been amongst the Jews for any one to have been priest who had not been of Aaron's posterity: for not only the priesthood in general being by divine institution, but the assignment of it" to the sole line and posterity of Aaron, made it impossible to be enjoyed or exercised by any one but those persons who were the offspring of Aaron: whose succession therefore was carefully observed, and by that the persons who had a right to the priesthood certainly known.

§ 108. Let us see then what care our author has taken to make us know who is "this heir, who by divine institution has a right to be king over all men." The first account of him we meet with is p. 12, in these words: "This subjection of children being the fountain of all regal authority, by the ordination of God himself; it follows that civil power, not only in general, is by divine institution, but even the assignment of it, specifically to the eldest parents." Matters of such consequence as this is should be in plain words, as little liable as might be to doubt or equivocation; and I think if language be capable of expressing any thing distinctly and clearly, that of kindred, and the several degrees of nearness of blood, is one. It were therefore to be wished that our author had used a little more intelligible expressions here, that we might have better known who it is to whom the assignment of civil power is made by divine institution; or at least would have told us what he meant by eldest parents: for I believe if land had been assigned or granted to him, and the eldest parents of his family, he would have thought it had needed an interpreter; and it would scarce have been known to whom next it belonged.

§ 109. In propriety of speech, (and certainly propriety of speech is necessary in a discourse of this nature) eldest parents signifies either the eldest men and women that have had children, or those who have longest had issue; and then our author's assertion will be, that those fathers and mothers who have been longest in the world, or longest fruitful, have by divine institution a right to civil power. If there be any absurdity in this, our author must answer for it: and if his meaning be different from my explication, he is to be blamed, that he would not speak it plainly. This I am sure, parents cannot signify heirs male, nor eldest parents an infant child: who yet may sometimes be the true heir, if there can be but one. And we are hereby still as much at a loss who civil power belongs to, notwithstanding this "assignment by divine institution," as if there had been no such assignment at all, or our author had said nothing of it. This of eldest parents leaving us more in the dark, who by divine institution has a right to civil power, than those who never heard any thing at all of heir or descent, of which our author is so full. And though the chief matter of his writing be to teach obedience to those who have a right to it, which he tells us is conveyed by descent; yet who those are, to whom this right by descent belongs, he leaves like the philosopher's stone in politics, out of the reach of any one to discover from his writings.

§ 110. This obscurity cannot be imputed to want of language in so great a master of style as sir Robert is, when he is resolved with himself what he would say: and therefore, I fear, finding how hard it would be to settle rules of descent by divine institution, and how little it would be to his purpose, or conduce to the clearing and establishing the titles of princes, if such rules of descent were settled, he chose rather to content himself with doubtful and general terms, which might make no ill sound in men's ears who were willing to be pleased with them; rather than offer any clear rules of descent of this fatherhood of Adam, by which men's consciences might be satisfied to whom it descended, and know the persons who had a right to regal power, and with it to their obedience.

§ 111. How else is it possible, that laying so much stress, as he does, upon descent, and Adam's heir, next heir, true heir, he should never tell us what heir means, nor the way to know who the next or true heir is? This I do not remember he does any where expressly handle; but, where it comes in his way, very warily and doubtfully touches; though it be so necessary, that without it all discourses of government and obedience upon his principles would be to no purpose, and fatherly power, ever so well made out, will be of no use to any body. Hence he tells us, O. 244, "That not only the constitution of power in general, but the limitation of it to one kind, *i. e.* monarchy, and the determination of it to the individual person and line of Adam, are all three ordinances of God; neither Eve nor her children could either limit Adam's power, or join others with him; and what was given unto Adam was given in his person to his posterity." Here again our author informs us, that the divine ordinance hath limited the descent of Adam's monarchical power. To whom? "To Adam's line and posterity," says our author. A notable limitation, a limitation to all mankind: for if our author can find any one amongst mankind that is not of the line and posterity of Adam, he may perhaps tell him who this next heir of Adam is: but for us, I despair how this limitation of Adam's empire to his line and posterity will help us to find out one heir. This limitation indeed of our author will save those the labour who would look for him amongst the race of brutes, if any such there were; but will very little contribute to the discovery of one next heir amongst men, though it make a short and easy determination of the

question about the descent of Adam's regal power, by telling us that the line
and posterity of Adam is to have it, that is, in plain English, any one may
have it, since there is no person living that hath not the title of being of the
line and posterity of Adam; and while it keeps there, it keeps within our
author's limitation by God's ordinance. Indeed, p. 19, he tells us, "that
such heirs are not only lords of their own children, but of their brethren;"
whereby, and by the words following, which we shall consider anon, he
seems to insinuate that the eldest son is heir; but he nowhere, that I know,
says it in direct words, but by the instances of Cain and Jacob, that there
follow, we may allow this to be so far his opinion concerning heirs, that
where there are divers children, the eldest son has the right to be heir. That
primogeniture cannot give any title to paternal power, we have already
showed. That a father may have a natural right to some kind of power over
his children, is easily granted; but that an elder brother has so over his
brethren, remains to be proved: God or nature has not any where, that I
know, placed such jurisdiction in the first-born; nor can reason find any
such natural superiority amongst brethren. The law of Moses gave a double
portion of the goods and possessions to the eldest; but we find not any
where that naturally, or by God's institution, superiority or dominion belonged to him; and the instances there brought by our author are but slender
proofs of a right to civil power and dominion in the first born, and do rather
show the contrary.

§ 112. His words are in the forecited place: "And therefore we find God
told Cain of his brother Abel, his desire shall be subject unto thee, and thou
shalt rule over him." To which I answer,

1. These words of God to Cain are by many interpreters, with great
reason, understood in a quite different sense than what our author uses
them in.

2. Whatever was meant by them, it could not be that Cain, as elder, had a
natural dominion over Abel; for the words are conditional, "If thou dost
well;" and so personal to Cain: and whatever was signified by them did
depend on his carriage, and not follow his birthright; and therefore could by
no means be an establishment of dominion in the first-born in general: for
before this Abel had his "distinct territories by right of private dominion,"
as our author himself confesses, O. 210, which he could not have had to the
prejudice of the heir's title, "if by divine institution" Cain as heir were to
inherit all his father's dominion.

3. If this were intended by God as the charter of primogeniture, and the
grant of dominion to the elder brothers in general as such, by right of
inheritance, we might expect it should have included all his brethren: for

we may well suppose, Adam, from whom the world was to be peopled, had by this time, that these were grown up to be men, more sons than these two: whereas Abel himself is not so much as named; and the words in the original can scarce, with any good construction, be applied to him.

4. It is too much to build a doctrine of so mighty consequence upon so doubtful and obscure a place of Scripture, which may well, nay better, be understood in a quite different sense, and so can be but an ill proof, being as doubtful as the thing to be proved by it; especially when there is nothing else in Scripture or reason to be found, that favours or supports it.

§ 113. It follows, p. 19, "Accordingly when Jacob bought his brother's birthright, Isaac blessed him thus; Be lord over thy brethren, and let the sons of thy mother bow before thee." Another instance, I take it, brought by our author to evince dominion due to birthright, and an admirable one it is: for it must be no ordinary way of reasoning in a man, that is pleading for the natural power of kings, and against all compact, to bring, for proof of it, an example, where his own account of it founds all the right upon compact, and settles empire in the younger brother, unless buying and selling be no compact; for he tells us, "when Jacob bought his birthright." But passing by that, let us consider the history itself, with what use our author makes of it, and we shall find the following mistakes about it.

1. That our author reports this, as if Isaac had given Jacob this blessing immediately upon his purchasing the birthright; for he says, "when Jacob bought, Isaac blessed him;" which is plainly otherwise in the Scripture: for it appears, there was a distance of time between, and if we will take the story in the order it lies, it must be no small distance: all Isaac's sojourning in Gerar, and transactions with Abimelech, Gen. xxvi. coming between; Rebecca being then beautiful, and consequently young: but Isaac, when he blessed Jacob, was old and decrepit: and Esau also complains of Jacob, Gen. xxvii. 36, that two times he had supplanted him; "he took away my birthright, (says he) and behold now he hath taken away my blessing;" words, that I think signify distance of time and difference of action.

2. Another mistake of our author's is, that he supposes Isaac gave Jacob the blessing, and bid him be "lord over his brethren," because he had the birthright; for our author brings this example to prove, that he that has the birthright, has thereby a right to "be lord over his brethren." But it is also manifest by the text, that Isaac had no consideration of Jacob's having bought the birthright; for when he blessed him, he considered him not as Jacob, but took him for Esau. Nor did Esau understand any such connexion between birthright and the blessing; for he says, "He hath supplanted me

these two times; he took away my birthright, and behold now he hath taken away my blessing:" whereas had the blessing, which was to be "lord over his brethren," belonged to the birthright, Esau could not have complained of this second as a cheat, Jacob having got nothing but what Esau had sold him, when he sold him his birthright; so that it is plain, dominion, if these words signify it, was not understood to belong to the birthright.

§ 114. And that, in those days of the patriarchs, dominion was not understood to be the right of the heir, but only a greater portion of goods, is plain from Gen. xxi. 10; for Sarah, taking Isaac to be heir, says, "cast out this bondwoman and her son, for the son of this bondwoman shall not be heir with my son:" whereby could be meant nothing, but that he should not have a pretence to an equal share of his father's estate after his death, but should have his portion presently, and be gone. Accordingly we read, Gen. xxv. 5, 6, "That Abraham gave all that he had unto Isaac: but unto the sons of the concubines which Abraham had, Abraham gave gifts, and sent them away from Isaac his son, while he yet lived." That is, Abraham having given portions to all his other sons, and sent them away, that which he had reserved, being the greatest part of his substance, Isaac as heir possessed after his death: but by being heir, he had no right to be "lord over his children;" for if he had, why should Sarah endeavour to rob him of one of his subjects, or lessen the number of his slaves, by desiring to have Ishmael sent away.

§ 115. Thus, as under the law, the privilege of birthright was nothing but a double portion: so we see that before Moses, in the patriarchs' time, from whence our author pretends to take his model, there was no knowledge, no thought, that birthright gave rule or empire, paternal or kingly authority, to any one over his brethren. If this be not plain enough in the story of Isaac and Ishmael, he that will look into 1 Chron. v. 1, may there read these words: "Reuben was the first-born: but forasmuch as he defiled his father's bed, his birthright was given unto the sons of Joseph, the son of Israel: and the genealogy is not to be reckoned after the birthright; for Judah prevailed above his brethren, and of him came the chief ruler; but the birthright was Joseph's." What this birthright was, Jacob blessing Joseph, Gen. xlviii. 22 telleth us in these words, "Moreover I have given thee one portion above thy brethren, which I took out of the hand of the Amorite, with my sword and with my bow." Whereby it is not only plain that the birthright was nothing but a double portion, but the text in Chronicles is express against our author's doctrine, and shows that dominion was no part of the birthright; for it tells us, that Joseph had the birthright, but Judah the dominion.

One would think our author were very fond of the very name of birthright, when he brings this instance of Jacob and Esau, to prove that dominion belongs to the heir over his brethren.

§ 116. 1. Because it will be but an ill example to prove, that dominion by God's ordination belonged to the eldest son, because Jacob the youngest here had it, let him come by it how he would: for if it prove any thing, it can only prove, against our author, that the "assignment of dominion to the eldest is not by divine institution," which would then be unalterable: for if by the law of God, or nature, absolute power and empire belongs to the eldest son and his heirs, so that they are supreme monarchs, and all the rest of their brethren slaves, our author gives us reason to doubt whether the eldest son has a power to part with it, to the prejudice of his posterity, since he tells us, O. 158, "That in grants and gifts that have their original from God or nature, no inferior power of man can limit, or make any law of prescription against them."

§ 117. 2. Because this place, Gen. xxvii. 29, brought by our author, concerns not at all the dominion of one brother over the other, nor the subjection of Esau to Jacob: for it is plain in history, that Esau was never subject to Jacob, but lived apart in mount Seir, where he founded a distinct people and government, and was himself prince over them, as much as Jacob was in his own family. The text, if considered, can never be understood of Esau himself, or the personal dominion of Jacob over him: for the words brethren and sons of thy mother, could not be used literally by Isaac, who knew Jacob had only one brother; and these words are so far from being true in a literal sense, or establishing any dominion in Jacob over Esau, that in the story we find the quite contrary; for Gen. xxxii. Jacob several times calls Esau lord, and himself his servant; and Gen. xxxiii. "he bowed himself seven times to the ground to Esau." Whether Esau then were a subject and vassal (nay, as our author tells us, all subjects are slaves to Jacob), and Jacob his sovereign prince by birthright, I leave the reader to judge; and to believe, if he can, that these words of Isaac, "be lord over thy brethren, and let thy mother's sons bow down to thee," confirmed Jacob in a sovereignty over Esau, upon the account of the birthright he had got from him.

§ 118. He that reads the story of Jacob and Esau, will find there never was any jurisdiction or authority, that either of them had over the other, after their father's death: they lived with the friendship and equality of brethren, neither lord, neither slave to his brother; but independent of each other, were both heads of their distinct families, where they received no laws from one another, but lived separately, and were the roots out of which sprang

two distinct people under two distinct governments. This blessing then of
Isaac, whereon our author would build the dominion of the elder brother,
signifies no more, but what Rebecca has been told from God, Gen. xxv. 23,
"Two nations are in thy womb, and two manner of people shall be separated
from thy bowels; and the one people shall be stronger than the other people,
and the elder shall serve the younger:" and so Jacob blessed Judah, Gen.
xlix., and gave him the sceptre and dominion; from whence our author
might have argued as well, that jurisdiction and dominion belongs to the
third son over his brethren, as well as from this blessing of Isaac, that it
belonged to Jacob: both these places contain only predictions of what
should long after happen to their posterities, and not any declaration of the
right of inheritance to dominion in either. And thus we have our author's
two great and only arguments to prove, that "heirs are lords over their
brethren."

1. Because God tells Cain, Gen. iv. that however sin might set upon him,
he ought or might be master of it: for the most learned interpreters understood the words of sin, and not of Abel, and give so strong reasons for it,
that nothing can convincingly be inferred from so doubtful a text to our
author's purpose.

2. Because in this of Gen. xxvii. Isaac foretels that the Israelites, the
posterity of Jacob, should have dominion over the Edomites, the posterity
of Esau; therefore, says our author, "heirs are lords of their brethren:" I
leave any one to judge of the conclusion.

§ 119. And now we see our author has provided for the descending, and
conveyance down of Adam's monarchical power, or paternal dominion, to
posterity, by the inheritance of his heir, succeeding to all his father's authority, and becoming upon his death as much lord as his father was, "not only
over his own children, but over his brethren," and all descended from his
father, and so in infinitum. But yet who this heir is, he does not once tell us;
and all the light we have from him in this so fundamental a point, is only
that in his instance of Jacob, by using the word birthright, as that which
passed from Esau to Jacob, he leaves us to guess, that by heir he means the
eldest son; though I do not remember he any where mentions expressly the
title of the first-born, but all along keeps himself under the shelter of the in-
definite term heir. But taking it to be his meaning, that the eldest son is heir
(for if the eldest be not, there will be no pretence why the sons should not be
all heirs alike) and so by right of primogeniture has dominion over his
brethren; this is but one step towards the settlement of succession, and the
difficulties remain still as much as ever, till he can show us who is meant by
right heir, in all those cases which may happen where the present possessor

hath no son. This he silently passes over, and perhaps wisely too: for what can be wiser, after one has affirmed, that "the person having that power, as well as the power and form of government, is the ordinance of God, and by divine institution," vid. O. 254, p. 12, than to be careful, not to start any question concerning the person, the resolution whereof will certainly lead him into a confession, that God and nature hath determined nothing about him? And if our author cannot show who by right of nature, or a clear positive law of God, has the next right to inherit the dominion of this natural monarch he has been at such pains about, when he died without a son, he might have spared his pains in all the rest; it being more necessary for the settling men's consciences, and determining their subjection and allegiance, to show them who, by original right, superior and antecedent to the will, or any act of men, hath a title to this paternal jurisdiction, than it is to show that by nature there was such a jurisdiction; it being to no purpose for me to know there is such a paternal power, which I ought, and am disposed to obey, unless where there are many pretenders, I also know the person that is rightfully invested and endowed with it.

§ 120. For the main matter in question being concerning the duty of my obedience, and the obligation of conscience I am under to pay it to him that is of right my lord and ruler, I must know the person that this right of paternal power reside in, and so empowers him to claim obedience from me. For let it be true what he says, p. 12, "That civil power not only in general is by divine institution, but even the assignment of it specially to the eldest parents;" and O. 254, "That not only the power or right of government, but the form of the power of governing, and the person having that power, are all the ordinance of God;" yet unless he show us in all cases who is this person ordained by God, who is this eldest parent: all his abstract notions of monarchical power will signify just nothing, when they are to be reduced to practice, and men are conscientiously to pay their obedience: for paternal jurisdiction being not the thing to be obeyed, because it cannot command, but is only that which gives one man a right which another hath not, and if it come by inheritance, another man cannot have, to command and be obeyed; it is ridiculous to say, I pay obedience to the paternal power, when I obey him, to whom paternal power gives no right to my obedience: for he can have no divine right to my obedience, who cannot show his divine right to the power of ruling over me, as well as that by divine right there is such a power in the world.

§ 121. And hence not being able to make out any prince's title to government, as heir to Adam, which therefore is of no use, and had been better let alone, he is fain to resolve all into present possession, and makes civil obedience as due to an usurper as to a lawful king; and thereby the usurper's title as good. His words are, O. 253, and they deserve to be remembered: " If an usurper dispossess the true heir, the subjects' obedience to the fatherly power must go along, and wait upon God's providence." But I shall leave his title of usurpers to be examined in its due place, and desire my sober reader to consider what thanks princes owe such politics as this, which can suppose paternal power, *i. e.* a right to government in the hands of a Cade or a Cromwell; and so all obedience being due to paternal power, the obedience of subject will be due to them, by the same right, and upon as good grounds, as it is to lawful princes; and yet this, as dangerous a doctrine as it is, must necessarily follow from making all political power to be nothing else but Adam's paternal power by right and divine institution, descending from him without being able to show to whom it descended, or who is heir to it.

§ 122. To settle government in the world, and to lay obligations to obedience on any man's conscience, it is as necessary (supposing with our author that all power be nothing but the being possessed of Adam's fatherhood) to satisfy him, who has a right to this power, this fatherhood, when the possessor dies, without sons to succeed immediately to it; as it was to tell him, that upon the death of the father, the eldest son had a right to it: for it is still to be remembered, that the great question is, (and that which our author would be thought to contend for, if he did not sometimes forget it) what persons have a right to be obeyed, and not whether there be a power in the world, which is to be called paternal, without knowing in whom it resides: for so it be a power, *i. e.* right to govern, it matters not, whether it be termed paternal or regal, natural or acquired; whether you call it supreme fatherhood, or supreme brotherhood, will be all one, provided we know who has it.

§ 123. I go on then to ask, whether in the inheriting of this paternal power, this supreme fatherhood, the grandson by a daughter hath a right before a nephew by a brother? Whether the grandson by the eldest son, being an infant, before the younger son, a man and able? Whether the daughter before the uncle? or any other man, descended by a male line? Whether a grandson, by a younger daughter, before a grand-daughter by an elder daughter? Whether the elder son by a concubine, before a younger son by a wife? From whence also will arise many questions of legitimation, and what in nature is the difference betwixt a wife and a concubine? For as to the municipal or positive laws of men, they can signify nothing here. It may farther be asked, Whether the eldest son, being a fool, shall inherit this paternal power, before the younger, a wise man? and what degree of folly it

must be that shall exclude him? and who shall be judge of it? Whether the
son of a fool, excluded for his folly, before the son of his wise brother who
reigned? Who has the paternal power whilst the widow-queen is with child
by the deceased king, and nobody knows whether it will be a son or a
daughter? Which shall be heir of the two male twins, who by the dissection
of the mother were laid open to the world? Whether a sister by the half-
blood, before a brother's daughter by the whole blood?

§ 124. These, and many more such doubts, might be proposed about the
titles of succession, and the right of inheritance; and that not as idle spec-
ulations, but such as in history we shall find have concerned the inheritance
of crowns and kingdoms; and if our's want them, we need not go farther for
famous examples of it than the other kingdom in this very island, which
having been fully related by the ingenious and learned author of Patriarcha
non Monarcha, I need say no more of. Till our author hath resolved all the
doubts that may arise about the next heir, and showed that they are plainly
determined by the law of nature, or the revealed law of God, all his suppositions of a monarchical, absolute, supreme, paternal power in Adam, and the
descent of that power to his heirs, would not be of the least use to establish
the authority, or make out the title of any one prince now on earth; but
would rather unsettle and bring all into question: for let our author tell us as
long as he pleases, and let all men believe it too, that Adam had a paternal,
and thereby a monarchical power; that this (the only power in the world)
descended to his heirs; and that there is no other power in the world but
this: let this be all as clear demonstration, as it is manifest error; yet if it be
not past doubt to whom this paternal power descends, and whose now it is,
nobody can be under any obligation of obedience; unless any one will say
that I am bound to pay obedience to paternal power in a man who has no
more paternal power than I myself; which is all one as to say, I obey a man,
because he has a right to govern; and if I be asked how I know he has a right
to govern, I should answer it cannot be known that he has any at all: for
that cannot be the reason of my obedience, which I know not to be so; much
less can that be a reason of my obedience, which nobody at all can know to
be so.

§ 125. And therefore all this ado about Adam's fatherhood, the greatness
of its power, and the necessity of its supposal, helps nothing to establish the
power of those that govern, or to determine the obedience of subjects who
are to obey, if they cannot tell whom they are to obey, or it cannot be known
who are to govern, and who to obey. In the state the world is now, it is
irrecoverably ignorant who is Adam's heir. This fatherhood, this monarchical power of Adam, descending to his heirs, would be of no more use to the

government of mankind, than it would be to the quieting of men's consciences, or securing their healths, if our author had assured them that Adam had a power to forgive sins, or cure diseases, which by divine institution descended to his heir, whilst this heir is impossible to be known. And should not he do as rationally, who upon this assurance of our author went and confessed his sins, and expected a good absolution; or took physic with expectation of health, from any one who had taken on himself the name of priest or physician, or thrust himself into those employments, saying, I acquiesce in the absolving power descending from Adam, or I shall be cured by the medicinal power descending from Adam; as he who says, I submit to and obey the paternal power descending from Adam, when it is confessed all these powers descend only to his single heir, and that heir is unknown?

§ 126. It is true the civil lawyers have pretended to determine some of these cases concerning the succession of princes; but by our author's principles they have meddled in a matter that belongs not to them: for if all political power be derived only from Adam, and be to descend only to his successive heirs, by the ordinance of God and divine institution, this is a right antecedent and paramount to all government; and therefore the positive laws of men cannot determine that which is itself the foundation of all law and government, and is to receive its rule only from the law of God and nature. And that being silent in the case, I am apt to think there is no such right to be conveyed this way: I am sure it would be to no purpose if there were, and men would be more at a loss concerning government, and obedience to governors, than if there were no such right; since by positive laws and compact, which divine institution (if there be any) shuts out, all these endless inextricable doubts can be safely provided against: but it can never be understood how a divine natural right, and that of such moment as is all order and peace in the world, should be conveyed down to posterity, without any plain natural or divine rule concerning it. And there would be an end of all civil government, if the assignment of civil power were by divine institution to the heir, and yet by that divine institution the person of the heir could not be known. This paternal regal power being by divine right only his, it leaves no room for human prudence, or consent, to place it any where else; for if only one man hath a divine right to the obedience of mankind, nobody can claim that obedience but he that can show that right; nor can men's consciences by any other pretence be obliged to it. And thus this doctrine cuts up all government by the roots.

§ 127. Thus we see how our author, laying it for a sure foundation, that the very person that is to rule is the ordinance of God, and by divine institution; tells us at large only that this person is the heir, but who this heir is he leaves us to guess; and so this divine institution, which assigns it to a person whom we have no rule to know, is just as good as an assignment to nobody at all. But whatever our author does, divine institution makes no such ridiculous assignments: nor can God be supposed to make it a sacred law, that one certain person should have a right to something, and yet not give rules to mark out, and know that person by; or give an heir a divine right to power, and yet not point out who that heir is. It is rather to be thought that an heir had no such right by divine institution, than that God should give such a right to the heir, but yet leave it doubtful and undeterminable who such heir is.

§ 128. If God had given the land of Canaan to Abraham, and in general terms to somebody after him, without naming his seed, whereby it might be known who that somebody was; it would have been as good and useful an assignment to determine the right to the land of Canaan, as it would be the determining the right of crowns, to give empire to Adam and his successive heirs after him, without telling who his heir is: for the word heir, without a rule to know who it is, signifies no more than somebody, I know not whom. God making it a divine institution that men should not marry those who were of near kin, thinks it not enough to say, "none of you shall approach to any that is near of kin to him, to uncover their nakedness;" but moreover gives rules to know who are those near of kin, forbidden by divine institution; or else that law would have been of no use; it being to no purpose to lay restraint or give privileges to men, in such general terms, as the particular person concerned cannot be known by. But God not having any where said the next heir shall inherit all his father's estate or dominion, we are not to wonder that he hath nowhere appointed who that heir should be; for never having intended any such thing, never designed any heir in that sense, we cannot expect he should any where nominate or appoint any person to it, as we might, had it been otherwise. And therefore in Scripture, though the word heir occur, yet there is no such thing as heir in our author's sense, one that was by right of nature to inherit all that his father had, exclusive of his brethren. Hence Sarah supposes that if Ishmael staid in the house to share in Abraham's estate after his death, this son of a bond-woman might be heir with Isaac; and therefore, says she, "cast out this bond-woman and her son, for the son of this bond-woman shall not be heir with my son:" but this cannot excuse our author, who telling us there is, in every number of men, one who is right and next heir to Adam, ought to have told us what the laws of descent are: but he having been so sparing to instruct us by rules how to know who is heir; let us see in the next place what his history out of Scripture, on which he pretend wholly to build his government, gives us in this necessary and fundamental point.

§ 129. Our author, to make good the title of his book, p. 13, begins his history of the descent of Adam's regal power, p. 13, in these words: "This lordship which Adam by command had over the whole world, and by right descending from him, the patriarchs did enjoy, was a large," &c. How does he prove that the patriarchs by descent did enjoy it? for "dominion of life and death, says he, we find Judah the father pronounced sentence of death against Thamar his daughter-in-law for playing the harlot," p. 13. How does this prove that Judah had absolute and sovereign authority? "he pronounced sentence of death." The pronouncing of sentence of death is not a certain mark of sovereignty, but usually the officer of inferior magistrates. The power of making laws of life and death is indeed a mark of sovereignty, but pronouncing the sentence according to those laws may be done by others, and therefore this will but ill prove that he had sovereign authority: as if one should say, judge Jefferies pronounced sentence of death in the late times, therefore judge Jefferies had sovereign authority. But it will be said Judah did it not by commission from another, and therefore did it in his own right. Who knows whether he had any right at all? Heat of passion might carry him to do that which he had no authority to do. "Judah had dominion of life and death:" how does that appear? He exercised it, he "pronounced sentence of death against Thamar." Our author thinks it is very good proof that because he did it, therefore he had a right to do it. He lay with her also; by the same way of proof he had a right to do that too. If the consequence be good from doing, to a right of doing, Absalom too may be reckoned amongst our author's sovereigns; for he pronounced such a sentence of death against his brother Amnon, and much upon a like occasion, and had it executed too, if that be sufficient to prove a dominion of life and death.

But allowing this all to be clear demonstration of sovereign power, who was it that had this "lordship by right descending to him from Adam, as large and ample as the absolutest dominion of any monarch?" Judah, says our author, Judah, a younger son of Jacob, his father and elder brethren living; so that if our author's own proof be to be taken, a younger brother may, in the life of his father and elder brothers, "by right of descent, enjoy Adam's monarchical power;" and if one so qualified may be a monarch by descent, why may not every man? If Judah, his father and elder brethren living, were one of Adam's heirs, I know not who can be excluded from this inheritance; all men by inheritance may be monarchs as well as Judah.

§ 130. "Touching war, we see that Abraham commanded an army of 318 soldiers of his own family, and Esau met his brother Jacob with 400 men at arms: for matter peace, Abraham made a league with Abimelech," &c. p. 13. Is it not possible for a man to have 318 men in his family without being heir to Adam? A planter in the West Indies has more, and might, if he pleased (who doubts?) muster them up and lead them out against the Indians to seek reparation upon any injury received from them; and all this without the "absolute dominion of a monarch, descending to him from Adam." Would it not be an admirable argument to prove, that all power by God's institution descended from Adam by inheritance, and that the very person and power of this planter were the ordinance of God, because he had power in his family over servants born in his house, and bought with his money? For this was just Abraham's case; those who were rich in the patriarch's days, as in the West Indies now, bought men and maid-servants, and by their increase, as well as purchasing of new, came to have large and numerous families, which though they made use of in war or peace, can it be thought the power they had over them was an inheritance descended from Adam, when it was the purchase of their money? A man's riding, in an expedition against an enemy, his horse bought in a fair, would be as good a proof that the owner enjoyed the lordship which Adam by command had over the whole world, by right descending to him," as Abraham's leading out the servants of his family is, that the patriarchs enjoyed this lordship by descent from Adam: since the title to the power the master had in both cases, whether over slaves or horses, was only from his purchase; and the getting a dominion over any thing by bargain and money, is a new way of proving one had it by descent and inheritance.

§ 131. "But making war and peace are marks of sovereignty." Let it be so in politic societies: may not therefore a man in the West Indies, who hath with him sons of his own, friends or companions, soldiers under pay; or slaves bought with money, or perhaps a band made up of all these, make war and peace, if there should be occasion, and "ratify the articles too with an oath, without being a sovereign, an absolute king over those who went with him? He that says he cannot, must then allow many masters of ships, many private planters, to be absolute monarchs, for as much as this they have done. War and peace cannot be made for politic societies, but by the supreme power of such societies; because war and peace giving a different motion to the force of such a politic body, none can make war or peace but that which has the direction of the force of the whole body, and that in politic societies is only the supreme power. In voluntary societies for the time, he that has such a power by consent may make war and peace, and so may a single man for himself, the state of war not consisting in the number of partisans, but the enmity of the parties, where they have no superior to appeal to.

§ 132. The actual making of war or peace is no proof of any other power, but only of disposing those to exercise or cease acts of enmity for whom he makes it; and this power in many cases any one may have without any politic supremacy: and therefore the making of war or peace will not prove that every one that does so is a politic ruler, much less a king; for then commonwealths must be kings too, for they do as certainly make war and peace as monarchical government.

§ 133. But granting this a "mark of sovereignty in Abraham," is it a proof of the descent to him of Adam's sovereignty over the whole world? If it be, it will surely be as good a proof of the descent of Adam's lordship to others too. And then commonwealths, as well as Abraham, will be heirs of Adam, for they make war and peace as well as he. If you say that the "lordship of Adam" doth not by right descend to commonwealths, though they make war and peace, the same say I of Abraham, and then there is an end of your argument: if you stand to your argument, and say those that do make war and peace, as commonwealths do without doubt, "do inherit Adam's lordship," there is an end of your monarchy, unless you will say that commonwealths "by descent enjoying Adam's lordship" are monarchies; and that indeed would be a new way of making all the governments in the world monarchical.

§ 134. To give our author the honour of this new invention, for I confess it is not I have first found it out by tracing his principles, and so charged it on him, it is fit my readers know that (as absurd as it may seem) he teaches it himself, p. 23, where he ingenuously says, "In all kingdoms and commonwealths in the world, whether the prince be the supreme father of the people, or but the true heir to such a father, or come to the crown by usurpation or election, or whether some few or a multitude govern the commonwealth; yet still the authority that is in any one, or in many, or in all these, is the only right and natural authority of a supreme father;" which right of fatherhood, he often tells us, is "regal and royal authority:" as particularly p. 12, the page immediately preceding this instance of Abraham. This regal authority, he says, those that govern commonwealths have; and if it be true, that regal and royal authority be in those that govern commonwealths, it is as true that commonwealths are governed by kings; for if regal authority be in him that governs, he that governs must needs be a king, and so all commonwealths are nothing but downright monarchies; and then what need any more ado about the matter? The governments of the world are as they should be, there is nothing but monarchy in it. This, without doubt, was the surest way our author could have found to turn all other governments, but monarchical, out of the world.

§ 135. But all this scarce proves Abraham to have been a king as heir to Adam. If by inheritance he had been king, Lot, who was of the same family, must needs have been his subject by that title, before the servants in his family; but we see they lived as friends and equals, and when their herdsmen could not agree, there was no pretence of jurisdiction or superiority between them, but they parted by consent, Gen. xiii. hence he is called, both by Abraham and by the text, Abraham's brother, the name of friendship and equality, and not of jurisdiction and authority, though he were really but his nephew. And if our author knows that Abraham was Adam's heir, and a king, it was more, it seems, than Abraham himself knew, or his servant whom he sent a wooing for his son; for when he sets out the advantages of the match, Gen. xxiv. 35, thereby to prevail with the young woman and her friends, he says, "I am Abraham's servant, and the Lord hath blessed my master greatly, and he is become great; and he hath given him flocks and herds, and silver and gold, and men-servants and maid-servants, and camels and asses; and Sarah, my master's wife, bare a son to my master when she was old, and unto him hath he given all he hath." Can one think that a discreet servant, that was thus particular to set out his master's greatness, would have omitted the crown Isaac was to have, if he had known of any such? Can it be imagined he should have neglected to have told them, on such an occasion as this, that Abraham was a king, a name well known at that time, for he had nine of them his neighbours, if he or his master had thought any such thing, the likeliest matter of all the rest, to make his errand successful?

§ 136. But this discovery it seems was reserved for our author to make two or 3000 years after, and let him enjoy the credit of it; only he should have taken care that some of Adam's land should have descended to this his heir, as well as all Adam's lordship: for though this lordship which Abraham, (if we may believe our author) as well as the other patriarchs, "by right descending to him, did enjoy, was as large and ample as the absolutest dominion of any monarch which hath been since the creation;" yet his estate, his territories, his dominions, were very narrow and scanty; for he had not the possession of a foot of land, till he bought a field and a cave of the sons of Heth to bury Sarah in.

§ 137. The instance of Esau joined with this of Abraham, to prove that the "lordship which Adam had over the whole world, by right descending from him, the patriarchs did enjoy," is yet more pleasant than the former. "Esau met his brother Jacob with 400 men at arms;" he therefore was a king by right of heir to Adam. Four hundred armed men then, however got together, are enough to prove him that leads them to be a king, and Adam's heir. There have been Tories in Ireland, (whatever there are in other countries) who would have thanked our author for so honourable an opinion of them, especially if there had been nobody near with a better title of 500 armed men, to question their royal authority of 400. It is a shame for men to trifle so, to say no worse of it, in so serious an argument. Here Esau is brought as a proof that Adam's lordship, "Adam's absolute dominion, as large as that of any monarch, descended by right to the patriarchs;" and in this very chap. p. 19, Jacob is brought as an instance of one, that by "birthright was lord over his brethren." So we have here two brothers absolute monarchs by the same title, and at the same time heirs to Adam; the eldest, heir to Adam, because he met his brother with 400 men; and the youngest heir to Adam by birth right: "Esau enjoyed the lordship which Adam had over the whole world by right descending to him, in as large and ample manner as the absolutest dominion of any monarch; and at the same time, Jacob lord over him, by the right heirs have to be lords over their brethren." *Risum teneatis ?* I never, I confess, met with any man of parts so dexterous as sir Robert at this way of arguing: but it was his misfortune to light upon an hypothesis that could not be accommodated to the nature of things, and human affairs; his principles could not be made to agree with that constitution and order which God had settled in the world, and therefore must needs often clash with common sense and experience.

§ 138. In the next section, he tells us, "This patriarchal power continued not only till the flood, but after it, as the name patriarch doth in part prove." The word patriarch doth more than in part prove, that patriarchal power continued in the world as long as there were patriarchs; for it is necessary that patriarchal power should be whilst there are patriarchs, as it is necessary there should be paternal or conjugal power whilst there are fathers or husbands; but this is but playing with names. That which he would fallaciously insinuate is the thing in question to be proved, viz. that the "lordship which Adam had over the world, the supposed absolute universal dominion of Adam by right descending from him, the patriarchs did enjoy." If he affirms such an absolute monarchy continued to the flood in the world, I would be glad to know what records he has it from; for I confess I cannot find a word of it in my Bible: if by patriarchal power he means any thing else, it is nothing to the matter in hand. And how the name patriarch in some part proves, that those who are called by that name had absolute monarchical power, I confess I do not see, and therefore I think needs no answer till the argument from it be made out a little clearer.

§ 139. "The three sons of Noah had the world," says our author, "divided amongst them by their father, for of them was the whole world overspread," p. 14. The world might be overspread by the offspring of Noah's sons, though he never divided the world amongst them; for the earth might be replenished without being divided: so that all our author's argument here proves no such division. However, I allow it to him, and then ask, the world being divided amongst them, which of the three was Adam's heir? If Adam's lordship, Adam's monarchy, by right descended only to the eldest, then the other two could be but his subjects, his slaves: if by right it descended to all three brothers, by the same right it will descend to all mankind; and then it will be impossible what he says, p. 19, that "heirs are lords of their brethren," should be true; but all brothers, and consequently all men, will be equal and independent, all heirs to Adam's monarchy, and consequently all monarchs too, one as much as another. But it will be said, Noah their father divided the world amongst them; so that our author will allow more to Noah than he will to God Almighty, for O. 211, he thought it hard, that God himself should give the world to Noah and his sons, to the prejudice of Noah's birthright. His words are, "Noah was left sole heir to the world: why should it be thought that God would disinherit him of his birthright, and make him, of all men in the world, the only tenant in common with his children?" and yet he here thinks it fit that Noah should disinherit Shem of his birthright, and divide the world betwixt him and his brethren; so that his birthright, when our author pleases, must, and when he pleases, must not, be sacred and inviolable.

§ 140. If Noah did divide the world between his sons, and his assignment of dominions to them were good, there is an end of divine institution; all our author's discourse of Adam's heir, with whatsoever he builds on it, is quite out of doors; the natural power of kings falls to the ground; and then "the form of the power governing, and the person having that power, will not be (as he says they are, O. 254), the ordinance of God, but they will be ordinances of man:" for if the right of the heir be the ordinance of God, a divine right; no man, father or not father, can alter it: if it be not a divine right, it is only human, depending on the will of man: and so where human institution gives it not, the first-born has no right at all above his brethren; and men may put government into what hands, and under what form they please.

§ 141. He goes on, "most of the civilest nations of the earth labour to fetch their original from some of the sons or nephews of Noah," p. 14. How many do most of the civilest nations amount to? and who are they? I fear the Chinese, a very great and civil people, as well as several other people of the East, West, North, and South, trouble not themselves much about this matter. All that believe the Bible, which I believe are our author's "most of the civilest nations," must necessarily derive themselves from Noah; but for the rest of the world, they think little of his sons or nephews. But if the heralds and antiquaries of all nations, for it is these men generally that labour to find out the originals of nations, or all the nations themselves, "should labour to fetch their original from some of the sons or nephews of Noah," what would this be to prove, that the "lordship which Adam had over the whole world, by a right descended to the patriarchs?" Whoever, nations, or races of men, "labour to fetch their original from," may be concluded to be thought by them men of renown, famous to posterity for the greatness of their virtues and actions; but beyond these they look not, nor consider who they were heirs to, but look on them as such as raised themselves by their own virtue to a degree that would give lustre to those who in future ages could pretend to derive themselves from them. But if it were Ogyges, Hercules, Brama, Tamerlain, Pharamond; nay, if Jupiter and Saturn were the names, from whence divers races of men, both ancient and modern, have laboured to derive their original; will that prove, that those men "enjoyed the "lordship of Adam by right descending to them?" If not, this is but a flourish of our author's to mislead his reader, that in itself signifies nothing.

§ 142. To as much purpose is what he tells us, p. 15, concerning this division of the world, "That some say it was by lot, and others that Noah sailed round the Mediterranean in ten years, and divided the world into Asia, Afric, and Europe, portions for his three sons." America then, it seems, was left to be his that could catch it. Why our author takes such pains to prove the division of the world by Noah to his sons, and will not leave out an imagination, though no better than a dream, that he can find any where to favour it, is hard to guess, since such a division, if it prove any thing, must necessarily take away the title of Adam's heir; unless three brothers can all together be heirs of Adam; and therefore the following words, "howsoever the manner of this division be uncertain, yet it is most certain the division was by families from Noah and his children, over which the parents were heads and princes," p. 15, if allowed him to be true, and of any force to prove, that all the power in the world is nothing but the lordship of Adam's descending by right, they will only prove, that the fathers of the children are all heirs to this lordship of Adam: for if in those days Cham and Japhet, and other parents, besides the eldest son, were heads and princes over their families, and had a right to divide the earth by families, what hinders younger brothers, being fathers of families, from having the same right? If Cham and Japhet were princes by right descending to them, notwithstanding any title of heir in their eldest brother, younger brothers by the same right descending to them are princes now; and so all our author's natural power of kings will reach no farther than their own children; and no kingdom, by this natural right, can be bigger than a family: for either this lordship of Adam over the whole world, by right descends only to the eldest son, and then there can be but one heir, as our author says, p. 19; or else it by right descends to all the sons equally, and then every father of a family will have it, as well as the three sons of Noah: take which you will, it destroys the present governments and kingdoms, that are now in the world; since whoever has this natural power of a king, by right descending to him, must have it, either as our author tells us Cain had it, and be lord over his brethren, and so be alone king of the whole world; or else, as he tells us here, Shem, Cham, and Japhet had it, three brothers, and so be only prince of his own family, and all families independent one of another: all the world must be only one empire by the right of the next heir, or else every family be a distinct government of itself, by the "lordship of Adam's descending to parents of families." And to this only tend all the proofs he here gives us of the descent of Adam's lordship: for continuing his story of this descent, he says,

§ 143. "In the dispersion of Babel, we must certainly find the establishment of royal power, throughout the kingdoms of the world," p. 14. If you must find it, pray do, and you will help us to a new piece of history: but you must show it us before we shall be bound to believe, that regal power was established in the world upon your principles: for, that regal power was established "in the kingdoms of the world," I think nobody will dispute; but that there should be kingdoms in the world, whose several kings enjoyed their crowns, "by right descending to them from 'Adam,'" that we think not only apocryphal, but also utterly impossible. If our author has no better foundation for his monarchy than a supposition of what was done at the dispersion of Babel, the monarchy he erects thereon, whose top is to reach to heaven to unite mankind, will serve only to divide and scatter them as that tower did; and, instead of establishing civil government and order in the world, will produce nothing but confusion.

§ 144. For he tells us, the nations they were divided into "were distinct families, which had fathers for rulers over them; whereby it appears, that even in the confusion, God was careful to preserve the fatherly authority, by distributing the diversity of languages according to the diversity of fami-

lies," p. 14. It would have been a hard matter for any one but our author to
have found out so plainly, in the text he here brings, that all the nations in
that dispersion were governed by fathers, and that "God was careful to
preserve the fatherly authority." The words of the text are, "These are the
sons of Shem after their families, after their tongues in their lands, after
their nations;" and the same thing is said of Cham and Japhet, after an
enumeration of their posterities: in all which there is not one word said of
their governors, or forms of government; of fathers, or fatherly authority.
But our author, who is very quick-sighted to spy out fatherhood, where
nobody else could see any the least glimpses of it, tells us positively their
"rulers were fathers, and God was careful to preserve the fatherly authority;" and why? Because those of the same family spoke the same language,
and so of necessity in the division kept together. Just as if one should argue
thus: Hannibal in his army, consisting of divers nations, kept those of the
same language together; therefore fathers were captains of each band, and
Hannibal was careful of the fatherly authority: or in peopling of Carolina,
the English, French, Scotch, and Welsh, that are there plant themselves
together, and by them the country is divided "in their lands after their
tongues, after their families, after their nations;" therefore care was taken
of the fatherly authority: or because, in many parts of America, every little
tribe was a distinct people, with a different language, one should infer that
therefore "God was careful to preserve the fatherly authority," or that
therefore their rulers "enjoyed Adam's lordship by right descending to
them" though we know not who were their governors, nor what their form
of government: but only that they were divided into little independent
societies, speaking different languages.

§ 145. The Scripture says not a word of their rulers or forms of government, but only gives an account how mankind came to be divided into
distinct languages and nations; and therefore it is not to argue from the
authority of Scripture, to tell us positively fathers were their rulers, when
the Scripture says no such thing; but to set up fancies in one's own brain,
when we confidently aver matter of fact, where records are utterly silent.
Upon a like ground, *i. e.* none at all, he says, "That they were not confused
multitudes without heads and governors, and at liberty to choose what
governors or governments they pleased."

§ 146. For I demand, when mankind were all yet of one language, all
congregated in the plain of Shinar, were they then all under one monarch,
"who enjoyed the lordship of Adam by right descending to him?" If they
were not, there were then no thoughts, it is plain, of Adam's heir, no right to
government known then upon that title; no care taken, by God or man, of

Adam's fatherly authority. If when mankind were but one people, dwelt altogether, and were of one language, and were upon building a city together; and when it is plain they could not but know the right heir; for Shem lived till Isaac's time, a long while after the division at Babel; if then, I say, they were not under the monarchical government of Adam's fatherhood, by right descending to the heir, it is plain there was no regard had to the fatherhood, no monarchy acknowledged due to Adam's heir, no empire of Shem's in Asia, and consequently no such division of the world by Noah, as our author has talked of. As far as we can conclude any thing from Scripture in this matter, it seems from this place, that if they had any government, it was rather a commonwealth than an absolute monarchy: for the Scripture tells us, Gen. xi. "They said:" it was not a prince commanded the building of this city and tower, it was not by the command of one monarch, but by the consultation of many, a free people; "let us build us a city:" they built it for themselves as free men, not as slaves for their lord and master: "that we be not scattered abroad;" having a city once built, and fixed habitations to settle our abodes and families. This was the consultation and design of a people, that were at liberty to part asunder, but desired to keep in one body; and could not have been either necessary or likely in men tied together under the government of one monarch, who if they had been, as our author tells us, all slaves under the absolute dominion of a monarch, needed not have taken such care to hinder themselves from wandering out of the reach of his dominion. I demand whether this be not plainer in Scripture than any thing of Adam's heir or fatherly authority?

§ 147. But if being, as God says, Gen. xi. 6, one people, they had one ruler, one king by natural right, absolute and supreme over them, "what care had God to preserve the paternal authority of the supreme fatherhood," if on a sudden he suffer 72 (for so many our author talks of) distinct nations to be erected out of it, under distinct governors, and at once to withdraw themselves from the obedience of their sovereign? This is to intitle God's care how, and to what we please. Can it be sense to say, that God was careful to preserve the fatherly authority in those who had it not? For if these were subjects under a supreme prince, what authority had they? Was it an instance of God's care to preserve the fatherly authority, when he took away the true supreme fatherhood of the natural monarch? Can it be reason to say, that God, for the preservation of fatherly authority, lets several new governments with their governors start up, who could not all have fatherly authority? And is it not as much reason to say, that God is careful to destroy fatherly authority, when he suffers one, who is in possession of it, to have his government torn in pieces, and shared by several of his subjects? Would it not be an argument just like this, for monarchical government to say, when any monarchy was shattered to pieces, and divided amongst revolted subjects, that Gold was careful to preserve monarchical power, by rending a settled empire into a multitude of little governments? If any one will say, that what happens in providence to be preserved, God is careful to preserve as a thing therefore to be esteemed by men as necessary or useful; it is a peculiar propriety of speech, which every one will not think fit to imitate: but this I am sure is impossible to be either proper or true speaking, that Shem, for example (for he was then alive), should have fatherly authority, or sovereignty by right of fatherhood, over that one people at Babel, and that the next moment, Shem yet living, 72 others should have fatherly authority, or sovereignty by right of fatherhood, over the same people, divided into so many distinct governments: either these 72 fathers actually were rulers, just before the confusion, and then they were not one people, but that God himself says they were; or else they were a commonwealth, and then where was monarchy? or else these 72 fathers had fatherly authority, but knew it not. Strange! that fatherly authority should be the only original of government amongst men, and yet all mankind not know it; and stranger yet, that the confusion of tongues should reveal it to them all of a sudden, that in an instant these 72 should know that they had fatherly power, and all others know that they were to obey it in them, and every one know that particular fatherly authority to which he was a subject. He that can think this arguing from Scripture, may from thence make out what model of an Utopia will best suit with his fancy or interest; and this fatherhood, thus disposed of, will justify both a prince who claims an universal monarchy, and his subjects, who, being fathers of families, shall quit all subjection to him, and canton his empire into less governments for themselves: for it will always remain a doubt in which of these the fatherly authority resided, till our author resolves us, whether Shem, who was then alive, or these 72 new princes, beginning so many new empires in his dominions, and over his subjects, had right to govern; since our author tells us, that both one and the other had fatherly, which is supreme authority, and are brought in by him as instances of those who did "enjoy the lordships of Adam by right descending to them, which was as large and ample as the absolutest dominion of any monarch." This at least is unavoidable, that if "God was careful to preserve the fatherly authority, in the 72 new-erected nations," it necessarily follows, that he was as careful to destroy all pretences of Adam's heir; since he took care, and therefore did preserve the fatherly authority in so many, at least 71, that could not possibly be Adam's heirs, when the right heir (if God had ever ordained any such inheritance) could not but be known; Shem then living, and they being all one people.

§ 148. Nimrod is his next instance of enjoying this patriarchal power, p. 16, but I know not for what reason our author seems a little unkind to him, and says, that he "against right enlarged his empire, by seizing violently on the rights of other lords of families." These lords of families here were called fathers of families, in his account of the dispersion at Babel: but it matters not how they were called, so we know who they are; for this fatherly authority must be in them, either as heirs to Adam, and so there could not be 72, nor above one at once; or else as natural parents over their children, and so every father will have paternal authority over his children by the same right, and in as large extent as those 72 had, and so be independent princes over their own offspring. Taking his lords of families in this latter sense (as it is hard to give those words any other sense in this place), he gives us a very pretty account of the original of monarchy, in these following words, p. 16. "And in this sense he may be said to be the author and founder of monarchy," viz. As against right seizing violently on the rights of fathers over their children; which paternal authority, if it be in them, by right of nature (for else how could those 72 come by it?) nobody can take from them without their own consents; and then I desire our author and his friends to consider, how far this will concern other princes, and whether it will not, according to his conclusion of that paragraph, resolve all regal power of those, whose dominions extend beyond their families, either into tyranny and usurpation, or election and consent of fathers of families, which will differ very little from consent of the people.

§ 149. All his instances, in the next section, p. 17, of the 12 dukes of Edom, the nine kings in a little corner of Asia in Abraham's days, the 31 kings in Canaan destroyed by Joshua, and the care he takes to prove that these were all sovereign princes, and that every town in those days had a king, are so many direct proofs against him, that it was not the lordship of Adam by right descending to them, that made kings: for if they had held their royalties by that title, either there must have been but one sovereign over them all, or else every father of a family had been as good a prince, and had as good a claim to royalty, as these: for if all the sons of Esau had each of them, the younger as well as the eldest, the right of fatherhood, and so were sovereign princes after their father's death; the same right had their sons after them, and so on to all posterity; which will limit all the natural power of fatherhood, only to be over the issue of their own bodies, and their descendents; which power of fatherhood dies with the head of each family, and makes way for the like power of fatherhood to take place in each of his sons over their respective posterities: whereby the power of fatherhood will be preserved indeed, and is intelligible, but will not be at all to our author's purpose. None of the instances he brings are proofs of any power they had, as heirs of Adam's paternal authority, by the title of his fatherhood descending to them; no, nor of any power they had by virtue of their own: for Adam's fatherhood being over all mankind, it could descend to but one at once, and from him to his right heir only, and so there could by that title be but one king in the world at a time: and by right of fatherhood, not descending from Adam, it must be only as they themselves were fathers, and so could be over none but their own posterity. So that if those 12 dukes of Edom; if Abraham and the nine kings his neighbours; if Jacob and Esau, and the 31 kings in Canaan, the 72 kings mutilated by Adonibeseck, the 32 kings that came to Benhadad, the 70 kings of Greece making war at Troy; were, as our author contends, all of them sovereign princes; it is evident that kings derived their power from some other original than fatherhood, since some of these had power over more than their own posterity; and it is demonstration, they could not be all heirs to Adam: for I challenge any man to make any pretence to power by right of fatherhood either intelligible or possible in any one, otherwise, than either as Adam's heir, or as progenitor over his own descendents, naturally sprung from him. And if our author could show that any one of these princes, of which he gives us here so large a catalogue, had his authority by either of these titles, I think I might yield him the cause; though it is manifest they are all impertinent, and directly contrary to what he brings them to prove, viz. "That the lordship which Adam had over the world by right descended to the patriarchs."

§ 150. Having told us, p. 16, That "the patriarchal government continued in Abraham, Isaac, and Jacob, until the Egyptian bondage," p. 17, he tells us, "by manifest footsteps we may trace this paternal government unto the Israelites coming into Egypt, where the exercise of the supreme patriarchal government was intermitted, because they were in subjection to a stronger prince." What these footsteps are of paternal government, in our author's sense, *i. e.* of absolute monarchical power descending from Adam, and exercised by right of fatherhood, we have seen; that is, for 2290 years no footsteps at all; since in all that time he cannot produce any one example of any person who claimed or exercised regal authority by right of fatherhood; or show any one who being a king was Adam's heir: all that his proofs amount to is only this, that there were fathers, patriarchs, and kings, in that age of the world; but that the fathers and patriarchs had any absolute arbitrary power, or by what titles those kings had theirs, and of what extent it was, the Scripture is wholly silent; it is manifest by right of fatherhood they neither did, nor could claim any title to dominion or empire.

§ 151. To say, "That the exercise of supreme patriarchal government was intermitted, because they were in subjection to a stronger prince," proves nothing but what I before suspected, viz. "That patriarchal jurisdiction or government" is a fallacious expression, and does not in our author signify (what he would yet insinuate by it) paternal and regal power, such an absolute sovereignty as he supposes was in Adam.

§ 152. For how can he say that patriarchal jurisdiction was intermitted in Egypt, where there was a king, under whose regal government the Israelites were, if patriarchal were absolute monarchical jurisdiction? And if it were not, but something else, why does he make such ado about a power not in question, and nothing to the purpose? The exercise of patriarchal jurisdiction, if patriarchal be regal, was not intermitted whilst the Israelites were in Egypt. It is true, the exercise of regal power was not then in the hands of any of the promised seeds of Abraham, nor before neither that I know: but what is that to the intermission of regal authority, as descending from Adam; unless our author will have it, that this chosen line of Abraham had the right of inheritance to Adam's lordship? and then to what purpose are his instances of the 72 rulers, in whom the fatherly authority was preserved in the confusion at Babel? Why does he bring the 12 princes sons of Ishmael, and the dukes of Edom, and join them with Abraham, Isaac, and Jacob, as examples of the exercise of true patriarchal government, if the exercise of patriarchal jurisdiction were intermitted in the world, whenever the heirs of Jacob had not supreme power? I fear, supreme patriarchal jurisdiction was not only intermitted, but from the time of the Egyptian bondage quite lost in the world; since it will be hard to find, from that time downwards, any one who exercised it as an inheritance descending to him from the patriarchs, Abraham, Isaac, and Jacob. I imagined monarchical government would have served his turn in the hands of Pharaoh, or any body. But one cannot easily discover in all places what his discourse tends to, as, particularly in this place, it is not obvious to guess what he drives at, when he says, "the exercise of supreme patriarchal jurisdiction in Egypt," or how this serves to make out the descent of Adam's lordship to the patriarchs, or any body else.

§ 153. For I thought he had been giving us out of Scripture proofs and examples of monarchical government, founded on paternal authority, descending from Adam; and not an history of the Jews: amongst whom yet we find no kings, till many years after they were a people: and when kings were their rulers, there is not the least mention or room for a pretence that they were heirs to Adam, or kings by paternal authority. I expected, talking so much as he does of Scripture, that he would have produced thence a series of monarchs, whose titles were clear to Adam's fatherhood, and who, as heirs to him, owned and exercised paternal jurisdiction over their subjects, and that this was the true patriarchal government: whereas he neither proves that the patriarchs were kings, nor that either kings or patriarchs were heirs to Adam, or so much as pretended to it: and one may as well prove that the patriarchs were all absolute monarchs; that the power both of patriarchs and kings was only paternal; and that this power descended to them from Adam: I say all these propositions may be as well proved by a confused account of a multitude of little kings in the West-Indies, out of Ferdinando Soto, or any of our late histories of the Northern America, or by our author's 70 kings of Greece, out of Homer, as by any thing he brings out of Scripture, in that multitude of kings he has reckoned up.

§ 154. And methinks he should have let Homer and his wars of Troy alone, since his great zeal to truth or monarchy carried him to such a pitch of transport against philosophers and poets, that he tells us in his preface, that "there are too many in these days who please themselves in running after the opinions of philosophers and poets, to find out such an original of government as might promise them some title to liberty, to the great scandal of Christianity and bringing in of atheism." And yet these heathens, philosopher Aristotle, and poet Homer, are not rejected by our zealous Christian politician, whenever they offer any thing that seems to serve his turn: whether "to the great scandal of Christianity and bringing in of atheism," let him look. This I cannot but observe in authors who it is visible write not for truth, how ready zeal for interest and party is to entitle Christianity to their designs, and to charge atheism on those who will not, without examining, submit to their doctrines, and blindly swallow their nonsense.

But to return to his Scripture history, our author farther tells us, p. 18, that "after the return of the Israelites out of bondage, God, out of a special care of them, chose Moses and Joshua successively to govern as princes in the place and stead of the supreme fathers." If it be true that they returned out of bondage, it must be in a state of freedom, and must imply, that both before and after this bondage they were free; unless our author will say that changing of masters is returning out of bondage; or that a slave returns out of bondage when he is removed from one gally to another. If then they returned out of bondage, it is plain that in those days, whatever our author in his preface says to the contrary, there was a difference between a son, a subject, and a slave; and that neither the patriarchs before, nor their rulers after this "Egyptian bondage, numbered their sons or subjects amongst their possessions," and disposed of them with as absolute a dominion, as they did their other goods.

§ 155. This is evident in Jacob to whom Reuben offered his two sons as pledges; and Judah was at last surety for Benjamin's safe return out of Egypt: which all had been vain, superfluous, and but a sort of mockery, if Jacob had had the same power over every one of his family as he had over his ox or his ass, as an owner over his substance; and the offers that Reuben or Judah made had been such a security for returning of Benjamin, as if a man should take two lambs out of his lord's flock, and offer one as security that he will safely restore the other.

§ 156. When they were out of this bondage, what then? "God out of a special care of them, the Israelites." It is well that once in his book he will allow God to have any care of the people: for in other places he speaks of mankind as if God had no care of any part of them, but only of their monarchs, and that the rest of the people, the societies of men, were made as so many herds of cattle, only for the service, use, and pleasure of their princes.

§ 157. "Chose Moses and Joshua successively to govern as princes;" a shrewd argument our author has found out to prove God's care of the fatherly authority, and Adam's heirs, that here, as an expression of his care of his own people, he chooses those for princes over them that had not the least pretence to either. The persons chosen were Moses, of the tribe of Levi, and Joshua of the tribe of Ephraim, neither of which had any title of fatherhood. But, says our author, they were in the place and stead of the supreme fathers. If God had any where as plainly declared his choice of such fathers to be rulers, as he did of Moses and Joshua, we might believe Moses and Joshua were in their place and stead: but that being the question in debate, till that be better proved, Moses being chosen by God to be ruler of his people, will no more prove that government belonged to Adam's heir, or to the fatherhood, than God's choosing Aaron of the tribe of Levi to be priest, will prove that the priesthood belonged to Adam's heir, or the prime fathers; since God would choose Aaron to be priest, and Moses ruler in Israel, though neither of those offices were settled on Adam's heir or the fatherhood.

§ 158. Our author goes on, "And after them likewise for a time he raised up judges, to defend his people in time of peril," p. 18. This proves fatherly authority to be the original of government, and that it descended from Adam to his heirs just as well as what went before: only here our author seems to confess that these judges, who were all the governors they then had, were only men of valour, whom they made their generals to defend them in time of peril; and cannot God raise up such men, unless fatherhood have a title to government?

§ 159. But says our author, "when God gave the Israelites kings, he re-established the ancient and prime right of lineal succession to paternal government." p. 18.

§ 160. How did God re-establish it? by a law, a positive command? We find no such thing. Our author means then, that when God gave them a king, in giving them a king, he re-established the right, &c. To re-establish *de facto* the right of lineal succession to paternal government is to put a man in possession of that government which his fathers did enjoy, and he by lineal succession had a right to: for, first, if it were another government than what his ancestor had, it was not succeeding to an ancient right, but beginning a new one: for if a prince should give a man, besides his ancient patrimony, which for some ages his family had been disseised of, an additional estate, never before in the possession of his ancestors, he could not be said to re-establish the right of lineal succession to any more than what had been formerly enjoyed by his ancestors. If therefore the power the kings of Israel had were any thing more than Isaac or Jacob had, it was not the re-establishing in them the right of succession to a power, but giving them a new power, however you please to call it, paternal or not: and whether Isaac and Jacob had the same power that the kings of Israel had, I desire any one, by what has been above said, to consider; and I do not think he will find that either Abraham, Isaac, or Jacob, had any regal power at all.

§ 161. Next, there can be "no re-establishment of the prime and ancient right of lineal succession" to any thing, unless he that is put in possession of it has the right to succeed, and be the true and next heir to him he succeeds to. Can that be a re-establishment which begins in a new family? or that the "re-establishment of an ancient right of lineal succession," when a crown is given to one who has no right of succession to it; and who, if the lineal succession had gone on, had been out of all possibility of pretence to it? Saul, the first king God gave the Israelites, was of the tribe of Benjamin. Was the "ancient and prime right of lineal succession re-established" in him? The next was David, the youngest son of Jesse, of the posterity of Judah, Jacob's third son. Was the "ancient and prime right of lineal succession to paternal government re-established in him?" or in Solomon, his younger son and successor in the throne? or in Jeroboam over the ten tribes? or in Athaliah, a woman who reigned six years, an utter stranger to the royal blood? "If the ancient and prime right of lineal succession to paternal government were re-established" in any of these or their posterity, "the ancient and prime right of lineal succession to paternal government" belongs to younger brothers as well as elder, and may be re-established in any man living: for whatever younger brothers, "by ancient and prime right of lineal succession," may have as well as the elder, that every man living may have a right to by lineal succession, and Sir Robert as well as any other. And so what a brave right of lineal succession to his paternal or regal government our author has re-established, for the securing the rights and inheritance of crowns, where every one may have it, let the world consider.

§ 162. But says our author, however, p. 19, "Whensoever God made choice of any special person to be king, he intended that the issue also should have benefit thereof, as being comprehended sufficiently in the person of the father, although the father was only named in the grant." This yet will not help out succession: for if, as our author says, the benefit of the grant be intended to the issue of the grantee, this will not direct the succession; since, if God give any thing to a man and his issue in general, the claim cannot be to any one of that issue in particular; every one that is of his race will have an equal right. If it be said, our author meant heir, I believe our author was as willing as any body to have used that word, if it would have served his turn: but Solomon, who succeeded David in the throne, being no more his heir than Jeroboam, who succeeded him in the government of the ten tribes, was his issue, our author had reason to avoid saying, that God intended it to the heirs, when that would not hold in a succession, which our author could not except against; and so he has left his succession as undetermined, as if he had said nothing about it: for if the regal power be given by God to a man and his issue, as the land of Canaan was to Abraham and his seed, must they not all have a title to it, all share in it? And one may as well say, that by God's grant to Abraham and his seed, the land of Canaan was to belong only to one of his seed, exclusive of all others, as by God's grant of dominion to a man and his issue, this dominion was to belong in peculiar to one of his issue exclusive of all others.

§ 163. But how will our author prove that whensoever God made choice of any special person to be a king, he intended that "the (I suppose he means his) issue also should have benefit thereof?" has he so soon forgot Moses and Joshua, whom in this very section, he says, "God out of a special care chose to govern as princes," and the judges that God raised up? Had not these princes, having the same authority of the supreme fatherhood, the same power that the kings had; and being specially chosen by God himself, should not their issue have the benefit of that choice, as well as David's or Solomon's? If these had the paternal authority put into their hands immediately by God, why had not their issue the benefit of this grant in a succession to this power? Or if they had it as Adam's heirs, why did not their heirs enjoy it after them by right descending to them? for they could not be heirs to one another. Was the power the same, and from the same original, in Moses, Joshua, and the Judges, as it was in David and the kings; and was it inheritable in one and not in the other? If it was not paternal authority, then God's own people were governed by those that had not paternal authority, and those governors did well enough without it: if it were paternal authority, and God chose the persons that were to exercise it, our author's rule fails, that "whensoever God makes choice of any person to be supreme ruler," (for I suppose the name king has no spell in it, it is not the title, but the power makes the difference), "he intends that the issue also should have the benefit of it," since from their coming out of Egypt to David's time, 400 years, the issue was never "so sufficiently comprehended in the person of the father," as that any son, after the death of his father, succeeded to the government amongst all those judges that judged Israel. If to avoid this, it be said, God always chose the person of the successor, and so, transferring the fatherly authority to him, excluded his issue from succeeding to it, that is manifestly not so in the story of Jephthah, where he articled with the people, and they made him judge over them, as is plain, Judg. xi.

§ 164. It is in vain then to say, that "whensoever God chooses any special person to have the exercise of paternal authority," (for if that be not to be king, I desire to know the difference between a king and one having the exercise of paternal authority), "he intends the issue also should have the benefit of it," since we find the authority the judges had ended with them, and descended not to their issue; and if the judges had not paternal authority, I fear it will trouble our author, or any of the friends to his principles, to tell who had then the paternal authority, that is, the government and supreme power amongst the Israelites: and I suspect they must confess that the chosen people of God continued a people several hundreds of years, without any knowledge or thought of this paternal authority, or any appearance of monarchical government at all.

§ 165. To be satisfied of this, he need but read the story of the Levite, and the war thereupon with the Benjamites, in the three last chapters of Judges; and when he finds, that the Levite appeals to the people for justice, that it was the tribes and the congregation that debated, resolved, and directed all that was done on that occasion; he must conclude, either that God was not "careful to preserve the fatherly authority" amongst his own chosen people; or else that the fatherly authority may be preserved where there is no monarchical government: if the latter, then it will follow, that though fatherly authority be ever so well proved, yet it will not infer a necessity of monarchical government; if the former, it will seem very strange and improbable, that God should ordain fatherly authority to be so sacred amongst the sons of men, that there could be no power or government without it, and yet that amongst his own people, even whilst he is providing a government for them, and therein prescribes rules to the several states and relations of men, this great and fundamental one, this most material and necessary of all the rest, should be concealed, and lie neglected for 400 years after.

§ 166. Before I leave this, I must ask how our author knows that "whensoever God makes choice of any special person to be king, he intends that the issue should have the benefit thereof?" Does God by the law of nature or revelation say so? By the same law also he must say, which of his issue must enjoy the crown in succession, and so point out the heir, or else leave his issue to divide or scramble for the government: both alike absurd, and such as will destroy the benefit of such grant to the issue. When any such declaration of God's intention is produced, it will be our duty to believe God intends it so; but till that be done, our author must show us some better warrant, before we shall be obliged to receive him as the authentic revealer of God's intentions.

§ 167. "The issue," says our author, "is comprehended sufficiently in the person of the father, although the father only was named in the grant:" and yet God, when he gave the land of Canaan to Abraham, Gen. xiii. 15, thought fit to put his seed into the grant too: so the priesthood was given to Aaron and his seed; and the crown God gave not only to David, but his seed also: and however our author assures us that "God intends that the issue should have the benefit of it, when he chooses any person to be king," yet we see that the kingdom which he gave to Saul, without mentioning his seed after him, never came to any of his issue: and why, when God chose a person to be king, he should intend that his issue should have the benefit of it, more than when he chose one to be judge in Israel, I would fain know a reason; or why does a grant of fatherly authority to a king more comprehend the issue, than when a like grant is made to a judge? Is paternal authority by right to descend to the issue of one, and not of the other? There will need some reason to be shown of this difference more than the name, when the thing given is the same fatherly authority, and the manner of giving it, God's choice of the person, the same too; for I suppose our author, when he says, "God raised up judges," will by no means allow they were chosen by the people.

§ 168. But since our author has so confidently assured us of the care of God to preserve the fatherhood, and pretends to build all he says upon the authority of the Scripture, we may well expect that that people, whose law, constitution, and history are chiefly contained in the Scripture, should furnish him with the clearest instances of God's care of preserving the fatherly authority in that people who it is agreed he had a most peculiar care of. Let us see than what state this paternal authority or government was in amongst the Jews from their beginning to be a people. It was omitted by our author's confession, from their coming into Egypt, till their return out of that bondage, above 200 years: from thence till God gave the Israelites a king, about 400 years more, our author gives but a very slender account of it; nor indeed all that time are there the least footsteps of paternal or regal government amongst them. But then, says our author, "God re-established the ancient and prime right of lineal succession to paternal government."

§ 169. What a "lineal succession to paternal government" was then established we have already seen. I only now consider how long this lasted, and that was to their captivity, about 500 years: from thence to their destruction by the Romans, above 650 years after, the "ancient and prime right of lineal succession to paternal government" was again lost, and they continued a people in the promised land without it. So that of 1750 years that they were God's peculiar people, they had hereditary kingly government amongst them not one-third of the time; and of that time there is not the least footstep of one moment of "paternal government, nor the re-establishment of the ancient and prime right of lineal succession to it," whether we suppose it to be derived, as from its fountain, from David, Saul, Abraham, or, which upon our author's principles is the only true, from Adam.

Of
Civil Government.

BOOK II: SECOND TREATISE

CHAPTER I.

§1. It having been shown in the foregoing discourse, 1. That Adam had not, either by natural right of fatherhood, or by positive donation from God, any such authority over his children, or dominion over the world, as is pretended:

2. That if he had, his heirs yet had no right to it:

3. That if his heirs had, there being no law of nature nor positive law of God that determines which is the right heir in all cases that may arise, the right of succession, and consequently of bearing rule, could not have been certainly determined:

4. That if even that had been determined, yet the knowledge of which is the eldest line of Adam's posterity being so long since utterly lost, that in the races of mankind and families of the world there remains not to one above another the least pretence to be the eldest house, and to have the right of inheritance:

All these premises having, as I think, been clearly made out, it is impossible that the rulers now on earth should make any benefit, or derive any the least shadow of authority from that, which is held to be the fountain of all power, "Adam's private dominion and paternal jurisdiction;" so that he that will not give just occasion to think that all government in the world is the product only of force and violence, and that men live together by no other rules but that of beasts, where the strongest carries it, and so lay a foundation for perpetual disorder and mischief, tumult, sedition, and rebellion, (things that the followers of that hypothesis so loudly cry out against) must of necessity find out another rise of government, another original of political power, and another way of designing and knowing the persons that have it, than what sir Robert Filmer hath taught us.

§ 2. To this purpose, I think it may not be amiss to set down what I take to be political power; that the power of a magistrate over a subject may be distinguished from that of a father over his children, a master over his servants, a husband over his wife, and a lord over his slave. All which distinct powers happening sometimes together in the same man, if he be considered under these different relations, it may help us to distinguish these powers one from another, and show the difference betwixt a ruler of a commonwealth, a father of a family, and a captain of a galley.

§ 3. Political power, then, I take to be a right of making laws with penalties of death, and consequently all less penalties, for the regulating and preserving of property, and of employing the force of the community, in the execution of such laws, and in the defence of the commonwealth from foreign injury; and all this only for the public good.

CHAPTER II.

Of the State of Nature.

§ 4. To understand political power right, and derive it from its original, we must consider what state all men are naturally in, and that is, a state of perfect freedom to order their actions and dispose of their possessions and persons, as they think fit, within the bounds of the law of nature; without asking leave, or depending upon the will of any other man.

A state also of equality, wherein all the power and jurisdiction is reciprocal, no one having more than another; there being nothing more evident than that creatures of the same species and rank, promiscuously born to all the same advantages of nature, and the use of the same faculties, should also be equal one amongst another without subordination or subjection; unless the Lord and Master of them all should, by any manifest declaration of his will, set one above another, and confer on him, by an evident and clear appointment, an undoubted right to dominion and sovereignty.

§ 5. This equality of men by nature the judicious Hooker looks upon as so evident in itself, and beyond all question, that he makes it the foundation of that obligation to mutual love amongst men, on which he builds the duties we owe one another, and from whence he derives the great maxims of justice and charity. His words are,

"The like natural inducement hath brought men to know that it is no less their duty to love others than themselves; for seeing those things which are equal must needs all have one measure; if I cannot but wish to receive good, even as much at every man's hands as any man can wish unto his own soul, how should I look to have any part of my desire herein satisfied, unless myself be careful to satisfy the like desire, which is undoubtedly in other men, being of one and the same nature? To have any thing offered them repugnant to this desire must needs in all respects grieve them as much as me; so that, if I do harm, I must look to suffer, there being no reason that others should show greater measure of love to me than they have by me showed unto them: my desire therefore to be loved of my equals in nature, as much as possibly may be, imposeth upon me a natural duty of bearing to them-ward fully the like affection: from which relation of equality between ourselves and them that are as ourselves, what several rules and canons natural reason hath drawn, for direction of life, no man is ignorant."

§ 6. But though this be a state of liberty, yet it is not a state of licence: though man in that state have an uncontrollable liberty to dispose of his person or possessions, yet he has not liberty to destroy himself, or so much as any creature in his possession, but where some nobler use than its bare preservation calls for it. The state of nature has a law of nature to govern it, which obliges every one: and reason, which is that law, teaches all mankind, who will but consult it, that being all equal and independent, no one ought to harm another in his life, health, liberty, or possessions: for men being all the workmanship of one omnipotent and infinitely wise Maker; all the servants of one sovereign Master, sent into the world by his order, and about his business; they are his property, whose workmanship they are, made to last during his, not another's pleasure: and being furnished with like faculties, sharing all in one community of nature, there cannot be supposed any such subordination among us that may authorize us to destroy another, as if we were made for one another's uses, as the inferior ranks of creatures are for ours. Every one, as he is bound to preserve himself, and not to quit his station wilfully, so by the like reason, when his own preservation comes not in competition, ought he, as much as he can, to preserve the rest of mankind, and may not, unless it be to do justice to an offender, take away or impair the life, or what tends to the preservation of life, the liberty, health, limb, or goods of another.

§ 7. And that all men may be restrained from invading others' rights, and from doing hurt to one another, and the law of nature be observed, which willeth the peace and preservation of all mankind, the execution of the law of nature is, in that state, put into every man's hands, whereby every one has a right to punish the transgressors of that law to such a degree as may hinder its violation: for the law of nature would, as all other laws that concern men in this world, be in vain, if there were nobody that in the state of nature had a power to execute that law, and thereby preserve the innocent, and restrain offenders. And if any one in the state of nature may punish another for any evil he has done, every one may do so: for in that state of perfect equality, where naturally there is no superiority or jurisdiction of one over another, what any may do in prosecution of that law every one must needs have a right to do.

§ 8. And thus, in the state of nature, "one man comes by a power over another;" but yet no absolute or arbitrary power to use a criminal, when he has got him in his hands, according to the passionate heats or boundless extravagancy of his own will; but only to retribute to him, so far as calm reason and conscience dictate, what is proportionate to his transgression; which is so much as may serve for reparation and restraint: for these two are the only resons why one man may lawfully do harm to another, which is that we call punishment. In transgressing the law of nature, the offender declares himself to live by another rule than that of reason and common equity, which is that measure God has set to the actions of men for their mutual security; and so he becomes dangerous to mankind, the tie, which is to secure them from injury and violence, being slighted and broken by him: which being a trespass against the whole species, and the peace and safety of it, provided for by the law of nature; every man upon this score, by the right he hath to preserve mankind in general, may restrain, or, where it is necessary, destroy things noxious to them, and so may bring such evil on any one, who hath transgressed that law, as may make him repent the doing of it, and thereby deter him, and by his example others, from doing the like mischief. And in this case, and upon this ground, "every man hath a right to punish the offender, and be executioner of the law of nature."

§ 9. I doubt not but this will seem a very strange doctrine to some men: but, before they condemn it, I desire them to resolve me by what right any prince or state can put to death or punish an alien for any crime he commits in their country. It is certain their laws, by virtue of any sanction they receive from the promulgated will of the legislative, reach not a stranger: they speak not to him, nor, if they did, is he bound to hearken to them. The legislative authority, by which they are in force over the subjects of that commonwealth, hath no power over him. Those who have the supreme power of making laws in England, France, or Holland, are to an Indian but like the rest of the world, men without authority: and therefore, if by the law of nature every man hath not a power to punish offences against it, as he soberly judges the case to require, I see not how the magistrates of any community can punish an alien of another country; since, in reference to him, they can have no more power than what every man naturally may have over another.

§ 10. Besides the crime which consists in violating the law, and varying from the right rule of reason, whereby a man so far becomes degenerate, and declares himself to quit the principles of human nature, and to be a noxious creature, there is commonly injury done to some person or other, and some other man receives damage by his transgression: in which case he who hath received any damage, has, besides the right of punishment common to him with other men, a particular right to seek reparation from him that has done it: and any other person, who finds it just, may also join with him that is injured, and assist him in recovering from the offender so much as may make satisfaction for the harm he has suffered.

§ 11. From these two distinct rights, the one of punishing the crime for restraint, and preventing the like offence, which right of punishing is in every body; the other of taking reparation, which belongs only to the injured party; comes it to pass that the magistrate, who by being magistrate hath the common right of punishing put into his hands, can often, where the public good demands not the execution of the law, remit the punishment of criminal offences by his own authority, but yet cannot remit the satisfaction due to any private man for the damage he has received. That he who has suffered the damage has a right to demand in his own name, and he alone can remit: the damnified person has this power of appropriating to himself the goods or service of the offender, by right of self-preservation, as every man has a power to punish the crime, to prevent its being committed again, "by the right he has of preserving all mankind," and doing all reasonable things he can in order to that end: and thus it is that every man, in the state of nature, has a power to kill a murderer, both to deter others from doing the like injury, which no reparation can compensate, by the example of the punishment that attends it from every body; and also to secure men from the attempts of a criminal, who having renounced reason, the common rule and measure God hath given to mankind, hath, by the unjust violence and slaughter he hath committed upon one, declared war against all mankind; and therefore may be destroyed as a lion or a tiger, one of those wild savage beasts with whom men can have no society nor security: and upon this is grounded that great law of nature, "Whoso sheddeth man's blood, by man shall his blood be shed." And Cain was so fully convinced that every one had a right to destroy such a criminal, that, after the murder of his brother, he cries out, "Every one that findeth me shall slay me;" so plain was it writ in the hearts of mankind.

§ 12. By the same reason may a man in the state of nature punish the lesser breaches of that law. It will perhaps be demanded, with death? I answer, each transgression may be punished to that degree, and with so much severity, as will suffice to make it an ill bargain to the offender, give him cause to repent, and terrify others from doing the like. Every offence, that can be committed in the state of nature, may in the state of nature be also punished equally, and as far forth, as it may in a commonwealth: for though it would be beside my present purpose to enter here into the particulars of the law of nature, or its measures of punishment, yet it is certain there is such a law, and that too as intelligible and plain to a rational creature, and a studier of that law, as the positive laws of commonwealths; nay, possibly plainer, as much as reason is easier to be understood than the fancies and intricate contrivances of men, following contrary and hidden interests put into words; for so truly are a great part of the municipal laws of countries, which are only so far right, as they are founded on the law of nature, by which they are to be regulated and interpreted.

§ 13. To this strange doctrine, viz. That "in the state of nature every one has the executive power" of the law of nature, I doubt not but it will be objected, that it is unreasonable for men to be judges in their own cases, that self-love will make men partial to themselves and their friends: and, on the other side, that ill-nature, passion, and revenge will carry them too far in punishing others; and hence nothing but confusion and disorder will follow: and that therefore God hath certainly appointed government to restrain the partiality and violence of men. I easily grant, that civil government is the proper remedy for the inconveniencies of the state of nature, which must certainly be great, where men may be judges in their own case; since it is easy to be imagined, that he who was so unjust as to do his brother an injury, will scarce be so just as to condemn himself for it: but I shall desire those who make this objection to remember, that absolute monarchs are but men; and if government is to be the remedy of those evils, which necessarily follow from men's being judges in their own cases, and the state of nature is therefore not to be endured; I desire to know what kind of government that is, and how much better it is than the state of nature, where one man, commanding a multitude, has the liberty to be judge in his own case, and may do to all his subjects whatever he pleases, without the least liberty to any one to question or control those who execute his pleasure? and in whatsoever he doth, whether led by reason, mistake, or passion, must be submitted to? Much better it is in the state of nature, wherein men are not bound to submit to the unjust will of another: and if he that judges, judges amiss in his own, or any other case, he is answerable for it to the rest of mankind.

§ 14. It is often asked, as a mighty objection, "where are or ever were there any men in such a state of nature?" To which it may suffice as an answer at present, that since all princes and rulers of independent governments, all through the world, are in a state of nature, it is plain the world never was, nor ever will be, without numbers of men in that state. I have named all governors of independent communities, whether they are, or are not, in league with others: for it is not every compact that puts an end to the state of nature between men, but only this one of agreeing together mutually to enter into one community, and make one body politic; other promises and compacts men may make one with another, and yet still be in the state of nature. The promises and bargains for truck, &c. between the two men in the desert island, mentioned by Garcilasso de la Vega, in his history of Peru; or between a Swiss and an Indian, in the woods of America; are binding to them, though they are perfectly in a state of nature, in reference to one another: for truth and keeping of faith belongs to men as men, and not as members of society.

§ 15. To those that say, there were never any men in the state of nature, I will not only oppose the authority of the judicious Hooker, Eccl. Pol. lib. i. sect. 10, where he says, "The laws which have been hitherto mentioned," *i.e.* the laws of nature, "do bind men absolutely, even as they are men, although they have never any settled fellowship, never any solemn agreement amongst themselves what to do, or not to do: but forasmuch as we are not by ourselves sufficient to furnish ourselves with competent store of things, needful for such a life as our nature doth desire, a life fit for the dignity of man; therefore to supply those defects and imperfections which are in us, as living singly and solely by ourselves, we are naturally induced to seek communion and fellowship with others. This was the cause of men's uniting themselves at first in politic societies." But I moreover affirm, that all men are naturally in that state, and remain so, till by their own consents they make themselves members of some politic society; and I doubt not in the sequel of this discourse to make it very clear.

State

State of nature ≠ *Of the State of War.* only → state of slavery

State

use of force, so to get him in his power, as to take away his money, or what he pleases, from him; because using force, where he has no right, to get me into his power, let his pretence be what it will, I have no reason to suppose, that he, who would take away my liberty, would not, when he had me in his power, take away every thing else. And therefore it is lawful for me to treat him as one who has put himself into a state of war with me, *i. e.* kill him if I can; for to that hazard does he justly expose himself, whoever introduces a state of war, and is aggressor in it.

§ 19. And here we have the plain "difference between the state of nature and the state of war;" which, however some men have confounded, are as far distant as a state of peace, good-will, mutual assistance and preservation, and a state of enmity, malice, violence, and mutual destruction, are one from another. Men living together according to reason, without a common superior on earth, with authority to judge between them, is properly the state of nature. But force, or a declared design of force, upon the person of another, where there is no common superior on earth to appeal to for relief, is the state of war: and it is the want of such an appeal gives a man the right of war even against an aggressor, though he be in society, and a fellow-subject. Thus a thief, whom I cannot harm, but by appeal to the law, for having stolen all that I am worth, I may kill, when he sets on me to rob me but of my horse or coat; because the law, which was made for my preservation, where it cannot interpose to secure my life from present force, which, if lost, is capable of no reparation, permits me my own defence, and the right of war, a liberty to kill the aggressor, because the aggressor allows not time to appeal to our common judge, nor the decision of the law, for remedy in a case where the mischief may be irreparable. Want of a common judge with authority puts all men in a state of nature: force without right, upon a man's person, makes a state of war, both where there is, and is not, a common judge.

§ 20. But when the actual force is over, the state of war ceases between those that are in society, and are equally on both sides subjected to the fair determination of the law; because then there lies open the remedy of appeal for the past injury, and to prevent future harm: but where no such appeal is, as in the state of nature, for want of positive laws, and judges with authority to appeal to, the state of war once begun, continues with a right to the innocent party to destroy the other whenever he can, until the aggressor offers peace, and desires reconciliation on such terms as may repair any wrongs he has already done, and secure the innocent for the future; nay, where an appeal to the law, and constituted judges, lies open, but the remedy is denied by a manifest perverting of justice, and a barefaced wresting of the laws to protect or indemnify the violence or injuries of some men, or party of men; there it is hard to imagine any thing but a state of war: for wherever violence is used, and injury done, though by hands appointed to administer justice, it is still violence and injury, however coloured with the name, pretences, or forms of law, the end whereof being to protect and redress the innocent, by an unbiassed application of it, to all who are under it; wherever that is not *bona fide* done, war is made upon the sufferers, who having no appeal on earth to right them, they are left to the only remedy in such cases, an appeal to Heaven.

§ 21. To avoid this state of war (wherein there is no appeal but to Heaven, and wherein every the least difference is apt to end, where there is no authority to decide between the contenders) is one great reason of men's putting themselves into society, and quitting the state of nature: for where there is an authority, a power on earth, from which relief can be had by appeal, there the continuance of the state of war is excluded, and the controversy is decided by that power. Had there been any such court, any superior jurisdiction on earth, to determine the right between Jephthah and the Ammonites, they had never come to a state of war: but we see he was forced to appeal to Heaven: "The Lord the Judge (says he) be judge this day, between the children of Israel and the children of Ammon," Judg. xi. 27; and then prosecuting, and relying on his appeal, he leads out his army to battle: and therefore in such controversies, where the question is put, who shall be judge? it cannot be meant, who shall decide the controversy; every one knows what Jephthah here tells us, that "the Lord the Judge" shall judge. Where there is no judge on earth, the appeal lies to God in heaven. That question then cannot mean, who shall judge whether another hath put himself in a state of war with me, and whether I may, as Jephthah did, appeal to Heaven in it? of that I myself can only be judge in my own conscience, as I will answer it, at the great day, to the supreme Judge of all men.

CHAPTER IV.

Of Slavery.

§ 22. The natural liberty of man is to be free from any superior power on earth, and not to be under the will or legislative authority of man, but to have only the law of nature for his rule. The liberty of man, in society, is to be under no other legislative power, but that established, by consent, in the commonwealth; nor under the dominion of any will, or restraint of any law, but what that legislative shall enact, according to the trust put in it. Freedom, then, is not what sir Robert Filmer tells us, O.A. 55, "a liberty for every one to do what he lists, to live as he pleases, and not to be tied by any laws:" but freedom of men under government is, to have a standing rule to live by, common to every one of the society, and made by the legislative power erected in it; a liberty to follow my own will in all things, where the rule prescribes not; and not to be subject to the inconstant, uncertain, unknown, arbitrary will of another man: as freedom of nature is, to be under no other restraint but the law of nature.

§ 23. This freedom from absolute, arbitrary power, is so necessary to, and closely joined with, a man's preservation, that he cannot part with it, but by what forfeits his preservation and life together: for a man, not having the power of his own life, cannot, by compact, or his own consent, enslave himself to any one, nor put himself under the absolute, arbitrary power of another, to take away his life when he pleases. Nobody can give more power than he has himself; and he that cannot take away his own life, cannot give another power over it. Indeed, having by his fault forfeited his own life, by some act that deserves death; he, to whom he has forfeited it, may (when he has him in his power) delay to take it, and make use of him to his own service, and he does him no injury by it: for, whenever he finds the hardship of his slavery outweigh the value of his life, it is in his power, by resisting the will of his master, to draw on himself the death he desires.

§ 24. This is the perfect condition of slavery, which is nothing else but "the state of war continued, between a lawful conqueror and a captive:" for, if once compact enter between them, and make an agreement for a limited power on the one side, and obedience on the other, the state of war and slavery ceases, as long as the compact endures: for, as has been said, no man can, by agreement, pass over to another that which he hath not in himself, a power over his own life.

I confess, we find among the Jews, as well as other nations, that men did sell themselves; but, it is plain, this was only to drudgery, not to slavery: for, it is evident, the person sold was not under an absolute, arbitrary, despotical power: for the master could not have power to kill him, at any time, whom, at a certain time, he was obliged to let go free out of his service; and the master of such a servant was so far from having an arbitrary power over his life, that he could not, at pleasure, so much as maim him, but the loss of an eye, or tooth, set him free, Exod. xxi.

Sold into drudgery,
not slavery,
Slaves could be killed

CHAPTER V.

Of Property.

[handwritten: limit = subsistence, no hoarding]

[handwritten: Labor + Property = Ownership]

§ 25. Whether we consider natural reason, which tells us, that men, being once born, have a right to their preservation, and consequently to meat and drink, and such other things as nature affords for their subsistence; or revelation, which gives us an account of those grants God made of the world to Adam, and to Noah, and his sons; it is very clear, that God, as king David says, Psal. cvx. 16, "has given the earth to the children of men;" given it to mankind in common. But this being supposed, it seems to some a very great difficulty how any one should ever come to have a property in any thing: I will not content myself to answer, that if it be difficult to make out property, upon a supposition that God gave the world to Adam and his posterity in common, it is impossible that any man, but one universal monarch, should have any property, upon a supposition that God gave the world to Adam, and his heirs in succession, exclusive of all the rest of his posterity. But I shall endeavour to show how men might come to have a property in several parts of that which God gave to mankind in common, and that without any express compact of all the commoners.

§ 26. God, who hath given the world to men in common, hath also given them reason to make use of it to the best advantage of life and convenience. The earth, and all that is therein, is given to men for the support and comfort of their being. And though all the fruits it naturally produces, and beasts it feeds, belong to mankind in common, as they are produced by the spontaneous hand of nature; and nobody has originally a private dominion, exclusive of the rest of mankind, in any of them, as they are thus in their natural state: yet being given for the use of men, there must of necessity be a means to appropriate them some way or other before they can be of any use, or at all beneficial to any particular man. The fruit, or venison, which nourishes the wild Indian, who knows no enclosure, and is still a tenant in common, must be his, or so his, *i. e.* a part of him, that another can no longer have any right to it, before it can do him any good for the support of his life.

§ 27. Though the earth, and all inferior creatures, be common to all men, yet every man has a property in his own person: this nobody has any right to but himself. The labour of his body, and the work of his hands, we may say, are properly his. Whatsoever then he removes out of the state that nature hath provided, and left it in, he hath mixed his labour with, and joined to it

[handwritten: end of state]
[handwritten Arabic: بلد معيشت]

something that is his own, and thereby makes it his property. It being by him removed from the common state nature hath placed it in, it hath by this labour something annexed to it that excludes the common right of other men. For this labour being the unquestionable property of the labourer, no man but he can have a right to what that is once joined to, at least where there is enough, and as good, left in common for others.

§ 28. He that is nourished by the acorns he picked up under an oak, or the apples he gathered from the trees in the wood, has certainly appropriated them to himself. Nobody can deny but the nourishment is his. I ask then, when did they begin to be his? when he digested? or when he ate? or when he boiled? or when he brought them home? or when he picked them up? and it is plain, if the first gathering made them not his, nothing else could. That labour put a distinction between them and common: that added something to them more than nature, the common mother of all, had done; and so they became his private right. And will any one say, he had no right to those acorns or apples he thus appropriated, because he had not the consent of all mankind to make them his? was it a robbery thus to assume to himself what belonged to all in common? If such a consent as that was necessary, man had starved, notwithstanding the plenty God had given him. We see in commons, which remain so by compact, that it is the taking any part of what is common, and removing it out of the state nature leaves it in, which begins the property; without which the common is of no use. And the taking of this or that part does not depend on the express consent of all the commoners. Thus the grass my horse has bit; the turfs my servant has cut; and the ore I have digged in any place, where I have a right to them in common with others; become my property, without the assignation or consent of any body. The labour that was mine, removing them out of that common state they were in, hath fixed my property in them.

§ 29. By making an explicit consent of every commoner necessary to any one's appropriating to himself any part of what is given in common, children or servants could not cut the meat, which their father or master had provided for them in common, without assigning to every one his peculiar part. Though the water running in the fountain be every one's, yet who can doubt but that in the pitcher is his only who drew it out? His labour hath taken it out of the hands of nature, where it was common, and belonged equally to all her children, and hath thereby appropriated it to himself.

§ 30. Thus this law of reason makes the deer that Indian's who hath killed it; it is allowed to be his goods who hath bestowed his labour upon it, though before it was the common right of every one. And amongst those who are counted the civilized part of mankind, who have made and multiplied positive laws to determine property, this original law of nature, for the beginning of property, in what was before common, still takes place; and by virtue thereof, what fish any one catches in the ocean, that great and still remaining common of mankind; or what ambergris any one takes up here, is by the labour that removes it out of that common state nature left it in made his property who takes that pains about it. And even amongst us, the hare that any one is hunting is thought his who pursues her during the chase: for being a beast that is still looked upon as common, and no man's private possession; whoever has employed so much labour about any of that kind, as to find and pursue her, has thereby removed her from the state of nature, wherein she was common, and hath begun a property.

§ 31. It will perhaps be objected to this, that "if gathering the acorns, or other fruits of the earth, &c. makes a right to them, then any one may engross as much as he will." To which I answer, Not so. The same law of nature, that does by this means give us property, does also bound that property too. "God has given us all things richly," 1 Tim. vi. 17, is the voice of reason confirmed by inspiration. But how far has he given it us? To enjoy. As much as any one can make use of to any advantage of life before it spoils, so much he may by his labour fix a property in: whatever is beyond this, is more than his share, and belongs to others. Nothing was made by God for man to spoil or destroy. And thus, considering the plenty of natural provisions there was a long time in the world, and the few spenders; and to how small a part of that provision the industry of one man could extend itself, and engross it to the prejudice of others; especially keeping within the bounds, set by reason, of what might serve for his use; there could be then little room for quarrels or contentions about property so established.

§ 32. But the chief matter of property being now not the fruits of the earth, and the beasts that subsist on it, but the earth itself; as that which takes in, and carries with it all the rest; I think it is plain, that property in that too is acquired as the former. As much land as a man tills, plants, improves, cultivates, and can use the product of, so much is his property. He by his labour does, as it were, enclose it from the common. Nor will it invalidate his right, to say every body else has an equal title to it, and therefore he cannot appropriate, he cannot enclose, without the consent of all his fellow-commoners, all mankind. God, when he gave the world in common to all mankind, commanded man also to labour, and the penury of his condition required it of him. God and his reason commanded him to subdue the earth, i. e. improve it for the benefit of life, and therein lay out something upon it that was his own, his labour. He that, in obedience to this command of God, subdued, tilled, and sowed any part of it, thereby annexed to it something that was his property, which another had no title to, nor could without injury take from him.

§ 33. Nor was this appropriation of any parcel of land, by improving it, any prejudice to any other man, since there was still enough, and as good left; and more than the yet unprovided could use. So that, in effect, there was never the less left for others because of his enclosure for himself: for he that leaves as much as another can make use of, does as good as take nothing at all. Nobody could think himself injured by the drinking of another man, though he took a good draught, who had a whole river of the same water left him to quench his thirst; and the case of land and water, where there is enough of both, is perfectly the same.

§ 34. God gave the world to men in common; but since he gave it them for their benefit, and the greatest conveniencies of life they were capable to draw from it, it cannot be supposed he meant it should always remain common and uncultivated. He gave it to the use of the industrious and rational (and labour was to be his title to it), not to the fancy or covetousness of the quarrelsome and contentious. He that had as good left for his improvement as was already taken up, needed not complain, ought not to meddle with what was already improved by another's labour: if he did, it is plain he desired the benefit of another's pains, which he had no right to, and not the ground which God had given him in common with others to labour on, and whereof there was as good left as that already possessed, and more than he knew what to do with, or his industry could reach to.

§ 35. It is true, in land that is common in England, or any other country, where there is plenty of people under government, who have money and commerce, no one can enclose or appropriate any part without the consent of all his fellow-commoners; because this is left common by compact, *i. e.* by the law of the land, which is not to be violated. And though it be common, in respect of some men, it is not so to all mankind, but is the joint property of this county, or this parish. Besides, the remainder, after such enclosure, would not be as good to the rest of the commoners as the whole was when they could all make use of the whole; whereas in the beginning and first peopling of the great common of the world it was quite otherwise. The law man was under was rather for appropriating. God commanded, and his wants forced him to labour. That was his property which could not be taken from him wherever he had fixed it. And hence subduing or cultivating the earth, and having dominion, we see are joined together. The one gave title to the other. So that God, by commanding to subdue, gave authority so far to appropriate: and the condition of human life, which requires labour and materials to work on, necessarily introduces private possessions.

§ 36. The measure of property nature has well set by the extent of men's labour and the conveniencies of life: no man's labour could subdue, or appropriate all; nor could his enjoyment consume more than a small part; so that it was impossible for any man, this way, to intrench upon the right of another, or acquire to himself a property, to the prejudice of his neighbour, who would still have room for as good and as large a possession (after the other had taken out his) as before it was appropriated. This measure did confine every man's possession to a very moderate proportion, and such as he might appropriate to himself, without injury to any body, in the first ages of the world, when men were more in danger to be lost, by wandering from their company, in the then vast wilderness of the earth, than to be straitened for want of room to plant in. And the same measure may be allowed still without prejudice to any body, as full as the world seems: for supposing a man, or family, in the state they were at first peopling of the world by the children of Adam, or Noah; let him plant in some inland, vacant places of America, we shall find that the possessions he could make himself, upon the measures we have given, would not be very large, nor, even to this day, prejudice the rest of mankind, or give them reason to complain, or think themselves injured by this man's encroachment; though the race of men have now spread themselves to all the corners of the world, and do infinitely exceed the small number was at the beginning. Nay, the extent of ground is of so little value, without labour, that I have heard it affirmed, that in Spain itself a man may be permitted to plough, sow, and reap, without being disturbed, upon land he has no other title to, but only his making use of it. But, on the contrary, the inhabitants think themselves beholden to him, who, by his industry on neglected, and consequently waste land, has increased the stock of corn, which they wanted. But be this as it will, which I lay no stress on; this I dare boldly affirm, that the same rule of propriety, viz. that every man should have as much as he could make use of, would hold still in the world, without straitening any body; since there is land enough in the world to suffice double the inhabitants, had not the invention of money, and the tacit agreement of men to put a value on it, introduced (by consent) larger possessions, and a right to them; which, how it has done, I shall by and by show more at large.

§ 37. This is certain, that in the beginning, before the desire of having more than man needed had altered the intrinsic value of things, which depends only on their usefulness to the life of man; or had agreed, that a little piece of yellow metal, which would keep without wasting or decay, should be worth a great piece of flesh, or a whole heap of corn; though men had a right to appropriate, by their labour, each one to himself, as much of the things of nature as he could use: yet this could not be much, nor to the prejudice of others, where the same plenty was still left to those who would use the same industry. To which let me add, that he who appropriates land to himself by his labour, does not lessen, but increase the common stock of mankind: for the provisions serving to the support of human life, produced by one acre of enclosed and cultivated land, are (to speak much within compass) ten times more than those which are yielded by an acre of land of an equal richness lying waste in common. And therefore he that encloses land, and has a greater plenty of the conveniencies of life from ten acres, than he could have from an hundred left to nature, may truly be said to give ninety acres to mankind: for his labour now supplies him with provisions out of ten acres, which were by the product of an hundred lying in common. I have here rated the improved land very low, in making its product but as ten to one, when it is much nearer an hundred to one: for I ask, whether in the wild woods and uncultivated waste of America, left to nature, without any improvement, tillage, or husbandry, a thousand acres yield the needy and wretched inhabitants as many conveniencies of life as ten acres equally fertile land do in Devonshire, where they are well cultivated?

Before the appropriation of land, he who gathered as much of the wild fruit, killed, caught, or tamed, as many of the beasts, as he could; he that so employed his pains about any of the spontaneous products of nature, as any way to alter them from the state which nature put them in, by placing any of his labour on them, did thereby acquire a propriety in them: but if they perished, in his possession, without their due use; if the fruits rotted, or the venison putrefied, before he could spend it; he offended against the common law of nature, and was liable to be punished; he invaded his neighbour's share, for he had no right, farther than his use called for any of them, and they might serve to afford him conveniencies of life.

§ 38. The same measures governed the possession of land too: whatsoever he tilled and reaped, laid up and made use of, before it spoiled, that was his peculiar right; whatsoever he enclosed, and could feed, and make use of, the cattle and product was also his. But if either the grass of his enclosure rotted on the ground, or the fruit of his planting perished without gathering and laying up; this part of the earth, notwithstanding his enclosure, was still to be looked on as waste, and might be the possession of any other. Thus, at the beginning, Cain might take as much ground as he could till, and make it his own land, and yet leave enough to Abel's sheep to feed on; a few acres would serve for both their possessions. But as families increased, and industry enlarged their stocks, their possessions enlarged with the need of them; but yet it was commonly without any fixed property in the ground they made use of, till they incorporated, settled themselves together, and built cities; and then, by consent, they came in time to set out the bounds of their distinct territories, and agree on limits between them and their neighbours; and by laws within themselves settled the properties of those of the same society: for we see that in that part of the world which was first inhabited, and therefore like to be best peopled, even as low down as Abraham's time, they wandered with their flocks, and their herds, which was their substance, freely up and down; and this Abraham did, in a country where he was a stranger. Whence it is plain, that at least a great part of the land lay in common; that the inhabitants valued it not, nor claimed property in any more than they made use of. But when there was not room enough in the same place for their herds to feed together, they by consent, as Abraham and Lot did, Gen. xiii. 5, separated and enlarged their pasture, where it best liked them. And for the same reason Esau went from his father, and his brother, and planted in mount Seir, Gen. xxxvi. 6.

§ 39. And thus, without supposing any private dominion and property in Adam, over all the world, exclusive of all other men, which can no way be proved, nor any one's property be made out from it; but supposing the world given, as it was, to the children of men in common, we see how labour could make men distinct titles to several parcels of it, for their private uses; wherein there could be no doubt of right, no room for quarrel.

§ 40. Nor is it so strange, as perhaps before consideration it may appear, that the property of labour should be able to overbalance the community of land: for it is labour indeed that put the difference of value on every thing; and let any one consider what the difference is between an acre of land planted with tobacco or sugar, sown with wheat or barley, and an acre of the same land lying in common, without any husbandry upon it, and he will find, that the improvement of labour makes the far greater part of the value. I think it will be but a very modest computation to say, that of the products of the earth useful to the life of man, nine-tenths are the effects of labour: nay, if we will rightly estimate things as they come to our use, and cast up the several expenses about them, what in them is purely owing to nature, and what to labour, we shall find, that in most of them ninety-nine hundredths are wholly to be put on the account of labour.

§ 41. There cannot be a clearer demonstration of any thing, than several nations of the Americans are of this, who are rich in land, and poor in all the comforts of life; whom nature having furnished as liberally as any other people with the materials of plenty, i. e. a fruitful soil, apt to produce in abundance what might serve for food, raiment, and delight; yet, for want of improving it by labour, have not one-hundredth part of the conveniencies we enjoy: and a king of a large and fruitful territory there feeds, lodges, and is clad worse than a day-labourer in England.

§ 42. To make this a little clear, let us but trace some of the ordinary provisions of life, through their several progresses, before they come to our use, and see how much of their value they receive from human industry. Bread, wine, and cloth, are things of daily use, and great plenty; yet notwithstanding, acorns, water, and leaves, or skins, must be our bread, drink, and clothing, did not labour furnish us with these more useful commodities: for whatever bread is more worth than acorns, wine than water, and cloth or silk than leaves, skins, or moss, that is wholly owing to labour and industry; the one of these being the food and raiment which unassisted nature furnishes us with; the other, provisions which our industry and pains prepare for us; which, how much they exceed the other in value, when any one hath computed, he will then see how much labour makes the far greatest part of the value of things we enjoy in this world: and the ground which produces the materials is scarce to be reckoned in as any, or, at most, but a very small part of it; so little, that even amongst us, land that is left wholly to nature, that hath no improvement of pasturage, tillage, or planting, is called, as indeed it is, waste; and we shall find the benefit of it amount to little more than nothing.

This shows how much numbers of men are to be preferred to largeness of dominions; and that the increase of lands, and the right of employing of them, is the great art of government: and that prince, who shall be so wise and godlike, as by established laws of liberty to secure protection and encouragement to the honest industry of mankind, against the oppression of power and narrowness of party, will quickly be too hard for his neighbours: but this by the by. To return to the argument in hand.

§ 43. An acre of land, that bears here twenty bushels of wheat, and another in America, which, with the same husbandry, would do the like, are, without doubt, of the same natural intrinsic value: but yet the benefit mankind receives from the one in a year is worth 5l. and from the other possibly not worth a penny, if all the profit an Indian received from it were to be valued, and sold here; at least, I may truly say, not one thousandth. It is labour, then, which puts the greatest part of the value upon land, without which it would scarcely be worth any thing: it is to that we owe the greatest part of all its useful products; for all that the straw, bran, bread, of that acre of wheat, is more worth than the product of an acre of as good land, which lies waste, is all the effect of labour: for it is not barely the ploughman's pains, the reaper's and thresher's toil, and the baker's sweat, is to be counted into the bread we eat; the labour of those who broke the oxen, who digged and wrought the iron and stones, who felled and framed the timber employed about the plough, mill, oven, or any other utensils, which are a vast number, requisite to this corn, from its being seed to be sown to its being made bread, must all be charged on the account of labour, and received as an effect of that: nature and the earth furnished only the almost worthless materials, as in themselves. It would be a strange "catalogue of things, that industry provided and made use of, about every loaf of bread," before it came to our use, if we could trace them; iron, wood, leather, bark, timber, stone, bricks, coals, lime, cloth, dyeing, drugs, pitch, tar, masts, ropes, and all the materials made use of in the ship, that brought any of the commodities used by any of the workmen, to any part of the work: all which it would be almost impossible, at least too long, to reckon up.

§ 44. From all which it is evident, that though the things of nature are given in common, yet man, by being master of himself, and "proprietor of his own person, and the actions or labour of it, had still in himself the great foundation of property;" and that which made up the greater part of what he applied to the support or comfort of his being, when invention and arts had improved the conveniencies of life, was perfectly his own, and did not belong in common to others.

§ 45. Thus labour, in the beginning, gave a right of property wherever any one was pleased to employ it upon what was common, which remained a long while the far greater part, and is yet more than mankind makes use of. Men, at first, for the most part, contented themselves with what unassisted nature offered to their necessities: and though afterwards, in some parts of the world, (where the increase of people and stock, with the use of money, had made land scarce, and so of some value) the several communities settled the bounds of their distinct territories, and by laws within themselves regulated the properties of the private men of their society, and so, by compact and agreement, settled the property which labour and industry began: and the leagues that have been made between several states and kingdoms, either expressly or tacitly disowning all claim and right to the land in the others' possession, have, by common consent, given up their pretences to their natural common right, which originally they had to those countries, and so have, by positive agreement, settled a property amongst themselves, in distinct parts and parcels of the earth; yet there are still great tracts of ground to be found, which (the inhabitants thereof not having joined with the rest of mankind in the consent of the use of their common money) lie waste, and are more than the people who dwell on it do or can make use of, and so still lie in common; though this can scarce happen amongst that part of mankind that have consented to the use of money.

§ 46. The greatest part of things really useful to the life of man, and such as the necessity of subsisting made the first commoners of the world look after, as it doth the Americans now, are generally things of short duration; such as, if they are not consumed by use, will decay and perish of themselves: gold, silver, and diamonds, are things that fancy or agreement hath put the value on, more than real use, and the necessary support of life. Now of those good things which nature hath provided in common, every one had a right (as hath been said) to as much as he could use, and property in all that he could effect with his labour; all that his industry could extend to, to alter from the state nature had put it in, was his. He that gathered a hundred bushels of acorns or apples, had thereby a property in them; they were his goods as soon as gathered. He was only to look that he used them before they spoiled, else he took more than his share, and robbed others. And indeed it was a foolish thing, as well as dishonest, to hoard up more than he could make use of. If he gave away a part to any body else, so that it perished not uselessly in his possession, these he also made use of. And if he also bartered away plums, that would have rotted in a week, for nuts that would last good for his eating a whole year, he did no injury; he wasted not the common stock; destroyed no part of the portion of the goods that belonged to others, so long as nothing perished uselessly in his hands. Again, if he would give his nuts for a piece of metal, pleased with its colour; or exchange his sheep for shells, or wool for a sparkling pebble or a diamond, and keep those by him all his life, he invaded not the right of others; he might heap as much of these durable things as he pleased; the exceeding of the bounds of his just property not lying in the largeness of his possession, but the perishing of any thing uselessly in it.

§ 47. And thus came in the use of money, some lasting thing that men might keep without spoiling, and that by mutual consent men would take in exchange for the truly useful, but perishable supports of life.

§ 48. And as different degrees of industry were apt to give men possessions in different proportions, so this invention of money gave them the opportunity to continue and enlarge them: for supposing an island, separate from all possible commerce with the rest of the world, wherein there were but an hundred families, but there were sheep, horses, and cows, with other useful animals, wholesome fruits, and land enough for corn for a hundred thousand times as many, but nothing in the island, either because of its commonness, or perishableness, fit to supply the place of money; what reason could any one have there to enlarge his possessions beyond the use of his family and a plentiful supply to its consumption, either in what their own industry produced, or they could barter for like perishable, useful commodities with others? Where there is not something, both lasting and scarce, and so valuable, to be hoarded up, there men will not be apt to enlarge their possessions of land, were it ever so rich, ever so free for them to take: for I ask, what would a man value ten thousand, or an hundred thousand acres of excellent land, ready cultivated, and well stocked too with cattle, in the middle of the inland parts of America, where he had no hopes of commerce with other parts of the world, to draw money to him by the sale of the product? It would not be worth the enclosing, and we should see him give up again to the wild common of nature, whatever was more than would supply the conveniencies of life to be had there for him and his family.

§ 49. Thus in the beginning all the world was America, and more so than that is now; for no such thing as money was any where known. Find out something that hath the use and value of money amongst his neighbours, you shall see the same man will begin presently to enlarge his possessions.

§ 50. But since gold and silver, being little useful to the life of man in proportion to food, raiment, and carriage, has its value only from the consent of men, whereof labour yet makes, in great part, the measure; it is plain, that men have agreed to a disproportionate and unequal possession of the earth; they having, by a tacit and voluntary consent, found out a way how a man may fairly possess more land than he himself can use the product of, by receiving, in exchange for the overplus, gold and silver, which may be hoarded up without injury to any one; these metals not spoiling or decaying in the hands of the possessor. This partage of things in an inequality of private possessions, men have made practicable out of the bounds of society, and without compact; only by putting a value on gold and silver, and tacitly agreeing in the use of money: for in governments, the laws regulate the right of property, and the possession of land is determined by positive constitutions.

§ 51. And thus, I think, it is very easy to conceive, "how labour could at first begin a title of property" in the common things of nature, and how the spending it upon our uses bounded it. So that there could then be no reason of quarrelling about title, nor any doubt about the largeness of possession it gave. Right and conveniency went together; for as a man had a right to all he could employ his labour upon, so he had no temptation to labour for more than he could make use of. This left no room for controversy about the title, nor for encroachment on the right of others; what portion a man carved to himself was easily seen: and it was useless, as well as dishonest, to carve himself too much, or take more than he needed.

CHAPTER VI.

Of paternal Power.

§ 52. It may perhaps be censured as an impertinent criticism, in a discourse of this nature, to find fault with words and names that have obtained
in the world: and yet possibly it may not be amiss to offer new ones when
the old are apt to lead men into mistakes, as this of paternal power probably
has done; which seems so to place the power of parents over their children
wholly in the father, as if the mother had no share in it: whereas, if we
consult reason or revelation, we shall find she hath an equal title. This may
give one reason to ask, whether this might not be more properly called
parental power? for whatever obligation nature and the right of generation
lays on children, it must certainly bind them equally to both concurrent
causes of it. And accordingly we see the positive law of God every where
joins them together, without distinction, when it commands the obedience
of children: "Honour thy father and thy mother," Exod. xx. 12. "Whosoever curseth his father or his mother," Lev. xx. 9. "Ye shall fear every man
his mother and his father," Lev. xix. 5. "Children, obey your parents," &c.
Eph. vi. 1, is the style of the Old and New Testament.

§ 53. Had but this one thing been well considered, without looking any
deeper into the matter, it might perhaps have kept men from running into
those gross mistakes they have made, about this power of parents; which,
however it might, without any great harshness, bear the name of absolute
dominion, and regal authority, when under the title of paternal power it
seemed appropriated to the father, would yet have sounded but oddly, and in
the very name shown the absurdity, if this supposed absolute power over
children had been called parental; and thereby have discovered, that it
belonged to the mother too: for it will but very ill serve the turn of those
men who contend so much for the absolute power and authority of the
fatherhood, as they call it, that the mother should have any share in it; and it
would have but ill supported the monarchy they contend for, when by the
very name it appeared that that fundamental authority, from whence they
would derive their government of a single person only, was not placed in
one, but two persons jointly. But to let this of names pass.

§ 54. Though I have said above, chap. ii. "That all men by nature are
equal," I cannot be supposed to understand all sorts of equality: age or
virtue may give men a just precedency: excellency of parts and merit may
place others above the common level: birth may subject some, and alliance

or benefits others, to pay an observance to those whom nature, gratitude, or other respects, may have made it due: and yet all this consists with the equality which all men are in, in respect of jurisdiction or dominion one over another; which was the equality I there spoke of, as proper to the business in hand, being that equal right that every man hath to his natural freedom, without being subjected to the will or authority of any other man.

§ 55. Children, I confess, are not born in this state of equality, though they are born to it. Their parents have a sort of rule and jurisdiction over them when they come into the world, and for some time after; but it is but a temporary one. The bonds of this subjection are like the swaddling-clothes they are wrapt up in, and supported by, in the weakness of their infancy: age and reason, as they grow up, loosen them, till at length they drop quite off, and leave a man at his own free disposal.

§ 56. Adam was created a perfect man, his body and mind in full possession of their strength and reason, and so was capable from the first instant of his being to provide for his own support and preservation, and govern his actions according to the dictates of the law of reason which God had implanted in him. From him the world is peopled with his descendants, who are all born infants, weak and helpless, without knowledge or understanding: but to supply the defects of this imperfect state, till the improvement of growth and age hath removed them, Adam and Eve, and after them all parents were, by the law of nature, "under an obligation to preserve, nourish, and educate the children" they had begotten; not as their own workmanship, but the workmanship of their own maker, the Almighty, to whom they were to be accountable for them.

§ 57. The law that was to govern Adam was the same that was to govern all his posterity, the law of reason. But his offspring having another way of entrance into the world, different from him, by a natural birth, that produced them ignorant and without the use of reason, they were not presently under that law; for nobody can be under a law which is not promulgated to him; and this law being promulgated or made known by reason only, he that is not come to the use of his reason cannot be said to be under this law; and Adam's children, being not presently as soon as born under this law of reason, were not presently free: for law, in its true notion, is not so much the limitation, as the direction of a free and intelligent agent to his proper interest, and prescribes no farther than is for the general good of those under that law: could they be happier without it, the law, as an useless thing, would of itself vanish; and that ill deserves the name of confinement which hedges us in only from bogs and precipices. So that, however it may be mistaken, the end of law is not to abolish or restrain, but to preserve and enlarge freedom: for in all the states of created beings capable of laws, "where there is no law, there is no freedom;" for liberty is to be free from restraint and violence from others; which cannot be where there is not law: but freedom is not, as we are told, "a liberty for every man to do what he lists:" (for who could be free, when every other man's humour might domineer over him?) but a liberty to dispose and order as he lists his person, actions, possessions, and his whole property, within the allowance of those laws under which he is, and therein not to be subject to the arbitrary will of another, but freely follow his own.

§ 58. The power, then, that parents have over their children arises from that duty which is incumbent on them, to take care of their offspring during the imperfect state of childhood. To inform the mind, and govern the actions of their yet ignorant nonage, till reason shall take its place, and ease them of that trouble, is what the children want, and the parents are bound to: for God having given man an understanding to direct his actions, has allowed him a freedom of will, and liberty of acting, as properly belonging thereunto, within the bounds of that law he is under. But whilst he is in an estate wherein he has not understanding of his own to direct his will, he is not to have any will of his own to follow: he that understands for him, must will for him too; he must prescribe to his will, and regulate his actions; but when he comes to the estate that made his father a freeman, the son is a freeman too.

§ 59. This holds in all the laws a man is under, whether natural or civil. Is a man under the law of nature? What made him free of that law? what gave him a free disposing of his property, according to his own will, within the compass of that law? I answer, a state of maturity, wherein he might be supposed capable to know that law, that so he might keep his actions within the bounds of it. When he has acquired that state, he is presumed to know how far that law is to be his guide, and how far he may make use of his freedom, and so comes to have it; till then, somebody else must guide him, who is presumed to know how far the law allows a liberty. If such a state of reason, such an age of discretion made him free, the same shall make his son free too. Is a man under the law of England? What made him free of that law? that is, to have the liberty to dispose of his actions and possessions according to his own will, within the permission of that law? A capacity of knowing that law, which is supposed by that law at the age of one-and-twenty years, and in some cases sooner. If this made the father free, it shall make the son free too. Till then we see the law allows the son to have no will, but he is to be guided by the will of his father or guardian, who is to understand for him. And if the father die, and fail to substitute a deputy in his trust; if he hath not provided a tutor to govern his son during his minority, during his want of understanding, the law takes care to do it; some other must govern him, and be a will to him, till he hath attained to a state of freedom, and his understanding be fit to take the government of his will. But after that, the father and son are equally free as much as tutor and pupil after nonage; equally subjects of the same law together, without any dominion left in the father over the life, liberty, or estate of his son, whether they be only in the state and under the law of nature, or under the positive laws of an established government.

§ 60. But if, through defects that may happen out of the ordinary course of nature, any one comes not to such a degree of reason wherein he might be supposed capable of knowing the law, and so living within the rules of it, he is never capable of being a free man, he is never let loose to the disposure of his own will, (because he knows no bounds to it, has not understanding, its proper guide) but is continued under the tuition and government of others, all the time his own understanding is incapable of that charge. And so lunatics and idiots are never set free from the government of their parents. "Children, who are not as yet come unto those years whereat they may have; and innocents which are excluded by a natural defect from ever having; thirdly, mad men, which for the present cannot possibly have the use of right reason to guide themselves, have for their guide the reason that guideth other men which are tutors over them, to seek and procure their good for them," says Hooker, Eccl. Pol. lib. i. sect. 7. All which seems no more than that duty which God and nature has laid on man, as well as other creatures, to preserve their offspring till they can be able to shift for themselves, and will scarce amount to an instance or proof of parents' regal authority.

§ 61. Thus we are born free, as we are born rational; not that we have actually the exercise of either: age, that brings one, brings with it the other too. And thus we see how natural freedom and subjection to parents may consist together, and are both founded on the same principle. A child is free by his father's title, by his father's understanding, which is to govern him till he hath it of his own. The freedom of a man at years of discretion, and the subjection of a child to his parents, whilst yet short of that age, are so consistent, and so distinguishable, that the most blinded contenders for monarchy, by right of fatherhood, cannot miss this difference; the most obstinate cannot but allow their consistency: for were their doctrine all true, were the right heir of Adam now known, and by that title settled a monarch in his throne, invested with all the absolute unlimited power sir Robert Filmer talks of; if he should die as soon as his heir were born, must not the child, notwithstanding he were ever so free, ever so much sovereign, be in subjection to his mother and nurse, to tutors and governors, till age and education brought his reason and ability to govern himself and others? The necessities of his life, the health of his body, and the information of his mind, would require him to be directed by the will of others, and not his own; and yet will any one think that this restraint and subjection were inconsistent with, or spoiled him of that liberty of sovereignty he had a right to, or gave away his empire to those who had the government of his non-age? This government over him only prepared him the better and sooner for it. If any body should ask me, when my son is of age to be free? I shall answer, just when his monarch is of age to govern. "But at what time," says the judicious Hooker, Eccl. Pol. lib. i. sect. 6, "a man may be said to have attained so far forth the use of reason, as sufficeth to make him capable of those laws whereby he is then bound to guide his actions: this a great deal more easy for sense to discern than for any one by skill and learning to determine."

§ 62. Commonwealths themselves take notice of, and allow, that there is a time when men are to begin to act like freemen, and therefore till that time require not oaths of fealty or allegiance, or other public owning of, or submission to, the government of their countries.

§ 63. The freedom then of man, and liberty of acting according to his own will, is grounded on his having reason, which is able to instruct him in that law he is to govern himself by, and make him know how far he is left to the freedom of his own will. To turn him loose to an unrestrained liberty, before he has reason to guide him, is not the allowing him the privilege of his nature to be free; but to thrust him out amongst brutes, and abandon him to a state as wretched, and as much beneath that of a man, as theirs. This is that which puts the authority into the parents' hands to govern the minority of their children. God hath made it their business to employ this care on their offspring, and hath placed in them suitable inclinations of tenderness and concern to temper this power, to apply it, as his wisdom designed it, to the children's good, as long as they should need to be under it.

§ 64. But what reason can hence advance this care of the parents due to their offspring into an absolute arbitrary dominion of the father, whose power reaches no farther than, by such a discipline as he finds most effectual, to give such strength and health to their bodies, such vigour and rectitude to their minds, as may best fit his children to be most useful to themselves and others; and, if it be necessary to his condition, to make them work, when they are able, for their own subsistence. But in this power the mother too has her share with the father.

§ 65. Nay, this power so little belongs to the father by any peculiar right of nature, but only as he is guardian of his children, that when he quits his care of them, he loses his power over them, which goes along with their nourishment and education, to which it is inseparably annexed; and it belongs as much to the foster-father of an exposed child, as to the natural father of another. So little power does the bare act of begetting give a man over his issue, if all his care ends there, and this be all the title he hath to the name and authority of a father. And what will become of this paternal power in that part of the world where one woman hath more than one husband at a time? or in those parts of America, where, when the husband and wife part, which happens frequently, the children are all left to the mother, follow her, and are wholly under her care and provision? If the father die whilst the children are young, do they not naturally every where owe the same obedience to their mother, during their minority, as to their father were he alive? and will any one say, that the mother hath a legislative power over her children? that she can make standing rules, which shall be of perpetual obligation, by which they ought to regulate all the concerns of their property, and bound their liberty all the course of their lives? or can she enforce the observation of them with capital punishments? for this is the proper power of the magistrate, of which the father hath not so much as the shadow. His command over his children is but temporary, and reaches not their life or property: it is but a help to the weakness and imperfection of their nonage, a discipline necessary to their education: and though a father may dispose of his own possessions as he pleases, when his children are out of danger of perishing for want, yet his power extends not to the lives or goods, which either their own industry or another's bounty has made theirs; nor to their liberty neither, when they are once arrived to the enfranchisement of the years of discretion. The father's empire then ceases, and can from thenceforwards no more dispose of the liberty of his son than that of any other man: and it must be far from an absolute or perpetual jurisdiction, from which a man may withdraw himself, having license from divine authority to "leave father and mother, and cleave to his wife."

§ 66. But though there be a time when a child comes to be as free from subjection to the will and command of his father, as the father himself is free from subjection to the will of any body else, and they are each under no restraint but that which is common to them both, whether it be the law of nature, or municipal law of their country; yet this freedom exempts not a son from that honour which he ought, by the law of God and nature, to pay his parents. God having made the parents instruments in his great design of continuing the race of mankind, and the occasions of life to their children;

as he hath laid on them an obligation to nourish, preserve, and bring up their offspring; so he has laid on the children a perpetual obligation of honouring their parents, which containing in it an inward esteem and reverence to be shown by all outward expressions, ties up the child from any thing that may ever injure or affront, disturb or endanger, the happiness or life of those from whom he received his; and engages him in all actions of defence, relief, assistance, and comfort of those by whose means he entered into being, and has been made capable of any enjoyments of life: from this obligation no state, no freedom, can absolve children. But this is very far from giving parents a power of command over their children, or authority to make laws and dispose as they please of their lives and liberties. It is one thing to owe honour, respect, gratitude, and assistance; another to require an absolute obedience and submission. The honour due to parents, a monarch in his throne owes his mother; and yet this lessens not his authority, nor subjects him to her government.

§ 67. The subjection of a minor, places in the father a temporary government, which terminates with the minority of the child: and the honour due from a child, places in the parents perpetual right to respect, reverence, support, and compliance too, more or less, as the father's care, cost, and kindness in his education, have been more or less. This ends not with minority, but holds in all parts and conditions of a man's life. The want of distinguishing these two powers, viz. that which the father hath in the right of tuition, during minority, and the right of honour all his life, may perhaps have caused a great part of the mistakes about this matter: for, to speak properly of them, the first of these is rather the privilege of children, and duty of parents, than any prerogative of paternal power. The nourishment and education of their children is a charge so incumbent on parents for their children's good, that nothing can absolve them from taking care of it: and though the power of commanding and chastising them go along with it, yet God hath woven into the principles of human nature such a tenderness for their offspring, that there is little fear that parents should use their power with too much rigour; the excess is seldom on the severe side, the strong bias of nature drawing the other way. And therefore God Almighty, when he would express his gentle dealing with the Israelites, he tells them, that though he chastened them, " he chastened them as a man chastens his son," Deut. viii. 5. *i. e.* with tenderness and affection, and kept them under no severer discipline than what was absolutely best for them, and had been less kindness to have slackened. This is that power to which children are commanded obedience, that the pains and care of their parents may not be increased, or ill rewarded.

§ 68. On the other side, honour and support, all that which gratitude requires to return for the benefits received by and from them, is the indispensable duty of the child, and the proper privilege of the parents. This is intended for the parents' advantage, as the other is for the child's; though education, the parents' duty, seems to have most power, because the ignorance and infirmities of childhood stand in need of restraint and correction; which is a visible exercise of rule, and a kind of dominion. And that duty which is comprehended in the word honour requires less obedience, though the obligation be stronger on grown than younger children: for who can think the command, "Children obey your parents," requires in a man that has children of his own the same submission to his father, as it does in his yet young children to him; and that by this precept he were bound to obey all his father's commands, if, out of a conceit of authority, he should have the indiscretion to treat him still as a boy?

§ 69. The first part then of paternal power, or rather duty, which is education, belongs so to the father, that it terminates at a certain season; when the business of education is over, it ceases of itself, and is also alienable before: for a man may put the tuition of his son in other hands; and he that has made his son an apprentice to another, has discharged him, during that time, of a great part of his obedience both to himself and to his mother. But all the duty of honour, the other part, remains nevertheless entire to them; nothing can cancel that: it is so inseparable from them both, that the father's authority cannot dispossess the mother of this right, nor can any man discharge his son from honouring her that bore him. But both these are very far from a power to make laws, and enforcing them with penalties that may reach estate, liberty, limbs, and life. The power of commanding ends with nonage; and though after that, honour and respect, support and defence, and whatsoever gratitude can oblige a man to, for the highest benefits he is naturally capable of, be always due from a son to his parents; yet all this puts no sceptre into the father's hand, no sovereign power of commanding. He has no dominion over his son's property, or actions; nor any right that his will should prescribe to his son's in all things; however it may become his son in many things, not very inconvenient to him and his family, to pay a deference to it.

§ 70. A man may owe honour and respect to an ancient or wise man; defence to his child or friend; relief and support to the distressed; and gratitude to a benefactor, to such a degree, that all he has, all he can do, cannot sufficiently pay it: but all these give no authority, no right to any one, of making laws over him from whom they are owing. And it is plain, all this is due not only to the bare title of father; not only because, as has been said, it is owing to the mother too, but because these obligations to parents, and the degrees of what is required of children, may be varied by the different care and kindness, trouble and expense, which are often employed upon one child more than another.

§ 71. This shows the reason how it comes to pass, that parents in societies, where they themselves are subjects, retain a power over their children, and have as much right to their subjection as those who are in the state of nature. Which could not possibly be, if all political power were only paternal, and that in truth they were one and the same thing: for then, all paternal power being in the prince, the subject could naturally have none of it. But these two powers, political and paternal, are so perfectly distinct and separate, are built upon so different foundations, and given to so different ends, that every subject, that is a father, has as much a paternal power over his children as the prince has over his: and every prince, that has parents, owes them as much filial duty and obedience as the meanest of his subjects do to theirs; and cannot therefore contain any part or degree of that kind of dominion which a prince or magistrate has over his subjects.

§ 72. Though the obligation on the parents to bring up their children, and the obligation on children to honour their parents, contain all the power on the one hand, and submissions on the other, which are proper to this relation, yet there is another power ordinary in the father, whereby he has a tie on the obedience of his children; which though it be common to him with other men, yet the occasions of showing it almost constantly happening to fathers in their private families, and the instances of it elsewhere being rare, and less taken notice of, it passes in the world for a part of paternal jurisdiction. And this is the power men generally have to bestow their estates on those who please them best; the possession of the father being the expectation and inheritance of the children, ordinarily in certain proportions, according to the law and custom of each country; yet it is commonly in the father's power to bestow it with a more sparing or liberal hand, according as the behavior of this or that child hath comported with his will and humour.

§ 73. This is no small tie on the obedience of children: and there being always annexed to the enjoyment of land a submission to the government of the country, of which that land is a part; it has been commonly supposed, that a father could oblige his posterity to that government, of which he himself was a subject, and that his compact held them; whereas, it being only a necessary condition annexed to the land, and the inheritance of an estate which is under that government, reaches only those who will take it on that condition, and so is no natural tie or engagement, but a voluntary submission: for every man's children being by nature as free as himself, or any of his ancestors ever were, may, whilst they are in that freedom, choose what society they will join themselves to, what commonwealth they will put themselves under. But if they will enjoy the inheritance of their ancestors, they must take it on the same terms their ancestors had it, and submit to all the conditions annexed to such a possession. By this power indeed fathers oblige their children to obedience to themselves, even when they are past minority, and most commonly too subject them to this or that political power: but neither of these by any peculiar right of fatherhood, but by the reward they have in their hands to enforce and recompense such a compliance; and is no more power than what a Frenchman has over an Englishman, who, by the hopes of an estate he will leave him, will certainly have a strong tie on his obedience: and if, when it is left him, he will enjoy it, he must certainly take it upon the conditions annexed to the possession of land in that country where it lies, whether it be France or England.

§ 74. To conclude then, though the father's power of commanding extends no farther than the minority of his children, and to a degree only fit for the discipline and government of that age; and though that honour and respect, and all that which the Latins called piety, which they indispensably owe to their parents all their lifetime, and in all estates, with all that support and defence which is due to them, gives the father no power of governing, *i. e.* making laws and enacting penalties on his children; though by all this he has no dominion over the property or actions of his son: yet it is obvious to conceive how easy it was, in the first ages of the world, and in places still, where the thinness of people gives families leave to separate into unpossessed quarters, and they have room to remove or plant themselves in yet vacant habitations, for the father of the family to become the prince* of it;

* It is no improbable opinion, therefore, which the arch-philosopher was of, "That the chief person in every household was always, as it were, a king: so when numbers of households joined themselves in civil societies together, kings were the first kind of governors amongst them, which is also, as it seemeth, the reason why the name of fathers continued still in them, who, of fathers, were made rulers; as also the ancient custom of governors to do as Melchizedeck, and being kings, to exercise the office of priests, which fathers did at the first, grew perhaps by the same occasion. Howbeit, this is not the only kind of regiment that has been received in the world. The inconveniencies of one kind have caused sundry others to be devised; so that, in a word, all public regiment, of what kind soever, seemeth evidently to have risen from the deliberate advice, consultation, and composition between men, judging it convenient and behoveful; there being no impossibility in nature considered by itself, but that man might have lived without any public regiment." *Hooker*'s Eccl. P. lib. i. sect. 10.

he had been a ruler from the beginning of the infancy of his children: and since without some government it would be hard for them to live together, it was likeliest it should, by the express or tacit consent of the children when they were grown up, be in the father, where it seemed without any change barely to continue; when indeed nothing more was required to it than the permitting the father to exercise alone, in his family, that executive power of the law of nature, which every free man naturally hath, and by that permission resigning up to him a monarchical power, whilst they remained in it. But that this was not by any paternal right, but only by the consent of his children, is evident from hence, that nobody doubts, but if a stranger, whom chance or business had brought to his family, had there killed any of his children, or committed any other fact, he might condemn and put him to death, or otherwise punish him, as well as any of his children: which it was impossible he should do by virtue of any paternal authority over one who was not his child, but by virtue of that executive power of the law of nature, which, as a man, he had a right to: and he alone could punish him in his family, where the respect of his children had laid by the exercise of such a power, to give way to the dignity and authority they were willing should remain in him, above the rest of his family.

§ 75. Thus it was easy, and almost natural for children, by a tacit, and scarce avoidable consent, to make way for the father's authority and government. They had been accustomed in their childhood to follow his direction, and to refer their little differences to him; and when they were men, who fitter to rule them? Their little properties, and less covetousness, seldom afforded greater controversies; and when any should arise, where could they have a fitter umpire than he, by whose care they had every one been sustained and brought up, and who had a tenderness for them all? It is no wonder that they made no distinction betwixt minority and full age; nor looked after one-and-twenty, or any other age that might make them the free disposers of themselves and fortunes, when they could have no desire to be out of their pupilage: the government they had been under during it, continued still to be more their protection than restraint: and they could nowhere find a greater security to their peace, liberties, and fortunes, than in the rule of a father.

§ 76. Thus the natural fathers of families by an insensible change became the politic monarchs of them too: and as they chanced to live long, and leave able and worthy heirs, for several successions, or otherwise; so they laid the foundations of hereditary, or elective kingdoms, under several constitutions and manners, according as chance, contrivance, or occasions happened to mould them. But if princes have their titles in their fathers' right, and it be a sufficient proof of the natural right of fathers to political authority, because they commonly were those in whose hands we find, *de facto,* the exercise of government: I say, if this argument be good, it will as strongly prove, that all princes, nay princes only, ought to be priests, since it is as certain, that in the beginning, "the father of the family was priest, as that he was ruler in his own household."

CHAPTER VII.

Of political or civil Society.

§ 77. God having made man such a creature, that in his own judgment it was not good for him to be alone, put him under strong obligations of necessity, convenience, and inclination, to drive him into society, as well as fitted him with understanding and language to continue and enjoy it. The first society was between man and wife, which gave beginning to that between parents and children; to which, in time, that between master and servant came to be added: and though all these might, and commonly did meet together, and make up but one family, wherein the master or mistress of it had some sort of rule proper to a family; each of these, or all together, came short of political society, as we shall see, if we consider the different ends, ties, and bounds of each of these.

§ 78. Conjugal society is made by a voluntary compact between man and woman; and though it consist chiefly in such a communion and right in one another's bodies as is necessary to its chief end, procreation; yet it draws with it mutual support and assistance, and a communion of interests too, as necessary not only to unite their care and affection, but also necessary to their common offspring, who have a right to be nourished and maintained by them, till they are able to provide for themselves.

§ 79. For the end of conjunction between male and female being not barely procreation, but the continuation of the species; this conjunction betwixt male and female ought to last, even after procreation, so long as is necessary to the nourishment and support of the young ones, who are to be sustained by those that got them, till they are able to shift and provide for themselves. This rule, which the infinite wise Maker hath set to the works of his hands, we find the inferior creatures steadily obey. In those viviparous animals which feed on grass, the conjunction between male and female lasts no longer than the very act of copulation; because the teat of the dam being sufficient to nourish the young, till it be able to feed on grass, the male only begets, but concerns not himself for the female or young, to whose sustenance he can contribute nothing. But in beasts of prey the conjunction lasts longer: because the dam not being able well to subsist herself, and nourish her numerous offspring by her own prey alone, a more laborious, as well as more dangerous way of living, than by feeding on grass; the assistance of the male is necessary to the maintenance of their common family, which cannot subsist till they are able to prey for themselves, but by the joint care of male and female. The same is to be observed in all birds, (except some domestic ones, where plenty of food excuses the cock from feeding, and taking care of the young brood) whose young needing food in the nest, the cock and hen continue mates, till the young are able to use their wing, and provide for themselves.

§ 80. And herein I think lies the chief, if not the only reason, "why the male and female in mankind are tied to a longer conjunction" than other creatures, viz. because the female is capable of conceiving, and *de facto* is commonly with child again, and brings forth too a new birth, long before the former is out of a dependency for support on his parents' help, and able to shift for himself, and has all the assistance that is due to him from his parents: whereby the father, who is bound to take care for those he hath begot, is under an obligation to continue in conjugal society with the same woman longer than other creatures, whose young being able to subsist of themselves before the time of procreation returns again, the conjugal bond dissolves of itself, and they are at liberty, till Hymen at his usual anniversary season summons them again to choose new mates. Wherein one cannot but admire the wisdom of the great Creator, who having given to man foresight, and an ability to lay up for the future, as well as to supply the present necessity, hath made it necessary, that society of man and wife should be more lasting than of male and female amongst other creatures; that so their industry might be encouraged, and their interest better united, to make provision and lay up goods for their common issue, which uncertain mixture, or easy and frequent solutions of conjugal society, would mightily disturb.

§ 81. But though these are ties upon mankind, which make the conjugal bonds more firm and lasting in man than the other species of animals; yet it would give one reason to inquire, why this compact, where procreation and education are secured, and inheritance taken care for, may not be made determinable, either by consent, or at a certain time, or upon certain conditions, as well as any other voluntary compacts, there being no necessity in the nature of the thing, nor to the ends of it, that it should always be for life; I mean, to such as are under no restraint of any positive law, which ordains all such contracts to be perpetual.

§ 82. But the husband and wife, though they have but one common concern, yet having different understandings, will unavoidably sometimes have different wills too; it therefore being necessary that the last determination, i. e. the rule, should be placed somewhere; it naturally falls to the man's share, as the abler and the stronger. But this reaching but to the things of their common interest and property, leaves the wife in the full and free possession of what by contract is her peculiar right, and gives the husband no more power over her life than she has over his; the power of the husband being so far from that of an absolute monarch, that the wife has in many cases a liberty to separate from him, where natural right or their contract allows it; whether that contract be made by themselves in the state of nature, or by the customs or laws of the country they live in; and the children upon such separation fall to the father's or mother's lot, as such contract does determine.

§ 83. For all the ends of marriage being to be obtained under politic government, as well as in the state of nature, the civil magistrate doth not abridge the right or power of either naturally necessary to those ends, viz. procreation and mutual support and assistance whilst they are together; but only decides any controversy that may arise between man and wife about them. If it were otherwise, and that absolute sovereignty and power of life and death naturally belonged to the husband, and were necessary to the society between man and wife, there could be no matrimony in any of those countries where the husband is allowed no such absolute authority. But the ends of matrimony requiring no such power in the husband, the condition of conjugal society put it not in him, it being not at all necessary to that state. Conjugal society could subsist and attain its ends without it; nay, community of goods, and the power over them, mutual assistance and maintenance, and other things belonging to conjugal society, might be varied and regulated by that contract which unites man and wife in that society, as far as may consist with procreation and the bringing up of children till they could shift for themselves; nothing being necessary to any society, that is not necessary to the ends for which it is made.

§ 84. The society betwixt parents and children, and the distinct rights and powers belonging respectively to them, I have treated of so largely, in the foregoing chapter, that I shall not here need to say any thing of it. And I think it is plain, that it is far different from a politic society.

§ 85. Master and servant are names as old as history, but given to those of far different condition; for a freeman makes himself a servant to another, by selling him, for a certain time, the service he undertakes to do, in exchange for wages he is to receive: and though this commonly puts him into the family of his master, and under the ordinary discipline thereof: yet it gives the master but a temporary power over him, and no greater than what is contained in the contract between them. But there is another sort of servants, which by a peculiar name we call slaves, who being captives taken in a just war, are by the right of nature subjected to the absolute dominion and arbitrary power of their masters. These men having, as I say, forfeited their lives, and with it their liberties, and lost their estates; and being in the state of slavery, not capable of any property; cannot in that state be considered as any part of civil society; the chief end whereof is the preservation of property.

§ 86. Let us therefore consider a master of a family with all these subordinate relations of wife, children, servants, and slaves, united under the domestic rule of a family; which, what resemblance soever it may have in its order, offices, and number too, with a little commonwealth, yet is very far from it, both in its constitution, power, and end: or if it must be thought a monarchy, and the pater-familias the absolute monarch in it, absolute monarchy will have but a very shattered and short power, when it is plain, by what has been said before, that the master of the family has a very distinct and differently limited power, both as to time and extent, over those several persons that are in it: for excepting the slave (and the family is as much a family, and his power as pater-familias as great, whether there be any slaves in his family or no), he has no legislative power of life and death over any of them, and none too but what a mistress of a family may have as well as he. And he certainly can have no absolute power over the whole family, who has but a very limited one over every individual in it. But how a family, or any other society of men, differ from that which is properly political society, we shall best see by considering wherein political society itself consists.

§ 87. Man being born, as has been proved, with a title to perfect freedom, and uncontrolled enjoyment of all the rights and privileges of the law of nature, equally with any other man, or number of men in the world, hath by nature a power, not only to preserve his property, that is, his life, liberty, and estate, against the injuries and attempts of other men; but to judge of and punish the breaches of that law in others, as he is persuaded the offence deserves, even with death itself, in crimes where the heinousness of the fact, in his opinion, requires it. But because no political society can be, nor subsist, without having in itself the power to preserve the property, and, in order thereunto, punish the offences of all those of that society; there, and there only is political society, where every one of the members hath quitted this natural power, resigned it up into the hands of the community in all cases that exclude him not from appealing for protection to the law established by it. And thus all private judgment of every particular member being excluded, the community comes to be umpire, by settled standing rules, indifferent, and the same to all parties; and by men having authority from the community, for the execution of those rules, decides all the differences that may happen between any members of that society concerning any matter of right; and punishes those offences which any member hath committed against the society, with such penalties as the law has established: whereby it is easy to discern who are, and who are not, in political society together. Those who are united into one body, and have a common established law and judicature to appeal to, with authority to decide controversies between them, and punish offenders, are in civil society one with another: but those who have no such common appeal, I mean on earth, are still in the state of nature, each being, where there is no other, judge for himself, and executioner: which is, as I have before showed it, the perfect state of nature.

§ 88. And thus the commonwealth comes by a power to set down what punishment shall belong to the several transgressions which they think worthy of it, committed amongst the members of that society, (which is the power of making laws) as well as it has the power to punish any injury done unto any of its members, by any one that is not of it, (which is the power of war and peace:) and all this for the preservation of the property of all the members of that society, as far as is possible. But though every man who has entered into civil society, and is become a member of any commonwealth, has thereby quitted his power to punish offences against the law of nature, in prosecution of his own private judgment; yet with the judgment of offences, which he has given up to the legislative in all cases, where he can appeal to the magistrate, he has given a right to the commonwealth to employ his force, for the execution of the judgments of the commonwealth, wherever he shall be called to it; which indeed are his own judgments, they being made by himself, or his representative. And herein we have the original of the legislative and executive power of civil society, which is to judge by standing laws, how far offences are to be punished, when committed within the commonwealth; and also to determine, by occasional judgments founded on the present circumstances of the fact, how far injuries from without are to be vindicated; and in both these to employ all the force of all the members, when there shall be need.

§ 89. Whenever therefore any number of men are so united into one society, as to quit every one his executive power of the law of nature, and to resign it to the public, there and there only is a political or civil society. And this is done, wherever any number of men, in the state of nature, enter into society to make one people, one body politic, under one supreme government; or else when any one joins himself to, and incorporates with any government already made: for hereby he authorizes the society, or, which is all one, the legislative thereof, to make laws for him, as the public good of the society shall require; to the execution whereof, his own assistance (as to his own degrees) is due. And this puts men out of a state of nature into that of a commonwealth, by setting up a judge on earth, with authority to determine all the controversies, and redress the injuries that may happen to any member of the commonwealth; which judge is the legislative, or magistrate appointed by it. And wherever there are any number of men, however associated, that have no such decisive power to appeal to, there they are still in the state of nature.

§ 90. Hence it is evident, that absolute monarchy, which by some men is counted the only government in the world, is indeed inconsistent with civil society, and so can be no form of civil government at all: for the end of civil society being to avoid and remedy those inconveniencies of the state of nature which necessarily follow from every man being judge in his own case, by setting up a known authority, to which every one of that society may appeal upon any injury received, or controversy that may arise, and which every one of the society * ought to obey; wherever any persons are, who have not such an authority to appeal to, for the decision of any difference between them, there those persons are still in the state of nature; and so is every absolute prince, in respect of those who are under his dominion.

§ 91. For he being supposed to have all, both legislative and executive power in himself alone, there is no judge to be found, no appeal lies open to any one, who may fairly, and indifferently, and with authority decide, and from whose decision relief and redress may be expected of any injury or inconveniency, that may be suffered from the prince, or by his order: so that such a man, however entitled, czar, or grand seignior, or how you please, is as much in the state of nature, with all under his dominion, as he is with the rest of mankind: for wherever any two men are, who have no standing rule, and common judge to appeal to on earth, for the determination of controver-

---

* "The public power of all society is above every soul contained in the same society; and the principal use of that power is, to give laws unto all that are under it, which laws in such cases we must obey, unless there be reason showed which may necessarily inforce, that the law of reason, or of God, doth enjoin the contrary." — *Hook.* Eccl. Pol. l. i. sect. 16.

sies of right betwixt them, there they are still in the state of nature*, and under all the inconveniencies of it, with only this woful difference to the subject, or rather slave of an absolute prince: that whereas in the ordinary state of nature he has a liberty to judge of his right, and, according to the best of his power, to maintain it; now, whenever his property is invaded by the will and order of his monarch, he has not only no appeal, as those in society ought to have, but, as if he were degraded from the common state of rational creatures, is denied a liberty to judge of, or to defend his right: and so is exposed to all the misery and inconveniencies, that a man can fear from one, who being in the unrestrained state of nature, is yet corrupted with flattery, and armed with power.

§ 92. For he that thinks absolute power purifies men's blood, and corrects the baseness of human nature, need read but the history of this, or any other age, to be convinced of the contrary. He that would have been insolent and injurious in the woods of America, would not probably be much better in a throne; where perhaps learning and religion shall be found out to justify all that he shall do to his subjects, and the sword presently silence all those that dare question it: for what the protection of absolute monarchy is, what kind of fathers of their countries it makes princes to be, and to what a degree of happiness and security it carries civil society, where this sort of government is grown to perfection; he that will look into the late relation of Ceylon may easily see.

§ 93. In absolute monarchies indeed, as well as other governments of the world, the subjects have an appeal to the law, and judges to decide any

* "To take away all such mutual grievances, injuries, and wrongs," *i. e.* such as attend men in the state of nature, "there was no way but only by growing into composition and agreement amongst themselves by ordaining some kind of government public, and by yielding themselves subject thereunto, that unto whom they granted authority to rule and govern, by them the peace, tranquillity, and happy state of the rest might be procured. Men always knew that where force and injury was offered, they might be defenders of themselves; they knew that however men may seek their own commodity, yet if this were done with injury unto others, it was not to be suffered, but by all men, and all good means, to be withstood. Finally, they knew that no man might in reason take upon him to determine his own right, and according to his own determination proceed in maintenance thereof, inasmuch as every man is towards himself, and them whom he greatly affects, partial; and therefore that strifes and troubles would be endless, except they gave their common consent, all to be ordered by some, whom they should agree upon, without which consent there would be no reason that one man should take upon him to be lord or judge over another." *Hooker's* Eccl. Pol. l. i. sect. 10.

controversies, and restrain any violence that may happen betwixt the subjects themselves, one amongst another. This every one thinks necessary, and
believes he deserves to be thought a declared enemy to society and mankind
who should go about to take it away. But whether this be from a true love of
mankind and society, and such a charity as we all owe one to another, there is
reason to doubt: for this is no more than what every man, who loves his own
power, profit, or greatness, may and naturally must do, keep those animals
from hurting or destroying one another, who labour and drudge only for his
pleasure and advantage; and so are taken care of, not out of any love the
master has for them, but love of himself, and the profit they bring him: for if
it be asked, what security, what fence is there, in such a state, against the
violence and oppression of this absolute ruler? the very question can scarce
be borne. They are ready to tell you, that it deserves death only to ask after
safety. Betwixt subject and subject, they will grant, there must be measures,
laws, and judges, for their mutual peace and security: but as for the ruler, he
ought to be absolute, and is above all such circumstances; because he has
power to do more hurt and wrong, it is right when he does it. To ask how you
may be guarded from harm, or injury, on that side where the strongest hand
is to do it, is presently the voice of faction and rebellion: as if when men
quitting the state of nature entered into society, they agreed that all of them
but one should be under the restraint of laws, but that he should still retain all
the liberty of the state of nature, increased with power, and made licentious
by impunity. This is to think, that men are so foolish, that they take care to
avoid what mischiefs may be done them by pole-cats, or foxes; but are
content, nay think it safety, to be devoured by lions.

§ 94. But whatever flatterers may talk to amuse people's understandings,
it hinders not men from feeling; and when they perceive that any man, in
what station soever, is out of the bounds of the civil society which they are
of, and that they have no appeal on earth against any harm they may receive
from him, they are apt to think themselves in the state of nature in respect of
him whom they find to be so; and to take care, as soon as they can, to have
that safety and security in civil society for which it was instituted, and for
which only they entered into it. And therefore, though perhaps at first (as
shall be showed more at large hereafter in the following part of this discourse), some one good and excellent man having got a pre-eminency
amongst the rest, had this deference paid to his goodness and virtue, as to a
kind of natural authority, that the chief rule, with arbitration of their differences, by a tacit consent devolved into his hands, without any other caution
but the assurance they had of his uprightness and wisdom; yet when time,
giving authority, and (as some men would persuade us) sacredness to cus-

toms, which the negligent and unforeseeing innocence of the first ages began, had brought in successors of another stamp; the people finding their properties not secure under the government as then it was (whereas government has no other end but the preservation of* property), could never be safe nor at rest, nor think themselves in civil society, till the legislature was placed in collective bodies of men, call them senate, parliament, or what you please. By which means every single person became subject, equally with other the meanest men, to those laws which he himself, as part of the legislative, had established; nor could any one, by his own authority, avoid the force of the law when once made; nor by any pretence of superiority plead exemption, thereby to license his own, or the miscarriages of any of his dependents. † "No man in civil society can be exempted from the laws of it:" for if any man may do what he thinks fit, and there be no appeal on earth, for redress or security against any harm he shall do; I ask, whether he be not perfectly still in the state of nature, and so can be no part or member of that civil society; unless any one will say the state of nature and civil society are one and the same thing, which I have never yet found any one so great a patron of anarchy as to affirm.

CHAPTER VIII.

Of the Beginning of Political Societies.

§ 95. Men being, as has been said, by nature all free, equal, and independent, no one can be put out of this estate, and subjected to the political power of another, without his own consent. The only way whereby any one

---

* "At the first, when some certain kind of regiment was once appointed, it may be that nothing was then farther thought upon for the manner of governing, but all permitted unto their wisdom and discretion, which were to rule, till by experience they found this for all parts very inconvenient, so as the thing which they had devised for a remedy did indeed but increase the sore which it should have cured. They saw that to live by one man's will became the cause of all men's misery. This constrained them to come into laws, wherein all men might see their duty beforehand, and know the penalties of transgressing them." *Hooker's* Eccl. Pol. l. i. sect. 10.

† "Civil law, being the act of the whole body politic, doth therefore overrule each several part of the same body." *Hooker's* Eccl. Pol. l. i. sect. 10.

divests himself of his natural liberty, and puts on the bonds of civil society, is by agreeing with other men to join and unite into a community, for their comfortable, safe, and peaceable living one amongst another, in a secure enjoyment of their properties, and a greater security against any that are not of it. This any number of men may do, because it injures not the freedom of the rest; they are left as they were in the liberty of the state of nature. When any number of men have so consented to make one community or government, they are thereby presently incorporated, and make one body politic, wherein the majority have a right to act and conclude the rest.

§ 96. For when any number of men have, by the consent of every individual, made a community, they have thereby made that community one body, with a power to act as one body, which is only by the will and determination of the majority; for that which acts any community being only the consent of the individuals of it, and it being necessary to that which is one body to move one way; it is necessary the body should move that way whither the greater force carries it, which is the consent of the majority: or else it is impossible it should act or continue one body, one community, which the consent of every individual that united into it agreed that it should; and so every one is bound by that consent to be concluded by the majority. And therefore we see that in assemblies, empowered to act by positive laws, where no number is set by that positive law which empowers them, the act of the majority passes for the act of the whole, and of course determines; as having, by the law of nature and reason, the power of the whole.

§ 97. And thus every man, by consenting with others to make one body politic under one government, puts himself under an obligation to every one of that society to submit to the determination of the majority, and to be concluded by it; or else this original compact, whereby he with others incorporate into one society, would signify nothing, and be no compact, if he be left free, and under no other ties than he was in before in the state of nature. For what appearance would there be of any compact? what new engagement, if he were no farther tied by any decrees of the society than he himself thought fit, and did actually consent to? This would be still as great a liberty as he himself had before his compact, or any one else in the state of nature hath, who may submit himself and consent to any acts of it if he thinks fit.

§ 98. For if the consent of the majority shall not, in reason, be received as the act of the whole, and conclude every individual, nothing but the consent of every individual can make any thing to be the act of the whole: but such a consent is next to impossible ever to be had, if we consider the infirmities of health, and avocations of business, which in a number, though much less than that of a commonwealth, will necessarily keep many away from the public assembly. To which if we add the variety of opinions, and contrariety of interests which unavoidably happen in all collections of men, the coming into society upon such terms would be only like Cato's coming into the theatre, only to go out again. Such a constitution as this would make the mighty leviathan of a shorter duration than the feeblest creatures, and not let it outlast the day it was born in: which cannot be supposed, till we can think that rational creatures should desire and constitute societies only to be dissolved: for where the majority cannot conclude the rest, there they cannot act as one body, and consequently will be immediately dissolved again.

§ 99. Whosoever therefore out of a state of nature unite into a community, must be understood to give up all the power necessary to the ends for which they unite into society, to the majority of the community, unless they expressly agreed in any number greater than the majority. And this is done by barely agreeing to unite into one political society, which is all the compact that is, or needs be, between the individuals that enter into, or make up a commonwealth. And thus that which begins and actually constitutes any political society, is nothing but the consent of any number of freemen capable of a majority, to unite and incorporate into such a society. And this is that, and that only, which did or could give beginning to any lawful government in the world.

§ 100. To this I find two objections made.

First, "That there are no instances to be found in story, of a company of men independent and equal one amongst another, that met together, and in this way began and set up a government."

Secondly, "It is impossible of right, that men should do so, because all men being born under government, they are to submit to that, and are not at liberty to begin a new one."

§ 101. To the first there is this to answer, that it is not at all to be wondered, that history gives us but a very little account of men that lived together in the state of nature. The inconveniencies of that condition, and the love and want of society, no sooner brought any number of them together, but they presently united and incorporated, if they designed to continue together. And if we may not suppose men ever to have been in the state of nature, because we hear not much of them in such a state, we may as well suppose the armies of Salmanasser or Xerxes were never children, because we hear little of them till they were men, and embodied in armies. Government is every where antecedent to records, and letters seldom come in amongst a people till a long continuation of civil society has, by other more necessary arts, provided for their safety, ease, and plenty: and then they begin to look after the history of their founders, and search into their original, when they have outlined the memory of it: for it is with common-wealths as with particular persons, they are commonly ignorant of their own births and infancies: and if they know any thing of their original, they are beholden for it to the accidental records that others have kept of it. And those that we have of the beginning of any politics in the world, excepting that of the Jews, where God himself immediately interposed, and which favours not at all paternal dominion, are all either plain instances of such a beginning as I have mentioned, or at least have manifest footsteps of it.

§ 102. He must show a strange inclination to deny evident matter of fact, when it agrees not with his hypothesis, who will not allow, that the begin-nings of Rome and Venice were by the uniting together of several men free and independent one of another, amongst whom there was no natural supe-riority or subjection. And if Josephus Acosta's word may be taken, he tells us, that in many parts of America there was no government at all. "There are great and apparent conjectures," says he, "that these men, speaking of those of Peru, for a long time had neither kings nor commonwealths, but lived in troops, as they do this day in Florida, the Cheriquanas, those of Brasil, and many other nations, which have no certain kings, but as occa-sion is offered, in peace or war, they choose their captains as they please," l. i. c. 25. If it be said that every man there was born subject to his father, or the head of his family; that the subjection due from a child to a father took not away his freedom of uniting into what political society he thought fit, has been already proved. But be that as it will, these men, it is evident, were actually free; and whatever superiority some politicians now would place in any of them, they themselves claimed it not, but by consent were all equal, till by the same consent they set rulers over themselves. So that their politic societies all began from a voluntary union, and the mutual agreement of men freely acting in the choice of their governors and forms of government.

§ 103. And I hope those who went away from Sparta with Palantus, mentioned by Justin, l. iii. c. 4, will be allowed to have been freemen, independent one of another, and to have set up a government over them-selves, by their own consent. Thus I have given several examples out of history, of people free and in the state of nature, that being met together incorporated and began a commonwealth. And if the want of such instances be an argument to prove that governments were not, nor could not be so begun, I suppose the contenders for paternal empire were better let it alone than urge it against natural liberty: for if they can give so many instances out of history, of governments begun upon paternal right, I think (though at best an argument from what has been, to what should of right be, has no great force) one might, without any great danger, yield them the cause. But if I might advise them in the case, they would do well not to search too much into the original of governments, as they have begun *de facto;* lest they should find, at the foundation of most of them, something very little favourable to the design they promote, and such a power as they contend for.

§ 104. But to conclude, reason being plain on our side, that men are naturally free, and the examples of history showing, that the governments of the world, that were begun in peace, had their beginning laid on that foundation, and were made by the consent of the people; there can be little room for doubt, either where the right is, or what has been the opinion or practice of mankind about the first erecting of governments.

§ 105. I will not deny that if we look back as far as history will direct us, towards the original of commonwealths, we shall generally find them under the government and administration of one man. And I am also apt to believe, that where a family was numerous enough to subsist by itself, and continued entire together, without mixing with others, as it often happens, where there is much land and few people, the government commonly began in the father: for the father having, by the law of nature, the same power with every man else to punish, as he thought fit, any offences against that law, might thereby punish his transgressing children, even when they were men, and out of their pupilage; and they were very likely to submit to his punishment, and all join with him against the offender in their turns, giving him thereby power to execute his sentence against any transgression, and so in effect make him the law-maker and governor over all that remained in conjunction with his family. He was fittest to be trusted; paternal affection secured their property and interest under his care; and the custom of obeying him in their childhood, made it easier to submit to him rather than to any other. If, therefore, they must have one to rule them, as government is hardly to be avoided amongst men that live together, who so likely to be the man as he that was their common father, unless negligence, cruelty, or any other defect of mind or body made him unfit for it? But when either the father died, and left his next heir, for want of age, wisdom, courage, or any other qualities, less fit for rule, or where several families met and consented to continue together, there, it is not to be doubted, but they used their natural freedom to set up him whom they judged the ablest, and most likely to rule well over them. Conformable hereunto, we find the people of America, who (living out of the reach of the conquering swords and spreading domination of the two great empires of Peru and Mexico, enjoyed their own natural freedom, though, *cæteris paribus,* they commonly prefer the heir of their deceased king; yet if they find him any way weak or incapable, they pass him by, and set up the stoutest and bravest man for their ruler.

§ 106. Thus, though looking back as far as records give us any account of peopling the world, and the history of nations, we commonly find the government to be in one hand; yet it destroys not that which I affirm, viz. that the beginning of politic society depends upon the consent of the individuals, to join into, and make one society; who, when they are thus incorporated, might set up what form of government they thought fit. But this having given occasion to men to mistake, and think that by nature government was monarchical, and belonged to the father; it may not be amiss here to consider, why people in the beginning generally pitched upon this form: which though perhaps the father's preeminency might, in the first institution of some commonwealth, give a rise to, and place in the beginning the power in one hand; yet it is plain that the reason that continued the form of government in a single person, was not any regard or respect to paternal authority; since all petty monarchies, that is, almost all monarchies, near this original, have been commonly, at least upon occasion, elective.

§ 107. First then, in the beginning of things, the father's government of the childhood of those sprung from him, having accustomed them to the rule of one man, and taught them that where it was exercised with care and skill, with affection and love to those under it, it was sufficient to procure and preserve to men all the political happiness they sought for in society; it was no wonder that they should pitch upon, and naturally run into that form of government, which from their infancy they had been all accustomed to; and which, by experience, they had found both easy and safe. To which, if we add, that monarchy being simple, and most obvious to men, whom neither experience had instructed in forms of government, nor the ambition or insolence of empire had taught to beware of the encroachments of prerogative, or the inconveniencies of absolute power, which monarchy in succession was apt to lay claim to, and bring upon them; it was not at all strange that they should not much trouble themselves to think of methods of restraining any exorbitancies of those to whom they had given the authority over them, and of balancing the power of government, by placing several parts of it in different hands. They had neither felt the oppression of tyrannical dominion, nor did the fashion of the age, nor their possessions, or way of living (which afforded little matter for covetousness or ambition), give them any reason to apprehend or provide against it; and therefore it is no wonder they put themselves into such a frame of government, as was not only, as I said, most obvious and simple, but also best suited to their present state and condition, which stood more in need of defence against foreign invasions and injuries, than of multiplicity of laws. The equality of a simple poor way of living, confining their desires within the narrow bounds of each man's small property, made few controversies, and so no need of many laws to decide them, or variety of officers to superintend the process, or look after the execution of justice, where there were but few trespasses, and few offenders. Since then those who liked one another so well as to join into society, cannot but be supposed to have some acquaintance and friendship together, and some trust one in another; they could not but have greater apprehensions of others than of one another: and therefore their first care and thought cannot but be supposed to be, how to secure themselves against foreign force. It was natural for them to put themselves under a frame of government which might best serve to that end, and choose the wisest and bravest man to conduct them in their wars, and lead them out against their enemies, and in this chiefly be their ruler.

§ 108. Thus we see that the kings of the Indians in America, which is still a pattern of the first ages in Asia and Europe, whilst the inhabitants were too few for the country, and want of people and money gave men no temptation to enlarge their possessions of land, or contest for wider extent of ground, are little more than generals of their armies; and though they command absolutely in war, yet at home and in time of peace they exercise very little dominion, and have but a very moderate sovereignty; the resolutions of peace and war being ordinarily either in the people, or in a council. Though the war itself, which admits not of plurality of governors, naturally devolves the command into the king's sole authority.

§ 109. And thus, in Israel itself, the chief business of their judges and first kings, seems to have been to be captains in war, and leaders of their armies; which (besides what is signified by "going out and in before the people," which was to march forth to war, and home again at the heads of their forces) appears plainly in the story of Jephthah. The Ammonites making war upon Israel, the Gileadites in fear send to Jephthah, a bastard of their family whom they had cast off, and article with him, if he will assist them against the Ammonites, to make him their ruler; which they do in these words, "And the people made him head and captain over them," Judg. xi. 11. which was, as it seems, all one as to be judge. "And he judged Israel," Judg. xii. 7, that is, was their captain-general, "six years." So when Jotham upbraids the Shechemites with the obligation they had to Gideon, who had been their judge and ruler, he tells them, "He fought for you, and adventured his life far, and delivered you out of the hands of Midian," Judg. ix. 17. Nothing is mentioned of him but what he did as a general: and indeed that is all is found in his history, or in any of the rest of the judges. And Abimelech particularly is called king, though at most he was but their general. And when, being weary of the ill conduct of Samuel's sons, the children of Israel desired a king, "like all the nations, to judge them, and to go out before them, and to fight their battles," 1 Sam. viii. 20, God, granting their desire, says to Samuel, "I will send thee a man, and thou shalt anoint him to be captain over my people Israel, that he may save my people out of the hands of the Philistines," ix. 16. As if the only business of a king had been to lead out their armies, and fight in their defence; and accordingly Samuel, at his inauguration, pouring a vial of oil upon him, declares to Saul, that "the Lord had anointed him to be captain over his inheritance," x. 1. And therefore those who, after Saul's being solemnly chosen and saluted king by the tribes of Mispeh, were unwilling to have him their king, made no other objection but this, "How shall this man save us?" v. 27; as if they should have said, this man is unfit to be our king, not having skill and conduct enough in war to be able to defend us. And when God resolved to transfer the government to David, it is in these words, "But now thy king-dom shall not continue: the Lord hath sought him a man after his own heart, and the Lord hath commanded him to be captain over his people," xiii. 14. As if the whole kingly authority were nothing else but to be their general: and therefore the tribes who had stuck to Saul's family, and opposed David's reign, when they came to Hebron with terms of submission to him, they tell him, amongst other arguments they had to submit to him as to their king, that he was in effect their king in Saul's time, and therefore they had no reason but to receive him as their king now. "Also (say they) in time past, when Saul was king over us, thou wast he that leddest out and broughtest in Israel, and the Lord said unto thee, Thou shalt feed my people Israel, and thou shalt be a captain over Israel."

§ 110. Thus, whether a family by degrees grew up into a commonwealth, and the fatherly authority being continued on to the elder son, every one in his turn growing up under it, tacitly submitted to it; and the easiness and equality of it not offending any one, every one acquiesced, till time seemed to have confirmed it, and settled a right of succession by prescription: or whether several families, or the descendants of several families, whom chance, neighbourhood, or business brought together, uniting into society: the need of a general, whose conduct might defend them against their enemies in war, and the great confidence the innocence and sincerity of that poor but virtuous age, (such as are almost all those which begin govern-ments, that ever come to last in the world) gave men of one another, made the first beginners of commonwealths generally put the rule into one man's hand, without any other express limitation or restraint, but what the nature of the thing and the end of government required: whichever of those it was that at first put the rule into the hands of a single person, certain it is that nobody was intrusted with it but for the public good and safety, and to those ends, in the infancies of commonwealths, those who had it, commonly used it. And unless they had done so, young societies could not have subsisted; without such nursing fathers, tender and careful of the public weal, all governments would have sunk under the weakness and infirmities of their infancy, and the prince and the people had soon perished together.

§ 111. But though the golden age (before vain ambition, and *amor sceleratus habendi,* evil concupiscence, had corrupted men's minds into a mistake of true power and honour) had more virtue, and consequently better governors, as well as less vicious subjects; and there was then no stretching prerogative on the one side, to oppress the people; nor consequently on the other, any dispute about privilege, to lessen or restrain the power of the magistrate; and so no contest betwixt rulers and people about governors or government: yet, when ambition and luxury in future ages* would retain and increase the power, without doing the business for which it was given; and, aided by flattery, taught princes to have distinct and separate interests from their people; men found it necessary to examine more carefully the original and rights of government, and to find out ways to restrain the exorbitancies, and prevent the abuses of that power, which they having intrusted in another's hands only for their own good, they found was made use of to hurt them.

§ 112. Thus we may see how probable it is, that people that were naturally free, and by their own consent either submitted to the government of their father, or united together out of different families to make a government, should generally put the rule into one man's hands, and choose to be under the conduct of a single person, without so much as by express

---

* " At first, when some certain kind of regiment was once approved, it may be nothing was then farther thought upon for the manner of governing, but all permitted unto their wisdom and discretion which were to rule, till by experience they found this for all parts very inconvenient, so as the thing which they had devised for a remedy, did indeed but increase the sore which it should have cured. They saw, that to live by one man's will, became the cause of all men's misery. This constrained them to come unto laws wherein all men might see their duty beforehand, and know the penalties of transgressing them." Hooker's Eccl. Pol. l. i. sect. 10.

conditions limiting or regulating his power, which they thought safe enough in his honesty and prudence: though they never dreamed of monarchy being *jure divino,* which we never heard of among mankind, till it was revealed to us by the divinity of this last age; nor ever allowed paternal power to have a right to dominion, or to be the foundation of all government. And thus much may suffice to show, that, as far as we have any light from history, we have reason to conclude, that all peaceful beginnings of government have been laid in the consent of the people. I say peaceful, because I shall have occasion in another place to speak of conquest, which some esteem a way of beginning of governments.

The other objection I find urged against the beginning of politics, in the way I have mentioned, is this, viz.

§ 113. "That all men being born under government, some or other, it is impossible any of them should ever be free, and at liberty to unite together, and begin a new one, or ever be able to erect a lawful government."

If this argument be good, I ask, how came so many lawful monarchies into the world? for if any body, upon this supposition, can show me any one man in any age of the world free to begin a lawful monarchy, I will be bound to show him ten other free men at liberty at the same time to unite and begin a new government under a regal, or any other form; it being demonstration, that if any one, born under the dominion of another, may be so free as to have a right to command others in a new and distinct empire, every one that is born under the dominion of another may be so free too, and may become a ruler, or subject of a distinct separate government. And so by this their own principle, either all men, however born, are free, or else there is but one lawful prince, one lawful government in the world. And then they have nothing to do, but barely to show us which that is; which when they have done, I doubt not but all mankind will easily agree to pay obedience to him.

§ 114. Though it be a sufficient answer to their objection, to show that it involves them in the same difficulties that it doth those they use it against; yet I shall endeavour to discover the weakness of this argument a little farther.

"All men, say they, are born under government, and therefore they cannot be at liberty to begin a new one. Every one is born a subject to his father, or his prince, and is therefore under the perpetual tie of subjection and allegiance." It is plain mankind never owned nor considered any such natural subjection that they were born in, to one or to the other, that tied them, without their own consents, to a subjection to them and their heirs.

§ 115. For there are no examples so frequent in history, both sacred and profane, as those of men withdrawing themselves, and their obedience, from the jurisdiction they were born under, and the family or community they were bred up in, and setting up new governments in other places; from whence sprang all that number of petty commonwealths in the beginning of ages, and which always multiplied as long as there was room enough, till the stronger, or more fortunate, swallowed the weaker; and those great ones again breaking to pieces, dissolved into lesser dominions. All which are so many testimonies against paternal sovereignty, and plainly prove that it was not the natural right of the father descending to his heirs, that made governments in the beginning, since it was impossible, upon that ground, there should have been so many little kingdoms; all must have been but only one universal monarchy, if men had not been at liberty to separate themselves from their families and the government, be it what it will, that was set up in it, and go and make distinct commonwealths and other governments, as they thought fit.

§ 116. This has been the practice of the world from its first beginning to this day; nor is it now any more hinderance to the freedom of mankind, that they are born under constituted and ancient polities, that have established laws and set forms of government, than if they were born in the woods, amongst the unconfined inhabitants that run loose in them: for those who would persuade us, that "by being born under any government, we are naturally subjects to it," and have no more any title or pretence to the freedom of the state of nature; have no other reason (bating that of paternal power, which we have already answered) to produce for it, but only because our fathers or progenitors passed away their natural liberty, and thereby bound up themselves and their posterity to a perpetual subjection to the government which they themselves submitted to. It is true, that whatever engagement or promises any one has made for himself, he is under the obligation of them, but cannot, by any compact whatsoever, bind his children or posterity: for his son, when a man, being altogether as free as the father, any "act of the father can no more give away the liberty of the son," than it can of any body else: he may indeed annex such conditions to the land he enjoyed as a subject of any commonwealth, as may oblige his son to be of that community, if he will enjoy those possessions which were his father's; because that estate being his father's property; he may dispose or settle it as he pleases.

§ 117. And this has generally given the occasion to mistake in this matter; because commonwealths not permitting any part of their dominions to be dismembered, nor to be enjoyed by any but those of their community, the son cannot ordinarily enjoy the possessions of his father, but under the same terms his father did, by becoming a member of the society; whereby he puts himself presently under the government he finds there established, as much as any other subject of that commonwealth. And thus, "the consent of freemen, born under government, which only makes them members of it," being given separately in their turns, as each comes to be of age, and not in a multitude together; people take no notice of it, and thinking it not done at all, or not necessary, conclude they are naturally subjects as they are men.

§ 118. But it is plain governments themselves understand it otherwise; they claim "no power over the son, because of that they had over the father;" nor look on children as being their subjects, by their fathers being so. If a subject of England have a child by an English woman in France, whose subject is he? Not the king of England's; for he must have leave to be admitted to the privileges of it: nor the king of France's; for how then has his father a liberty to bring him away, and breed him as he pleases? and who ever was judged as a traitor or deserter, if he left or warred against a country, for being barely born in it of parents that were aliens there? It is plain then, by the practice of governments themselves, as well as by the law of right reason, that "a child is born a subject of no country or government." He is under his father's tuition and authority till he comes to age of discretion; and then he is a freeman, at liberty what government he will put himself under, what body politic he will unite himself to: for if an Englishman's son, born in France, be at liberty, and may do so, it is evident there is no tie upon him by his father's being a subject of this kingdom; nor is he bound up by any compact of his ancestors. And why then hath not his son, by the same reason, the same liberty, though he be born any where else? Since the power that a father hath naturally over his children is the same, wherever they be born, and the ties of natural obligations are not bounded by the positive limits of kingdoms and commonwealths.

§ 119. Every man being, as has been showed, naturally free, and nothing being able to put him into subjection to any earthly power, but only his own consent; it is to be considered, what shall be understood to be a sufficient declaration of a man's consent, to make him subject to the laws of any government. There is a common distinction of an express and a tacit consent, which will concern our present case. Nobody doubts but an express consent of any man entering into any society, makes him a perfect member of that society, a subject of that government. The difficulty is, what ought to be looked upon as a tacit consent, and how far it binds, *i. e.* how far any one shall be looked on to have consented, and thereby submitted to any government, where he has made no expressions of it at all. And to this I say, that every man, that hath any possessions, or enjoyment of any part of the dominions of any government, doth thereby give his tacit consent, and is as far forth obliged to obedience to the laws of that government, during such enjoyment, as any one under it; whether this his possession be of land, to him and his heirs for ever, or a lodging only for a week; or whether it be barely travelling freely on the highway; and, in effect, it reaches as far as the very being of any one within the territories of that government.

§ 120. To understand this the better, it is fit to consider, that every man, when he at first incorporates himself into any commonwealth, he, by his uniting himself thereunto, annexes also, and submits to the community those possessions which he has, or shall acquire, that do not already belong to any other government: for it would be a direct contradiction for any one to enter into society with others for the securing and regulating of property, and yet to suppose his land, whose property is to be regulated by the laws of the society, should be exempt from the jurisdiction of that government, to which he himself, the proprietor of the land, is a subject. By the same act therefore, whereby any one unites his person, which was before free, to any commonwealth, by the same he unites his possessions, which were before free, to it also: and they become, both of them, person and possession, subject to the government and dominion of that commonwealth, as long as it hath a being. Whoever, therefore, from thenceforth, by inheritance, purchase, permission, or otherways, enjoys any part of the land so annexed to, and under the government of that commonwealth, must take it with the condition it is under; that is, of submitting to the government of the commonwealth, under whose jurisdiction it is, as far forth as any subject of it.

§ 121. But since the government has a direct jurisdiction only over the land, and reaches the possessor of it (before he has actually incorporated himself in the society) only as he dwells upon, and enjoys that; the obligation any one is under, by virtue of such enjoyment, to "submit to the government, begins and ends with the enjoyment:" so that whenever the owner, who has given nothing but such a tacit consent to the government, will, by donation, sale, or otherwise, quit the said possession, he is at liberty to go and incorporate himself into any other commonwealth; or to agree with others to begin a new one, in *vacuis locis,* in any part of the world they can find free and unpossessed: whereas he that has once, by actual agreement, and any express declaration, given his consent to be of any commonwealth, is perpetually and indispensably obliged to be, and remain unalterably a subject to it, and can never be again in the liberty of the state of nature; unless, by any calamity, the government he was under comes to be dissolved, or else by some public act cuts him off from being any longer a member of it.

§ 122. But submitting to the laws of any country, living quietly, and enjoying privileges and protection under them, makes not a man a member of that society: this is only a local protection and homage due to and from all those, who, not being in a state of war, come within the territories belonging to any government, to all parts whereof the force of its laws extends. But this no more makes a man a member of that society, a perpetual subject of that commonwealth, than it would make a man a subject to another, in whose family he found it convenient to abide for some time; though, whilst he continued in it, he were obliged to comply with the laws, and submit to the government he found there. And thus we see, that foreigners, by living all their lives under another government, and enjoying the privileges and protection of it, though they are bound, even in conscience, to submit to its administration, as far forth as any denison; yet do not thereby come to be subjects or members of that commonwealth. Nothing can make any man so, but his actually entering into it by positive engagement, and express promise and compact. This is that which I think concerning the beginning of political societies, and that consent which makes any one a member of any commonwealth.

CHAPTER IX.

Of the Ends of political Society and Government.

§ 123. If man in the state of nature be so free as has been said; if he be absolute lord of his own person and possessions, equal to the greatest, and subject to nobody, why will he part with his freedom, why will he give up this empire, and subject himself to the dominion and control of any other power? To which it is obvious to answer, that though in the state of nature he hath such a right, yet the enjoyment of it is very uncertain, and constantly exposed to the invasion of others; for all being kings as much as he, every man his equal, and the greater part no strict observers of equity and justice, the enjoyment of the property he has in this state is very unsafe, very unsecure. This makes him willing to quit a condition, which, however free, is full of fears and continual dangers: and it is not without reason that he seeks out, and is willing to join in society with others, who are already united, or have a mind to unite, for the mutual preservation of their lives, liberties, and estates, which I call by the general name property.

§ 124. The great and chief end, therefore, of men's uniting into commonwealths, and putting themselves under government, is the preservation of their property. To which in the state of nature there are many things wanting.

First, There wants an established, settled, known law, received and allowed by common consent to be the standard of right and wrong, and the common measure to decide all controversies between them: for though the law of nature be plain and intelligible to all rational creatures; yet men being biassed by their interest, as well as ignorant for want of studying it, are not apt to allow of it as a law binding to them in the application of it to their particular cases.

§ 125. Secondly, In the state of nature there wants a known and indifferent judge, with authority to determine all differences according to the established law: for every one in that state being both judge and executioner of the law of nature, men being partial to themselves, passion and revenge is very apt to carry them too far, and with too much heat, in their own cases; as well as negligence and unconcernedness, to make them too remiss in other men's.

§ 126. Thirdly, In the state of nature there often wants power to back and support the sentence when right, and to give it due execution. They who by any injustice offend, will seldom fail, where they are able, by force to make good their injustice; such resistance many times makes the punishment dangerous, and frequently destructive to those who attempt it.

§ 127. Thus mankind, notwithstanding all the privileges of the state of nature, being but in an ill condition, while they remain in it, are quickly driven into society. Hence it comes to pass, that we seldom find any number of men live any time together in this state. The inconveniencies that they are therein exposed to, by the irregular and uncertain exercise of the power every man has of punishing the transgressions of others, make them take sanctuary under the established laws of government, and therein seek the preservation of their property. It is this makes them so willingly give up every one his single power of punishing, to be exercised by such alone as shall be appointed to it amongst them; and by such rules as the community, or those authorized by them to that purpose, shall agree on. And in this we have the original right of both the legislative and executive power, as well as of the governments and societies themselves.

§ 128. For in the state of nature, to omit the liberty he has of innocent delights, a man has two powers.

The first is to do whatsoever he thinks fit for the preservation of himself and others within the permission of the law of nature: by which law, common to them all, he and all the rest of mankind are one community, make up one society, distinct from all other creatures. And, were it not for the corruption and viciousness of degenerate men, there would be no need of any other; no necessity that men should separate from this great and natural community, and by positive agreements combine into smaller and divided associations.

The other power a man has in the state of nature, is the power to punish the crimes committed against that law. Both these he gives up when he joins in a private, if I may so call it, or particular politic society, and incorporates into any commonwealth, separate from the rest of mankind.

§ 129. The first power, viz. "of doing whatsoever he thought fit for the preservation of himself" and the rest of mankind, he gives up to be regulated by laws made by the society, so far forth as the preservation of himself and the rest of that society shall require; which laws of the society in many things confine the liberty he had by the law of nature.

§ 130. Secondly, The power of punishing he wholly gives up, and engages his natural force (which he might before employ in the execution of the law of nature, by his own single authority, as he thought fit), to assist the executive power of the society, as the law thereof shall require: for being now in a new state, wherein he is to enjoy many conveniencies, from the labour, assistance, and society of others in the same community, as well as protection from its whole strength; he is to part also with as much of his natural liberty, in providing for himself, as the good, prosperity, and safety of the society shall require; which is not only necessary, but just, since the other members of the society do the like.

§ 131. But though men, when they enter into society, give up the equality, liberty, and executive power they had in the state of nature, into the hands of the society, to be so far disposed of by the legislative as the good of the society shall require; yet it being only with an intention in every one the better to preserve himself, his liberty and property (for no rational creature can be supposed to change his condition with an intention to be worse); the power of the society, or legislative constituted by them, can never be supposed to extend farther than the common good; but is obliged to secure every one's property, by providing against those three defects above-mentioned, that made the state of nature so unsafe and uneasy. And so whoever has the legislative or supreme power of any commonwealth, is bound to govern by established standing laws, promulgated and known to the people, and not by extemporary decrees; by indifferent and upright judges, who are to decide controversies by those laws; and to employ the force of the community at home, only in the execution of such laws; or abroad to prevent or redress foreign injuries, and secure the community from inroads and invasion. And all this to be directed to no other end but the peace, safety, and public good of the people.

CHAPTER X.

Of the Forms of a Commonwealth.

§ 132. The majority having, as has been showed, upon men's first uniting into society, the whole power of the community naturally in them, may employ all that power in making laws for the community from time to time, and executing those laws by officers of their own appointing; and then the form of the government is a perfect democracy: or else may put the power of making laws into the hands of a few select men, and their heirs or successors; and then it is an oligarchy: or else into the hands of one man, and then it is a monarchy: if to him and his heirs, it is an hereditary monarchy: if to him only for life, but upon his death the power only of nominating a successor to return to them, an elective monarchy. And so accordingly of these the community may make compounded and mixed forms of government, as they think good. And if the legislative power be at first given by the majority to one or more persons only for their lives, or any limited time, and then the supreme power to revert to them again; when it is so reverted, the community may dispose of it again anew into what hands they please, and so constitute a new form of government: for the form of government depending upon the placing the supreme power, which is the legislative (it being impossible to conceive that an inferior power should prescribe to a superior, or any but the supreme make laws), according as the power of making laws is placed, such is the form of the commonwealth.

§ 133. By commonwealth, I must be understood all along to mean, not a democracy, or any form of government, but any independent community, which the Latines signified by the word *civitas;* to which the word which best answers in our language is commonwealth, and most properly expresses such a society of men, which community or city in English does not: for there may be subordinate communities in government; and city amongst us has a quite different notion from commonwealth: and therefore, to avoid ambiguity, I crave leave to use the word commonwealth in that *all law* (handwritten annotation)

sense, in which I find it used by king James the First; and I take it to be its genuine signification; which if any body dislike, I consent with him to change it for a better.

CHAPTER XI.

Of the Extent of the legislative Power.

§ 134. The great end of men's entering into society being the enjoyment of their properties in peace and safety, and the great instrument and means of that being the laws established in that society; the first and fundamental positive law of all commonwealths is the establishing of the legislative power; as the first and fundamental natural law, which is to govern even the legislative itself, is the preservation of the society, and (as far as will consist with the public good) of every person in it. This legislative is not only the supreme power of the commonwealth, but sacred and unalterable in the hands where the community have once placed it; nor can any edict of any body else, in what form soever conceived, or by what power soever backed, have the force and obligation of a law, which has not its sanction from that legislative which the public has chosen and appointed: for without this the law could not have that which is absolutely necessary to its being a law*, the consent of the society; over whom nobody can have a power to make laws, but by their own consent, and by authority received from them. And

---

* "The lawful power of making laws to command whole politic societies of men, belonging so properly unto the same entire societies, that for any prince or potentate of what kind soever upon earth, to exercise the same of himself, and not by express commission immediately and personally received from God, or else by authority derived at the first from their consent, upon whose persons they impose laws, it is no better than mere tyranny. Laws they are not, therefore, which public approbation hath not made so." Hooker's Eccl. Pol. l. i. sect. 10. "Of this point therefore we are to note, that sith men naturally have no full and perfect power to command whole politic multitudes of men, therefore utterly without our consent, we could in such sort be at no man's commandment living. And to be commanded we do consent, when that society, whereof we be a part, hath at any time before consented, without revoking the same by the like universal agreement.

"Laws therefore human, of what kind soever, are available by consent." *Ibid.*

as sovereign as it gets in Locke – (handwritten annotation) therefore all the obedience, which by the most solemn ties any one can be obliged to pay, ultimately terminates in this supreme power, and is directed by those laws which it enacts: nor can any oaths to any foreign power whatsoever, or any domestic subordinate power, discharge any member of the society from his obedience to the legislative, acting pursuant to their trust; nor oblige him to any obedience contrary to the laws so enacted, or farther than they do allow; it being ridiculous to imagine one can be tied ultimately to obey any power in the society which is not supreme.

§ 135. Though the legislative, whether placed in one or more, whether it be always in being, or only by intervals, though it be the supreme power in every commonwealth; yet,

First, It is not, nor can possibly be absolutely arbitrary over the lives and fortunes of the people: for it being but the joint power of every member of the society given up to that person or assembly which is legislator; it can be no more than those persons had in a state of nature before they entered into society, and gave up to the community: for nobody can transfer to another more power than he has in himself; and nobody has an absolute arbitrary power over himself, or over any other, to destroy his own life, or take away the life or property of another. A man, as has been proved, cannot subject himself to the arbitrary power of another; and having in the state of nature no arbitrary power over the life, liberty, or possession of another, but only so much as the law of nature gave him for the preservation of himself and the rest of mankind; this is all he doth, or can give up to the commonwealth, and by it to the legislative power, so that the legislative can have no more than this. Their power, in the utmost bounds of it, is limited to the public good of the society. It is a power that hath no other end but preservation, and therefore can never* have a right to destroy, enslave, or designedly to

---

* Two foundations there are which bear up public societies; the one a natural inclination, whereby all men desire sociable life and fellowship; the other an order, expressly or secretly agreed upon, touching the manner of their union in living together: the latter is that which we call the law of a commonweal, the very soul of a politic body, the parts whereof are by law animated, held together, and set on work in such actions as the common good requireth. Laws politic, ordained for external order and regiment amongst men, are never framed as they should be, unless presuming the will of man to be inwardly obstinate, rebellious, and averse from all obedience to the sacred laws of his nature; in a word, unless presuming man to be, in regard to his depraved mind, little better than a wild beast, they do accordingly provide, notwithstanding, so to frame his outward actions, that they be no hindrance unto the common good, for which societies are instituted. Unless they do this, they are not perfect." *Hooker*'s Eccl. Pol. l. i. sect. 10.

impoverish the subjects. The obligations of the law of nature cease not in society, but only in many cases are drawn closer, and have by human laws known penalties annexed to them, to enforce their observation. Thus the law of nature stands as an eternal rule to all men, legislators as well as others. The rules that they make for other men's actions must, as well as their own and other men's actions be conformable to the law of nature, *i. e.* to the will of God, of which that is a declaration; and the "fundamental law of nature being the preservation of mankind," no human sanction can be good or valid against it."

§ 136. Secondly, *The legislative or supreme authority cannot assume to itself a power to rule by extemporary, arbitrary decrees; but is bound to dispense justice, and to decide the rights of the subject, by promulgated, standing laws, and known authorized judges. For the law of nature being unwritten, and so nowhere to be found, but in the minds of men, they who, through passion, or interest, shall miscite, or misapply it, cannot so easily be convinced of their mistake, where there is no established judge: and so it serves not, as it ought, to determine the rights, and fence the properties of those that live under it; especially where every one is judge, interpreter, and executioner of it too, and that in his own case: and he that has right on his side, having ordinarily but his own single strength, hath not force enough to defend himself from injuries, or to punish delinquents. To avoid these inconveniencies, which disorder men's properties in the state of nature, men unite into societies, that they may have the united strength of the whole society to secure and defend their properties, and may have standing rules to bound it, by which every one may know what is his. To this end it is that men give up all their natural power to the society which they enter into, and the community put the legislative power into such hands as they think fit; with this trust, that they shall be governed by declared laws, or else their peace, quiet, and property will still be at the same uncertainty as it was in the state of nature.

§ 137. Absolute arbitrary power, or governing without settled standing laws, can neither of them consist with the ends of society and government,

---

* "Human laws are measures in respect of men whose actions they must direct, howbeit such measures they are as have also their higher rules to be measured by, which rules are two, the law of God, and the law of nature; so that laws human must be made according to the general laws of nature, and without contradiction to any positive law of scripture, otherwise they are ill made." *Hooker*'s Eccl. Pol. l. iii. sect. 9.

"To constrain men to any thing inconvenient doth seem unreasonable." *Ibid.* l. i. sect. 10.

which men would not quit the freedom of the state of nature for, and tie themselves up under, were it not to preserve their lives, liberties, and fortunes, and by stated rules of right and property to secure their peace and quiet. It cannot be supposed that they should intend, had they a power so to do, to give to any one, or more, an absolute arbitrary power over their persons and estates, and put a force into the magistrate's hand to execute his unlimited will arbitrarily upon them. This were to put themselves into a worse condition than the state of nature, wherein they had a liberty to defend their right against the injuries of others, and were upon equal terms of force to maintain it, whether invaded by a single man, or many in combination. Whereas by supposing they have given up themselves to the absolute arbitrary power and will of a legislator, they have disarmed themselves, and armed him, to make a prey of them when he pleases; he being in a much worse condition, who is exposed to the arbitrary power of one man, who has the command of 100,000, than he that is exposed to the arbitrary power of 100,000 single men; nobody being secure that his will, who has such a command, is better than that of other men, though his force be 100,000 times stronger. And therefore, whatever form the commonwealth is under, the ruling power ought to govern by declared and received laws, and not by extemporary dictates and undetermined resolutions; for then mankind will be in a far worse condition than in the state of nature, if they shall have armed one or a few men with the joint power of a multitude, to force them to obey at pleasure the exorbitant and unlimited degrees of their sudden thoughts, or unrestrained, and till that moment unknown wills, without having any measures set down which may guide and justify their actions: for all the power the government has being only for the good of the society, as it ought not to be arbitrary and at pleasure, so it ought to be exercised by established and promulgated laws; that both the people may know their duty, and be safe and secure within the limits of the law; and the rulers too kept within their bounds, and not be tempted, by the power they have in their hands, to employ it to such purposes, and by such measures, as they would not have known, and own not willingly.

§ 138. Thirdly, The supreme power cannot take from any man part of his property without his own consent: for the preservation of property being the end of government, and that for which men enter into society, it necessarily supposes and requires, that the people should have property, without which they must be supposed to lose that, by entering into society, which was the end for which they entered into it; too gross an absurdity for any man to own. Men therefore in society having property, they have such right to the goods, which by the law of the community are theirs, that nobody hath a right to take their substance or any part of it from them, without their own consent: without this they have no property at all; for I have truly no property in that, which another can by right take from me, when he pleases, against my consent. Hence it is a mistake to think, that the supreme or legislative power of any commonwealth can do what it will, and dispose of the estates of the subject arbitrarily, or take any part of them at pleasure. This is not much to be feared in governments where the legislative consists, wholly or in part, in assemblies which are variable, whose members, upon the dissolution of the assembly, are subjects under the common laws of their country, equally with the rest. But in governments where the legislative is in one lasting assembly always in being, or in one man, as in absolute monarchies, there is danger still that they will think themselves to have a distinct interest from the rest of the community; and so will be apt to increase their own riches and power, by taking what they think fit from the people: for a man's property is not at all secure, though there be good and equitable laws to set the bounds of it between him and his fellow-subjects, if he who commands those subjects have power to take from any private man what part he pleases of his property, and use and dispose of it as he thinks good.

§ 139. But government, into whatsoever hands it is put, being, as I have before showed, entrusted with this condition, and for this end, that men might have and secure their properties; the prince, or senate, however it may have power to make laws for the regulating of property between the subjects one amongst another, yet can never have a power to take to themselves the whole or any part of the subject's property without their own consent: for this would be in effect to leave them no property at all. And to let us see, that even absolute power, where it is necessary, is not arbitrary by being absolute, but is still limited by that reason, and confined to those ends, which required it in some cases to be absolute, we need look no farther than the common practice of martial discipline: for the preservation of the army, and in it of the whole commonwealth, requires an absolute obedience to the command of every superior officer, and it is justly death to disobey or dispute the most dangerous or unreasonable of them; but yet we see, that neither the serjeant, that could command a soldier to march up to the mouth of a cannon, or stand in a breach, where he is almost sure to perish, can command that soldier to give him one penny of his money; nor the general, that can condemn him to death for deserting his post, or for not obeying the most desperate orders, can yet, with all his absolute power of life and death, dispose of one farthing of that soldier's estate, or seize one jot of his goods; whom yet he can command any thing, and hang for the least disobedience;

because such a blind obedience is necessary to that end for which the commander has his power, viz. the preservation of the rest; but disposing of his goods has nothing to do with it.

§ 140. It is true, governments cannot be supported without great charge, and it is fit every one who enjoys his share of the protection, should pay out of his estate his proportion for the maintenance of it. But still it must be with his own consent, *i. e.* the consent of the majority, giving it either by themselves, or their representatives chosen by them: for if any one shall claim a power to lay and levy taxes on the people by his own authority, and without such consent of the people, he thereby invades the fundamental law of property, and subverts the end of government: for what property have I in that which another may by right take, when he pleases, to himself?

§ 141. Fourthly, The legislative cannot transfer the power of making laws to any other hands: for it being but a delegated power from the people, they who have it cannot pass it over to others. The people alone can appoint the form of the commonwealth, which is by constituting the legislative, and appointing in whose hands that shall be. And when the people have said, we will submit to rules, and be governed by laws made by such men, and in such forms, nobody else can say other men shall make laws for them; nor can the people be bound by any laws but such as are enacted by those whom they have chosen, and authorized to make laws for them. The power of the legislative being derived from the people by a positive voluntary grant and institution, can be no other than what that positive grant conveyed, which being only to make laws, and not to make legislators, the legislative can have no power to transfer their authority of making laws and place it in other hands.

§ 142. These are the bounds which the trust that is put in them by the society, and the law of God and nature, have set to the legislative power of every commonwealth, in all forms of government.

First, They are to govern by promulgated established laws, not to be varied in particular cases, but to have one rule for rich and poor, for the favourite at court, and the countryman at plough.

Secondly, These laws also ought to be designed for no other end ultimately, but the good of the people.

Thirdly, They must not raise taxes on the property of the people, without the consent of the people, given by themselves or their deputies. And this properly concerns only such governments where the legislative is always in being, or at least where the people have not reserved any part of the legislative to deputies, to be from time to time chosen by themselves.

Fourthly, The legislative neither must nor can transfer the power of making laws to any body else, or place it any where, but where the people have.

CHAPTER XII.

Of the legislative, executive, and federative Power of the Commonwealth.

§ 143. The legislative power is that, which has a right to direct how the force of the commonwealth shall be employed for preserving the community and the members of it. But because those laws which are constantly to be executed, and whose force is always to continue, may be made in a little time, therefore there is no need that the legislative should be always in being, not having always business to do. And because it may be too great a temptation to human frailty, apt to grasp at power, for the same persons who have the power of making laws, to have also in their hands the power to execute them; whereby they may exempt themselves from obedience to the laws they make, and suit the law, both in its making and execution, to their own private advantage, and thereby come to have a distinct interest from the rest of the community, contrary to the end of society and government: therefore in well ordered commonwealths, where the good of the whole is so considered, as it ought, the legislative power is put into the hands of divers persons, who, duly assembled, have by themselves, or jointly with others, a power to make laws; which when they have done, being separated again, they are themselves subject to the laws they have made; which is a new and near tie upon them, to take care that they make them for the public good.

§ 144. But because the laws, that are at once, and in a short time made, have a constant and lasting force, and need a perpetual execution, or an attendance thereunto; therefore it is necessary there should be a power always in being, which should see to the execution of the laws that are made, and remain in force. And thus the legislative and executive power come often to be separated.

§ 145. There is another power in every commonwealth, which one may call natural, because it is that which answers to the power every man naturally had before it entered into society: for though in a commonwealth, the members of it are distinct persons still in reference to one another, and as such are governed by the laws of the society; yet in reference to the rest of mankind, they make one body, which is, as every member of it before was, still in the state of nature with the rest of mankind. Hence it is, that the controversies that happen between any man of the society with those that are out of it, are managed by the public; and an injury done to a member of their body engages the whole in the reparation of it. So that, under this consideration, the whole community is one body in the state of nature, in respect of all other states of persons out of its community.

§ 146. This therefore contains the power of war and peace, leagues and alliances, and all the transactions with all persons and communities without the commonwealth; and may be called federative, if any one pleases. So the thing be understood, I am indifferent as to the name.

§ 147. These two powers, executive and federative, though they be really distinct in themselves, yet one comprehending the execution of the municipal laws of the society within itself, upon all that are parts of it; the other the management of the security and interest of the public without, with all those that it may receive benefit or damage from; yet they are always almost united. And though this federative power in the well or ill management of it be of great moment to the commonwealth, yet it is much less capable to be directed by antecedent, standing, positive laws, than the executive; and so must necessarily be left to the prudence and wisdom of those whose hands it is in, to be managed for the public good: for the laws that concern subjects one amongst another, being to direct their actions, may well enough precede them. But what is to be done in reference to foreigners, depending much upon their actions, and the variation of designs, and interests, must be left in great part to the prudence of those who have this power committed to them, to be managed by the best of their skill, for the advantage of the commonwealth.

§ 148. Though, as I said, the executive and federative power of every community be really distinct in themselves, yet they are hardly to be separated, and placed at the same time in the hands of distinct persons: for both of them requiring the force of the society for their exercise, it is almost impracticable to place the force of the commonwealth in distinct, and not subordinate hands; or that the executive and federative power should be placed in persons that might act separately, whereby the force of the public would be under different commands; which would be apt some time or other to cause disorder and ruin.

CHAPTER XIII.

Of the Subordination of the Powers of the Commonwealth.

§ 149. Though in a constituted commonwealth, standing upon its own basis, and acting according to its own nature, that is, acting for the preservation of the community, there can be but one supreme power, which is the legislative, to which all the rest are and must be subordinate; yet the legislative being only a fiduciary power to act for certain ends, there remains still "in the people a supreme power to remove or alter the legislative," when they find the legislative act contrary to the trust reposed in them: for all power given with trust for the attaining an end, being limited by that end: whenever that end is manifestly neglected or opposed, the trust must necessarily be forfeited, and the power devolve into the hands of those that gave it, who may place it anew where they shall think best for their safety and security. And thus the community perpetually retains a supreme power of saving themselves from the attempts and designs of any body, even of their legislators, whenever they shall be so foolish, or so wicked, as to lay and carry on designs against the liberties and properties of the subject: for no man, or society of men, having a power to deliver up their preservation, or consequently the means of it, to the absolute will and arbitrary dominion of another; whenever any one shall go about to bring them into such a slavish condition, they will always have a right to preserve what they have not a power to part with; and to rid themselves of those who invade this fundamental, sacred, and unalterable law of self-preservation, for which they entered into society. And thus the community may be said in this respect to be always the supreme power, but not as considered under any form of government, because this power of the people can never take place till the government be dissolved.

§ 150. In all cases, whilst the government subsists, the legislative is the supreme power: for what can give laws to another, must needs be superior to him; and since the legislative is no otherwise legislative of the society, but by the right it has to make laws for all the parts, and for every member of the society, prescribing rules to their actions, and giving power of execution, where they are transgressed; the legislative must needs be the supreme, and all other powers, in any members or parts of the society, derived from and subordinate to it.

§ 151. In some commonwealths, where the legislative is not always in being, and the executive is vested in a single person, who has also a share in the legislative; there that single person in a very tolerable sense may also be called supreme; not that he has in himself all the supreme power, which is that of law-making; but because he has in him the supreme execution, from whom all inferior magistrates derive all their several subordinate powers, or at least the greatest part of them: having also no legislative superior to him, there being no law to be made without his consent, which cannot be expected should ever subject him to the other part of the legislative, he is properly enough in this sense supreme. But yet it is to be observed, that though oaths of allegiance and fealty are taken to him, it is not to him as supreme legislator, but as supreme executor of the law, made by a joint power of him with others: allegiance being nothing but an obedience according to law, which when he violates, he has no right to obedience, nor can claim it otherwise than as the public person invested with the power of the law; and so is to be considered as the image, phantom, or representative of the commonwealth, acted by the will of the society, declared in its laws; and thus he has no will, no power, but that of the law. But when he quits this representation, this public will, and acts by his own private will, he degrades himself, and is but a single private person without power, and without will, that has no right to obedience; the members owing no obedience but to the public will of the society.

§ 152. The executive power, placed any where but in a person that has also a share in the legislative, is visibly subordinate and accountable to it, and may be at pleasure changed and displaced; so that it is not the supreme executive power that is exempt from subordination: but the supreme executive power vested in one, who having a share in the legislative, has no distinct superior legislative to be subordinate and accountable to, farther than he himself shall join and consent; so that he is no more subordinate than he himself shall think fit, which one may certainly conclude will be but very little. Of other ministerial and subordinate powers in a commonwealth we need not speak, they being so multiplied with infinite variety, in the different customs and constitutions of distinct commonwealths, that it is impossible to give a particular account of them all. Only thus much, which is necessary to our present purpose, we may take notice of concerning them, that they have no manner of authority, any of them, beyond what is by positive grant and commission delegated to them, and are all of them accountable to some other power in the commonwealth.

§ 153. It is not necessary, no, nor so much as convenient, that the legislative should be always in being; but absolutely necessary that the executive power should; because there is not always need for new laws to be made, but always need of execution of the laws that are made. When the legislative hath put the execution of the laws they make into other hands, they have a power still to resume it out of those hands, when they find cause, and to punish for any maladministration against the laws. The same holds also in regard of the federative power, that and the executive being both ministerial and subordinate to the legislative, which, as has been showed, in a constituted commonwealth is the supreme. The legislative also in this case being supposed to consist of several persons, (for if it be a single person, it cannot but be always in being, and so will, as supreme, naturally have the supreme executive power, together with the legislative) may assemble, and exercise their legislature, at the times that either their original constitution, or their own adjournment, appoints, or when they please; if neither of these hath appointed any time, or there be no other way prescribed to convoke them: for the supreme power being placed in them by the people, it is always in them, and they may exercise it when they please, unless by their original constitution they are limited to certain seasons, or by an act of their supreme power they have adjourned to a certain time; and when that time comes, they have a right to assemble and act again.

§ 154. If the legislative, or any part of it, be made up of representatives chosen for that time by the people, which afterwards return into the ordinary state of subjects, and have no share in the legislature but upon a new choice, this power of choosing must also be exercised by the people, either at certain appointed seasons, or else when they are summoned to it; and in this latter case the power of convoking the legislative is ordinarily placed in the executive, and has one of these two limitations in respect of time: that either the original constitution requires their assembling and acting at certain intervals, and then the executive power does nothing but ministerially issue directions for their electing and assembling according to due forms; or else it is left to his prudence to call them by new elections, when the occasions or exigencies of the public require the amendment of old, or making of new laws, or the redress or prevention of any inconveniences, that lie on, or threaten the people.

§ 155. It may be demanded here, What if the executive power, being possessed of the force of the commonwealth, shall make use of that force to hinder the meeting and acting of the legislative, when the original constitution or the public exigencies require it? I say, using force upon the people without authority, and contrary to the trust put in him that does so, is a state of war with the people, who have a right to reinstate their legislative in the exercise of their power: for having erected a legislative, with an intent they should exercise the power of making laws, either at certain set times, or when there is need of it; when they are hindered by any force from what is so necessary to the society, and wherein the safety and preservation of the people consists, the people have a right to remove it by force. In all states and conditions, the true remedy of force without authority is to oppose force to it. The use of force without authority always puts him that uses it into a state of war, as the aggressor, and renders him liable to be treated accordingly.

§ 156. The power of assembling and dismissing the legislative, placed in the executive, gives not the executive a superiority over it, but is a fiduciary trust placed in him for the safety of the people, in a case where the uncertainty and variableness of human affairs could not bear a steady fixed rule: for it not being possible that the first framers of the government should, by any foresight, be so much masters of future events as to be able to prefix so just periods of return and duration to the assemblies of the legislative, in all times to come, that might exactly answer all the exigencies of the commonwealth; the best remedy could be found for this defect was to trust this to the prudence of one who was always to be present, and whose business it was to watch over the public good. Constant frequent meetings of the legislative, and long continuations of their assemblies, without necessary occasion, could not but be burdensome to the people, and must necessarily in time produce more dangerous inconveniencies, and yet the quick turn of affairs might be sometimes such as to need their present help; any delay of their convening might endanger the public; and sometimes too their business might be so great, that the limited time of their sitting might be too short for their work, and rob the public of that benefit which could be had only from their mature deliberation. What then could be done in this case to prevent the community from being exposed some time or other to eminent hazard, on one side or the other, by fixed intervals and periods, set to the meeting and acting of the legislative; but to intrust it to the prudence of some, who being present, and acquainted with the state of public affairs, might make use of this prerogative for the public good? and where else could this be so well placed as in his hands, who was intrusted with the execution of the laws for the same end? Thus supposing the regulation of times for the assembling and sitting of the legislative not settled by the original constitution, it naturally fell into the hands of the executive, not as an arbitrary power depending on his good pleasure, but with this trust always to have it exercised only for the public weal, as the occurrences of times and change of affairs might require. Whether settled periods of their convening, or a liberty left to the prince for convoking the legislative, or perhaps a mixture of both, hath the least inconvenience attending it, it is not my business here to inquire; but only to show, that though the executive power may have the prerogative of convoking and dissolving such conventions of the legislative, yet it is not thereby superior to it.

§ 157. Things of this world are in so constant a flux, that nothing remains long in the same state. Thus people, riches, trade, power, change their stations, flourishing mighty cities come to ruin, and prove in time neglected desolate corners, whilst other unfrequented places grow into populous countries, filled with wealth and inhabitants. But things not always changing equally, and private interest often keeping up customs and privileges, when the reasons of them are ceased; it often comes to pass, that in governments, where part of the legislative consists of representatives chosen by the people, that in tract of time this representation becomes very unequal and disproportionate to the reasons it was at first established upon. To what gross absurdities the following of custom, when reason has left it, may lead, we may be satisfied, when we see the bare name of a town, of which there remains not so much as the ruins, where scarce so much housing as a sheep-cote, or more inhabitants than a shepherd is to be found, sends as many representatives to the grand assembly of law-makers as a whole county, numerous in people, and powerful in riches. This strangers stand amazed at, and every one must confess needs a remedy; though most think it hard to find one; because the constitution of the legislative being the original and supreme act of the society, antecedent to all positive laws in it, and depending wholly on the people, no inferior power can alter it. And therefore the people, when the legislative is once constituted, having, in such a government as we have been speaking of, no power to act as long as the government stands; this inconvenience is thought incapable of a remedy.

§ 158. *Salus populi suprema lex,* is certainly so just and fundamental a rule, that he, who sincerely follows it, cannot dangerously err. If therefore the executive, who has the power of convoking the legislative, observing rather the true proportion than fashion of representation, regulates not by old custom, but true reason, the number of members in all places that have a right to be distinctly represented, which no part of the people, however incorporated, can pretend to, but in proportion to the assistance which it affords to the public; it cannot be judged to have set up a new legislative, but to have restored the old and true one, and to have rectified the disorders which succession of time had insensibly, as well as inevitably introduced; for it being the interest as well as intention of the people, to have a fair and equal representative; whoever brings it nearest to that, is an undoubted friend to, and establisher of the government, and cannot miss the consent and approbation of the community: prerogative being nothing but a power in the hands of the prince, to provide for the public good, in such cases, which depending upon unforeseen and uncertain occurrences, certain and unalterable laws could not safely direct; whatsoever shall be done manifestly for the good of the people, and the establishing the government upon its true foundations, is, and always will be, just prerogative. The power of erecting new corporations, and therewith new representatives, carries with it a supposition that in time the measures of representation might vary, and those places have a just right to be represented which before had none; and by the same reason, those cease to have a right, and be too inconsiderable for such a privilege, which before had it. It is not a change from the present state, which perhaps corruption or decay has introduced, that makes an inroad upon the government; but the tendency of it to injure or oppress the people, and to set up one part or party, with a distinction from, and an unequal subjection of the rest. Whatsoever cannot but be acknowledged to be of advantage to the society, and people in general, upon just and lasting measures, will always, when done, justify itself; and whenever the people shall choose their representatives upon just and undeniably equal measures, suitable to the original frame of the government, it cannot be doubted to be the will and act of the society, whoever permitted or caused them so to do.

CHAPTER XIV.

Of Prerogative.

§ 159. Where the legislative and executive power are in distinct hands, (as they are in all moderated monarchies and well-framed governments) there the good of the society requires, that several things should be left to the discretion of him that has the executive power: for the legislators not being able to foresee, and provide by laws, for all that may be useful to the community, the executor of the laws having the power in his hands, has by the common law of nature a right to make use of it for the good of the society, in many cases, where the municipal law has given no direction, till the legislative can conveniently be assembled to provide for it. Many things there are, which the law can by no means provide for; and those must necessarily be left to the discretion of him that has the executive power in his hands, to be ordered by him as the public good and advantage shall require: nay, it is fit that the laws themselves should in some cases give way to the executive power, or rather to this fundamental law of nature and government, viz. That, as much as may be, all the members of the society are to be preserved: for since many accidents may happen, wherein a strict and rigid observation of the laws may do harm; (as not to pull down an innocent man's house to stop the fire, when the next to it is burning) and a man may come sometimes within the reach of the law, which makes no distinction of persons, by an action that may deserve reward and pardon; it is fit the ruler should have a power, in many cases, to mitigate the severity of the law, and pardon some offenders: for the end of government being the preservation of all, as much as may be, even the guilty are to be spared, where it can prove no prejudice to the innocent.

§ 160. This power to act according to discretion for the public good, without the prescription of the law, and sometimes even against it, is that which is called prerogative: for since in some governments the lawmaking power is not always in being, and is usually too numerous, and so too slow for the despatch requisite to execution; and because also it is impossible to foresee, and so by laws to provide for all accidents and necessities that may concern the public, or to make such laws as will do no harm, if they are executed with an inflexible rigour on all occasions, and upon all persons that may come in their way; therefore there is a latitude left to the executive power, to do many things of choice which the laws do not prescribe.

§ 161. This power, whilst employed for the benefit of the community, and suitably to the trust and ends of the government, is undoubted prerogative, and never is questioned; for the people are very seldom or never scrupulous or nice in the point; they are far from examining prerogative, whilst it is in any tolerable degree employed for the use it was meant; that is, for the good of the people, and not manifestly against it: but if there comes to be a question between the executive power and the people, about a thing claimed as a prerogative, the tendency of the exercise of such prerogative to the good or hurt of the people will easily decide that question.

§ 162. It is easy to conceive, that in the infancy of governments, when commonwealths differed little from families in number of people, they differed from them too but little in number of laws: and the governors being as the fathers of them, watching over them for their good, the government was almost all prerogative. A few established laws served the turn, and the discretion and care of the ruler supplied the rest. But when mistake or flattery prevailed with weak princes to make use of this power for private ends of their own, and not for the public good, the people were fain by express laws to get prerogative determined in those points wherein they found disadvantage from it: and thus declared limitations of prerogative were by the people found necessary in cases which they and their ancestors had left, in the utmost latitude, to the wisdom of those princes who made no other but a right use of it; that is, for the good of their people.

§ 163. And therefore they have a very wrong notion of government, who say, that the people have encroached upon the prerogative, when they have got any part of it to be defined by positive laws: for in so doing they have not pulled from the prince any thing that of right belonged to him, but only declare, that that power which they indefinitely left in his or his ancestors' hands, to be exercised for their good, was not a thing which they intended him when he used it otherwise: for the end of government being the good of the community, whatsoever alterations are made in it, tending to that end, cannot be an encroachment upon any body, since nobody in government can have a right tending to any other end: and those only are encroachments which prejudice or hinder the public good. Those who say otherwise, speak as if the prince had a distinct and separate interest from the good of the community, and was not made for it; the root and source from which spring almost all those evils and disorders which happen in kingly governments. And indeed, if that be so, the people under his government are not a society of rational creatures, entered into a community for their mutual good; they are not such as have set rulers over themselves, to guard and promote that good; but are to be looked on as an herd of inferior creatures under the dominion of a master, who keeps them and works them for his own pleasure or profit. If men were so void of reason, and brutish, as to enter into society upon such terms, prerogative might indeed be, what some men would have it, an arbitrary power to do things hurtful to the people.

§ 164. But since a rational creature cannot be supposed, when free, to put himself into subjection to another, for his own harm; (though, where he finds a good and wise ruler, he may not perhaps think it either necessary or useful to set precise bounds to his power in all things) prerogative can be nothing but the people's permitting their rulers to do several things, of their own free choice, where the law was silent, and sometimes too against the direct letter of the law, for the public good; and their acquiescing in it when so done: for as a good prince, who is mindful of the trust put into his hands, and careful of the good of his people, cannot have too much prerogative, that is, power to do good; so a weak and ill prince, who would claim that power which his predecessors exercised without the direction of the law, as a prerogative belonging to him by right of his office, which he may exercise at his pleasure, to make or promote an interest distinct from that of the public; gives the people an occasion to claim their right, and limit that power, which, whilst it was exercised for their good, they were content should be tacitly allowed.

§ 165. And therefore he that will look into the history of England, will find, that prerogative was always largest in the hands of our wisest and best princes; because the people, observing the whole tendency of their actions to be the public good, contested not what was done without law to that end: or, if any human frailty or mistake (for princes are but men, made as others) appeared in some small declinations from that end; yet it was visible, the main of their conduct tended to nothing but the care of the public. The people, therefore, finding reason to be satisfied with these princes, whenever they acted without, or contrary to the letter of the law, acquiesced in what they did, and, without the least complaint, let them enlarge their prerogative as they pleased; judging rightly, that they did nothing herein to the prejudice of their laws, since they acted conformably to the foundation and end of all laws, the public good.

§ 166. Such God-like princes, indeed, had some title to arbitrary power by that argument, that would prove absolute monarchy the best government, as that which God himself governs the universe by; because such kings partook of his wisdom and goodness. Upon this is founded that saying, That the reigns of good princes have been always most dangerous to the liberties of their people: for when their successors, managing the government with different thoughts, would draw the actions of those good rulers into precedent, and make them the standard of their prerogative, as if what had been done only for the good of the people was a right in them to do for the harm of the people, if they so pleased; it has often occasioned contest, and sometimes public disorders, before the people could recover their original right, and get that to be declared not to be prerogative, which truly was never so: since it is impossible that any body in the society should ever have a right to do the people harm; though it be very possible and reasonable that the people should not go about to set any bounds to the prerogative of those kings or rulers, who themselves transgressed not the bounds of the public good; for "prerogative is nothing but the power of doing public good without a rule."

§ 167. The power of calling parliaments in England, as to precise time, place, and duration, is certainly a prerogative of the king, but still with this trust, that it shall be made use of for the good of the nation, as the exigencies of the times, and variety of occasions shall require: for it being impossible to foresee which should always be the fittest place for them to assemble in, and what the best season, the choice of these was left with the executive power, as might be most subservient to the public good, and best suit the ends of parliaments.

§ 168. The old question will be asked in this matter of prerogative, "But who shall be judge when this power is made a right use of?" I answer: between an executive power in being, with such a prerogative, and a legislative that depends upon his will for their convening, there can be no judge on earth; as there can be none between the legislative and the people, should either the executive or the legislative, when they have got the power in their hands, design or go about to enslave or destroy them. The people have no other remedy in this, as in all other cases where they have no judge on earth, but to appeal to heaven: for the rulers, in such attempts, exercising a power the people never put into their hands (who can never be supposed to consent that any body should rule over them for their harm), do that which they have not a right to do. And where the body of the people, or any single man, is deprived of their right, or under the exercise of a power without right, and have no appeal on earth, then they have a liberty to appeal to heaven, whenever they judge the cause of sufficient moment. And therefore, though the people cannot be judge, so as to have, by the constitution of that society, any superior power to determine and give effective sentence in the case; yet they have, by a law antecedent and paramount to all positive laws of men, reserved that ultimate determination to themselves which belongs to all mankind, where there lies no appeal on earth, viz. to judge whether they have just cause to make their appeal to heaven. — And this judgment they cannot part with, it being out of a man's power so to submit himself to another, as to give him a liberty to destroy him; God and nature never allowing a man so to abandon himself, as to neglect his own preservation: and since he cannot take away his own life, neither can he give another power to take it. Nor let any one think this lays a perpetual foundation for disorder; for this operates not till the inconveniency is so great that the majority feel it, and are weary of it, and find a necessity to have it amended. But this the executive power, or wise princes, never need come in the danger of: and it is the thing, of all others, they have most need to avoid, as of all others the most perilous.

CHAPTER XV.

Of paternal, political, and despotical Power, considered together.

§ 169. Though I have had occasion to speak of these separately before, yet the great mistakes of late about government having, as I suppose, arisen from confounding these distinct powers one with another, it may not, perhaps, be amiss to consider them here together.

§ 170. First, then, paternal or parental power is nothing but that which parents have over their children, to govern them for the children's good, till they come to the use of reason, or a state of knowledge, wherein they may be supposed capable to understand that rule, whether it be the law of nature, or the municipal law of their country, they are to govern themselves by: capable, I say, to know it, as well as several others, who live as freemen under that law. The affection and tenderness which God hath planted in the breast of parents towards their children, makes it evident, that this is not intended to be a severe arbitrary government, but only for the help, instruction, and preservation of their offspring. But happen it as it will, there is, as I have proved, no reason why it should be thought to extend to life and death, at any time, over their children, more than over any body else; neither can there be any pretence why this parental power should keep the child, when grown to a man, in subjection to the will of his parents, any farther than having received life and education from his parents, obliges him to respect, honour, gratitude, assistance, and support, all his life, to both father and mother. And thus, it is true, the paternal is a natural government, but not at all extending itself to the ends and jurisdictions of that which is political. The power of the father doth not reach at all to the property of the child, which is only in his own disposing.

§ 171. Secondly, political power is that power which every man having in the state of nature, has given up into the hands of the society, and therein to the governors, whom the society hath set over itself, with this express or tacit trust, that it shall be employed for their good, and the preservation of their property: now this power, which every man has in the state of nature, and which he parts with to the society in all such cases where the society can secure him, is to use such means for the preserving of his own property as he thinks good, and nature allows him; and to punish the breach of the law of nature in others, so as (according to the best of his reason) may most conduce to the preservation of himself and the rest of mankind. So that the end and measure of this power, when in every man's hands in the state of nature, being the preservation of all of his society, that is, all mankind in general, it can have no other end or measure, when in the hands of the magistrate, but to preserve the members of that society in their lives, liberties, and possessions; and so cannot be an absolute arbitrary power over their lives and fortunes, which are as much as possible to be preserved; but a power to make laws, and annex such penalties to them, as may tend to the preservation of the whole, by cutting off those parts, and those only, which are so corrupt that they threaten the sound and healthy, without which no severity is lawful. And this power has its original only from compact and agreement, and the mutual consent of those who make up the community.

§ 172. Thirdly, despotical power is an absolute, arbitrary power one man has over another, to take away his life whenever he pleases. This is a power, which neither nature gives, for it has made no such distinction between one man and another, nor compact can convey; for man not having such an arbitrary power over his own life, cannot give another man such a power over it; but it is the effect only of forfeiture, which the aggressor makes of his own life, when he puts himself into the state of war with another: for having quitted reason, which God hath given to be the rule betwixt man and man, and the common bond whereby human kind is united into one fellowship and society, and having renounced the way of peace which that teaches, and made use of the force of war, to compass his unjust ends upon another, where he has no right; and so revolting from his own kind to that of beasts, by making force, which is theirs, to be his rule of right; he renders himself liable to be destroyed by the injured person, and the rest of mankind, that will join with him in the execution of justice, as any other wild beast, or noxious brute, with whom mankind can have neither society nor security*. And thus captives, taken in a just and lawful war, and such only, are subject to a despotical power; which, as it arises not from compact, so neither is it capable of any, but is the state of war continued: for what compact can be made with a man that is not master of his own life? what condition can he perform? and if he be once allowed to be master of his own life, the despotical arbitrary power of his master ceases. He that is master of himself, and his own life, has a right too to the means of preserving it; so that, as soon as compact enters, slavery ceases, and he so far quits his absolute power, and puts an end to the state of war, who enters into conditions with his captive.

* Another copy, corrected by Mr. Locke, has it thus, "Noxious brute that is destructive to their being."

§ 173. Nature gives the first of these, viz. paternal power, to parents for the benefit of their children during their minority, to supply their want of ability and understanding how to manage their property. (By property I must be understood here, as in other places, to mean that property which men have in their persons as well as goods.) Voluntary agreement gives the second, viz. political power to governors for the benefit of their subjects, to secure them in the possession and use of their properties. And forfeiture gives the third despotical power to lords, for their own benefit, over those who are stripped of all property.

§ 174. He that shall consider the distinct rise and extent, and the different ends of these several powers, will plainly see, that paternal power comes as far short of that of the magistrate, as despotical exceeds it; and that absolute dominion, however placed, is so far from being one kind of civil society, that it is as inconsistent with it, as slavery is with property. Paternal power is only where minority makes the child incapable to manage his property; political, where men have property in their own disposal; and despotical, over such as have no property at all.

CHAPTER XVI.

Of Conquest.

§ 175. Though governments can originally have no other rise than that before-mentioned, nor politics be founded on any thing but the consent of the people; yet such have been the disorders ambition has filled the world with, that in the noise of war, which makes so great a part of the history of mankind, this consent is little taken notice of: and therefore many have mistaken the force of arms for the consent of the people, and reckon conquest as one of the originals of government. But conquest is as far from setting up any government, as demolishing a house is from building a new one in the place. Indeed, it often makes way for a new frame of a commonwealth, by destroying the former; but, without the consent of the people, can never erect a new one.

§ 176. That the aggressor, who puts himself into the state of war with another, and unjustly invades another man's right, can, by such an unjust war, never come to have a right over the conquered, will be easily agreed by all men, who will not think that robbers and pirates have a right of empire over whomsoever they have force enough to master, or that men are bound by promises which unlawful force extorts from them. Should a robber break into my house, and with a dagger at my throat make me seal deeds to convey my estate to him, would this give him any title? Just such a title, by his sword, has an unjust conqueror, who forces me into submission. The injury and the crime are equal, whether committed by the wearer of the crown or some petty villain. The title of the offender, and the number of his followers, make no difference in the offence, unless it be to aggravate it. The only difference is, great robbers punish little ones, to keep them in their obedience; but the great ones are rewarded with laurels and triumphs, because they are too big for the weak hands of justice in this world, and have the power in their own possession which should punish offenders. What is my remedy against a robber, that so broke into my house? Appeal to the law for justice. But perhaps justice is denied, or I am crippled and cannot stir, robbed and have not the means to do it. If God has taken away all means of seeking remedy, there is nothing left but patience. But my son, when able, may seek the relief of the law, which I am denied: he or his son may renew his appeal, till he recover his right. But the conquered, or their children, have no court, no arbitrator on earth to appeal to. Then they may appeal, as Jephthah did, to heaven, and repeat their appeal till they have recovered the native right of their ancestors, which was, to have such a legislative over them as the majority should approve, and freely acquiesce in. If it be objected, this would cause endless trouble; I answer, no more than justice does, where she lies open to all that appeal to her. He that troubles his neighbour without a cause, is punished for it by the justice of the court he appeals to; and he that appeals to heaven must be sure he has right on his side, and a right too that is worth the trouble and cost of the appeal, as he will answer at a tribunal that cannot be deceived, and will be sure to retribute to every one according to the mischiefs he hath created to his fellow-subjects; that is, any part of mankind: from whence it is plain, that he that "conquers in an unjust war, can thereby have no title to the subjection and obedience of the conquered."

§ 177. But supposing victory favours the right side, let us consider a conqueror in a lawful war, and see what power he gets, and over whom.

First, It is plain he "gets no power by his conquest over those that conquered with him." They that fought on his side cannot suffer by the conquest, but must at least be as much freeman as they were before. And most commonly they serve upon terms, and on conditions to share with their leader, and enjoy a part of the spoil, and other advantages that attended the conquering sword; or at least have a part of the subdued country bestowed upon them. And "the conquering people are not, I hope, to be slaves by conquest," and wear their laurels only to show they are sacrifices to their leader's triumph. They that found absolute monarchy upon the title of the sword, make their heroes, who are the founders of such monarchies, arrant Drawcansirs, and forget they had any officers and soldiers that fought on their side in the battles they won, or assisted them in the subduing, or shared in possessing, the countries they mastered. We are told by some, that the English monarchy is founded in the Norman conquest, and that our princes have thereby a title to absolute dominion: which if it were true (as by the history it appears otherwise), and that William had a right to make war on this island, yet his dominion by conquest could reach no farther than to the Saxons and Britons, that were then inhabitants of this country. The Normans that came with him, and helped to conquer, and all descended from them, are freemen, and no subjects by conquest, let that give what dominion it will. And if I, or any body else, shall claim freedom, as derived from them, it will be very hard to prove the contrary; and it is plain the law, that has made no distinction between the one and the other, intends not there should be any difference in their freedom or privileges.

§ 178. But supposing, which seldom happens, that the conquerors and conquered never incorporate into one people, under the same laws and freedom; let us see next "what power a lawful conqueror has over the subdued:" and that I say is purely despotical. He has an absolute power over the lives of those who by an unjust war have forfeited them: but not over the lives or fortunes of those who engaged not in the war, nor over the possessions even of those who were actually engaged in it.

§ 179. Secondly, I say then the conqueror gets no power but only over those who have actually assisted, concurred, or consented to that unjust force that is used against him: for the people having given to their governors no power to do an unjust thing, such as is to make an unjust war (for they never had such a power in themselves) they ought not to be charged as guilty of the violence and injustice that is committed in an unjust war, any farther than they actually abet it, no more than they are to be thought guilty of any violence or oppression their governors should use upon the people themselves, or any part of their fellow-subjects, they having empowered them no more to the one than to the other. Conquerors, it is true, seldom trouble themselves to make the distinction, but they willingly permit the confusion of war to sweep all together: but yet this alters not the right; for the conqueror's power over the lives of the conquered being only because they have used force to do, or maintain an injustice, he can have that power only over those who have concurred in that force; all the rest are innocent;

and he has no more title over the people of that country, who have done him no injury, and so have made no forfeiture of their lives, than he has over any other, who, without any injuries or provocations, have lived upon fair terms with him.

§ 180. Thirdly, The power a conqueror gets over those he overcomes in a just war, is perfectly despotical: he has an absolute power over the lives of those, who, by putting themselves in a state of war, have forfeited them; but he has not thereby a right and title to their possessions. This I doubt not but at first sight will seem a strange doctrine, it being so quite contrary to the practice of the world; there being nothing more familiar in speaking of the dominion of countries, than to say such an one conquered it; as if conquest, without any more ado, conveyed a right of possession. But when we consider, that the practice of the strong and powerful, how universal soever it may be, is seldom the rule of right, however it be one part of the subjection of the conquered, not to argue against the conditions cut out to them by the conquering sword.

§ 181. Though in all war there be usually a complication of force and damage, and the aggressor seldom fails to harm the estate, when he uses force against the persons of those he makes war upon; yet it is the use of force only that puts a man into the state of war: for whether by force he begins the injury, or else having quietly, and by fraud, done the injury, he refuses to make reparation, and by force maintains it (which is the same thing, as at first to have done it by force), it is the unjust use of force that makes the war: for he that breaks open my house, and violently turns me out of doors; or, having peaceably got in, by force keeps me out, does in effect the same thing; supposing we are in such a state that we have no common judge on earth whom I may appeal to, and to whom we are both obliged to submit; for of such I am now speaking. It is the "unjust use of force then, that puts a man into the state of war" with another; and thereby he that is guilty of it makes a forfeiture of his life: for quitting reason, which is the rule given between man and man, and using force, the way of beasts, he becomes liable to be destroyed by him he uses force against, as any savage ravenous beast, that is dangerous to his being.

§ 182. But because the miscarriages of the father are no faults of the children, and they may be rational and peaceable, notwithstanding the brutishness and injustice of the father; the father, by his miscarriages and violence, can forfeit but his own life, but involves not his children in his guilt or destruction. His goods, which nature, that willeth the preservation of all mankind as much as is possible, hath made to belong to the children to keep them from perishing, do still continue to belong to his children; for supposing them not to have joined in the war, either through infancy, absence, or choice, they have done nothing to forfeit them: nor has the conqueror any right to take them away, by the bare title of having subdued him that by force attempted his destruction; though perhaps he may have some right to them, to repair the damages he has sustained by the war, and the defence of his own right; which how far it reaches to the possessions of the conquered, we shall see by and by. So that he that by conquest has a right over a man's person to destroy him if he pleases, has not thereby a right over his estate to possess and enjoy it; for it is the brutal force the aggressor has used that gives his adversary a right to take away his life, and destroy him, if he pleases, as a noxious creature; but it is damage sustained that alone gives him title to another man's goods: for though I may kill a thief that sets on me in the highway, yet I may not (which seems less) take away his money and let him go: this would be robbery on my side. His force, and the state of war he put himself in, made him forfeit his life, but gave me no title to his goods. The right then of conquest extends only to the lives of those who joined in the war, not to their estates, but only in order to make reparation for the damages received, and the charges of the war; and that too with reservation of the right of the innocent wife and children.

§ 183. Let the conqueror have as much justice on his side as could be supposed, he has no right to seize more than the vanquished could forfeit: his life is at the victor's mercy; and his service and goods he may appropriate to make himself reparation; but he cannot take the goods of his wife and children: they too had a title to the goods he enjoyed, and their shares in the estate he possessed: for example, I in the state of nature (and all commonwealths are in the state of nature one with another) have injured another man, and refusing to give satisfaction, it comes to a state of war, wherein my defending by force what I had gotten unjustly makes me the aggressor. I am conquered: my life, it is true, as forfeit, is at mercy, but not my wife's and children's. They made not the war, nor assisted in it. I could not forfeit their lives; they were not mine to forfeit. My wife had a share in my estate; that neither could I forfeit. And my children also, being born of me, had a right to be maintained out of my labour or substance. Here then is the case: the conqueror has a title to reparation for damages received, and the children have a title to their father's estate for their subsistence: for as to the wife's share, whether her own labour, or compact, gave her a title to it, it is plain her husband could not forfeit what was hers. What must be done in the case? I answer; the fundamental law of nature being, that all, as much as may be, should be preserved, it follows, that if there be not enough fully to satisfy both, viz. for the conqueror's losses, and children's maintenance, he that hath, and to spare, must remit something of his full satisfaction, and give way to the pressing and preferable title of those who are in danger to perish without it.

§ 184. But supposing the charge and damages of the war are to be made up to the conqueror, to the utmost farthing; and that the children of the vanquished, spoiled of all their father's goods, are to be left to starve and perish; yet the satisfying of what shall, on this score, be due to the conqueror, will scarce give him a title to any country he shall conquer: for the damages of war can scarce amount to the value of any considerable tract of land, in any part of the world, where all the land is possessed, and none lies waste. And if I have not taken away the conqueror's land, which, being vanquished, it is impossible I should; scarce any other spoil I have done him can amount to the value of mine, supposing it equally cultivated, and of an extent any way coming near what I have over-run of his. The destruction of a year's product or two (for it seldom reaches four or five) is the utmost spoil that usually can be done: for as to money, and such riches and treasures taken away, these are none of nature's goods, they have but a fantastical imaginary value: nature has put no such upon them: they are of no more account by her standard, than the wampompeke of the Americans to an European prince, or the silver money of Europe would have been formerly to an American. And five years product is not worth the perpetual inheritance of land, where all is possessed, and none remains waste, to be taken up by him that is disseized: which will be easily granted, if one do but take away the imaginary value of money, the disproportion being more than between five and five hundred; though, at the same time, half a year's product is more worth than the inheritance, where there being more land than the inhabitants possess and make use of, any one has liberty to make use of the waste: but there conquerors take little care to possess themselves of the lands of the vanquished. No damage, therefore, that men in the state of nature (as all princes and governments are in reference to one another) suffer from one another, can give a conqueror power to dispossess the posterity of the vanquished, and turn them out of that inheritance, which ought to be the possession of them and their descendants to all generations. The conqueror indeed will be apt to think himself master: and it is the very condition of the subdued not to be able to dispute their right. But if that be all, it gives no other title than what bare force gives to the stronger over the weaker: and, by this reason, he that is strongest will have a right to whatever he pleases to seize on.

§ 185. Over those then that joined with him in the war, and over those of the subdued country that opposed him not, and the posterity even of those that did, the conqueror, even in a just war, hath, by his conquest, no right of dominion: they are free from any subjection to him, and if their former government be dissolved, they are at liberty to begin and erect another to themselves.

§ 186. The conqueror, it is true, usually, by the force he has over them, compels them, with a sword at their breasts, to stoop to his conditions, and submit to such a government as he pleases to afford them; but the inquiry is, what right he has to do so? If it be said, they submit by their own consent, then this allows their own consent to be necessary to give the conqueror a title to rule over them. It remains only to be considered, whether promises extorted by force, without right, can be thought consent, and how far they bind. To which I shall say, they bind not at all; because whatsoever another gets from me by force, I still retain the right of, and he is obliged presently to restore. He that forces my horse from me, ought presently to restore him, and I have still a right to retake him. By the same reason, he that forced a promise from me, ought presently to restore it, *i. e.* quit me of the obligation of it; or I may resume it myself, *i. e.* choose whether I will perform it: for the law of nature laying an obligation on me only by the rules she pre-scribes, cannot oblige me by the violation of her rules: such is the extorting any thing from me by force. Nor does it at all alter the case to say, "I gave my promise," no more than it excuses the force, and passes the right, when I put my hand in my pocket and deliver my purse myself to a thief, who demands it with a pistol at my breast.

§ 187. From all which it follows, that the government of a conqueror, imposed by force on the subdued, against whom he had no right of war, or who joined not in the war against him, where he had right, has no obligation upon them.

§ 188. But let us suppose that all the men of that community, being all members of the same body politic, may be taken to have joined in that unjust war wherein they are subdued, and so their lives are at the mercy of the conqueror.

§ 189. I say, this concerns not their children who are in their minority: for since a father hath not, in himself, a power over the life or liberty of his child, no act of his can possibly forfeit it. So that the children, whatever may have happened to the fathers, are freemen, and the absolute power of the conqueror reaches no farther than the persons of the men that were subdued by him, and dies with them: and should he govern them as slaves, subjected to his absolute arbitrary power, he has no such right or dominion over their children. He can have no power over them but by their own consent, whatever he may drive them to say or do; and he has no lawful authority, whilst force, and not choice, compels them to submission.

§ 190. Every man is born with a double right: first, a right of freedom to his person, which no other man has a power over, but the free disposal of it lies in himself. Secondly, a right, before any other man, to inherit with his brethren his father's goods.

§ 191. By the first of these, a man is naturally free from subjection to any government, though he be born in a place under its jurisdiction; but if he disclaim the lawful government of the country he was born in, he must also quit the right that belonged to him by the laws of it, and the possessions there descending to him from his ancestors, if it were a government made by their consent.

§ 192. By the second, the inhabitants of any country, who are descended, and derive a title to their estates from those who are subdued, and had a government forced upon them against their free consents, retain a right to the possession of their ancestors, though they consent not freely to the government, whose hard conditions were by force imposed on the possessors of that country: for, the first conqueror never having had a title to the land of that country, the people who are the descendants of, or claim under those who were forced to submit to the yoke of a government by constraint, have always a right to shake it off, and free themselves from the usurpation or tyranny which the sword hath brought in upon them, till their rulers put them under such a frame of government as they willingly and of choice consent to. Who doubts but the Grecian Christians, descendants of the ancient possessors of that country, may justly cast off the Turkish yoke, which they have so long groaned under, whenever they have an opportunity to do it? For no government can have a right to obedience from a people who have not freely consented to it; which they can never be supposed to do, till either they are put in a full state of liberty to choose their government and governors, or at least till they have such standing laws, to which they have by themselves or their representatives given their free consent; and also till they are allowed their due property, which is so to be proprietors of what they have, that nobody can take away any part of it without their own consent, without which, men under any government are not in the state of freemen, but are direct slaves under the force of war.

§ 193. But granting that the conqueror in a just war has a right to the estates, as well as power over the persons of the conquered; which, it is plain, he hath not: nothing of absolute power will follow from hence, in the continuance of the government; because the descendants of these being all freemen, if he grants them estates and possessions to inhabit his country, (without which it would be worth nothing) whatsoever he grants them, they have, so far as it is granted, property in. — The nature whereof is, that "without a man's own consent, it cannot be taken from him."

§ 194. Their persons are free by a native right, and their properties, be they more or less, are their own, and at their own dispose, and not at his; or else it is no property. Supposing the conqueror gives to one man a thousand acres, to him and his heirs for ever; to another he lets a thousand acres for his life, under the rent of 50*l*. or 500*l*. per ann.: has not the one of these a right to his thousand acres for ever, and the other during his life, paying the said rent? and hath not the tenant for life a property in all that he gets over and above his rent, by his labour and industry during the said term, supposing it to be double the rent? Can any one say, the king, or conqueror, after his grant, may by his power of conqueror take away all, or part of the land from the heirs of one, or from the other during his life, he paying the rent? or can he take away from either the goods or money they have got upon the said land, at his pleasure? If he can, then all free and voluntary contracts cease, and are void in the world; there needs nothing to dissolve them at any time, but power enough; and all the grants and promises of men in power are but mockery and collusion: for can there be any thing more ridiculous than to say, I give you and yours this for ever, and that in the surest and most solemn way of conveyance can be devised; and yet it is to be understood, that I have right, if I please, to take it away from you again to-morrow?

§ 195. I will not dispute now, whether princes are exempt from the laws of their country; but this I am sure, they owe subjection to the laws of God and nature. Nobody, no power, can exempt them from the obligations of that eternal law. Those are so great, and so strong, in the case of promises, that omnipotency itself can be tied by them. Grants, promises, and oaths, are bonds that hold the Almighty: whatever some flatterers say to princes of the world, who all together, with all their people joined to them, are in comparison of the great God, but as a drop of the bucket, or a dust on the balance, inconsiderable, nothing.

§ 196. The short of the case in conquest is this: the conqueror, if he have a just cause, has a despotical right over the persons of all that actually aided, and concurred in the war against him, and a right to make up his damage and cost out of their labour and estates, so he injure not the right of any other. Over the rest of the people, if there were any that consented not to the war, and over the children of the captives themselves, or the possessions of either, he has no power; and so can have, by virtue of conquest, no lawful title himself to dominion over them, or derive it to his posterity; but is an aggressor, if he attempts upon their properties, and thereby puts himself in a state of war against them: and has no better a right of principality, he, nor any of his successors, than Hingar, or Hubba, the Danes, had here in England; or Spartacus, had he conquered Italy, would have had; which is to have their yoke cast off, as soon as God shall give those under their subjection courage and opportunity to do it. Thus, notwithstanding whatever title the kings of Assyria had over Judah, by the sword, God assisted Hezekiah to throw off the dominion of that conquering empire. "And the Lord was with Hezekiah, and he prospered; wherefore he went forth, and he rebelled against the king of Assyria; and served him not," 2 Kings, xviii. 7. Whence it is plain, that shaking off a power, which force, and not right, hath set over any one, though it hath the name of rebellion, yet is no offence before God, but is that which he allows and countenances, though even promises and covenants, when obtained by force, have intervened: for it is very probable, to any one that reads the story of Ahaz and Hezekiah attentively, that the Assyrians subdued Ahaz, and deposed him, and made Hezekiah king in his father's lifetime; and that Hezekiah by agreement had done him homage, and paid him tribute all this time.

CHAPTER XVII.

Of Usurpation.

§ 197. As conquest may be called a foreign usurpation, so usurpation is a kind of domestic conquest; with this difference, that an usurper can never have right on his side, it being no usurpation but where one is got into the possession of what another has right to. This, so far as it is usurpation, is a change only of persons, but not of the forms and rules of the government: for if the usurper extend his power beyond what of right belonged to the lawful princes or governors of the commonwealth, it is tyranny added to usurpation.

§ 198. In all lawful governments, the designation of the persons, who are to bear rule, is as natural and necessary a part as the form of the government itself; and is that which had its establishment originally from the people: the anarchy being much alike to have no form of government at all, or to agree that it shall be monarchical, but to appoint no way to design the person that shall have the power, and be the monarch.— Hence all commonwealths, with the form of government established, have rules also of appointing those who are to have any share in the public authority, and settled methods of conveying the right to them: for the anarchy is much alike to have no form of government at all, or to agree that it shall be monarchical, but to appoint no way to know or design the person that shall have the power, and be the monarch. Whoever gets into the exercise of any part of the power, by other ways than what the laws of the community have prescribed, hath no right to be obeyed, though the form of the commonwealth be still preserved; since he is not the person the laws have appointed, and consequently not the person the people have consented to. Nor can such an usurper, or any deriving from him, ever have a title, till the people are both at liberty to consent, and have actually consented to allow, and confirm in him the power he hath till then usurped.

CHAPTER XVIII.

Of Tyranny.

§ 199. As usurpation is the exercise of power, which another hath a right to, so tyranny is the exercise of power beyond right, which nobody can have a right to. And this is making use of the power any one has in his hands, not for the good of those who are under it, but for his own private, separate advantage. — When the governor, however entitled, makes not the law, but his will, the rule; and his commands and actions are not directed to the preservation of the properties of his people, but the satisfaction of his own ambition, revenge, covetousness, or any other irregular passion.

§ 200. If one can doubt this to be truth or reason, because it comes from the obscure hand of a subject, I hope the authority of a king will make it pass with him. King James the First, in his speech to the parliament, 1603, tells them thus: "I will ever prefer the weal of the public, and of the whole commonwealth, in making of good laws and constitutions, to any particular and private ends of mine; thinking ever the wealth and weal of the commonwealth to be my greatest weal and worldly felicity; a point wherein a lawful king doth directly differ from a tyrant: for I do acknowledge, that the special and greatest point of difference that is between a rightful king and an usurping tyrant is this, that whereas the proud and ambitious tyrant doth think his kingdom and people are only ordained for satisfaction of his desires and unreasonable appetites, the righteous and just king doth, by the contrary, acknowledge himself to be ordained for the procuring of the wealth and property of his people." And again, in his speech to the parliament, 1609, he hath these words: "The king binds himself by a double oath to the observation of the fundamental laws of his kingdom; tacitly, as by being a king, and so bound to protect as well the people, as the laws of his kingdom; and expressly, by his oath at his coronation; so as every just king, in a settled kingdom, is bound to observe that paction made to his people by his laws, in framing his government agreeable thereunto, according to that paction which God made with Noah after the deluge: Hereafter, seed-time and harvest, and cold and heat, and summer and winter, and day and night, shall not cease while the earth remaineth. And therefore a king governing in a settled kingdom, leaves to be a king, and degenerates into a tyrant, as soon as he leaves off to rule according to his laws." And a little after, "Therefore all kings that are not tyrants, or perjured, will be glad to bound themselves within the limits of their laws; and they that persuade them the contrary, are vipers, and pests both against them and the commonwealth." Thus that learned king, who well understood the notions of things, makes the difference betwixt a king and a tyrant to consist only in this, that one makes the laws the bounds of his power, and the good of the public the end of his government; the other makes all give way to his own will and appetite.

§ 201. It is a mistake to think this fault is proper only to monarchies; other forms of government are liable to it, as well as that: for wherever the power, that is put in any hands for the government of the people, and the preservation of their properties, is applied to other ends, and made use of to impoverish, harass, or subdue them to the arbitrary and irregular commands of those that have it; there it presently becomes tyranny, whether those that thus use it are one or many. Thus we read of the thirty tyrants at Athens, as well as one at Syracuse; and the intolerable dominion of the decemviri at Rome was nothing better.

§ 202. Wherever law ends, tyranny begins, if the law be transgressed to another's harm; and whosoever in authority exceeds the power given him by the law, and makes use of the force he has under his command, to compass that upon the subject which the law allows not, ceases in that to be a magistrate; and, acting without authority, may be opposed as any other man who by force invades the right of another. This is acknowledged in subordinate magistrates. He that hath authority to seize my person in the street, may be opposed as a thief and a robber if he endeavours to break into my house to execute a writ, notwithstanding that I know he has such a warrant, and such a legal authority as will impower him to arrest me abroad. And why this should not hold in the highest, as well as in the most inferior magistrate, I would gladly be informed. Is it reasonable that the eldest brother, because he has the greatest part of his father's estate, should thereby have a right to take away any of his younger brother's portions? or that a rich man, who possessed a whole country, should from thence have a right to seize, when he pleased, the cottage and garden of his poor neighbour? The being rightfully possessed of great power and riches, exceedingly beyond the greatest part of the sons of Adam, is so far from being an excuse, much less a reason, for rapine and oppression, which the endamaging another without authority is, that it is a great aggravation of it: for the exceeding the bounds of authority is no more a right in a great, than in a petty officer; no more justifiable in a king than a constable; but is so much the worse in him, in that he has more trust put in him, has already a much greater share than the rest of his brethren, and is supposed, from the advantages of his education, employment, and counsellors, to be more knowing in the measures of right and wrong.

§ 203. "May the commands then of a prince be opposed? may he be resisted as often as any one shall find himself aggrieved, and but imagine he has not right done him? This will unhinge and overturn all politics, and, instead of government and order, leave nothing but anarchy and confusion."

§ 204. To this I answer, that force is to be opposed to nothing but to unjust and unlawful force; whoever makes any opposition in any other case, draws on himself a just condemnation both from God and man; and so no such danger or confusion will follow, as is often suggested: for,

§ 205. First, As, in some countries, the person of the prince by the law is sacred; and so, whatever he commands or does, his person is still free from all question or violence, not liable to force, or any judicial censure or condemnation. But yet opposition may be made to the illegal acts of any inferior officer, or other commissioned by him, unless he will, by actually putting himself into a state of war with his people, dissolve the government, and leave them to that defence which belongs to every one in the state of nature: for of such things who can tell what the end will be? and a neighbour kingdom has showed the world an odd example. In all other cases the sacredness of the person exempts him from all inconveniences, whereby he is secure, whilst the government stands, from all violence and harm whatsoever; than which there cannot be a wiser constitution: for the harm he can do in his own person not being likely to happen often, nor to extend itself far; nor being able by his single strength to subvert the laws, nor oppress the body of the people; should any prince have so much weakness and ill-nature as to be willing to do it, the inconveniency of some particular mischiefs that may happen sometimes, when a heady prince comes to the throne, are well recompensed by the peace of the public, and security of the government, in the person of the chief magistrate, thus set out of the reach of danger: it being safer for the body, that some few private men should be sometimes in danger to suffer, than that the head of the republic should be easily, and upon slight occasions, exposed.

§ 206. Secondly, But this privilege belonging only to the king's person, hinders not, but they may be questioned, opposed, and resisted, who use unjust force, though they pretend a commission from him, which the law authorizes not; as is plain in the case of him that has the king's writ to arrest a man, which is a full commission from the king; and yet he that has it cannot break open a man's house to do it, nor execute this command of the king upon certain days, nor in certain places, though this commission have no such exception in it; but they are the limitations of the law, which if any one transgress, the king's commission excuses him not; for the king's authority being given him only by the law, he cannot empower any one to act against the law, or justify him, by his commission, in so doing; the commission or command of any magistrate, where he has no authority, being so void and insignificant as that of any private man; the difference between the one and the other being that the magistrate has some authority so far, and to such ends, and the private man has none at all: for it is not the commission, but the authority, that gives the right of acting; and against the laws there can be no authority. But, notwithstanding such resistance, the king's person and authority are still both secured, and so no danger to governor or government.

§ 207. Thirdly, Supposing a government wherein the person of the chief magistrate is not thus sacred; yet this doctrine of the lawfulness of resisting all unlawful exercises of his power, will not upon every slight occasion endanger him, or embroil the government: for where the injured party may be relieved, and his damages repaired by appeal to the law, there can be no pretence for force, which is only to be used where a man is intercepted from appealing to the law: for nothing is to be accounted hostile force, but where it leaves not the remedy of such an appeal; and it is such force alone that puts him that uses it into a state of war, and makes it lawful to resist him. A man with a sword in his hand demands my purse in the highway, when perhaps I have not twelve-pence in my pocket: this man I may lawfully kill. To another I deliver 100*l*. to hold only whilst I alight, which he refuses to restore me, when I am got up again, but draws his sword to defend the possession of it by force, if I endeavour to retake it. The mischief this man does me is an hundred, or possibly a thousand times more than the other perhaps intended me (whom I killed before he really did me any); and yet I might lawfully kill the one, and cannot so much as hurt the other lawfully. The reason whereof is plain; because the one using force, which threatened my life, I could not have time to appeal to the law to secure it; and when it was gone, it was too late to appeal. The law could not restore life to my dead carcase, the loss was irreparable: which to prevent, the law of nature gave me a right to destroy him, who had put himself into a state of war with me, and threatened my destruction. But in the other case, my life not being in danger, I may have the benefit of appealing to the law, and have reparation for my 100*l.* that way.

§ 208. Fourthly, But if the unlawful acts done by the magistrate be maintained (by the power he has got), and the remedy which is due by law be by the same power obstructed, yet the right of resisting, even in such manifest acts of tyranny, will not suddenly, or on slight occasions, disturb the government: for if it reach no farther than some private men's cases, though they have a right to defend themselves, and to recover by force what by unlawful force is taken from them; yet the right to do so will not easily engage them in a contest, wherein they are sure to perish; it being as impossible for one, or a few oppressed men to disturb the government, where the body of the people do not think themselves concerned in it, as for a raving madman, or heady malecontent, to overturn a well-settled state; the people being as little apt to follow the one as the other.

§ 209. But if either these illegal acts have extended to the majority of the people, or if the mischief and oppression has lighted only on some few, but in such cases, as the precedent and consequences seem to threaten all; and they are persuaded in their consciences, that their laws, and with them their estates, liberties, and lives are in danger, and perhaps their religion too; how they will be hindered from resisting illegal force, used against them, I cannot tell. This is an inconvenience, I confess, that attends all governments whatsoever, when the governors have brought it to this pass, to be generally suspected of their people; the most dangerous state which they can possibly put themselves in; wherein they are less to be pitied, because it is so easy to be avoided; it being as impossible for a governor, if he really means the good of his people, and the preservation of them, and their laws together, not to make them see and feel it, as it is for the father of a family not to let his children see he loves and takes care of them.

§ 210. But if all the world shall observe pretences of one kind, and actions of another; arts used to elude the law, and the trust of prerogative (which is an arbitrary power in some things left in the prince's hand to do good, not harm to the people) employed contrary to the end for which it was given: if the people shall find the ministers and subordinate magistrates chosen suitable to such ends, and favoured, or laid by, proportionably as they promote or oppose them: if they see several experiments made of arbitrary power, and that religion underhand favoured (though publicly proclaimed against), which is readiest to introduce it; and the operators in it supported, as much as may be; and when that cannot be done, yet approved still, and liked the better: if a long train of actions show the councils all tending that way, how can a man any more hinder himself from being persuaded in his own mind which way things are going; or from casting about how to save himself, than he could from believing the captain of the ship he was in, was carrying him, and the rest of the company, to Algiers, when he found him always steering that course, though cross winds, leaks in his ship, and want of men and provisions did often force him to turn his course another way for some time, which he steadily returned to again, as soon as the wind, weather, and other circumstances would let him?

CHAPTER XIX.

Of the Dissolution of Government.

§ 211. He that will with any clearness speak of the dissolution of government, ought in the first place to distinguish between the dissolution of the society and the dissolution of the government. That which makes the community, and brings men out of the loose state of nature into one politic society, is the agreement which every one has with the rest to incorporate, and act as one body, and so be one distinct commonwealth. The usual, and almost only way whereby this union is dissolved, is the inroad of foreign force making a conquest upon them: for in that case (not being able to maintain and support themselves as one entire and independent body), the union belonging to that body which consisted therein, must necessarily cease, and so every one return to the state he was in before, with a liberty to shift for himself, and provide for his own safety, as he thinks fit, in some other society. Whenever the society is dissolved, it is certain the government of that society cannot remain. Thus conquerors' swords often cut up governments by the roots, and mangle societies to pieces, separating the subdued or scattered multitude from the protection of, and dependence on, that society which ought to have preserved them from violence. The world is too well instructed in, and too forward to allow of, this way of dissolving of governments, to need any more to be said of it; and there wants not much argument to prove, that where the society is dissolved, the government cannot remain; that being as impossible, as for the frame of a house to subsist when the materials of it are scattered and dissipated by a whirlwind, or jumbled into a confused heap by an earthquake.

§ 212. Besides this overturning from without, governments are dissolved from within.

First, When the legislative is altered. Civil society being a state of peace, amongst those who are of it from whom the state of war is excluded by the umpirage, which they have provided in their legislative, for the ending all differences that may arise amongst any of them; it is in their legislative, that the members of a commonwealth are united, and combined together into one coherent living body. This is the soul that gives form, life, and unity to the commonwealth: from hence the several members have their mutual influence, sympathy, and connexion: and therefore, when the legislative is broken or dissolved, dissolution and death follows: for, the essence and union of the society consisting in having one will, the legislative, when once established by the majority, has the declaring, and as it were keeping of that will. The constitution of the legislative is the first and fundamental act of society, whereby provision is made for the continuation of their union, under the direction of persons, and bonds of laws, made by persons authorized thereunto, by the consent and appointment of the people; without which no one man, or number of men, amongst them, can have authority of making laws that shall be binding to the rest. When any one, or more, shall take upon them to make laws, whom the people have not appointed so to do, they make laws without authority, which the people are not therefore bound to obey; by which means they come again to be out of subjection, and may constitute to themselves a new legislative, as they think best, being in full liberty to resist the force of those, who without authority would impose any thing upon them. Every one is at the disposure of his own will, when those who had, by the delegation of the society, the declaring of the public will, are excluded from it, and others usurp the place, who have no such authority or delegation.

§ 213. This being usually brought about by such in the commonwealth who misuse the power they have, it is hard to consider it aright, and know at whose door to lay it, without knowing the form of government in which it happens. Let us suppose then the legislative placed in the concurrence of three distinct persons.

1. A single hereditary person, having the constant, supreme, executive power, and with it the power of convoking and dissolving the other two, within certain periods of time.

2. An assembly of hereditary nobility.

3. An assembly of representatives chosen, *pro tempore,* by the people. Such a form of government supposed, it is evident,

§ 214. First, That when such a single person, or prince, sets up his own arbitrary will in place of the laws, which are the will of the society, declared by the legislative, then the legislative is changed: for that being in effect the legislative, whose rules and laws are put in execution, and required to be obeyed; when other laws are set up, and other rules pretended, and enforced, than what the legislative, constituted by the society, have enacted, it is plain that the legislative is changed. Whoever introduces new laws, not being thereunto authorized by the fundamental appointment of the society, or subverts the old; disowns and overturns the power by which they were made, and so sets up a new legislative.

§ 215. Secondly, When the prince hinders the legislative from assembling in its due time, or from acting freely, pursuant to those ends for which it was constituted, the legislative is altered: for it is not a certain number of men, no, nor their meeting, unless they have also freedom of debating, and leisure of perfecting, what is for the good of the society, wherein the legislative consists: when these are taken away or altered, so as to deprive the society of the due exercise of their power, the legislative is truly altered: for it is not names that constitute governments, but the use and exercise of those powers that were intended to accompany them; so that he, who takes away the freedom, or hinders the acting of the legislative in its due seasons, in effect takes away the legislative, and puts an end to the government.

§ 216. Thirdly, When, by the arbitrary power of the prince, the electors, or ways of election, are altered, without the consent, and contrary to the common interest of the people, there also the legislative is altered: for if others than those whom the society hath authorized thereunto, do choose, or in another way than what the society hath prescribed, those chosen are not the legislative appointed by the people.

§ 217. Fourthly, The delivery also of the people into the subjection of a foreign power, either by the prince or by the legislative, is certainly a change of the legislative, and so a dissolution of the government: for the end why people entered into society being to be preserved one entire, free, independent society, to be governed by its own laws; this is lost, whenever they are given up into the power of another.

§ 218. Why, in such a constitution as this, the dissolution of the government in these cases is to be imputed to the prince, is evident; because he, having the force, treasure, and offices of the state to employ, and often persuading himself, or being flattered by others, that as supreme magistrate he is uncapable of control; he alone is in a condition to make great advances toward such changes, under pretence of lawful authority, and has it in his hands to terrify or suppress opposers, as factious, seditious, and enemies to the government: whereas no other part of the legislative, or people, is capable by themselves to attempt any alteration of the legislative, without open and visible rebellion, apt enough to be taken notice of; which, when it prevails, produces effects very little different from foreign conquest. Besides, the prince in such a form of government having the power of dissolving the other parts of the legislative, and thereby rendering them private persons, they can never in opposition to him, or without his concurrence, alter the legislative by a law, his consent being necessary to give any of their decrees that sanction. But yet, so far as the other parts of the legislative any way contribute to any attempt upon the government, and do either promote, or not (what lies in them) hinder such designs; they are guilty, and partake in this, which is certainly the greatest crime men can be guilty of one towards another.

§ 219. There is one way more whereby such a government may be dissolved, and that is, when he who has the supreme executive power, neglects and abandons that charge, so that the laws already made can no longer be put in execution. This is demonstratively to reduce all to anarchy, and so effectually to dissolve the government: for laws not being made for themselves, but to be, by their execution, the bonds of the society, to keep every part of the body politic in its due place and function; when that totally ceases, the government visibly ceases, and the people become a confused multitude, without order or connexion. Where there is no longer the administration of justice, for the securing of men's rights, nor any remaining power within the community to direct the force, or provide for the necessities of the public; there certainly is no government left. Where the laws cannot be executed, it is all one as if there were no laws; and a government without laws is, I suppose, a mystery in politics, inconceivable to human capacity, and inconsistent with human society.

§ 220. In these and the like cases, when the government is dissolved, the people are at liberty to provide for themselves, by erecting a new legislative, differing from the other, by the change of persons, or form, or both, as they shall find it most for their safety and good: for the society can never, by the fault of another, lose the native and original right it has to preserve itself; which can only be done by a settled legislative, and a fair and impartial execution of the laws made by it. But the state of mankind is not so miserable that they are not capable of using this remedy, till it be too late to look for any. To tell people they may provide for themselves, by erecting a new legislative, when by oppression, artifice, or being delivered over to a foreign power, their old one is gone, is only to tell them, they may expect relief when it is too late, and the evil is past cure. This is in effect no more than to bid them first be slaves, and then to take care of their liberty; and when their chains are on, tell them they may act like freemen. This, if barely so, is rather mockery than relief; and men can never be secure from tyranny, if there be no means to escape it till they are perfectly under it; and therefore it is, that they have not only a right to get out of it, but to prevent it.

§ 221. There is therefore, secondly, another way whereby governments are dissolved, and that is, when the legislative, or the prince, either of them, act contrary to their trust.

First, the legislative acts against the trust reposed in them, when they endeavour to invade the property of the subject, and to make themselves, or any part of the community, masters, or arbitrary disposers of the lives, liberties, or fortunes of the people.

§ 222. The reason why men enter into society is the preservation of their property; and the end why they choose and authorize a legislative is, that there may be laws made, and rules set, as guards and fences to the properties of all the members of the society: to limit the power, and moderate the dominion, of every part and member of the society: for since it can never be supposed to be the will of the society that the legislative should have a power to destroy that which every one designs to secure by entering into society, and for which the people submitted themselves to legislators of their own making; whenever the legislators endeavour to take away and destroy the property of the people, or to reduce them to slavery under arbitrary power, they put themselves into a state of war with the people, who are thereupon absolved from any farther obedience, and are left to the common refuge, which God hath provided for all men, against force and violence. Whensoever therefore the legislative shall transgress this fundamental rule of society; and either by ambition, fear, folly, or corruption, endeavour to grasp themselves, or put into the hands of any other, an absolute power over the lives, liberties, and estates of the people; by this breach of trust they forfeit the power the people had put into their hands for quite contrary ends, and it devolves to the people, who have a right to resume their original liberty, and, by the establishment of a new legislative, (such as they shall think fit) provide for their own safety and security, which is the end for which they are in society. What I have said here, concerning the legislative in general, holds true also concerning the supreme executor, who having a double trust put in him, both to have a part in the legislative, and the supreme execution of the law, acts against both, when he goes about to set up his own arbitrary will as the law of the society. He acts also contrary to his trust, when he either employs the force, treasure, and offices of the society to corrupt the representatives, and gain them to his purposes; or openly pre-engages the electors, and prescribes to their choice, such, whom he has, by solicitations, threats, promises, or otherwise, won to his designs; and employs them to bring in such, who have promised beforehand what to vote, and what to enact. Thus to regulate candidates and electors, and new-model the ways of election, what is it but to cut up the government by the roots, and poison the very fountain of public security? for the people having reserved to themselves the choice of their representatives, as the fence to their properties, could do it for no other end, but that they might always be freely chosen, and so chosen, freely act, and advise, as the necessity of the commonwealth and the public good should, upon examination and mature debate, be judged to require. This, those who give their votes before they hear the debate, and have weighed the reasons on all sides, are not capable of doing. To prepare such an assembly as this, and endeavour to set up the declared abettors of his own will, for the true representatives of the people, and the law-makers of the society, is certainly as great a breach of trust, and as perfect a declaration of a design to subvert the government, as is possible to be met with. To which if one shall add rewards and punishments visibly employed to the same end, and all the arts of perverted law made use of, to take off and destroy all that stand in the way of such a design, and will not comply and consent to betray the liberties of their country, it will be past doubt what is doing. What power they ought to have in the society, who thus employ it contrary to the trust that went along with it in its first institution, is easy to determine; and one cannot but see, that he, who has once attempted any such thing as this, cannot any longer be trusted.

§ 223. To this perhaps it will be said, that the people being ignorant, and always discontented, to lay the foundation of government in the unsteady opinion and uncertain humour of the people, is to expose it to certain ruin; and no government will be able long to subsist, if the people may set up a new legislative, whenever they take offence at the old one. To this I answer, quite the contrary. People are not so easily got out of their old forms, as some are apt to suggest. They are hardly to be prevailed with to amend the acknowledged faults in the frame they have been accustomed to. And if there be any original defects, or adventitious ones introduced by time, or

ITEM CHECKED OUT

Due Date: 10/29/2013 02:30 PM

Title: CSSSI C48/C49 Remote

Author:

Call Number:

Enumeration:

Chronology:

Copy:

Item Barcode: 39002110628014

See Your Library Account information at:
http://orbis.library.yale.edu

corruption; it is not an easy thing to get them changed, even when all the world sees there is an opportunity for it. This slowness and aversion in the people to quit their old constitutions, has in the many revolutions, which have been seen in this kingdom, in this and former ages, still kept us to, or, after some interval of fruitless attempts, still brought us back again to, our old legislative of king, lords, and commons: and whatever provocations have made the crown be taken from some of our princes' heads, they never carried the people so far as to place it in another line.

§ 224. But it will be said, this hypothesis lays a ferment for frequent rebellion. To which I answer,

First, No more than any other hypothesis: for when the people are made miserable, and find themselves exposed to the ill usage of arbitrary power, cry up their governors as much as you will, for sons of Jupiter; let them be sacred and divine, descended, or authorized from heaven; give them out for whom or what you please, the same will happen. The people generally ill-treated, and contrary to right, will be ready upon any occasion to ease themselves of a burden that sits heavy upon them. They will wish, and seek for the opportunity, which in the change, weakness, and accidents of human affairs, seldom delays long to offer itself. He must have lived but a little while in the world, who has not seen examples of this in his time; and he must have read very little, who cannot produce examples of it in all sorts of governments in the world.

§ 225. Secondly, I answer, such revolutions happen not upon every little mismanagement in public affairs. Great mistakes in the ruling part, many wrong and inconvenient laws, and all the slips of human frailty, will be born by the people without mutiny or murmur. But if a long train of abuses, prevarications, and artifices, all tending the same way, make the design visible to the people, and they cannot but feel what they lie under, and see whither they are going; it is not to be wondered, that they should then rouse themselves, and endeavour to put the rule into such hands which may secure to them the ends for which government was at first erected; and without which, ancient names, and specious forms, are so far from being better, that they are much worse, than the state of nature, or pure anarchy; the inconveniencies, being all as great and as near, but the remedy farther off and more difficult.

§ 226. Thirdly, I answer, that this doctrine of a power in the people of providing for their safety anew, by a new legislative, when their legislators have acted contrary to their trust, by invading their property, is the best fence against rebellion, and the probablest means to hinder it: for rebellion being an opposition, not to persons, but authority, which is founded only in the constitutions and laws of the government; those, whoever they be, who by force break through, and by force justify their violation of them, are truly and properly rebels: for when men, by entering into society and civil government, have excluded force, and introduced laws for the preservation of property, peace, and unity amongst themselves; those who set up force again in opposition to the laws, do *rebellare,* that is, bring back again the state of war, and are properly rebels: which they who are in power, (by the pretence they have to authority, the temptation of force they have in their hands, and the flattery of those about them) being likeliest to do; the properest way to prevent the evil is to show them the danger and injustice of it, who are under the greatest temptation to run into it.

§ 227. In both the fore-mentioned cases, when either the legislative is changed, or the legislators act contrary to the end for which they were constituted, those who are guilty are guilty of rebellion: for if any one by force takes away the established legislative of any society, and the laws by them made pursuant to their trust, he thereby takes away the umpirage, which every one had consented to, for a peaceable decision of all their controversies, and a bar to the state of war amongst them. They, who remove, or change the legislative, take away this decisive power, which nobody can have but by the appointment and consent of the people; and so destroying the authority which the people did, and nobody else can set up, and introducing a power which the people hath not authorized, they actually introduce a state of war, which is that of force without authority; and thus, by removing the legislative established by the society (in whose decisions the people acquiesced and united, as to that of their own will) they untie the knot, and expose the people anew to the state of war. And if those, who by force take away the legislative, are rebels, the legislators themselves, as has been shown, can be no less esteemed so; when they, who were set up for the protection and preservation of the people, their liberties and properties, shall by force invade and endeavour to take them away; and so they putting themselves into a state of war with those who made them the protectors and guardians of their peace, are properly, and with the greatest aggravation, *rebellantes,* rebels.

§ 228. But if they, who say, "it lays a foundation for rebellion," mean that it may occasion civil wars, or intestine broils, to tell the people they are absolved from obedience when illegal attempts are made upon their liberties or properties, and may oppose the unlawful violence of those who were their magistrates, when they invade their properties contrary to the trust put in them; and that therefore this doctrine is not to be allowed, being so destructive to the peace of the world: they may as well say, upon the same

differ from Hobbes

ground, that honest men may not oppose robbers or pirates, because this may occasion disorder or bloodshed. If any mischief come in such cases, it is not to be charged upon him who defends his own right, but on him that invades his neighbour's. If the innocent honest man must quietly quit all he has, for peace sake, to him who will lay violent hands upon it, I desire it may be considered, what a kind of peace there will be in the world, which consists only in violence and rapine; and which is to be maintained only for the benefit of robbers and oppressors. Who would not think it an admirable peace betwixt the mighty and the mean, when the lamb, without resistance, yielded his throat to be torn by the imperious wolf? Polyphemus's den gives us a perfect pattern of such a peace, and such a government, wherein Ulysses and his companions had nothing to do, but quietly to suffer themselves to be devoured. And no doubt Ulysses, who was a prudent man, preached up passive obedience, and exhorted them to a quiet submission, by representing to them of what concernment peace was to mankind; and by showing the inconveniencies might happen, if they should offer to resist Polyphemus, who had now the power over them.

§ 229. The end of government is the good of mankind: and which is best for mankind, that the people should be always exposed to the boundless will of tyranny; or that the rulers should be sometimes liable to be opposed, when they grow exorbitant in the use of their power, and employ it for the destruction, and not the preservation of the properties of their people?

§ 230. Nor let any one say, that mischief can arise from hence, as often as it shall please a busy head, or turbulent spirit, to desire the alteration of the government. It is true, such men may stir, whenever they please; but it will be only to their own just ruin and perdition: for till the mischief be grown general, and the ill designs of the rulers become visible, or their attempts sensible to the greater part, the people, who are more disposed to suffer than right themselves by resistance, are not apt to stir. The examples of particular injustice or oppression, of here and there an unfortunate man, moves them not. But if they universally have a persuasion, grounded upon manifest evidence, that designs are carrying on against their liberties, and the general course and tendency of things cannot but give them strong suspicions of the evil intention of their governors, who is to be blamed for it? Who can help it, if they, who might avoid it, bring themselves into this suspicion? Are the people to be blamed, if they have the sense of rational creatures, and can think of things no otherwise than as they find and feel them? And is it not rather their fault, who put things into such a posture, that they would not have them thought to be as they are? I grant, that the pride, ambition, and turbulency of private men have sometimes caused great disorders in commonwealths, and factions have been fatal to states and kingdoms. But whether the mischief hath oftener begun in the people's wantonness, and a desire to cast off the lawful authority of their rulers, or in the rulers' insolence, and endeavours to get and exercise an arbitrary power over their people; whether oppression, or disobedience, gave the first rise to the disorder; I leave it to impartial history to determine. This I am sure, whoever, either ruler or subject, by force goes about to invade the rights of either prince or people, and lays the foundation for overturning the constitution and frame of any just government, is highly guilty of the greatest crime, I think, a man is capable of; being to answer for all those mischiefs of blood, rapine, and desolation, which the breaking to pieces of governments bring on a country. And he who does it, is justly to be esteemed the common enemy and pest of mankind, and is to be treated accordingly.

§ 231. That subjects or foreigners, attempting by force on the properties of any people, may be resisted with force, is agreed on all hands. But that magistrates, doing the same thing, may be resisted, hath of late been denied: as if those who had the greatest privileges and advantages by the law, had thereby a power to break those laws, by which alone they were set in a better place than their brethren: whereas their offence is thereby the greater, both as being ungrateful for the greater share they have by the law, and breaking also that trust, which is put into their hands by their brethren.

§ 232. Whosoever uses force without right, as every one does in society, who does it without law, puts himself into a state of war with those against whom he so uses it; and in that state all former ties are cancelled, all other rights cease, and every one has a right to defend himself, and to resist the aggressor. This is so evident, that Barclay himself, that great assertor of the power and sacredness of kings, is forced to confess, that it is lawful for the people, in some cases, to resist their king; and that too in a chapter, wherein he pretends to show, that the divine law shuts up the people from all manner of rebellion. Whereby it is evident, even by his own doctrine, that, since they may in some cases resist, all resisting of princes is not rebellion. His words are these. "Quod siquis dicat, Ergone populus tyrannicæ crudelitati et furori jugulum semper præbebit? Ergone multitudo civitates suas fame, ferro, et flammâ vastari, seque, conjuges, et liberos fortunæ ludibrio et tyranni libidini exponi, inque omnia vitæ pericula omnesque miserias et molestias à rege deduci patientur? Num illis quod omni animantium generi est à naturâ tributum, denegari debet, ut sc. vim vi repellant, seseque ab injuria tueantur? Huic breviter responsum sit, Populo universo negari defensionem, quæ juris naturalis est, neque ultionem quæ præter naturam est adversus regem concedi debere. Quapropter si rex non in singulares tantum personas aliquot privatum odium exerceat, sed corpus etiam reipublicæ, cujus ipse caput est, *i. e.* totum populum, vel insignem aliquam ejus partem immani et intolerandâ sævitiâ seu tyrannide divexet; populo quidem hoc casu resistendi ac tuendi se ab injuriâ potestas competit; sed tuendi se tantum, non enim in principem invadendi: et restituendæ injuriæ illatæ, non recedendi à debitâ reverentiâ propter acceptam injuriam. Præsentem denique impetum propulsandi non vim præteritam ulciscendi jus habet. Horum enim alterum à naturâ est, ut vitam scilicet corpusque tueamur. Alterum vero contra naturam, ut inferior de superiori supplicium sumat. Quod itaque populus malum, antequam factum sit, impedire potest, ne fiat; id postquam factum est, in regem authorem sceleris vindicare non potest: populus igitur hoc amplius quam privatus quispiam habet: quod huic, vel ipsis adversariis judicibus, excepto Buchanano, nullum nisi in patientia remedium superest. Cùm ille si intolerabilis tyrannus est (modicum enim ferre omnino debet) resistere cum reverentiâ possit." Barclay contra Monarchom. l. iii. c. 8.

In English thus:

§ 233. "But if any one should ask, Must the people then always lay themselves open to the cruelty and rage of tyranny? Must they see their cities pillaged and laid in ashes, their wives and children exposed to the tyrant's lust and fury, and themselves and families reduced by their king to ruin, and all the miseries of want and oppression; and yet sit still? Must men alone be debarred the common privilege of opposing force with force, which nature allows so freely to all other creatures for their preservation from injury? I answer: Self-defence is a part of the law of nature; nor can it be denied the community, even against the king himself: but to revenge themselves upon him, must by no means be allowed them; if being not agreeable to that law. Wherefore if the king should show an hatred, not only to some particular persons, but sets himself against the body of the commonwealth, whereof he is the head, and shall, with intolerable ill usage, cruelly tyrannise over the whole, or a considerable part of the people, in this case the people have a right to resist and defend themselves from injury: but it must be with this caution, that they only defend themselves, but do not attack their prince: they may repair the damages received, but must not for any provocation exceed the bounds of due reverence and respect. They may repulse the present attempt, but must not revenge past violences: for it is natural for us to defend life and limb; but that an inferior should punish a superior, is against nature. The mischief which is designed them the people may prevent before it be done: but when it is done, they must not revenge it on the king, though author of the villany. This therefore is the privilege of the people in general, above what any private person hath; that particular men are allowed by our adversaries themselves (Buchanan only excepted) to have no other remedy but patience; but the body of the people may with reverence resist intolerable tyranny; for, when it is but moderate, they ought to endure it."

§ 234. Thus far that great advocate of monarchical power allows of resistance.

§ 235. It is true, he has annexed two limitations to it, to no purpose:

First, He says, it must be with reverence.

Secondly, It must be without retribution, or punishment; and the reason he gives is, "Because an inferior cannot punish a superior."

First, How to resist force without striking again, or how to strike with reverence, will need some skill to make intelligible. He that shall oppose an assault only with a shield to receive the blows, or in any more respectful posture, without a sword in his hand, to abate the confidence and force of the assailant, will quickly be at an end of his resistance, and will find such a defence serve only to draw on himself the worse usage. This is as ridiculous a way of resisting, as Juvenal thought it of fighting; "ubi tu pulsas, ego vapulo tantum." And the success of the combat will be unavoidably the same he there describes it:

— "Libertas pauperis hæc est:
Pulsatus rogat, et pugnis concisus, adorat,
Ut liceat paucis cum dentibus inde reverti."

This will always be the event of such an imaginary resistance, where men may not strike again. He therefore who may resist, must be allowed to strike. And then let our author, or any body else, join a knock on the head, or a cut on the face, with as much reverence and respect as he thinks fit. He that can reconcile blows and reverence, may, for aught I know, deserve for his pains a civil, respectful cudgelling, wherever he can meet with it.

Secondly, As to his second, "An inferior cannot punish a superior;" that is true, generally speaking, whilst he is his superior. But to resist force with force, being the state of war that levels the parties, cancels all former relation of reverence, respect, and superiority: and then the odds that remains, is, that he, who opposes the unjust aggressor, has this superiority over him, that he has a right, when he prevails, to punish the offender, both for the breach of the peace, and all the evils that followed upon it. Barclay therefore, in another place, more coherently to himself, denies it to be lawful to resist a king in any case. But he there assigns two cases, whereby a king may unking himself. His words are.

"Quid ergo, nulline casus incidere possunt quibus populo sese erigere atque in regem impotentius dominantem arma capere et invadere jure suo suâque authoritate liceat? Nulli certe quamdiu rex manet. Semper enim ex divinis id obstat, Regem honorificato; et qui potestati, resistit, Dei ordinationi resistit: non aliàs igitur in eum populo potestas est quam si id committat propter quod ipso jure rex esse desinat. Tunc enim se ipse principatu exuit atque in privatis constituit liber: hoc modo populus et superior efficitur, reverso ad eum sc. jure illo quod ante regem inauguratum in interregno habuit. At sunt paucorum generum commissa ejusmodi quæ hunc effectum pariunt. At ego cum plurima animo perlustrem, duo tantam ínvenio, duos, inquam, casus quibus rex ipso facto ex rege non regem se facit et omni honore et dignítate regali atque in subditos potestate destituit; quorum etiam meminit Winzerus. Horum unus est, Si regnum disperdat, quemadmodum de Nerone fertur, quod is nempe senatum populumque Romanum, atque adeo urbem ipsam ferro flammaque vastare, ac novas sibi sedes quærere, decrevisset. Et de Caligula, quod palam denunciarit se neque civem neque principem senatui amplius fore, inque animo habuerit interempto utriusque ordinis electissimo quoque Alexandriam commigrare, ac ut populum uno ictu interimeret, unam ei cervicem optavit. Talia cum rex aliquis meditatur et molitur serio, omnem regnandi curam et animum ilico abjicit, ac proinde imperium in subditos amittit, ut dominus servi pro derelicto habiti dominium."

§ 236. "Alter casus est, Si rex in alicujus clientelam se contulit, ac regnum quod liberum à majoribus et populo traditum accepit, alienæ ditioni mancipavit. Nam tunc quamvis forte non eâ mente id agit populo plane ut incommodet: tamen quia quod præcipuum est regiæ dignitatis amisit, ut summus scilicet in regno secundum Deum sit, et solo Deo inferior, atque populum etiam totum ignorantem vel invitum, cujus libertatem sartam et tectam conservare debuit, in alterius gentis ditionem et potestatem dedidit; hâc velut quadam regni ab alienatione efficit, ut nec quod ipse in regno imperium habuit retineat, nec in eum cui collatum voluit, juris quicquam transferat; atque ita eo facto liberum jam et suæ potestatis populum relinquit, cujus rei exemplum unum annales Scotici suppeditant." Barclay contra Monarchom. l. iii. c. 16.

Which in English runs thus:

§ 237. "What then, can there no case happen wherein the people may of right, and by their own authority, help themselves, take arms, and set upon their king, imperiously domineering over them? None at all, whilst he remains a king. Honour the king, and he that resists the power, resists the ordinance of God, are divine oracles that will never permit it. The people therefore can never come by a power over him, unless he does something that makes him cease to be a king: for then he divests himself of his crown and dignity, and returns to the state of a private man, and the people become free and superior, the power which they had in the interregnum, before they crowned him king, devolving to them again. But there are but few miscarriages which bring the matter to this state. After considering it well on all sides, I can find but two. Two cases there are, I say, whereby a king, *ipso facto,* becomes no king, and loses all power and regal authority over his people; which are also taken notice of by Winzerus.

"The first is, If he endeavour to overturn the government, that is, if he have a purpose and design to ruin the kingdom and commonwealth; as it is recorded of Nero, that he resolved to cut off the senate and people of Rome, lay the city waste with fire and sword, and then remove to some other place. — And of Caligula, that he openly declared, that he would be no longer a head to the people or senate, and that he had it in his thoughts to cut off the worthiest men of both ranks, and then retire to Alexandria; and he wished that the people had but one neck, that he might despatch them all at a blow. — Such designs as these, when any king harbours in his thoughts, and seriously promotes, he immediately gives up all care and thought of the commonwealth; and consequently forfeits the power of governing his subjects, as a master does the dominion over his slaves whom he hath abandoned."

§ 238. "The other case is, When a king makes himself the dependent of another, and subjects his kingdom which his ancestors left him, and the people put free into his hands, to the dominion of another: for however perhaps it may not be his intention to prejudice the people, yet because he has hereby lost the principal part of regal dignity, viz. to be next and immediately under God supreme in his kingdom; and also because he betrayed or forced his people, whose liberty he ought to have carefully preserved, into the power and dominion of a foreign nation. By this, as it were, alienation of his kingdom he himself loses the power he had in it before, without transferring any the least right to those on whom he would have bestowed it; and so by this act sets the people free, and leaves them at their own disposal. One example of this is to be found in the Scottish Annals."

§ 239. In these cases, Barclay, the great champion of absolute monarchy, is forced to allow that a king may be resisted, and ceases to be a king. That is, in short, not to multiply cases, in whatsoever he has no authority, there he is no king, and may be resisted: for wheresoever the authority ceases, the king ceases too, and becomes like other men who have no authority — And these two cases he instances differ little from those above-mentioned to be destructive to governments, only that he has omitted the principle from which his doctrine flows; and that is, the breach of trust, in not preserving the form of government agreed on, and in not intending the end of government itself, which is the public good and preservation of property. When a king has dethroned himself, and put himself in a state of war with his people, what shall hinder them from prosecuting him who is no king, as they would any other man, who has put himself into a state of war with them; Barclay and those of his opinion would do well to tell us. This farther I desire may be taken notice of out of Barclay, that he says, "The mischief that is designed them, the people may prevent before it be done: whereby he allows resistance when tyranny is but in design. Such designs as these (says he) when any king harbours in his thoughts and seriously promotes, he immediately gives up all care and thought of the commonwealth;" so that, according to him, the neglect of the public good is to be taken as an evidence of such design, or at least for a sufficient cause of resistance. And the reason of all he gives in these words, "Because he betrayed or forced his people, whose liberty he ought carefully to have preserved." What he adds, "into the power and dominion of a foreign nation," signifies nothing, the fault and forfeiture lying in the loss of their liberty, which he ought to have preserved, and not in any distinction of the persons to whose dominion they were subjected. The people's right is equally invaded, and their liberty lost, whether they are made slaves to any of their own, or a foreign nation; and in this lies the injury, and against this only have they the right of defence. And there are instances to be found in all countries, which show that it is not the change of nations in the persons of their governors, but the change of government, that gives the offence. Bilson, a bishop of our church, and a great stickler for the power and prerogative of princes, does, if I mistake not, in his treatise of Christian subjection, acknowledge that princes may forfeit their power, and their title to the obedience of their subjects; and if there needed authority in a case where reason is so plain, I could send my reader to Bracton, Fortescue, and the author of the Mirror, and others, writers that cannot be suspected to be ignorant of our government, or enemies to it. But I thought Hooker alone might be enough to satisfy those men, who relying on him for their ecclesiastical polity, are by a strange fate carried to deny those principles upon which he builds it. Whether they are herein made the tools of cunninger workmen, to pull down their own fabric, they were best look. This I am sure, their civil policy is so new, so dangerous, and so destructive to both rulers and people, that as former ages never could bear the broaching of it; so it may be hoped those to come, redeemed from the impositions of these Egyptian under-taskmasters, will abhor the memory of such servile flatterers, who, whilst it seemed to serve their turn, resolved all government into absolute tyranny, and would have all men born to, what their mean souls fitted them for, slavery.

§ 240. Here, it is like, the common question will be made, "Who shall be judge, whether the prince or legislative act contrary to their trust?" This, perhaps, ill-affected and factious men may spread amongst the people, when the prince only makes use of his due prerogative. To this I reply, "The people shall be judge;" for who shall be judge whether his trustee or deputy acts well, and according to the trust reposed in him, but he who deputes him, and must, by having deputed him, have still a power to discard him, when he fails in his trust? If this be reasonable in particular cases of private men, why should it be otherwise in that of the greatest moment, where the welfare of millions is concerned, and also where the evil, if not prevented, is greater, and the redress very difficult, dear, and dangerous?

§ 241. But farther, this question, ("Who shall be judge?") cannot mean, that there is no judge at all: for where there is no judicature on earth, to decide controversies amongst men, God in heaven is judge. He alone, it is true, is judge of the right. But every man is judge for himself, as in all other cases, so in this, whether another hath put himself into a state of war with him, and whether he should appeal to the supreme Judge, as Jephthah did.

§ 242. If a controversy arise betwixt a prince and some of the people, in a matter where the law is silent or doubtful, and the thing be of great conse-quence, I should think the proper umpire, in such a case, should be the body of the people: for in cases where the prince hath a trust reposed in him, and is dispensed from the common ordinary rules of the law; there, if any men find themselves aggrieved, and think the prince acts contrary to, or beyond that trust, who so proper to judge as the body of the people, (who, at first, lodged that trust in him) how far they meant it should extend? But if the prince, or whoever they be in the administration, decline that way of deter-mination, the appeal then lies nowhere but to Heaven; force between either persons, who have no known superior on earth, or which permits no appeal to a judge on earth, being properly a state of war, wherein the appeal lies only to Heaven; and in that state the injured party must judge for himself, when he will think fit to make use of that appeal, and put himself upon it.

§ 243. To conclude, The power that every individual gave the society, when he entered into it, can never revert to the individuals again, as long as the society lasts, but will always remain in the community; because without this there can be no community, no commonwealth, which is contrary to the original agreement: so also when the society hath placed the legislative in any assembly of men, to continue in them and their successors, with direction and authority for providing such successors, the legislative can never revert to the people whilst that government lasts; because, having provided a legislative with power to continue for ever, they have given up their political power to the legislative, and cannot resume it. But if they have set limits to the duration of their legislative, and made this supreme power in any person, or assembly, only temporary; or else, when by the miscarriages of those in authority it is forfeited; upon the forfeiture, or at the determination of the time set, it reverts to the society, and the people have a right to act as supreme, and continue the legislative in themselves; or erect a new form, or under the old form place it in new hands, as they think good.

A Letter Concerning Toleration

To the Reader

The ensuing letter concerning Toleration, first printed in Latin this very year, in Holland, has already been translated both into Dutch and French. So general and speedy an approbation may therefore bespeak its favourable reception in England. I think indeed there is no nation under heaven, in which so much has already been said upon that subject as ours. But yet certainly there is no people that stand in more need of having something further both said and done amongst them, in this point, than we do.

Our government has not only been partial in matters of religion, but those also who have suffered under that partiality, and have therefore endeavoured by their writings to vindicate their own rights and liberties, have for the most part done it upon narrow principles, suited only to the interests of their own sects.

This narrowness of spirit on all sides has undoubtedly been the principal occasion of our miseries and confusions. But whatever have been the occasions, it is now high time to seek for a thorough cure. We have need of more generous remedies than what have yet been made use of in our distemper. It is neither declarations of indulgence, nor acts of comprehension, such as have yet been practised or projected amongst us, that can do the work. The first will but palliate, the second increase our evil.

Absolute liberty, just and true liberty, equal and impartial liberty, is the thing that we stand in need of. Now, though this has indeed been much talked of, I doubt it has not been much understood; I am sure not at all practised, either by our governors towards the people in general, or by any dissenting parties of the people towards one another.

I cannot, therefore, but hope that this discourse, which treats of that subject, however briefly, yet more exactly than any we have yet seen, demonstrating both the equitableness and practicableness of the thing, will be esteemed highly seasonable by all men who have souls large enough to prefer the true interest of the public, before that of a party.

It is for the use of such as are already so spirited, or to inspire that spirit into those that are not, that I have translated it into our language. But the thing itself is so short, that it will not bear a longer preface. I leave it, therefore, to the consideration of my countrymen; and heartily wish they may make the use of it that it appears to be designed for.

A
Letter
Concerning
Toleration.

HONOURED SIR,

Since you are pleased to inquire what are my thoughts about the mutual toleration of Christians in their different professions of religion, I must needs answer you freely, that I esteem that toleration to be the chief characteristical mark of the true church. For whatsoever some people boast of the antiquity of places and names, or of the pomp of their outward worship; others, of the reformation of their discipline; all, of the orthodoxy of their faith, for every one is orthodox to himself: these things, and all others of this nature, are much rather marks of men's striving for power and empire over one another, than of the church of Christ. Let any one have ever so true a claim to all these things, yet if he be destitute of charity, meekness, and goodwill in general towards all mankind, even to those that are not Christians, he is certainly yet short of being a true Christian himself. "The kings of the Gentiles exercise lordship over them," said our Saviour to his disciples, but ye shall not be so, Luke xxii. 25, 26. The business of true religion is quite another thing. It is not instituted in order to the erecting an external pomp, nor to the obtaining of ecclesiastical dominion, nor to the exercising of compulsive force; but to the regulating of men's lives according to the rules of virtue and piety. Whosoever will list himself under the banner of Christ, must, in the first place, and above all things, make war upon his own lusts and vices. It is in vain for any man to usurp the name of Christian, without holiness of life, purity of manners, and benignity and meekness of spirit. "Let every one that nameth the name of Christ depart from iniquity," 2 Tim. ii. 19. "Thou, when thou art converted, strengthen thy brethren," said our Lord to Peter, Luke xxii. 32. It would indeed be very hard for one that appears careless about his own salvation, to persuade me that he were extremely concerned for mine. For it is impossible that those should sincerely and heartily apply themselves to make other people Christians, who have not really embraced the Christian religion in their own hearts. If the Gospel and the apostles may be credited, no man can be a Christian without charity, and without that faith which works, not by force, but by love. Now I appeal to the consciences of those that persecute, torment, destroy, and kill other men upon pretence of religion, whether they do it out of friendship and kindness towards them, or no: and I shall then indeed, and not till then, believe they do so, when I shall see those fiery zealots correcting, in the same manner, their friends and familiar acquaintance, for the manifest sins they commit against the precepts of the Gospel; when I shall see them prosecute with fire and sword the members of their own communion that are tainted with enormous vices, and without amendment are in danger of eternal perdition; and when I shall see them thus express their love and desire of the salvation of their souls by the infliction of torments, and exercise of all manner of cruelties. For if it be out of a principle of charity, as they pretend, and love to men's souls, that they deprive them of their estates, maim them with corporal punishments, starve and torment them in noisome prisons, and in the end even take away their lives; I say, if all this be done merely to make men Christians, and procure their salvation, why then do they suffer "whoredom, fraud, malice, and such like enormities," which, according to the apostle, Rom.i. manifestly relish of heathenish corruption, to predominate so much and abound amongst their flocks and people? These, and such like things, are certainly more contrary to the glory of God, to the purity of the church, and to the salvation of souls, than any conscientious dissent from ecclesiastical decision, or separation from public worship, whilst accompanied with innocency of life. Why then does this burning zeal for God, for the church, and for the salvation of souls; burning, I say, literally with fire and faggot; pass by those moral vices and wickednesses, without any chastisement, which are acknowledged by all men to be diametrically opposite to the profession of Christianity, and bend all its nerves either to the introducing of ceremonies, or to the establishment of opinions, which for the most part are about nice and intricate matters, that exceed the capacity of ordinary understandings? Which of the parties contending about these things is in the right, which of them is guilty of schism, or heresy, whether those that domineer or those that suffer, will then at last be manifest, when the cause of their separation comes to be judged of. He certainly that follows Christ, embraces his doctrine, and bears his yoke, though he forsake both father and mother, separate from the public assemblies and ceremonies of his country, or whomsoever, or whatsoever else he relinquishes, will not then be judged an heretic.

Now, though the divisions that are amongst sects should be allowed to be ever so obstructive of the salvation of souls, yet, nevertheless, "adultery, fornication, uncleanness, lasciviousness, idolatry, and such like things, cannot be denied to be works of the flesh;" concerning which the apostle has expressly declared, that "they who do them shall not inherit the kingdom of God," Gal. v. 21. Whosoever, therefore, is sincerely solicitous about the kingdom of God, and thinks it his duty to endeavour the enlargement of it amongst men, ought to apply himself with no less care and industry to the rooting out of these immoralities, than to the extirpation of sects. But if any one do otherwise, and, whilst he is cruel and implacable towards those that differ from him in opinion, he be indulgent to such iniquities and immoralities as are unbecoming the name of a Christian, let such a one talk ever so much of the church, he plainly demonstrates by his actions, that it is another kingdom he aims at, and not the advancement of the kingdom of God.

That any man should think fit to cause another man, whose salvation he heartily desires, to expire in torments, and that even in an unconverted estate, would, I confess, seem very strange to me, and, I think, to any other also. But nobody, surely, will ever believe that such a carriage can proceed from charity, love, or goodwill. If any one maintain that men ought to be compelled by fire and sword to profess certain doctrines, and conform to this or that exterior worship, without any regard had unto their morals; if any one endeavour to convert those that are erroneous unto the faith, by forcing them to profess things that they do not believe, and allowing them to practise things that the Gospel does not permit; it cannot be doubted, indeed, that such a one is desirous to have a numerous assembly joined in the same profession with himself; but that he principally intends by those means to compose a truly Christian church, is altogether incredible. It is not therefore to be wondered at, if those who do not really contend for the advancement of the true religion, and of the church of Christ, make use of arms that do not belong to the Christian warfare. If, like the Captain of our salvation, they sincerely desired the good of souls, they would tread in the steps and follow the perfect example of that Prince of Peace, who sent out his soldiers to the subduing of nations, and gathering them into his church, not armed with the sword, or other instruments of force, but prepared with the Gospel of peace, and with the exemplary holiness of their conversation. This was his method. Though if infidels were to be converted by force, if those that are either blind or obstinate were to be drawn off from their errors by armed soldiers, we know very well that it was much more easy for him to do it with armies of heavenly legions, than for any son of the church, how potent soever, with all his dragoons.

The toleration of those that differ from others in matters of religion, is so agreeable to the Gospel of Jesus Christ, and to the genuine reason of mankind, that it seems monstrous for men to be so blind, as not to perceive the necessity and advantage of it, in so clear a light. I will not here tax the pride and ambition of some, the passion and uncharitable zeal of others. These are faults from which human affairs can perhaps scarce ever be perfectly freed; but yet such as nobody will bear the plain imputation of, without covering them with some specious colour; and so pretend to commendation, whilst they are carried away by their own irregular passions. But, however, that some may not colour their spirit of persecution and unchristian cruelty with a pretence of care of the public weal, and observation of the laws, and that others, under pretence of religion, may not seek impunity for their libertinism and licentiousness; in a word, that none may impose either upon himself or others, by the pretences of loyalty and obedience to the prince, or of tenderness and sincerity in the worship of God; I esteem it above all things necessary to distinguish exactly the business of civil government from that of religion, and to settle the just bounds that lie between the one and the other. If this be not done, there can be no end put to the controversies that will be always arising between those that have, or at least pretend to have, on the one side, a concernment for the interest of men's souls, and, on the other side, a care of the commonwealth.

The commonwealth seems to me to be a society of men constituted only for the procuring, preserving, and advancing their own civil interests.

Civil interest I call life, liberty, health, and indolency of body; and the possession of outward things, such as money, lands, houses, furniture, and the like.

It is the duty of the civil magistrate, by the impartial execution of equal laws, to secure unto all the people in general, and to every one of his subjects in particular, the just possession of these things belonging to this life. If any one presume to violate the laws of public justice and equity, established for the preservation of these things, his presumption is to be checked by the fear of punishment, consisting in the deprivation or diminution of those civil interests, or goods, which otherwise he might and ought to enjoy. But seeing no man does willingly suffer himself to be punished by the deprivation of any part of his goods, and much less of his liberty or life, therefore is the magistrate armed with the force and strength of all his subjects, in order to the punishment of those that violate any other man's rights.

Now that the whole jurisdiction of the magistrate reaches only to these civil concernments; and that all civil power, right, and dominion, is bounded and confined to the only care of promoting these things; and that it neither can nor ought in any manner to be extended to the salvation of souls; these following considerations seem unto me abundantly to demonstrate.

First, Because the care of souls is not committed to the civil magistrate, any more than to other men. It is not committed unto him, I say, by God; because it appears not that God has ever given any such authority to one man over another, as to compel any one to his religion. Nor can any power be vested in the magistrate by the consent of the people; because no man can so far abandon the care of his own salvation as blindly to leave it to the choice of any other, whether prince or subject, to prescribe to him what faith or worship he shall embrace. For no man can, if he would, conform his faith to the dictates of another. All the life and power of true religion consists in the inward and full persuasion of the mind; and faith is not faith without believing. Whatever profession we make, to whatever outward worship we conform, if we are not fully satisfied in our own mind that the one is true, and the other well-pleasing unto God, such profession and such practice, far from being any furtherance, are indeed great obstacles to our salvation. For in this manner, instead of expiating other sins by the exercise of religion, I say, in offering thus unto God Almighty such a worship as we esteem to be displeasing unto him, we add unto the number of our other sins, those also of hypocrisy, and contempt of his Divine Majesty.

In the second place. The care of souls cannot belong to the civil magistrate, because his power consists only in outward force: but true and saving religion consists in the inward persuasion of the mind, without which nothing can be acceptable to God. And such is the nature of the understanding, that it cannot be compelled to the belief of any thing by outward force. Confiscation of estate, imprisonment, torments, nothing of that nature can have any such efficacy as to make men change the inward judgment that they have framed of things.

It may indeed be alleged that the magistrate may make use of arguments, and thereby draw the heterodox into the way of truth, and procure their salvation. I grant it; but this is common to him with other men. In teaching, instructing, and redressing the erroneous by reason, he may certainly do what becomes any good man to do. Magistracy does not oblige him to put off either humanity or Christianity. But it is one thing to persuade, another to command; one thing to press with arguments, another with penalties. This the civil power alone has a right to do; to the other, good-will is authority enough. Every man has commission to admonish, exhort, convince another of error, and by reasoning to draw him into truth: but to give laws, receive obedience, and compel with the sword, belongs to none but the magistrate. And upon this ground I affirm, that the magistrate's power extends not to the establishing of any articles of faith, or forms of worship, by the force of his laws. For laws are of no force at all without penalties, and penalties in this case are absolutely impertinent; because they are not proper to convince the mind. Neither the profession of any articles of faith, nor the conformity to any outward form of worship, as has been already said, can be available to the salvation of souls, unless the truth of the one, and the acceptableness of the other unto God, be thoroughly believed by those that so profess and practise. But penalties are no ways capable to produce such belief. It is only light and evidence that can work a change in men's opinions; and that light can in no manner proceed from corporal sufferings, or any other outward penalties.

In the third place, The care of the salvation of men's souls cannot belong to the magistrate; because, though the rigour of laws and the force of penalties were capable to convince and change men's minds, yet would not that help at all to the salvation of their souls. For, there being but one truth, one way to heaven; what hopes is there that more men would be led into it, if they had no other rule to follow but the religion of the court, and were put under a necessity to quit the light of their own reason, to oppose the dictates of their own consciences, and blindly to resign up themselves to the will of their governors, and to the religion, which either ignorance, ambition, or superstition had chanced to establish in the countries where they were born? In the variety and contradiction of opinions in religion, wherein the princes of the world are as much divided as in their secular interests, the narrow way would be much straitened; one country alone would be in the right, and all the rest of the world put under an obligation of following their princes in the ways that lead to destruction: and that which heightens the absurdity, and very ill suits the notion of a Deity, men would owe their eternal happiness or misery to the places of their nativity.

These considerations, to omit many others that might have been urged to the same purpose, seem unto me sufficient to conclude, that all the power of civil government relates only to men's civil interests, is confined to the care of the things of this world, and hath nothing to do with the world to come.

Let us now consider what a church is. A church then I take to be a voluntary society of men, joining themselves together of their own accord, in order to the public worshipping of God, in such a manner as they judge acceptable to him, and effectual to the salvation of their souls.

I say, it is a free and voluntary society. Nobody is born a member of any church; otherwise the religion of parents would descend unto children, by the same right of inheritance as their temporal estates, and every one would hold his faith by the same tenure he does his lands; than which nothing can be imagined more absurd. Thus therefore that matter stands. No man by nature is bound unto any particular church or sect, but every one joins himself voluntarily to that society in which he believes he has found that profession and worship which is truly acceptable to God. The hopes of salvation, as it was the only cause of his entrance into that communion, so it can be the only reason of his stay there. For if afterwards he discover any thing either erroneous in the doctrine, or incongruous in the worship of that society to which he has joined himself, why should it not be as free for him to go out as it was to enter? No member of a religious society can be tied with any other bonds but what proceed from the certain expectation of eternal life. A church then is a society of members voluntarily uniting to this end.

It follows now that we consider what is the power of this church, and unto what laws it is subject.

Forasmuch as no society, how free soever, or upon whatsoever slight occasion instituted, (whether of philosophers for learning, of merchants for commerce, or of men of leisure for mutual conversation and discourse) no church or company, I say, can in the least subsist and hold together, but will presently dissolve and break to pieces, unless it be regulated by some laws, and the members all consent to observe some order. Place and time of meeting must be agreed on; rules for admitting and excluding members must be established; distinction of officers, and putting things into a regular course, and such like, cannot be omitted. But since the joining together of several members into this church-society, as has already been demonstrated, is absolutely free and spontaneous, it necessarily follows, that the right of making its laws can belong to none but the society itself, or at least, which is the same thing, to those whom the society by common consent has authorized thereunto.

Some perhaps may object, that no such society can be said to be a true church, unless it have in it a bishop, or presbyter, with ruling authority derived from the very apostles, and continued down unto the present time by an uninterrupted succession.

To these I answer. In the first place, Let them show me the edict by which Christ has imposed that law upon his church. And let not any man think me impertinent, if, in a thing of this consequence, I require that the terms of that edict be very express and positive. — For the promise he has made us, that "wheresoever two or three are gathered together in his name, he will be in the midst of them," Matth. xviii. 20, seems to imply the contrary. Whether such an assembly want any thing necessary to a true church, pray do you consider. Certain I am, that nothing can be there wanting unto the salvation of souls, which is sufficient for our purpose.

Next, pray observe how great have always been the divisions amongst even those who lay so much stress upon the divine institution, and continued succession of a certain order of rulers in the church. Now their very dissension unavoidably puts us upon a necessity of deliberating, and consequently allows a liberty of choosing that, which upon consideration we prefer.

And, in the last place, I consent that these men have a ruler of their church, established by such a long series of succession as they judge necessary, provided I may have liberty at the same time to join myself to that society, in which I am persuaded those things are to be found which are necessary to the salvation of my soul. In this manner ecclesiastical liberty will be preserved on all sides, and no man will have a legislator imposed upon him, but whom himself has chosen.

But since men are so solicitous about the true church, I would only ask them here by the way, if it be not more agreeable to the church of Christ to make the conditions of her communion consist in such things, and such things only, as the Holy Spirit has in the holy Scriptures declared, in express words, to be necessary to salvation? I ask, I say, whether this be not more agreeable to the church of Christ, than for men to impose their own inventions and interpretations upon others, as if they were of divine authority; and to establish by ecclesiatical laws, as absolutely necessary to the profession of Christianity such things as the holy Scriptures do either not mention, or at least not expressly command? Whosoever requires those things in order to ecclesiastical communion, which Christ does not require in order to life eternal, he may perhaps indeed constitute a society accommodated to his own opinion, and his own advantage; but how that can be called the church of Christ, which is established upon laws that are not his, and which excludes such persons from its communion as he will one day receive into the kingdom of heaven, I understand not. But this being not a proper place to inquire into the marks of the true church, I will only mind those that contend so earnestly for the decrees of their own society, and that cry out continually the CHURCH, the CHURCH, with as much noise, and perhaps upon the same principle, as the Ephesian silversmiths did for their Diana; this, I say, I desire to mind them of, that the Gospel frequently declares, that the true disciples of Christ must suffer persecution; but that the church of Christ should persecute others, and force others by fire and sword to embrace her faith and doctrine, I could never yet find in any of the books of the New Testament.

The end of a religious society, as has already been said, is the public worship of God, and by means thereof the acquisition of eternal life. All discipline ought therefore to tend to that end, and all ecclesiastical laws to be thereunto confined. Nothing ought, nor can be transacted in this society, relating to the possession of civil and worldly goods. No force is here to be made use of, upon any occasion whatsoever: for force belongs wholly to the civil magistrate, and the possession of all outward goods is subject to his jurisdiction.

But it may be asked, by what means then shall ecclesiastical laws be established, if they must be thus destitute of all compulsive power? I answer they must be established by means suitable to the nature of such things, whereof the external profession and observation, if not proceeding from a thorough conviction and approbation of the mind, is altogether useless and unprofitable. The arms by which the members of this society are to be kept within their duty, are exhortations, admonitions, and advice. If by these means the offenders will not be reclaimed, and the erroneous convinced, there remains nothing farther to be done, but that such stubborn and obstinate persons, who give no ground to hope for their reformation, should be cast out and separated from the society. This is the last and utmost force of ecclesiastical authority: no other punishment can thereby be inflicted, than that the relation ceasing between the body and the member which is cut off, the person so condemned ceases to be a part of that church.

These things being thus determined, let us inquire, in the next place, how far the duty of toleration extends, and what is required from every one by it.

And first, I hold, that no church is bound by the duty of toleration to retain any such person in her bosom, as after admonition continues obstinately to offend against the laws of the society. For these being the condition of communion, and the bond of society, if the breach of them were permitted without any animadversion, the society would immediately be thereby dissolved. But nevertheless, in all such cases care is to be taken that the sentence of excommunication, and the execution thereof, carry with it no rough usage, of word or action, whereby the ejected person may any ways be damnified in body or estate. For all force, as has often been said, belongs only to the magistrate, nor ought any private persons, at any time, to use force; unless it be in self-defence against unjust violence. Excommunication neither does nor can deprive the excommunicated person of any of those civil goods that he formerly possessed. All those things belong to the civil government, and are under the magistrate's protection. The whole force of excommunication consists only in this, that the resolution of the society in that respect being declared, the union that was between the body and some member, comes thereby to be dissolved; and that relation ceasing, the participation of some certain things, which the society communicated to its members, and unto which no man has any civil right, comes also to cease. For there is no civil injury done unto the excommunicated person, by the church minister's refusing him that bread and wine, in the celebration of the Lord's supper, which was not bought with his, but other men's money.

Secondly: No private person has any right in any manner to prejudice another person in his civil enjoyments, because he is of another church or religion. All the rights and franchises that belong to him as a man, or as a denison, are inviolably to be preserved to him. These are not the business of religion. No violence nor injury is to be offered him, whether he be Christian or pagan. Nay, we must not content ourselves with the narrow measures of bare justice: charity, bounty, and liberality must be added to it. This the Gospel enjoins, this reason directs, and this that natural fellowship we are born into requires of us. If any man err from the right way, it is his own misfortune, no injury to thee: nor therefore art thou to punish him in the things of this life, because thou supposest he will be miserable in that which is to come.

What I say concerning the mutual toleration of private persons differing from one another in religion, I understand also of particular churches; which stand as it were in the same relation to each other as private persons among themselves; nor has any one of them any manner of jurisdiction over any other, no, not even when the civil magistrate, as it sometimes happens, come to be of this or the other communion. For the civil government can give no new right to the church, nor the church to the civil government. So that whether the magistrate join himself to any church, or separate from it, the church remains always as it was before, a free and voluntary society. It neither acquires the power of the sword by the magistrate's coming to it, nor does it lose the right of instruction and excommunication by his going from it. This is the fundamental and immutable right of a spontaneous society, that is has to remove any of its members who transgress the rules of its institution: but it cannot, by the accession of any new members, acquire any right of jurisdiction over those that are not joined with it. And therefore peace, equity, and friendship, are always mutually to be observed by particular churches, in the same manner as by private persons, without any pretence of superiority or jurisdiction over one another.

That the thing may be made yet clearer by an example; let us suppose two churches, the one of Arminians, the other of Calvinists, residing in the city of Constantinople. Will any one say, that either of these churches has right to deprive the members of the other of their estates and liberty, as we see practised elsewhere, because of their differing from it in some doctrines or ceremonies; whilst the Turks in the meanwhile silently stand by, and laugh to see with what inhuman cruelty Christians thus rage against Christians? But if one of these churches hath this power of treating the other ill, I ask which of them it is to whom that power belongs, and by what right? It will be answered, undoubtedly, that it is the orthodox church which has the right of authority over the erroneous or heretical. This is, in great and specious words, to say just nothing at all. For every church is orthodox to itself; to others, erroneous or heretical. Whatsoever any church believes, it believes to be true; and the contrary thereunto it pronounces to be error. So that the controversy between these churches about the truth of their doctrines, and the purity of their worship, is on both sides equal; nor is there any judge, either at Constantinople, or elsewhere upon earth, by whose sentence it can be determined. The decision of that question belongs only to the Supreme Judge of all men, to whom also alone belongs the punishment of the erroneous. In the mean while, let those men consider how heinously they sin, who, adding injustice, if not to their error, yet certainly to their pride, do rashly and arrogantly take upon them to misuse the servants of another master, who are not at all accountable to them.

Nay, further: if it could be manifest which of these two dissenting churches were in the right way, there would not accrue thereby unto the orthodox any right of destroying the other. For churches have neither any jurisdiction in worldly matters, nor are fire and sword any proper instruments wherewith to convince men's minds of error, and inform them of the truth. Let us suppose, nevertheless, that the civil magistrate is inclined to favour one of them, and to put his sword into their hands, that, by his consent, they might chastise the dissenters as they pleased. Will any man say, that any right can be derived unto a Christian church, over its brethren, from a Turkish emperor? An infidel, who has himself no authority to punish Christians for the articles of their faith, cannot confer such an authority upon any society of Christians, nor give unto them a right which he has not himself. This would be the case at Constantinople. And the reason of the thing is the same in any Christian kingdom. The civil power is the same in every place: nor can that power, in the hands of a Christian prince, confer any greater authority upon the church, than in the hands of a heathen; which is to say, just none at all.

Nevertheless, it is worthy to be observed, and lamented, that the most violent of these defenders of the truth, the opposers of error, the exclaimers against schism, do hardly ever let loose this their zeal for God, with which they are so warmed and inflamed, unless where they have the civil magistrate on their side. But so soon as ever court favour has given them the better end of the staff, and they begin to feel themselves the stronger; then presently peace and charity are to be laid aside: otherwise they are religiously to be observed. Where they have not the power to carry on persecution, and to become masters, there they desire to live upon fair terms, and preach up toleration. When they are not strengthened with the civil power, then they can bear most patiently, and unmovedly, the contagion of idolatry, superstition, and heresy, in their neighbourhood; of which, on other occasions, the interest of religion makes them to be extremely apprehensive. They do not forwardly attack those errors which are in fashion at court, or are countenanced by the government. Here they can be content to spare their arguments: which yet, with their leave, is the only right method of propagating truth; which has no such way of prevailing, as when strong arguments and good reason are joined with the softness of civility and good usage.

Nobody therefore, in fine, neither single persons, nor churches, nay, nor even commonwealths, have any just title to invade the civil rights and worldly goods of each other, upon pretence of religion. Those that are of another opinion, would do well to consider with themselves how pernicious a seed of discord and war, how powerful a provocation to endless hatreds, rapines, and slaughters, they thereby furnish unto mankind. No peace and security, no, not so much as common friendship, can ever be established or preserved amongst men, so long as this opinion prevails, "that dominion is founded in grace, and that religion is to be propagated by force of arms."

In the third place: Let us see what the duty of toleration requires from those who are distinguished from the rest of mankind, from the laity, as they please to call us, by some ecclesiastical character and office; whether they be bishops, priests, presbyters, ministers, or however else dignified or distinguished. It is not my business to inquire here into the original of the power or dignity of the clergy. This only I say, that whencesoever their authority be sprung, since it is ecclesiastical, it ought to be confined within the bounds of the church, nor can it in any manner be extended to civil affairs; because the church itself is a thing absolutely separate and distinct from the commonwealth. The boundaries on both sides are fixed and immoveable. He jumbles heaven and earth together, the things most remote and opposite, who mixes these societies, which are, in their original, end, business, and in every thing, perfectly distinct, and infinitely different from each other. No man therefore, with whatsoever ecclesiastical office he be dignified, can deprive another man, that is not of his church and faith, either of liberty, or of any part of his worldly goods, upon the account of that difference which is between them in religion. For whatsoever is not lawful to the whole church cannot, by any ecclesiastical right, become lawful to any of its members.

But this is not all. It is not enough that ecclesiastical men abstain from violence and rapine, and all manner of persecution. He that pretends to be a successor of the apostles, and takes upon him the office of teaching, is obliged also to admonish his hearers of the duties of peace and good-will towards all men; as well towards the erroneous as the orthodox; towards those that differ from them in faith and worship, as well as towards those that agree with them therein: and he ought industriously to exhort all men, whether private persons or magistrates, if any such there be in his church, to charity, meekness, and toleration; and diligently endeavour to allay and temper all that heat, and unreasonable averseness of mind, which either any man's fiery zeal for his own sect, or the craft of others, has kindled against dissenters. I will not undertake to represent how happy and how great would be the fruit, both in church and state, if the pulpits every where sounded with this doctrine of peace and toleration; lest I should seem to reflect too severely upon those men whose dignity I desire not to detract from, nor would have it diminished either by others or themselves. But this I say, that thus it ought to be. And if any one that professes himself to be a minister of the word of God, a preacher of the Gospel of peace, teach otherwise; he either understands not, or neglects the business of his calling, and shall one day give account thereof unto the Prince of Peace. If Christians are to be admonished that they abstain from all manner of revenge, even after repeated provocations and multiplied injuries; how much more ought they who suffer nothing, who have had no harm done them, to forbear violence, and abstain from all manner of ill usage towards those from whom they have received none! This caution and temper they ought certainly to use towards those who mind only their own business, and are solicitous for nothing but that, whatever men think of them, they may worship God in that manner which they are persuaded is acceptable to him, and in which they have the strongest hopes of eternal salvation. In private domestic affairs, in the management of estates, in the conservation of bodily health, every man may consider what suits his own conveniency, and follow what course he likes best. No man complains of the ill management of his neighbour's affairs. No man is angry with another for an error committed in sowing his land, or in marrying his daughter. Nobody corrects a spendthrift for consuming his substance in taverns. Let any man pull down, or build, or make whatsoever expenses he pleases, nobody murmurs, nobody controls him; he has his liberty. But if any man do not frequent the church, if he do not there conform his behaviour exactly to the accustomed ceremonies, or if he brings not his children to be initiated in the sacred mysteries of this or the other congregation; this immediately causes an uproar, and the neighbourhood is filled with noise and clamour. Every one is ready to be the avenger of so great a crime. And the zealots hardly have patience to refrain from violence and rapine, so long till the cause be heard, and the poor man be, according to form, condemned to the loss of liberty, goods, or life. Oh that our ecclesiastical orators, of every sect, would apply themselves, with all the strength of argument that they are able, to the confounding of men's errors! But let them spare their persons. Let them not supply their want of reasons with the instruments of force, which belong to another jurisdiction, and do ill become a churchman's hands. Let them not call in the magistrate's authority to the aid of their eloquence or learning; lest perhaps, whilst they pretend only love for the truth, this their intemperate zeal, breathing nothing but fire and sword, betray their ambition, and show that what they desire is temporal dominion. For it will be very difficult to persuade men of sense, that he, who with dry eyes, and satisfaction of mind, can deliver his brother unto the executioner, to be burnt alive, does sincerely and heartily concern himself to save that brother from the flames of hell in the world to come.

In the last place. Let us now consider what is the magistrate's duty in the business of toleration: which is certainly very considerable.

We have already proved, that the care of souls does not belong to the magistrate: not a magisterial care, I mean, if I may so call it, which consists in prescribing by laws, and compelling by punishments. But a charitable care, which consists in teaching, admonishing, and persuading, cannot be denied unto any man. The care therefore of every man's soul belongs unto himself, and is to be left unto himself. But what if he neglect the care of his soul? I answer, what if he neglect the care of his health, or of his estate; which things are nearlier related to the government of the magistrate than the other? Will the magistrate provide by an express law, that such an one shall not become poor or sick? Laws provide, as much as is possible, that the goods and health of subjects be not injured by the fraud or violence of others; they do not guard them from the negligence or ill husbandry of the possessors themselves. No man can be forced to be rich or healthful, whether he will or no. Nay, God himself will not save men against their wills. Let us suppose, however, that some prince were desirous to force his subjects to accumulate riches, or to preserve the health and strength of their bodies. Shall it be provided by law, that they must consult none but Roman physicians, and shall every one be bound to live according to their prescriptions? What, shall no potion, no broth be taken, but what is prepared either in the Vatican, suppose, or in a Geneva shop? Or to make these subjects rich, shall they all be obliged by law to become merchants, or musicians?

Or, shall every one turn victualler, or smith, because there are some that maintain their families plentifully, and grow rich in those professions? But it may be said, there are a thousand ways to wealth, but one only way to heaven. It is well said indeed, especially by those that plead for compelling men into this or the other way; for if there were several ways that lead thither, there would not be so much as a pretence left for compulsion. But now, if I be marching on with my utmost vigour, in that way which, according to the sacred geography, leads straight to Jerusalem; why am I beaten and ill used by others, because, perhaps, I wear not buskins; because my hair is not of the right cut; because, perhaps, I have not been dipt in the right fashion; because I eat flesh upon the road, or some other food which agrees with my stomach; because I avoid certain by-ways, which seem unto me to lead into briars or precipices; because, amongst the several paths that are in the same road, I choose that to walk in which seems to be the straightest and cleanest; because I avoid to keep company with some travellers that are less grave, and others that are more sour than they ought to be; or in fine, because I follow a guide that either is, or is not, clothed in white, and crowned with a mitre? Certainly, if we consider right, we shall find that for the most part they are such frivolous things as these, that, without any prejudice to religion or the salvation of souls, if not accompanied with superstition or hypocrisy, might either be observed or omitted; I say, they are such like things as these, which breed implacable enmities among Christian brethren, who are all agreed in the substantial and truly fundamental part of religion.

But let us grant unto these zealots, who condemn all things that are not of their mode, that from these circumstances arise different ends. What shall we conclude from thence? There is only one of these which is the true way to eternal happiness. But, in this great variety of ways that men follow, it is still doubted which is this right one. Now, neither the care of the commonwealth, nor the right of enacting laws, does discover this way that leads to heaven more certainly to the magistrate, than every private man's search and study discovers it unto himself. I have a weak body, sunk under a languishing disease, for which I suppose there is only one remedy, but that unknown: does it therefore belong unto the magistrate to prescribe me a remedy, because there is but one, and because it is unknown? Because there is but one way for me to escape death, will it therefore be safe for me to do whatsoever the magistrate ordains? Those things that every man ought sincerely to inquire into himself, and by meditation, study, search, and his own endeavours, attain the knowledge of, cannot be looked upon as the perculiar profession of any sort of men. Princes, indeed, are born superior unto other men in power, but in nature equal. Neither the right, nor the art of ruling, does necessarily carry along with it the certain knowledge of other things; and least of all of the true religion; for if it were so, how could it come to pass that the lords of the earth should differ so vastly as they do in religious matters? But let us grant that it is probable the way to eternal life may be better known by a prince than by his subjects; or, at least, that in this incertitude of things, the safest and most commodious way for private persons is to follow his dictates. You will say, what then? If he should bid you follow merchandize for your livelihood, would you decline that course, for fear it should not succeed? I answer, I would turn merchant upon the prince's command, because in case I should have ill success in trade, he is abundantly able to make up my loss some other way. If it be true, as he pretends, that he desires I should thrive and grow rich, he can set me up again when unsuccessful voyages have broke me. But this is not the case in the things that regard the life to come. If there I take a wrong course, if in that respect I am once undone, it is not in the magistrate's power to repair my loss, to ease my suffering, or to restore me in any measure, much less entirely, to a good estate. What security can be given for the kingdom of heaven?

Perhaps some will say, that they do not suppose this infallible judgment, that all men are bound to follow in the affairs of religion, to be in the civil magistrate, but in the church. What the church has determined, that the civil magistrate orders to be observed; and he provides by his authority, that nobody shall either act or believe, in the business of religion, otherwise than the church teaches; so that the judgment of those things is in the church. The magistrate himself yields obedience thereunto, and requires the like obedience from others. I answer, Who sees not how frequently the name of the church, which was so venerable in the time of the apostles, has been made use of to throw dust in people's eyes, in following ages? But, however, in the present case it helps us not. The one only narrow way which leads to heaven is not better known to the magistrate than to private persons, and therefore I cannot safely take him for my guide, who may probably be as ignorant of the way as myself, and who certainly is less concerned for my salvation than I myself am. Amongst so many kings of the Jews, how many of them were there whom any Israelite, thus blindly following, had not fallen into idolatry, and thereby into destruction? Yet, nevertheless, you bid me be of good courage, and tell me that all is now safe and secure, because the magistrate does not now enjoin the observance of his own decrees in matters of religion, but only the decrees of the church. Of what church, I beseech you? Of that which certainly likes him best. As if he that compels me by laws and penalties to enter into this or the other church, did not interpose his own judgment in the matter. What difference is there whether he lead me himself, or deliver me over to be led by others? I depend both ways upon his will, and it is he that determines both ways of my eternal state. Would an Israelite, that had worshipped Baal upon the command of his king, have been in any better condition, because somebody had told him that the king ordered nothing in religion upon his own head, nor commanded any thing to be done by his subjects in divine worship, but what was approved by the counsel of priests, and declared to be of divine right by the doctors of the church? If the religion of any church become, therefore, true and saving, because the head of that sect, the prelates and priests, and those of that tribe, do all of them, with all their might, extol and praise it; what religion can ever be accounted erroneous, false, and destructive? I am doubtful concerning the doctrine of the Socinians, I am suspicious of the way of worship practised by the Papists or Lutherans; will it be ever a jot the safer for me to join either unto the one or the other of those churches, upon the magistrate's command, because he commands nothing in religion but by the authority and counsel of the doctors of that church?

But to speak the truth, we must acknowledge that the church, if a convention of clergymen, making canons, must be called by that name, is for the most part more apt to be influenced by the court, than the court by the church. How the church was under the vicissitude of orthodox and Arian emperors is very well known. Or if those things be too remote, our modern English history affords us fresher examples, in the reigns of Henry VIII. Edward VI. Mary, and Elizabeth, how easily and smoothly the clergy changed their decrees, their articles of faith, their form of worship, every thing, according to the inclination of those kings and queens. Yet were those kings and queens of such different minds, in points of religion, and enjoined thereupon such different things, that no man in his wits, I had almost said none but an atheist, will presume to say that any sincere and upright worshipper of God could, with a safe conscience, obey their several decrees. To conclude, it is the same thing whether a king that prescribes laws to another man's religion pretend to do it by his own judgment, or by the ecclesiastical authority and advice of others. The decisions of churchmen, whose differences and disputes are sufficiently known, cannot be any sounder or safer than his nor can all their suffrages joined together add any new strength unto the civil power. Though this also must be taken notice of, that princes seldom have any regard to the suffrages of ecclesiastics that are not favourers of their own faith and way of worship.

But after all, the principal consideration, and which absolutely determines this controversy, is this: although the magistrate's opinion in religion be sound, and the way that he appoints be truly evangelical, yet if I be not thoroughly persuaded thereof in my own mind, there will be no safety for me in following it. No way whatsoever that I shall walk in against the dictates of my conscience, will ever bring me to the mansions of the blessed. I may grow rich by an art that I take not delight in; I may be cured of some disease by remedies that I have not faith in; but I cannot be saved by a religion that I distrust, and by a worship that I abhor. It is in vain for an unbeliever to take up the outward show of another man's profession. Faith only, and inward sincerity, are the things that procure acceptance with God. The most likely and most approved remedy can have no effect upon the patient, if his stomach reject it as soon as taken; and you will in vain cram a medicine down a sick man's throat, which his particular constitution will be sure to turn into poison. In a word, whatsoever may be doubtful in religion, yet this at least is certain, that no religion, which I believe not to be true, can be either true or profitable unto me. In vain, therefore, do princes compel their subjects to come into their church-communion, under pretence of saving their souls. If they believe, they will come of their own accord; if they believe not, their coming will nothing avail them. How great, soever, in fine, may be the pretence of good-will and charity, and concern for the salvation of men's souls, men cannot be forced to be saved whether they will or no; and therefore, when all is done, they must be left to their own consciences.

Having thus at length freed men from all dominion over one another in matters of religion, let us now consider what they are to do. All men know and acknowledge that God ought to be publicly worshipped. Why otherwise do they compel one another unto the public assemblies? Men, therefore, constituted in this liberty are to enter into some religious society, that they may meet together, not only for mutual edification, but to own to the world that they worship God, and offer unto his divine majesty such service as they themselves are not ashamed of, and such as they think not unworthy of him, nor unacceptable to him; and finally, that by the purity of doctrine, holiness of life, and decent form of worship, they may draw others unto the love of the true religion, and perform such others things in religion as cannot be done by each private man apart.

These religious societies I call churches: and these I say the magistrate ought to tolerate: for the business of these assemblies of the people is nothing but what is lawful for every man in particular to take care of; I mean the salvation of their souls: nor, in this case, is there any difference between the national church and other separated congregations.

But as in every church there are two things especially to be considered; the outward form and rites of worship, and the doctrines and articles of faith; these things must be handled each distinctly, that so the whole matter of toleration may the more clearly be understood.

Concerning outward worship, I say, in the first place, that the magistrate has no power to enforce by law, either in his own church, or much less in another, the use of any rites or ceremonies whatsoever in the worship of God. And this, not only because these churches are free societies, but because whatsoever is practised in the worship of God is only so far justifiable as it is believed by those that practise it to be acceptable unto him. — Whatsoever is not done with that assurance of faith, is neither well in itself, nor can it be acceptable to God. To impose such things, therefore, upon any people, contrary to their own judgment, is, in effect, to command them to offend God; which, considering that the end of all religion is to please him, and that liberty is essentially necessary to that end, appears to be absurd beyond expression.

But perhaps it may be concluded from hence, that I deny unto the magistate all manner of power about indifferent things; which, if it be not granted, the whole subject matter of law-making is taken away. No, I readily grant that indifferent things, and perhaps none but such, are subjected to the legislative power. But it does not therefore follow, that the magistrate may ordain whatsoever he pleases concerning any thing that is indifferent. The public good is the rule and measure of all law-making. If a thing be not useful to the commonwealth, thought it be ever so indifferent, it may not presently be established by law.

But further: Things ever so indifferent in their own nature, when they are brought into the church and worship of God, are removed out of the reach of the magistrate's jurisdiction, because in that use they have no connexion at all with civil affairs. The only business of the church is the salvation of souls: and it no ways concerns the commonwealth, or any member of it, that this or the other ceremony be there made use of. Neither the use, nor the omission, of any ceremonies in those religious assemblies does either advantage or prejudice the life, liberty, or estate, of any man. For example: Let it be granted, that the washing of an infant with water is in itself an indifferent thing: let it be granted also, that if the magistrate understand such washing to be profitable to the curing or preventing of any disease that children are subject unto, and esteem the matter weighty enough to be taken care of by a law, in that case he may order it to be done. But will any one, therefore, say, that the magistrate has the same right to ordain, by law, that all children shall be baptized by priests, in the sacred font, in order

234 A Letter Concerning Toleration

to the purification of their souls? The extreme difference of these two cases is visible to every one at first sight. Or let us apply the last case to the child of a Jew, and the thing will speak itself: for what hinders but a Christian magistrate may have subjects that are Jews? Now, if we acknowledge that such an injury may not be done unto a Jew, as to compel him, against his own opinion, to practise in his religion a thing that is in its nature indifferent, how can we maintain that any thing of this kind may be done to a Christian?

Again: Things in their own nature indifferent, cannot, by any human authority, be made any part of the worship of God, for this very reason, because they are indifferent. For since indifferent things are not capable, by any virtue of their own, to propitiate the Deity, no human power or authority can confer on them so much dignity and excellency as to enable them to do it. In the common affairs of life, that use of indifferent things which God has not forbidden is free and lawful; and therefore in those things human authority has place. But it is not so in matters of religion. Things indifferent are not otherwise lawful in the worship of God than as they are instituted by God himself; and as he, by some positive command, has ordained them to be made a part of that worship which he will vouchsafe to accept of at the hands of poor sinful men. Nor when an incensed Deity shall ask us, "Who has required these or such like things at your hands?" will it be enough to answer him, that the magistrate commanded them. If civil jurisdiction extended thus far, what might not lawfully be introduced into religion? What hodge-podge of ceremonies, what superstitious inventions, built upon the magistrate's authority, might not, against conscience, be imposed upon the worshippers of God! For the greatest part of these ceremonies and superstitions consists in the religious use of such things as are in their own nature indifferent: nor are they sinful upon any other account, than because God is not the author of them. The sprinkling of water, and use of bread and wine, are both in their own nature, and in the ordinary occasions of life, altogether indifferent. Will any man, therefore, say that these things could have been introduced into religion, and made a part of divine worship, if not by divine institution? If any human authority or civil power could have done this, why might it not also enjoin the eating of fish, and drinking of ale, in the holy banquet, as a part of divine worship? Why not the sprinkling of the blood of beasts in churches, and expiations by water or fire, and abundance more of this kind? But these things, how indifferent soever they be in common uses, when they come to be annexed unto divine worship, without divine authority, they are as abominable to God as the sacrifice of a dog. And why a dog so abominable? What difference is there between a dog and a goat, in respect of the divine nature, equally and infinitely distant from all affinity with matter; unless it be that God required the use of the one in his worship, and not of the other? We see, therefore, that indifferent things, how much soever they be under the power of the civil magistrate, yet cannot, upon that pretence, be introduced into religion, and imposed upon religious assemblies; because in the worship of God they wholly cease to be indifferent. He that worships God, does it with design to please him, and procure his favour: but that cannot be done by him, who, upon the command of another, offers unto God that which he knows will be displeasing to him, because not commanded by himself. This is not to please God, or appease his wrath, but willingly and knowingly to provoke him, by a manifest contempt; which is a thing absolutely repugnant to the nature and end of worship.

But it will here be asked, If nothing belonging to divine worship be left to human discretion, how is it then that churches themselves have the power of ordering any thing about the time and place of worship, and the like? To this I answer; that in religious worship we must distinguish between what is part of the worship itself, and what is but a circumstance. That is a part of the worship which is believed to be appointed by God, and to be well pleasing to him; and therefore that is necessary. Circumstances are such things which, though in general they cannot be separated from worship, yet the particular instances or modifications of them are not determined; and therefore they are indifferent. Of this sort are the time and place of worship, the habit and posture of him that worships. These are circumstances, and perfectly indifferent, where God has not given any express command about them. For example: amongst the Jews, the time and place of their worship, and the habits of those that officiated in it, were not mere circumstances, but a part of the worship itself; in which, if any thing were defective, or different from the institution, they could not hope that it would be accepted by God. But these, to Christians, under the liberty of the Gospel, are mere circumstances of worship which the prudence of every church may bring into such use as shall be judged most subservient to the end of order, decency, and edification. Though even under the Gospel also, those who believe the first, or the seventh day to be set apart by God, and consecrated still to his worship, to them that portion of time is not a simple circumstance, but a real part of divine worship, which can neither be changed nor neglected.

In the next place: As the magistrate has no power to impose, by his laws, the use of any rites and ceremonies in any church; so neither has he any power to forbid the use of such rites and ceremonies as are already received, approved, and practised by any church: because, if he did so, he would destroy the church itself; the end of whose institution is only to worship God with freedom, after its own manner.

You will say, by this rule, if some congregations should have a mind to sacrifice infants, or, as the primitive Christians were falsely accused, lustfully pollute themselves in promiscuous uncleanness, or practise any other such heinous enormities, is the magistrate obliged to tolerate them, because they are committed in a religious assembly? I answer, No. These things are not lawful in the ordinary course of life, nor in any private house; and, therefore, neither are they so in the worship of God, or in any religious meeting. But, indeed, if any people congregated upon account of religion, should be desirous to sacrifice a calf, I deny that that ought to be prohibited by a law. Melibœus, whose calf it is, may lawfully kill his calf at home, and burn any part of it that he thinks fit: for no injury is thereby done to any one, no prejudice to another man's goods. And for the same reason he may kill his calf also in a religious meeting. Whether the doing so be well-pleasing to God or no, it is their part to consider that do it. — The part of the magistrate is only to take care that the commonwealth receive no prejudice, and that there be no injury done to any man, either in life or estate. And thus what may be spent on a feast may be spent on a sacrifice. But if, peradventure, such were the state of things, that the interest of the commonwealth required all slaughter of beasts should be forborn for some while, in order to the increasing of the stock of cattle, that had been destroyed by some extraordinary murrain; who sees not that the magistrate, in such a case, may forbid all his subjects to kill any calves for any use whatsoever? Only it is to be observed, that in this case the law is not made about a religious, but a political matter: nor is the sacrifice, but the slaughter of calves thereby prohibited.

By this we see what difference there is between the church and the commonwealth. Whatsoever is lawful in the commonwealth, cannot be prohibited by the magistrate in the church. Whatsoever is permitted unto any of his subjects for their ordinary use, neither can nor ought to be forbidden by him to any sect of people for their religious uses. If any man may lawfully take bread or wine, either sitting or kneeling, in his own house, the law ought not to abridge him of the same liberty in his religious worship; though in the church the use of bread and wine be very different, and be there applied to the mysteries of faith, and rites of divine worship. But those things that are prejudicial to the commonweal of a people in their ordinary use, and are therefore forbidden by laws, those things ought not to be permitted to churches in their sacred rites. Only the magistrate ought always to be very careful that he do not misuse his authority, to the oppression of any church, under pretence of public good.

It may be said, What if a church be idolatrous, is that also to be tolerated by the magistrate? In answer, I ask, what power can be given to the magistrate for the suppression of an idolatrous church, which may not, in time and place, be made use of to the ruin of an orthodox one? For it must be remembered, that the civil power is the same every where, and the religion of every prince is orthodox to himself. If, therefore, such a power be granted unto the civil magistrate in spirituals, as that at Geneva, for example; he may extirpate, by violence and blood, the religion which is there reputed idolatrous; by the same rule, another magistrate, in some neighbouring country, may oppress the reformed religion; and, in India, the Christian. The civil power can either change every thing in religion, according to the prince's pleasure, or it can change nothing. If it be once permitted to introduce any thing into religion, by the means of laws and penalties, there can be no bounds put to it; but it will, in the same manner, be lawful to alter every thing, according to that rule of truth which the magistrate has framed unto himself. No man whatsoever ought therefore to be deprived of his terrestrial enjoyments, upon account of his religion. Not even Americans, subjected unto a Christian prince, are to be punished either in body or goods, for not embracing our faith and worship. If they are persuaded that they please God in observing the rites of their own country, and that they shall obtain happiness by that means, they are to be left unto God and themselves. Let us trace this matter to the bottom. Thus it is: an inconsiderable and weak number of Christians, destitute of every thing, arrive in a pagan country; these foreigners beseech the inhabitants, by the bowels of humanity, that they would succour them with the necessaries of life; those necessaries are given them, habitations are granted, and they all join together, and grow up into one body of people. The Christian religion by this means takes root in that country, and spreads itself; but does not suddenly grow the strongest. While things are in this condition, peace, friendship, faith, and equal justice, are preserved amongst them. At length the magistrate becomes a Christian, and by that means their party becomes the most powerful. Then immediately all compacts are to be broken, all civil rights to be violated, that idolatry may be extirpated: and unless these innocent pagans, strict observers of the rules of equity and the law of nature, and no ways offending against the laws of the society, I say unless they will forsake their ancient religion, and embrace a new and strange one, they are to be turned out of the lands and possessions of their forefathers, and perhaps deprived of life itself. Then at last it appears what zeal for the church, joined with the desire of dominion, is capable to produce: and how easily the pretence of religion, and of the care of souls, serves for a cloke to covetousness, rapine, and ambition.

Now, whosoever maintains that idolatry is to be rooted out of any place by laws, punishments, fire, and sword, may apply this story to himself: for the reason of the thing is equal, both in America and Europe. And neither pagans there, nor any dissenting Christians here, can with any right be deprived of their worldly goods by the predominating faction of a court-church; nor are any civil rights to be either changed or violated upon account of religion in one place more than another.

But idolatry, say some, is a sin, and therefore not to be tolerated. If they said it were therefore to be avoided, the inference were good. But it does not follow, that because it is a sin, it ought therefore to be punished by the magistrate. For it does not belong unto the magistrate to make use of his sword in punishing every thing, indifferently, that he takes to be a sin against God. Covetousness, uncharitableness, idleness, and many other things are sins, by the consent of all men, which yet no man ever said were to be punished by the magistrate. The reason is, because they are not prejudicial to other men's rights, nor do they break the public peace of societies. Nay, even the sins of lying and perjury are nowhere punishable by laws; unless in certain cases, in which the real turpitude of the thing, and the offence against God, are not considered, but only the injury done unto men's neighbours, and to the commonwealth. And what if, in another country, to a Mahometan or a pagan prince, the Christian religion seem false and offensive to God; may not the Christians, for the same reason, and after the same manner, be extirpated there?

But it may be urged farther, that by the law of Moses idolaters were to be rooted out. True indeed, by the law of Moses; but that is not obligatory to us Christians. Nobody pretends that every thing, generally, enjoined by the law of Moses, ought to be practised by Christians. But there is nothing more frivolous than that common distinction of moral, judicial, and ceremonial law, which men ordinarily make use of: for no positive law whatsoever can oblige any people but those to whom it is given. "Hear, O Israel," sufficiently restrains the obligation of the law of Moses only to that people. And this consideration alone is answer enough unto those that urge the authority of the law of Moses, for the inflicting of capital punishments upon idolaters. But however I will examine this argument a little more particularly.

The case of idolaters, in respect of the Jewish commonwealth, falls under a double consideration. The first is of those, who, being initiated in the Mosaical rites, and made citizens of that commonwealth, did afterwards apostatize from the worship of the God of Israel. These were proceeded against as traitors and rebels, guilty of no less than high treason; for the commonwealth of the Jews, different in that from all others, was an absolute theocracy: nor was there, or could there be, any difference between that commonwealth and the church. The laws established there concerning the worship of one invisible Deity, were the civil laws of that people, and a part of their political government, in which God himself was the legislator. Now if any one can show me where there is a commonwealth, at this time, constituted upon that foundation, I will acknowledge that the ecclesiastical laws do there unavoidably become a part of the civil; and that the subjects of that government both may, and ought to be, kept in strict conformity with that church, by the civil power. But there is absolutely no such thing, under the Gospel, as a Christian commonwealth. There are, indeed, many cities and kingdoms that have embraced the faith of Christ; but they have retained their ancient forms of government, with which the law of Christ hath not at all meddled. He, indeed, hath taught men how, by faith and good works, they may attain eternal life. But he instituted no commonwealth; he prescribed unto his followers no new and peculiar form of government; nor put he the sword into any magistrate's hand, with commission to make use of it in forcing men to forsake their former religion, and receive his.

Secondly, Foreigners, and such as were strangers to the commonwealth of Israel, were not compelled by force to observe the rites of the Mosaical law: but, on the contrary, in the very same place where it is ordered that an Israelite that was an idolater should be put to death, there it is provided that strangers should not be "vexed nor oppressed," Exod. xxii. 21. I confess that the seven nations that possessed the land which was promised to the Israelites were utterly to be cut off. But this was not singly because they were idolaters; for if that had been the reason, why were the Moabites and other nations to be spared? No; the reason is this: God being in a peculiar manner the King of the Jews, he could not suffer the adoration of any other deity, which was properly an act of high treason against himself, in the land of Canaan, which was his kingdom; for such a manifest revolt could no ways consist with his dominion, which was perfectly political, in that country. All idolatry was therefore to be rooted out of the bounds of his kingdom; because it was an acknowledgment of another God, that is to say, another king, against the laws of empire. The inhabitants were also to be driven out, that the entire possession of the land might be given to the Israelites. And for the like reason the Emims and the Horims were driven out of their countries by the children of Esau and Lot; and their lands, upon the same grounds, given by God to the invaders, Deut. ii. 12. But though all idolatry was thus rooted out of the land of Canaan, yet every idolater was not brought to execution. The whole family of Rahab, the whole nation of the Gibeonites, articled with Joshua, and were allowed by treaty; and there were many captives amongst the Jews, who were idolaters. David and Solomon subdued many countries without the confines of the Land of Promise, and carried their conquests as far as Euphrates. Amongst so many captives taken, of so many nations reduced under their obedience, we find not one man forced into the Jewish religion, and the worship of the true God, and punished for idolatry, though all of them were certainly guilty of it. If any one indeed, becoming a proselyte, desired to be made a denizen of their commonwealth, he was obliged to submit unto their laws; that is, to embrace their religion. But this he did willingly, on his own accord, not by constraint. He did not unwillingly submit, to show his obedience; but he sought and solicited for it, as a privilege; and as soon as he was admitted, he became subject to the laws of the commonwealth, by which all idolatry was forbidden within the borders of the land of Canaan. But that law, as I have said, did not reach to any of those regions, however subjected unto the Jews, that were situated without those bounds.

Thus far concerning outward worship. Let us now consider articles of faith.

The articles of religion are some of them practical, and some speculative. Now, though both sorts consist in the knowledge of truth, yet these terminate simply in the understanding, those influence the will and manners. Speculative opinions, therefore, and articles of faith, as they are called, which are required only to be believed, cannot be imposed on any church by the law of the land; for it is absurd that things should be enjoined by laws which are not in men's power to perform; and to believe this or that to be true does not depend upon our will. But of this enough has been said already. But, will some say, let men at least profess that they believe. A sweet religion, indeed, that obliges men to dissemble, and tell lies both to God and man, for the salvation of their souls! If the magistrate thinks to save men thus, he seems to understand little of the way of salvation; and if he does it not in order to save them, why is he so solicitous about the articles of faith as to enact them by a law?

Further, The magistrate ought not to forbid the preaching or professing of any speculative opinions in any church, because they have no manner of relation to the civil rights of the subjects. If a Roman Catholic believe that to be really the body of Christ, which another man calls bread, he does no injury thereby to his neighbour. If a Jew does not believe the New Testament to be the word of God, he does not thereby alter any thing in men's civil rights. If a heathen doubt of both Testaments, he is not therefore to be punished as a pernicious citizen. The power of the magistrate, and the estates of the people, may be equally secure, whether any man believe these things or no. I readily grant that these opinions are false and absurd; but the business of laws is not to provide for the truth of opinions, but for the safety and security of the commonwealth, and of every particular man's goods and person. And so it ought to be; for truth certainly would do well enough, if she were once left to shift for herself. She seldom has received, and I fear never will receive, much assistance from the power of great men, to whom she is but rarely known, and more rarely welcome. She is not taught by laws, nor has she any need of force to procure her entrance into the minds of men. Errors indeed prevail by the assistance of foreign and borrowed succours. But if truth makes not her way into the understanding by her own light, she will be but the weaker for any borrowed force violence can add to her. Thus much for speculative opinions. Let us now proceed to the practical ones.

A good life, in which consists not the least part of religion and true piety, concerns also the civil government: and in it lies the safety both of men's souls and of the commonwealth. Moral actions belong therefore to the jurisdiction both of the outward and inward court; both of the civil and domestic governor; I mean, both of the magistrate and conscience. Here therefore is great danger, lest one of these jurisdictions intrench upon the other, and discord arise between the keeper of the public peace and the overseers of souls. But if what has been already said concerning the limits of both these governments be rightly considered, it will easily remove all difficulty in this matter.

Every man has an immortal soul, capable of eternal happiness or misery; whose happiness depending upon his believing and doing those things in this life, which are necessary to the obtaining of God's favour, and are prescribed by God to that end: it follows from thence, first, that the observance of these things is the highest obligation that lies upon mankind, and that our utmost care, application, and diligence, ought to be exercised in the search and performance of them; because there is nothing in this world that is of any consideration in comparison with eternity. Secondly, that seeing one man does not violate the right of another, by his erroneous opinions, and undue manner of worship, nor is his perdition any prejudice to another man's affairs; therefore the care of each man's salvation belongs only to himself. But I would not have this understood, as if I meant hereby to condemn all charitable admonitions, and affectionate endeavours to reduce men from errors; which are indeed the greatest duty of a Christian. Any one may employ as many exhortations and arguments as he pleases, towards the promoting of another man's salvation. But all force and compulsion are to be forborn. Nothing is to be done imperiously. — Nobody is obliged in that manner to yield obedience unto the admonitions or injunctions of another, farther than he himself is persuaded. Every man, in that, has the supreme and absolute authority of judging for himself; and the reason is, because nobody else is concerned in it, nor can receive any prejudice from his conduct therein.

But besides their souls, which are immortal, men have also their temporal lives here upon earth; the state whereof being frail and fleeting, and the duration uncertain, they have need of several outward conveniencies to the support thereof, which are to be procured or preserved by pains and industry; for those things that are necessary to the comfortable support of our lives, are not the spontaneous products of nature, nor do offer themselves fit and prepared for our use. This part, therefore, draws on another care, and necessarily gives another employment. But the pravity of mankind being such, that they had rather injuriously prey upon the fruits of other men's labours than take pains to provide for themselves; the necessity of preserving men in the possession of what honest industry has already acquired, and also of preserving their liberty and strength, whereby they may acquire what they farther want, obliges men to enter into society with one another; that by mutual assistance and joint force, they may secure unto each other their properties, in the things that contribute to the comforts and happiness of this life; leaving in the mean while to every man the care of his own eternal happiness, the attainment whereof can neither be facilitated by another man's industry, nor can the loss of it turn to another man's prejudice, nor the hope of it be forced from him by any external violence. But forasmuch as men thus entering into societies, grounded upon their mutual compacts of assistance, for the defence of their temporal goods, may nevertheless be deprived of them, either by the rapine and fraud of their fellow-citizens, or by the hostile violence of foreigners: the remedy of this evil consists in arms, riches, and multitudes of citizens: the remedy of others in laws: and the care of all things relating both to the one and the other is committed by the society to the civil magistrate. This is the original, this is the use, and these are the bounds of the legislative, which is the supreme power in every commonwealth. I mean, that provision may be made for the security of each man's private possessions; for the peace, riches, and public commodities of the whole people, and, as much as possible, for the increase of their inward strength against foreign invasions.

These things being thus explained, it is easy to understand to what end the legislative power ought to be directed, and by what measures regulated, and that is the temporal good and outward prosperity of the society, which is the sole reason of men's entering into society, and the only thing they seek and aim at in it; and it is also evident what liberty remains to men in reference to their eternal salvation, and that is, that every one should do what he in his conscience is persuaded to be acceptable to the Almighty, on whose good pleasure and acceptance depends his eternal happiness; for obedience is due in the first place to God, and afterwards to the laws.

But some may ask, "What if the magistrate should enjoin any thing by his authority, that appears unlawful to the conscience of a private person?" I answer, that if government be faithfully administered, and the counsels of the magistrate be indeed directed to the public good, this will seldom happen. But if perhaps it do so fall out, I say, that such a private person is to abstain from the actions that he judges unlawful; and he is to undergo the punishment, which is not unlawful for him to bear; for the private judgment of any person concerning a law enacted in political matters, for the public good, does not take away the obligation of that law, nor deserve a dispensation. But if the law indeed be concerning things that lie not within the verge of the magistrate's authority; as, for example, that the people, or any party amongst them, should be compelled to embrace a strange religion, and join in the worship and ceremonies of another church; men are not in these cases obliged by that law, against their consciences; for the political society is instituted for no other end, but only to secure every man's possession of the things of this life. The care of each man's soul, and of the things of heaven, which neither does belong to the commonwealth, nor can be subjected to it, is left entirely to every man's self. Thus the safeguard of men's lives, and of the things that belong unto this life, is the business of the commonwealth; and the preserving of those things unto their owners is the duty of the magistrate; and therefore the magistrate cannot take away these worldly things from this man, or party, and give them to that; nor change property amongst fellow-subjects, no not even by a law, for a cause that has no relation to the end of civil government; I mean for their religion; which, whether it be true or false, does no prejudice to the worldly concerns of their fellow-subjects, which are the things that only belong unto the care of the commonwealth.

"But what if the magistrate believe such a law as this to be for the public good?" I answer: as the private judgment of any particular person, if erroneous, does not exempt him from the obligation of law, so the private judgment, as I may call it, of the magistrate, does not give him any new right of imposing laws upon his subjects, which neither was in the

constitution of the government granted him, nor ever was in the power of
the people to grant: and least of all, if he make it his business to enrich and
advance his followers and fellow-sectaries with the spoils of others. But
what if the magistrate believe that he has a right to make such laws, and that
they are for the public good; and his subjects believe the contrary? Who
shall be judge between them? I answer, God alone; for there is no judge
upon earth between the supreme magistrate and the people. God, I say, is
the only judge in this case, who will retribute unto every one at the last day
according to his deserts; that is, according to his sincerity and uprightness
in endeavouring to promote piety, and the public weal and peace of mankind. But what shall be done in the mean while? I answer: the principal and
chief care of every one ought to be of his own soul first, and, in the next
place, of the public peace: though yet there are few will think it is peace
there, where they see all laid waste. There are two sorts of contests amongst
men; the one managed by law, the other by force: and they are of that
nature, that where the one ends, the other always begins. But it is not my
business to inquire into the power of the magistrate in the different constitutions of nations. I only know what usually happens where controversies
arise, without a judge to determine them. You will say then the magistrate
being the stronger will have his will, and carry his point. Without doubt. But
the question is not here concerning the doubtfulness of the event, but the
rule of right.

But to come to particulars. I say, first, No opinions contrary to human
society, or to those moral rules which are necessary to the preservation of
civil society, are to be tolerated by the magistrate. But of those indeed
examples in any church are rare. For no sect can easily arrive to such a
degree of madness, as that it should think fit to teach, for doctrines of
religion, such things as manifestly undermine the foundations of society,
and are therefore condemned by the judgment of all mankind: because their
own interest, peace, reputation, every thing would be thereby endangered.

Another more secret evil, but more dangerous to the commonwealth, is
when men arrogate to themselves, and to those of their own sect, some
peculiar prerogative, covered over with a specious show of deceitful words,
but in effect opposite to the civil rights of the community. For example: we
cannot find any sect that teaches expressly and openly, that men are not
obliged to keep their promise; that princes may be dethroned by those that
differ from them in religion; or that the dominion of all things belongs only
to themselves. For these things, proposed thus nakedly and plainly, would
soon draw on them the eye and hand of the magistrate, and awaken all the
care of the commonwealth to a watchfulness against the spreading of so

dangerous an evil. But nevertheless, we find those that say the same things in other words. What else do they mean, who teach that "faith is not to be kept with heretics?" Their meaning, forsooth, is, that the privilege of breaking faith belongs unto themselves: for they declare all that are not of their communion to be heretics, or at least may declare them so whensoever they think fit. What can be the meaning of their asserting that "kings excommunicated forfeit their crowns and kingdoms?" It is evident that they thereby arrogate unto themselves the power of deposing kings: because they challenge the power of excommunication as the peculiar right of their hierarchy. "That dominion is founded in grace," is also an assertion by which those that maintain it do plainly lay claim to the possession of all things. For they are not so wanting to themselves as not to believe, or at least as not to profess, themselves to be the truly pious and faithful. These therefore, and the like, who attribute unto the faithful, religious, and orthodox, that is, in plain terms, unto themselves, any peculiar privilege or power above other mortals, in civil concernments; or who, upon pretence of religion, do challenge any manner of authority over such as are not associated with them in their ecclesiastical communion; I say these have no right to be tolerated by the magistrate; as neither those that will not own and teach the duty of tolerating all men in matters of mere religion. For what do all these and the like doctrines signify, but that they may, and are ready upon any occasion to seize the government, and possess themselves of the estates and fortunes of their fellow-subjects; and that they only ask leave to be tolerated by the magistrates so long, until they find themselves strong enough to effect it.

Again: That church can have no right to be tolerated by the magistrate, which is constituted upon such a bottom, that all those who enter into it, do thereby, *ipso facto,* deliver themselves up to the protection and service of another prince. For by this means the magistrate would give way to the settling of a foreign jurisdiction in his own country, and suffer his own people to be listed, as it were, for soldiers against his own government. Nor does the frivolous and fallacious distinction between the court and the church afford any remedy to this inconvenience; especially when both the one and the other are equally subject to the absolute authority of the same person; who has not only power to persuade the members of his church to whatsoever he lists, either as purely religious, or as in order thereunto; but can also enjoin it them on pain of eternal fire. It is ridiculous for any one to profess himself to be a Mahometan only in religion, but in every thing else a faithful subject to a Christian magistrate, whilst at the same time he acknowledges himself bound to yield blind obedience to the mufti of

Constantinople; who himself is entirely obedient to the Ottoman emperor, and frames the famed oracles of that religion according to his pleasure. But this Mahometan, living amongst Christians, would yet more apparently renounce their government, if he acknowledged the same person to be head of his church, who is the supreme magistrate in the state.

Lastly, Those are not at all to be tolerated who deny the being of God. Promises, covenants, and oaths, which are the bonds of human society, can have no hold upon an atheist. The taking away of God, though but even in thought, dissolves all. Besides also, those that by their atheism undermine and destroy all religion, can have no pretence of religion whereupon to challenge the privilege of a toleration. As for other practical opinions, though not absolutely free from all error, yet if they do not tend to establish domination over others, or civil impunity to the church in which they are taught, there can be no reason why they should not be tolerated.

It remains that I say something concerning those assemblies, which being vulgarly called, and perhaps having sometimes been conventicles, and nurseries of factions and seditions, are thought to afford the strongest matter of objection against this doctrine of toleration. But this has not happened by any thing peculiar unto the genius of such assemblies, but by the unhappy circumstances of an oppressed or ill-settled liberty. These accusations would soon cease, if the law of toleration were once so settled, that all churches were obliged to lay down toleration as the foundation of their own liberty; and teach that liberty of conscience is every man's natural right, equally belonging to dissenters as to themselves; and that nobody ought to be compelled in matters of religion either by law or force. The establishment of this one thing would take away all ground of complaints and tumults upon account of conscience. And these causes of discontents and animosities being once removed, there would remain nothing in these assemblies that were not more peaceable, and less apt to produce disturbance of state, than in any other meetings whatsoever. But let us examine particularly the heads of these accusations.

You will say, that "assemblies and meetings endanger the public peace, and threaten the commonwealth." I answer: if this be so, why are there daily such numerous meetings in markets, and courts of judicature? Why are crowds upon the Exchange, and a concourse of people in cities suffered? You will reply, these are civil assemblies; but those we object against are ecclesiastical. I answer: it is a likely thing indeed, that such assemblies as are altogether remote from civil affairs should be most apt to embroil them. O, but civil assemblies are composed of men that differ from one another in matters of religion: but these ecclesiastical meetings are of persons that are all of one opinion. As if an agreement in matters of religion were in effect a conspiracy against the commonwealth: or as if men would not be so much the more warmly unanimous in religion, the less liberty they had of assembling. But it will be urged still, that civil assemblies are open, and free for any one to enter into; whereas religious conventicles are more private, and thereby give opportunity to clandestine machinations. I answer, that this is not strictly true: for many civil assemblies are not open to every one. And if some religious meetings be private, who are they, I beseech you, that are to be blamed for it? those that desire, or those that forbid their being public? Again: you will say, that religious communion does exceedingly unite men's minds and affections to one another, and is therefore the more dangerous. But if this be so, why is not the magistrate afraid of his own church; and why does he not forbid their assemblies, as things dangerous to his government? You will say, because he himself is a part, and even the head of them. As if he were not also a part of the commonwealth, and the head of the whole people.

Let us therefore deal plainly. The magistrate is afraid of other churches, but not of his own; because he is kind and favourable to the one, but severe and cruel to the other. These he treats like children, and indulges them even to wantonness. Those he uses as slaves; and how blamelessly soever they demean themselves, recompenses them no otherwise than by galleys, prisons, confiscations, and death. These he cherishes and defends: those he continually scourges and oppresses. Let him turn the tables: or let those dissenters enjoy but the same privileges in civils as his other subjects, and he will quickly find that these religious meetings will be no longer dangerous. For if men enter into seditious conspiracies, it is not religion inspires them to it in their meetings, but their sufferings and oppressions that make them willing to ease themselves. Just and moderate governments are every where quiet, every where safe. But oppression raises ferments, and makes men struggle to cast off an uneasy and tyrannical yoke. I know that seditions are very frequently raised upon pretence of religion. But it is as true, that, for religion, subjects are frequently ill treated, and live miserably. Believe me, the stirs that are made proceed not from any peculiar temper of this or that church or religious society; but from the common disposition of all mankind, who, when they groan under any heavy burthen, endeavour naturally to shake off the yoke that galls their necks. Suppose this business of religion were let alone, and that there were some other distinction made between men and men, upon account of their different complexions, shapes, and features, so that those who have black hair, for example, or gray eyes, should not enjoy the same privileges as other citizens; that they should not be permitted either to buy or sell, or live by their callings; that parents should not have the government and education of their own children; that they should either be excluded from the benefit of the laws, or meet with partial judges: can it be doubted but these persons, thus distinguished from others by the colour of their hair and eyes, and united together by one common persecution, would be as dangerous to the magistrate, as any others that had associated themselves merely upon the account of religion? Some enter into company for trade and profit: others, for want of business, have their clubs for claret. Neighbourhood joins some, and religion others. But there is one thing only which gathers people into seditious commotions, and that is oppression.

You will say; what, will you have people to meet at divine service against the magistrate's will? I answer; why, I pray, against his will? Is it not both lawful and necessary that they should meet? Against his will, do you say? This is what I complain of. That is the very root of all the mischief. Why are assemblies less sufferable in a church than in a theatre or market? Those that meet there are not either more vicious, or more turbulent, than those that meet elsewhere. The business in that is, that they are ill used, and therefore they are not to be suffered. Take away the partiality that is used towards them in matters of common right; change the laws, take away the penalties unto which they are subjected, and all things will immediately become safe and peaceable: nay, those that are averse to the religion of the magistrate, will think themselves so much the more bound to maintain the peace of the commonwealth, as their condition is better in that place than elsewhere; and all the several separate congregations, like so many guardians of the public peace, will watch one another, that nothing may be innovated or changed in the form of the government: because they can hope for nothing better than what they already enjoy; that is, an equal condition with their fellow-subjects, under a just and moderate government. Now if that church, which agrees in religion with the prince, be esteemed the chief support of any civil government, and that for no other reason, as has already been shown, than because the prince is kind, and the laws are favourable to it; how much greater will be the security of a government, where all good subjects, of whatsoever they be, without any distinction upon account of religion, enjoying the same favour of the prince, and the same benefit of the laws, shall become the common support and guard of it; and where none will have any occasion to fear the severity of the laws, but those that do injuries to their neighbours, and offend against the civil peace!

That we may draw towards a conclusion. "The sum of all we drive at is, that every man enjoy the same rights that are granted to others." Is it permitted to worship God in the Roman manner? Let it be permitted to do it in the Geneva form also. Is it permitted to speak Latin in the market-place? Let those that have a mind to it, be permitted to do it also in the church. Is it lawful for any man in his own house to kneel, stand, sit, or use any other posture; and clothe himself in white or black, in short or in long garments? Let it not be made unlawful to eat bread, drink wine, or wash with water in the church. In a word: whatsoever things are left free by law in the common occasions of life, let them remain free unto every church in divine worship. Let no man's life, or body, or house, or estate, suffer any manner of prejudice upon these accounts. Can you allow of the presbyterian discipline? why should not the episcopal also have what they like? Ecclesiastical authority, whether it be administered by the hands of a single person, or many, is every where the same; and neither has any jurisdiction in things civil, nor any manner of power of compulsion, nor any thing at all to do with riches and revenues.

Ecclesiastical assemblies and sermons, are justified by daily experience, and public allowance. These are allowed to people of some one persuasion: why not to all? If any thing pass in a religious meeting seditiously, and contrary to the public peace, it is to be punished in the same manner, and no otherwise, than as if it had happened in a fair or market. These meetings ought not to be sanctuaries of factious and flagitious fellows: nor ought it to be less lawful for men to meet in churches than in halls: nor are one part of the subjects to be esteemed more blamable for their meeting together than others. Every one is to be accountable for his own actions; and no man is to be laid under a suspicion, or odium, for the fault of another. Those that are seditious, murderers, thieves, robbers, adulterers, slanderers, &c. of whatsoever church, whether national or not, ought to be punished and suppressed. But those whose doctrine is peaceable, and whose manners are pure and blameless, ought to be upon equal terms with their fellow-subjects. Thus if solemn assemblies, observations of festivals, public worship, be permitted to any one sort of professors; all these things ought to be permitted to the presbyterians, independents, anabaptists, Arminians, quakers, and others, with the same liberty. Nay, if we may openly speak the truth, and as becomes one man to another, neither pagan, nor Mahometan, nor Jew, ought to be excluded from the civil rights of the commonwealth, because of his religion. The Gospel commands no such thing. The church, "which judgeth not those that are without," 1 Cor. v. 11, wants it not. And the commonwealth, which embraces indifferently all men that are honest, peaceable, and industrious, requires it not. Shall we suffer a pagan to deal and trade with us, and shall we not suffer him to pray unto and worship

God? If we allow the Jews to have private houses and dwellings amongst us, why should we not allow them to have synagogues? Is their doctrine more false, their worship more abominable, or is the civil peace more endangered, by their meeting in public, than in their private houses? But if these things may be granted to Jews and pagans, surely the condition of any Christians ought not to be worse than theirs, in a Christian commonwealth.

You will say, perhaps, yes, it ought to be: because they are more inclinable to factions, tumults, and civil wars. I answer: is this the fault of the Christian religion? If it be so, truly the Christian religion is the worst of all religions, and ought neither to be embraced by any particular person, nor tolerated by any commonwealth. For if this be the genius, this the nature of the Christian religion, to be turbulent and destructive of the civil peace, that church itself which the magistrate indulges will not always be innocent. But far be it from us to say any such thing of that religion, which carries the greatest opposition to covetousness, ambition, discord, contention, and all manner of inordinate desires; and is the most modest and peaceable religion that ever was. We must therefore seek another cause of those evils that are charged upon religion. And if we consider right, we shall find it consist wholly in the subject that I am treating of. It is not the diversity of opinions, which cannot be avoided; but the refusal of toleration to those that are of different opinions, which might have been granted, that has produced all the bustles and wars, that have been in the Christian world, upon account of religion. The heads and leaders of the church, moved by avarice and insatiable desire of dominion, making use of the immoderate ambition of magistrates, and the credulous superstition of the giddy multitude, have incensed and animated them against those that dissent from themselves, by preaching unto them, contrary to the laws of the Gospel, and to the precepts of charity, that schismatics and heretics are to be outed of their possessions, and destroyed. And thus have they mixed together, and confounded two things, that are in themselves most different, the church and the commonwealth. Now as it is very difficult for men patiently to suffer themselves to be stripped of the goods, which they have got by their honest industry; and contrary to all the laws of equity, both human and divine, to be delivered up for a prey to other men's violence and rapine; especially when they are otherwise altogether blameless; and that the occasion for which they are thus treated does not at all belong to the jurisdiction of the magistrate, but entirely to the conscience of every particular man, for the conduct of which he is accountable to God only; what else can be expected, but that these men, growing weary of the evils under which they labour, should in the end think it lawful for them to resist force with force, and to defend their natural rights, which are not forfeitable upon account of religion, with arms as well as they can? That this has been hitherto the ordinary course of things, is abundantly evident in history: and that it will continue to be so hereafter, is but too apparent in reason. It cannot indeed be otherwise, so long as the principle of persecution for religion shall prevail, as it has done hitherto, with magistrate and people; and so long as those that ought to be the preachers of peace and concord, shall continue, with all their art and strength, to excite men to arms, and sound the trumpet of war. But that magistrates should thus suffer these incendiaries, and disturbers of the public peace, might justly be wondered at, if it did not appear that they have been invited by them unto a participation of the spoil, and have therefore thought fit to make use of their covetousness and pride, as means whereby to increase their own power. For who does not see that these good men are indeed more ministers of the government than ministers of the Gospel; and that by flattering the ambition, and favouring the dominion of princes and men in authority, they endeavour with all their might to promote that tyranny in the commonwealth, which otherwise they should not be able to establish in the church? This is the unhappy agreement that we see between the church and the state. Whereas if each of them would contain itself within its own bounds, the one attending to the worldly welfare of the commonwealth, the other to the salvation of souls, it is impossible that any discord should ever have happened between them. "Sed pudet hæc opprobria," &c. God Almighty grant, I beseech him, that the Gospel of peace may at length be preached, and that civil magistrates, growing more careful to conform their own consciences to the law of God, and less solicitous about the binding of other men's consciences by human laws, may, like fathers of their country, direct all their counsels and endeavours to promote universally the civil welfare of all their children; except only of such as are arrogant, ungovernable, and injurious to their brethren; and that all ecclesiastical men, who boast themselves to be the successors of the apostles, walking peaceably and modestly in the apostles' steps, without intermeddling with state affairs, may apply themselves wholly to promote the salvation of souls. Farewell.

Perhaps it may not be amiss to add a few things concerning heresy and schism. A Turk is not, nor can be either heretic or schismatic to a Christian; and if any man fall off from the Christian faith to Mahometism, he does not thereby become a heretic, or a schismatic, but an apostate and an infidel. This nobody doubts of. And by this it appears that men of different religions cannot be heretics or schismatics to one another.

We are to inquire, therefore, what men are of the same religion:

concerning which, it is manifest that those who have one and the same rule of faith and worship are of the same religion, and those who have not the same rule of faith and worship are of different religions. For since all things that belong unto that religion are contained in that rule, it follows necessarily, that those who agree in one rule are of one and the same religion; and *vice versâ*. Thus Turks and Christians are of different religions; because these take the Holy Scriptures to be the rule of their religion, and those the Koran. And for the same reason, there may be different religions also, even amongst Christians. The papists and the Lutherans, though both of them profess faith in Christ, and are therefore called Christians, yet are not both of the same religion: because these acknowledge nothing but the Holy Scriptures to be the rule and foundation of their religion; those take in also traditions and decrees of popes, and of all these together make the rule of their religion. And thus the Christians of St. John, as they are called, and the Christians of Geneva, are of different religions: because these also take only the Scriptures, and those, I know not what traditions, for the rule of their religion.

This being settled, it follows, First, That heresy is a separation made in ecclesiastical communion between men of the same religion, for some opinions no way contained in the rule itself. And secondly, That amongst those who acknowledge nothing but the Holy Scriptures to be their rule of faith, heresy is a separation made in their Christian communion, for opinions not contained in the express words of Scripture.

Now this separation may be made in a twofold manner:

First, When the greater part, or, by the magistrate's patronage, the stronger part, of the church separates itself from others, by excluding them out of her communion, because they will not profess their belief of certain opinions which are not to be found in the express words of Scripture. For it is not the paucity of those that are separated, nor the authority of the magistrate, that can make any man guilty of heresy; but he only is an heretic who divides the church into parts, introduces names and marks of distinction, and voluntarily makes a separation because of such opinions.

Secondly, When any one separates himself from the communion of a church, because that church does not publicly profess some certain opinions which the Holy Scriptures do not expressly teach.

Both these are "heretics, because they err in fundamentals, and they err obstinately against knowledge." For when they have determined the Holy Scriptures to be the only foundation of faith, they nevertheless lay down certain propositions as fundamental, which are not in the Scripture; and because others will not acknowledge these additional opinions of theirs, nor build upon them as if they were necessary and fundamental, they therefore make a separation in the church, either by withdrawing themselves from the others, or expelling the others from them. Nor does it signify any thing for them to say that their confessions and symbols are agreeable to Scripture, and to the analogy of faith: for if they be conceived in the express words of Scripture, there can be no question about them; because those are acknowledged by all Christians to be of divine inspiration, and therefore fundamental. But if they say that the articles which they require to be professed are consequences deduced from the Scripture, it is undoubtedly well done of them to believe and profess such things as seem unto them so agreeable to the rule of faith: but it would be very ill done to obtrude those things upon others, unto whom they do not seem to be the indubitable doctrines of the Scripture. And to make a separation for such things as these, which neither are nor can be fundamental, is to become heretics. For I do not think there is any man arrived to that degree of madness, as that he dare give out his consequences and interpretations of Scripture as divine inspirations, and compare the articles of faith, that he has framed according to his own fancy, with the authority of the Scripture. I know there are some propositions so evidently agreeable to Scripture, that nobody can deny them to be drawn from thence: but about those therefore there can be no difference. This only I say, that however clearly we may think this or the other doctrine to be deduced from Scripture, we ought not therefore to impose it upon others as a necessary article of faith, because we believe it to be agreeable to the rule of faith; unless we would be content also that other doctrines should be imposed upon us in the same manner; and that we should be compelled to receive and profess all the different and contradictory opinions of Lutherans, Calvinists, remonstrants, anabaptists, and other sects, which the contrivers of symbols, systems, and confessions, are accustomed to deliver unto their followers as genuine and necessary deductions from the Holy Scripture. I cannot but wonder at the extravagant arrogance of those men who think that they themselves can explain things necessary to salvation more clearly than the Holy Ghost, the eternal and infinte wisdom of God.

Thus much concerning heresy; which word in common use is applied only to the doctrine part of religion. Let us now consider schism, which is a crime near akin to it: for both those words seem unto me to signify an "ill-grounded separation in ecclesiastical communion, made about things not necessary." But since use, which is the supreme law in matter of language, has determined that heresy relates to errors in faith, and schism to those in worship or discipline, we must consider them under that distinction.

Schism then, for the same reasons that have already been alleged, is nothing else but a separation made in the communion of the church, upon account of something in divine worship, or ecclesiastical discipline, that is not any necessary part of it. Now nothing in worship or discipline can be necessary to Christian communion, but what Christ our legislator, or the apostles, by inspiration of the Holy Spirit, have commanded in express words.

In a word: he that denies not any thing that the Holy Scriptures teach in express words, nor makes a separation upon occasion of any thing that is not manifestly contained in the sacred text; however he may be nicknamed by any sect of Christians, and declared by some, or all of them, to be utterly void of true Christianity; yet in deed and in truth this man cannot be either a heretic or schismatic.

These things might have been explained more largely, and more advantageously; but it is enough to have hinted at them, thus briefly, to a person of your parts.

Essays

Measuring Locke's Shadow

JOHN DUNN

How well human lives go still turns largely on the relations between our dependence, our intelligence, and our capacities and opportunities to choose for ourselves how to make those lives together.[1] John Locke was one of the great reshapers of how we conceive and interpret those relations. "Measuring Locke's Shadow" considers how we can best judge today what he contributed to that reshaping, within the context of the history of political thinking in the West, and increasingly in the world as a whole.

The Problem of Perspective: The View from Without or the View from Within?

As with any human life, Locke's can be viewed, at least in intention, both from the inside and from without. We can attempt to see it as it must have seemed or been for Locke himself, but we can also try to see it as it really was for others, then or (sometimes very much) later. We can view it as a more or less confused and dispersed sequence of battles, adventures, enjoyments, and sufferings, or as a practical pressure, potent or all but nugatory, on the lives of an endless series of other human beings. Except in the stern light of the Last Judgment,[2] it is at best a heroic assumption, and probably nothing more than a literary conceit, that any human life could truly be from any angle or at any point in time a unified whole.[3] But it would be merely quixotic to suppose that the most integrated such life, however grand and consequential, should also prove a unified whole as seen from the outside, whether by or on behalf of all the other human beings who in the end turn out to have had some stake in it. Locke's was a very grand and consequential life indeed, and in the nearly three centuries which have passed since his death, huge numbers of human beings across time and space have had (or thought they had) some real stake in what it was or meant for them in particular. Because they have seen so much as riding on that life,[4] and because they have differed so widely in their beliefs, thoughts, and feelings, and have disagreed so drastically on what that life itself meant, they have also disagreed very extensively on what it consisted in: on what in fact took place within it.

As time goes by and human beings continue to proliferate, the task of seeing Locke's life steadily and as a whole from the outside becomes ever more elaborate, and perhaps ever more evidently forlorn. It fans out wider and wider, and is ever further from being adequately discharged. This is certainly not because we now, between us, know less about Locke than our counterparts did fifty years ago. Here, if anything, the position is clearly the opposite. There has been a massive accumulation of knowledge about Locke in the years since the outbreak of the Second World War. It is a safe bet that more is now known, and known reliably, about the dead Locke than has ever been known before. Living human beings, all but inevitably, are known about in a very different way, and those who live long, and who touch many other lives quite emphatically whilst doing so, as Locke certainly did, are known directly, if with varying intimacy, to numerous others (Shaftesbury, James Tyrrell, Damaris Masham, Edward Clarke, Philipp van Limborch, Sylvester Brounower). The best of scholars, however imaginative, clear-headed, and patient they may be, can never hope to know an archive the way in which most of us know a few other human beings. We may reach for Locke's life, as it appeared from within, and do so as bravely and imaginatively as we can, but there is much about that life which we can never hope to recapture — much which is now lost for ever, gone with the companions who once lived and breathed and quarreled and cared beside him, and with the bearer who alone ever had the opportunity to know it from within.

The external, objectifying, eye of scholarship (or modern thought more generally) has limited concern with that irretrievably lost life, and is in any case apt to suspect the pathos of loss of being either confused or bogus. It volunteers to identify and convey relatively determinate aspects of the view from without and assess their significance to the highest current intellectual standards, anticipating neither comprehensive conversion to its own point of view, nor utter futility in the attempt to edify the stubborn and largely involuntary prejudices of everyone else. It settles for critical accountability, evidence, and the reasonably frank acknowledgment of its own agendas, modes of inquiry, and criteria of validation. For many purposes, the view from without is not merely all we now have open to us, and quite adequately interpretable from documents which Locke himself chose to make public, whether anonymously or under his own name; it is also all we need in order to interpret what that life has come to mean for very many others over the centuries which followed. In this optic, the historical Locke just happened to be the author of a set of immensely consequential texts, and what we need to take in is the history of the consequences of those texts, and the causal and rational basis of the scale and distribution of those consequences. It no longer matters what Locke was up to in writing them in the first place, or what he supposed himself to be doing at any point along his way. (Or, if it does matter to anyone, it does and can do so only to the purest of historians — those who prescind radically from all interest in consequences, for fear that any trace of such interest must sully the integrity of the past the way it simply was, those who fear that the least hint of affinity with Whig subject matter must be incompatible with the flatly Tory requirements of historical truth.[5])

The Persisting Imaginative Pressure of the Supposed View from Within

There is some force to each of these lines of thought. But it is instructive how hard modern interpreters of Locke's political thinking have found it to stand by the conclusions of either. For almost half a century, since Wolfgang Von Leyden's meticulous and impressively thoughtful edition of the relatively juvenile *Essays on the Law of Nature,*[6] scholars have found themselves endlessly dragged back from the well-formed and controlled technical exercises of modern philosophy to less comfortable or elegant grapplings with the epistemological treacheries of the struggle to recover at least the main intellectual (or even emotional) dynamics of Locke's life as he once viewed it from within. This is a matter of some interest in itself, and it is far from clear quite why it should have been so. But it seems unlikely that the answer turns merely on the relative confusion or stupidity of the scholars in question. Part of that answer, probably, is as much a matter of supply as one of demand, in the striking contingency of the survival of a huge mass of personal documentation, the fate of the Lovelace papers, the individual curiosity, taste and munificence of Paul Mellon, and the good fortune and sense of occasion of the Bodleian Library. Any serious Locke scholar today is heir to a remarkable treasury of well-explored and endlessly fascinating resources. But a larger part of the answer, surely, must rest firmly with effective demand.

   The historical Locke lived some time ago, but the refusal to leave him unmolested in his grave plainly comes from very much more recently. In many ways it has grown in insistence as the decades have gone by since Von

Leyden's edition. The impulse behind that refusal derives above all from
the United States. It is primarily as an ideologue that we cannot let Locke
rest even now in the massive peace of historical indifference. Today, over
two thirds of a century since Merle Curti's famous article,[7] Locke is still
intractably America's philosopher, and still very much America's philosopher for what still seems ever more peremptorily America's globe. He is the
sign on the banner of America's imperious external reach, her cultural,
imaginative, ideological, economic, and even political *Griff nach der Weltmacht*. The image on that banner, unsurprisingly, is very distant from its
historical archetype, and quite hazily delineated as time goes by. But its
stunning prominence ceaselessly raises the price of the apparently ingenu-
ous question of just what was or was not true of that far off historical
incarnation. (Contrast the relaxation of Michael Oakeshott's incomparable
assessment two thirds of a century ago: "It is at least remarkable that at the
present time the gospel of Locke is less able to secure adherents than any
other whatever . . . he was meek, and until recently he inherited the earth.")[8]

   The first impulse of the historian, naturally enough, has been to shield
the historical Locke from these intrusions: to insist on his own idiosyncratic
preoccupations, and emphasize the unbridgeable gap between those preoccupations and the high stakes of global ideological struggle three centuries
later.[9] But this impulse is less clear in its ultimate purposes, and hence far
less convincingly self-vindicating, than it initially appeared to some. It still
has no obvious insecurities as a claim of justice: an insistence on the dead
Locke's right to immunity from primitive errors of identification, or, more
generously, to his continuing entitlement, like any other human being alive
or dead, to at least the effort at sympathetic understanding on the part of any
other human being who claims to disclose the truth about them.[10] But it is
less prepossessing (and wholly devoid of authority) as an effort at appropriation: an attempt to exclude others (everyone but true historians) from the
great Common of the past. Here a disparity in interests is badly miscast as a
commitment to, or a flouting of, the epistemic decencies, or an index of
personal intellectual coherence or confusion.[11]

The Historical and Political Sources of
That Continuing Pressure

In the second half of the twentieth century two main groups of scholars
proved especially reluctant to leave Locke unmolested to history. One was
made up of the socialist critics of global capitalism, still drawing their core

political convictions from the tradition of Karl Marx. The second formed
the educational heritage of Leo Strauss. History since 1954 has been kinder
to the latter than to the former, but not necessarily in ways which do much
to clarify either the character of Locke's life viewed from within, or the
aspects of his thinking which will in the end prove to cast the longest
shadows of all. Locke's own most explicit (if disingenuous) assessment of
his achievements as a theorist of politics[12] drew attention to the unique
felicity of his treatment of property in the (still determinedly anonymous)
Two Treatises of Government.[13] Modern scholars who have studied this
aspect of his thinking at all attentively have seldom endorsed this evalua-
tion, but, between them, they have greatly clarified both the arguments
which he advanced and the scale of the continuing challenge to identify a
normative basis for capitalist appropriation which does not, under critical
reflection, effectively denounce itself.[14] The dispute as to whether capitalist
appropriation can and must in the end be understood as a process of aug-
menting the stock of natural goods, rather than depleting it by subtracting
resources from the common, is as deep and arduous as it has ever been
before.[15] No one could sanely believe that its resolution turns on interpreting Locke's own thought processes or polemical strategies. But, even three
centuries after he added his key argument to the final edition of chapter V of
the *Second Treatise*,[16] it remains hard to get to the heart of the issue faster or
more incisively than through Locke's thinking. Those few lines are still the
most spectacular point of intersection between that life viewed from the
inside and the same life viewed from without. If we see the history of
capitalism, as we emphatically should, as an endless collision between
forms of life,[17] institutional constructions, normative rhetorics, and ways of
focusing and deepening human powers, with no preguaranteed outcomes
for better or worse, and the bleakest indifference to the vulnerable human
animals who enact it, this elaborately contextualized episode in Locke's
thinking is still one of the great imaginative moments within that history;
and the argument as to how best to represent that episode when seen from
within is still a significant prize in the struggle to characterize authorita-
tively from the outside not merely Locke's own life, but the human significance of most recent history. The Marxists may have lost all residual political credibility. But they still seem to have had a better grasp of the key
issues at stake here than virtually any of the antagonists who have swept
them so humiliatingly from the field.[18] After a promising phase in the 1970s
and 1980s,[19] it is still unclear how much this sustained scholarly attention
has done to establish exactly what questions Locke himself was attempting
to answer, or quite what conclusions he sought to vindicate and just why, in

his reflections on property. They have been considerably more successful, however, in spelling out conclusions which his works certainly do not establish (whether or not he meant them to do so). Because of the continuing ideological resonance of the claim to connect economic entitlements under capitalism with clear personal merits (to ground entitlement, at least in enough salient instances, in desert), the relations between the limited cogency of some of these arguments and their continued imaginative attractions is still of great moment, irrespective of Locke's own historical concerns, ambitions, or endeavors.

The idea of grasping the content of an intellectual life seen from within necessarily privileges the temporal coordinates of the life itself, and rapidly loses coherence as it moves away from these. But the idea of grasping its contents from the outside has no such temporal moorings. It demands that we look backward as well as forward, and that we register what has happened in and through that life by contrasting its intellectual outcomes at least with what its own bearer came self-consciously to reject, and perhaps, too, with what she or he contrived inadvertently to lose sight of or betray. The relation between Locke's grandest work, the *Essay Concerning Human Understanding,* and the cultural dynamics of the Enlightenment, and the powerfully inimical relation between the mode of analysis which that work set out and the imaginative stability and theoretical coherence of Christian Natural Jurisprudence, both guaranteed that no adequate account of what happened in that life could rest solely on what Locke himself contrived to notice in the course of living it (let alone on what he cared to acknowledge openly whilst doing so). Nor could it rest solely on a conjunction of those recognitions and acknowledgments with what happened later. It demands, too, a clear vision of what slipped away, or was squandered inadvertently, in the same passage of thought and feeling, and hence a contrast, conceptually at least, with a vast, if indeterminate, miscellany of what had gone before. To take the measure of Locke's achievements, for better and for worse, we would first need to be able to take the measure of the main movements of modern western thought, and do so, not compulsively in its own pre-established terms, but somehow freely on ones for which we could assume full responsibility ourselves. The dream of such an assessment, scandalous, insanely arrogant, but undeniably thrilling, has tantalized European intellectuals since at least the days of Nietzsche; most flamboyantly, in recent years, in the strange odyssey of Michel Foucault.[20] No modern Locke scholar of any quality has had the effrontery to attempt anything of the kind. But in relation to the deepest issues with which Locke struggled, and also in relation to the most drastic challenges which his work poses to our own continuing efforts to apprehend politics, it is far from clear that anything less grandiose can possibly suffice.

Locke and the Dynamics of the Enlightenment

For Locke's life seen from within, the key question of ethical and political judgment posed by its centrality to the dynamics of the Enlightenment is how far Locke himself came in later life to recognize and embrace the destructive implications for Christian Natural Law of the analyses of language and knowledge which he eventually worked out in the *Essay*. That question may have been posed fairly crudely three or four decades ago, but it has attracted since, and especially since the mid 1980s, an exceptionally impressive array of scholarship from the most empathetic to the most analytically astringent. Predictably, the scholars in question remain divided in their conclusions principally by discrepancies in intellectual interests or attention, and by contrasts in ideological taste. Those most appreciative of the continuities in language and rhetoric between elements in Locke's texts and the public ideology of the United States have often been the most confident of the clarity of his recognition and endorsement of the destructively secularizing implications of his epistemology and psychology.[21] In face of an indisputably protracted and dogged reluctance on their author's part to acknowledge these implications for himself in public, they have buffered their interpretation of his purposes by attributing to him a corresponding agility and zest for obfuscation, following the hermeneutic lead long ago offered by Leo Strauss himself. Naturally enough, the result is seldom as convincing in its depiction of the historical Locke as the best work of those who confine their interests mainly to the latter.[22] It is, for one thing, consistently far more restrictive in the range of pertinent archival material which it elects to consider at all, or to analyze with any care.[23] But its relative historical insouciance has not necessarily impeded it from delineating the internal tensions within Locke's developing thinking in a powerfully illuminating way.[24] Setting aside the contributions of factional animosity (a topic on which Locke himself dwelt at some length), this disparity is in the end best seen as one of contrast in purposes. A synoptic interest in large-scale change over long periods of time is not readily combined with a keen concern for the intricacies of individual experience, even if the causal basis of all such change must always be an immense accumulation of individual intricacies of exactly that kind. Reconciling a synoptic interest in drastic intellectual transformations over long time spans with a zest for particular intellectual heroes or heroines favors a highly stylized representation of those selected.

The carefully stylized Straussian Locke reappears at varying distances and for a miscellany of purposes. Some of its most interesting and illuminating exemplars have been presented less in order to recharacterize, with greater or less patience and authority, the philosopher himself, than to clarify and consolidate an older picture of the significance of the American Founding in face of the republican lineage so masterfully disclosed by John Pocock,[25] and embraced more than a third of a century ago in Bernard Bailyn's classic Introduction to his Belknap Press edition of the *Pamphlets of the American Revolution,* [26] trenchantly reissued two years later as *The Ideological Origins of the American Revolution.*[27] This protracted historiographical mêlée has often been more than a little confused and, even cumulatively, has done less to enhance the understanding of Locke himself than more narrowly focused textual studies of similar provenance like those of Nathan Tarcov[28] or Ruth Grant[29] have contrived to do. The historical question of just how much American political perception or sentiment were at any point clearly attributable to the more or less attentive reading of passages from Locke's writings is extremely complicated and very hard to answer at all convincingly.[30] Little dependable headway has been made with it since the days of Merle Curti's article (or, more tersely, perhaps ever). It is easier to establish where, when, and to whom, copies of the relevant Locke texts were definitely available in eighteenth-century America, or when, and to some degree why, particular passages from his writings were cited, with greater or less precision and with or without acknowledgment,[31] in books, pamphlets, newspapers, manuscripts, or public pronouncements[32] in the colonies or early republic.[33] But most of the more important instances of the latter have been well known for a very long time, and continue to underline the very special significance of the construal of the relation between legitimate taxation and consent in the *Second Treatise of Government* in the context of the struggles which preceded and led up to American independence.

The anglophone reactions to Locke's political texts have recently been charted with exemplary patience by Mark Goldie,[34] with results which largely confirm the dislocation between preoccupation with the continuing presence of the texts themselves, and concern predominantly with the issue of what exactly Locke's own intellectual experiences and innovations have proved in due course to mean for human beings alive considerably later. The continuing presence of the texts, both in public life and in the comparative seclusion of academic inquiry and disputation, is comparatively tract-

able historiographically, however patchy the evidence eventually proves to
be. But the long-term implications of Locke's own intellectual experience,
invention, and indiscretion for his human successors are not an essentially
historiographical matter, and except in detail and within the carefully restrictive focus of particular disciplinary culs-de-sac, they are unlikely to
prove tractable to any reasonably determinate mode of inquiry. This yields
an unenviable dilemma: more than a suspicion that the sole available op-
tions are for triviality or charlatanism. To opt for pure history was to eschew
charlatanism like the plague, but since its purity was its sole specific against
the risk of triviality, it is easy to see why it was likely, sooner or later, to
seem gravely insufficient, and especially so for those whose principal concern was with understanding politics.[35] In the theory of politics, trade-offs
between precision of method and the claims of the subject matter, even in
the more Alexandrian phases of the development of modern academic
disciplines,[36] could never for long firmly favor the precision of method.
Hence the continuing importance for those who share neither the political
convictions of Karl Marx nor many of the methodological judgments of
Leo Strauss, of the bodies of scholarship which have issued from each of
these.

The Ideological Prizes at Stake

Besides the key issue of the relations between the normative standing of
rights to private property and the justice or otherwise of social arrangements in their entirety, the main axis of ideological contestation across the
globe for most of the time since Locke's death, there are a number of other
key domains of normative conflict in modern politics, where the bearing of
Locke's personal intellectual experience still carries profound significance.
Amongst the more important are the integrity and coherence of a normative
political vision grounded on assigning rights to individual human beings as
a distinctive type of natural creature, the realism and normative cogency of
grounding political authority on a process of personal authorization and
consent, and the clarity and conclusiveness of the claim that human thought
and speech must be seen and treated as free, and that each individual is
therefore entitled, however bizarre or irksome the judgments or pronouncements in which they issue, to a toleration from their fellows, limited only by
the unmistakable threat of physical harm. Other plausible, if in the end less
compelling, instances are the law-focused approach to the design and en-
actment of constitutions which entrench all three of these commitments, if

with varying degrees of security and priority, and the sociological presumption that, except in pathological or perhaps non-occidental cases, societies can, do, and should, subsist in some degree of causal independence from the inherently arbitrary dispositions of state power or the vagaries of operating markets, and that such societies therefore deserve, and may even be able to exact a measure of direct control over the former, and at least a limited immunity to the latter.[37] In the case of the United States all five of these complexes of normative and practical interpretation in some measure fit together and disclose an apparent elective affinity. Each complex can be associated, with varying degrees of selective inattention, with at least some aspects of Locke's writings, and Locke can therefore, less defensibly, be identified as the leading historical protagonist of all five. Even if all five did fit together perfectly in the case of the United States itself, this state of affairs would offer no guarantee that their affinity was anything more than a contingency of history and geography. Since it requires little effort to notice loosenesses in the fit even in the American case (between, for example, the natural universality of human rights and the institution of chattel slavery), any presumption that the linkages will prove robust across time and space (that they will turn out over time transhistorically and globally self-evident) is fairly heroic. America's *Griff nach der Weltmacht* is the most overwhelming, the furthest extended, and in many ways the most integral grasp for world power there has yet been, but it was always inherently unlikely to vindicate this presumption.

Locke and the Theorization of Rights

In the meantime, in any case, it is intellectually more prudent to try to assess the bearing of Locke's reflections in these five cases, one by one. The most strategically illuminating of the five is the theorization of individual rights, recently analyzed with the greatest care by A. John Simmons.[38] The grounds and implications of Locke's theory in this case have long been at the center of scholarly contestation to define the terms on which Locke himself is best understood. C. B. Macpherson,[39] and other interpreters who drew their main insights into Locke from a broadly Marxist orientation,[40] read his theorization of rights decisively through the prism of Chapter V of the *Second Treatise,* following the cue proffered in the *Essay's* comparatively casual observation that where there is no property there is no injustice.[41] Macpherson himself presumed, without obvious warrant, that property in this sense was to be taken in its restricted meaning of private

ownership, rather than in the wider usage glossed by Locke himself as
"lives, liberties and estates,"[42] in which it was always more reasonable to
interpret the term as virtually a synonym for rights, and the casual equation
of the scope of property and justice, instead of being a striking act of moral
and political effrontery, becomes an unexhilarating tautology. It would be
attractive to settle the matter once and for all by isolating the way in which
Locke himself understood the category of justice over time, and demonstrating the constraints which that understanding must have imposed in the
ways in which he conceived many other connected issues[43] — an approach
rendered still more enticing at present by the dominant concerns of contemporary liberal political philosophy with the criterion for justice in social
arrangements. But rich though the materials which Locke left behind certainly are, and fascinating though the scholarly materials extracted from
them over the half century or so since Von Leyden's edition have proved,
nothing in these materials confirms that justice had for Locke himself a
theoretical centrality analogous to that which it plainly carries for John
Rawls, Robert Nozick, Ronald Dworkin, or Tim Scanlon.

If it is still as implausible as ever to see Locke's intellectual life on the
model of John Rawls's (as a protracted struggle to pin down the scope of
justice in human social and political relations, and the requirements which
it places upon human agents), it is altogether more compelling to see that
same life as a sustained inquiry into the nature of the rights which human
beings as such hold against one another, and a somewhat more intermittent
investigation, differentially focused over time but sometimes pursued with
the utmost urgency, into just how these rights articulate with each other in
relation to particular issues: the true original, extent and end of civil government, the grounds and scope of the duty to tolerate the religious convictions
and practices of others, how far and why private ownership, more especially of land,[44] can be a genuine entitlement. The nature of the rights which
human beings hold against one another is the core intellectual problem of
Natural Law. For many centuries it lay at the center of European thought
about ethics, epistemology, and theology. The balance between these domains, notoriously, shifted over the course of Locke's life, and has continued to shift, more or less erratically, over the centuries since his death.[45]
A scholar with the fastidiousness and patience of Von Leyden was every bit
as attuned to the scale and significance of these shifts as more flamboyant
and macroscopic interpreters of the dynamics and implications of European
intellectual history, from Leo Strauss himself,[46] to Charles Taylor,[47] Alasdair MacIntyre,[48] Michel Foucault, or Richard Rorty. He may have focused on different aspects of them and analyzed them with a considerably

finer grain, but it would be simply an error to suppose that he was either obtuse to them, or foolishly blithe over their significance. Just the same is true of the more careful and reflective of the scholars, whether philosophers, historians, or political theorists by profession or intellectual formation, who have followed in his footsteps.[49]

The most conspicuous single shift in the structuring of western thought between Locke's birth and the present day has been the erasure of the all-structuring role of a single omnipotent and omniscient Deity (if not necessarily as a contingent focus for personal belief, at least as a publicly avowable premise of cognitive strategy). Uncontentiously, in Locke's early intellectual life that role was still firmly in place. Arguably, by his death, and to no small degree as a consequence of his own analytical reflections and conceptual innovations, it was not merely clearly less secure, but conclusively displaced. What remains acutely contentious is quite how clearly he himself was aware of the more disturbing implications of some of his own main lines of thought, and how clearly and calmly he embraced the most disruptive of these. (Plainly, insofar as he was unaware of them, he cannot plausibly be thought to have embraced them.) Since Strauss himself, the most confident and determined exponents of the view that Locke understood and welcomed all of these implications, and the most disruptive, the most warmly and whole-heartedly, have come from the ranks of the scholars whom Strauss inspired and did so much to shape. Although the initial diagnosis reaches back before Von Leyden's edition was even published, and was grounded quite independently of any of Locke's early texts, this group of scholars has labored purposefully to push the moment of recognition and endorsement of the shift by Locke himself as far back as possible within their author's life. Despite the ingenuity and incidental insight of some of the resultant readings, this exercise has not proved historiographically convincing. But the most grudging verdict on it could hardly deny that it has by now done much to sharpen a modern reader's awareness of the scale of what is at stake. What is less clear is whether, in doing so, it has advanced significantly on Locke's own apprehension of these stakes, which was in many ways both acute and extremely explicit.[50]

Nowhere in Locke's thinking does the conceptual presence or absence of an omnipotent and omniscient Deity bear more directly and conclusively than on his view of the character and practical import of the presumptively equal rights of all human beings as natural creatures.[51] In his view these rights are an articulation of an authoritative Law, and that Law itself expresses the will, the presumptively perfect judgment, and the overwhelming powers of enforcement of its supreme Law-Maker. The distribution of rights assigned under this Law can, of course, be reconceived less hectically, as Simmons suggests,[52] in terms of a metaphysically less ambitious moral realism, without necessarily undergoing drastic disturbance, at least in their conceptual architecture. But the sanctions of an explicitly concerned and overwhelmingly effective enforcer must then be replaced in their entirety by whatever other materials can be elicited from culture, history, deliberative rationality, and interactive prudence or imprudence. All of these resources, none of which can be said to be ignored by Locke himself, have been explored extensively since his death. Surprisingly many of the main outlines which he left behind, recapitulated, self-consciously or inadvertently, in the polemical strategies of the American revolutionaries and the constitutional expedients adopted by the founders of the new republic, have kept their shape and impetus, and greatly extended their territorial impact, in the centuries since his death.

If we see this complex apparatus of individual rights, constitutionally mediated state power, practically institutionalized representative consent, and increasingly confident capitalist property relations as embodying a somewhat inexplicit historical pragmatism, whether or not we also attribute its extension to the expanding power of the United States of America,[53] it is reasonable to see the theorization of rights not merely as a contingency of American cultural history, but also as a practical institutional expedient which has gained steadily in political plausibility as time has gone by. Here, plainly, nothing turns on the intimacy and precision of the causal connections, if any, between the apparatus thus extended and the historical inquiries, arguments, or conclusions of Locke himself. It is only if we press the question of whether this apparatus does reflect a coherent and compelling rationale that there is any strong reason for viewing it over against Locke's own intellectual experiences or creations. A self-defending and self-commending set of pragmatic expedients stands in no need of a coherent rationale,[54] and it would be unwise to desert it merely because no such rationale readily suggests itself. But the view that this apparatus plainly is both self-defending and self-commending is very much a view from within, and, even from within, is some way from exhausting the visual space. From without, it has always faced severe criticism, as well as acute animosity. In face of that criticism, the judgment that Nature carries no authoritative Law, and that any vision of the distribution of rights within it merely reflects the normative intuitions of particular individuals, groups, or cultures, depletes the language of rights of most of its power,[55] and undermines the presumption that there is anything determinate for it to answer to. Under a Law which holds authority over nature as a whole, rights might indeed be trumps.[56] They might dominate a normative space through a power which they carried in themselves, and do so without specious rhetorical amplification. But in the cacophony of cultures, and amidst the often murderous exigencies of political conflict, it is hard to see them as more than whimsically invoked pseudo-trumps, claims to an authority which in the end is wholly bogus, and which also has nothing left to fall back on, as soon as its targets choose actively to repudiate it.[57]

As far as we know, Locke himself never doubted that the prescriptive content of the Law of Nature (what it commanded and forbade) lay within the epistemic reach of every adult human being. But he certainly did not believe that most human beings in fact grasped that content at all fully and accurately, let alone recognized how overwhelming were their grounds for complying with it.[58] In his judgment, on sustained reflection, these grounds were less and less convincingly accessible from the interaction between human beings and the natural world alone. What was missing decisively from the epistemic resources yielded by that interaction was a knowledge of the sanctions required to enforce that law conclusively and in its entirety: more specifically the sanctions disclosed in the Christian Revelation.[59] Within Locke's own vision, this assignment of rights and duties issued from a Law which held full normative authority, and which was also backed to the hilt by overwhelming power. Shorn of that backing, the claim to normative authority lay at the mercy of the sensibilities of its individual human targets, and lost the air of externality, objectivity, and solidity, which it drew from its presumptive standing as the normative logic of a created universe.[60] Along with that air, it also lost any intelligible claim to a foundation independent of, and over against, the fluidities of cultural change or the quicksands of inter-group animosities. Instead of offering a normative matrix with the power to distinguish permissible from impermissible human actions in any possible space of interaction, it subsided into an altogether more Hobbesian version of the State of Nature, in which right extended no further than power, and every normative intuition was open to challenge by anyone with the confidence or obduracy to feel and judge differently. At the level of power, this has done little to impede the diffusion of the rights schemata of modern representative democratic states and the capitalist property orders which accompany them.[61] A vulgar pragmatism must confine itself to recording this historical movement. To explain it, and still more to vindicate it, demands an altogether more alert and critical pragmatism; and such a pragmatism (in intention, most of the more influential and impressive contemporary political philosophy) has had minimal success in explaining this movement, and has sought largely to vindicate a variety of economic, social, political, and legal arrangements which, for all their pronounced lack of utopian allure, are unmistakably at odds with those which at present prevail.[62] Within this body of disciplined critical appraisal pragmatic commitment and normative intuition have parted company ever more decisively.

The Intellectual Upshot of That Theorization

Studying the thought of Locke is no direct aid in mapping this process of disintegration: the cracking up of the juridical ice-fields once fused together in the model of Nature's unified Law. What Locke's vision still can offer is an immensely revealing vantage point from which to view that process of disintegration over time. It in no way precludes sympathy with (or even at points allegiance to) the enterprises of constructivist theoretical re-imagining, or systematically cooperative design and implementation of legal institutions, which are needed to establish a regime of human rights within and between all existing states. But it does compel us, if we are to think clearly and accurately about the matter, to view each of these exercises quite largely (and the latter all but exclusively) as hazardous, extreme, and necessarily improvisatory, political adventures, not as simple acts of recognition of the decencies implied by our standing as one particular kind of animal in a world where we already are, or could ever hope to become, fully at home.[63] In the world as Locke imagined it, theology was still the master science. God's Law ruled that world without restriction, both by right and by power, and all rights of human beings in the end issued from a single integrated framework of meaning and authority. In the world as we severally imagine it today, the ideas of a master science of the normative, of an all-encompassing and authoritative Law, or a unified framework of meaning, make no residual sense. The scope of human rights must be defined by whatever practices we prove to approve, and the authority of human rights is as flimsy, and their definition as fitful and centrifugal, as the vagaries of our approvals and disapprovals.

We still, therefore, have every reason to distinguish as sharply as we can the critical question of just what Locke's arguments rationally imply, in both their force and their failures, from the historical question of the continuity, extent, and depth of the ideological shadow cast by his great texts. The first question is one of philosophy or political theory; the second, an assortment of questions about the historical transmission of formulae, complexes of belief, or structures of argument, and the dynamics

of contemporary change, economic, social, cultural, and political, across
the globe. Studying Locke will be little, if any, help in addressing any of the
latter. But it remains the sole minimally prudent method for focusing on the
former, and thus an indispensable moment in judging how best to answer it.
Because Locke considered so many different topics in ethics, politics, theology, and philosophy with some care in the course of his life, and because
he did so with such intellectual energy and ability, it would be absurd to
attempt a complete listing of the range of such arguments which he advanced which might still repay the closest analysis. Any selection on
grounds of urgency or relative depth must principally reflect the tastes and
preoccupations of the selector. Over and above the key issue of property,
the leading contenders for the most pressing and significant of these arguments in the last decade and a half have come from his analyses of the
rationale for and limits to toleration, his treatments, explicit or implicit, of
the significance of gender,[64] and his relatively relaxed conceptualization of
political authorization. It is simply a mistake to see Locke as a champion, or
even an especially careful analyst, of the merits of constitutionalism.[65] But
he plainly did intend the *Second Treatise,* with its crisp account of the true
original, extent, and end of civil government, as a compelling picture of
how political power can be to some degree validly authorized. Over issues
of gender the degree to which his attention really was engaged is often
harder to judge. Only over the claims of toleration does the scale and
continuity of his concerns, the vigor with which he pursued his arguments,
and the imaginative and analytical force of his treatment establish for itself
the continuing centrality of his analysis for many connected matters now
and far into the future.

Locke and Toleration

For all the energy, and in some cases the distinction, of scholarly accounts of
Locke's views on toleration since the 1980s, there is still room for a full and
balanced analysis of the changing ways in which he saw the issue of toleration over time, and the range of experiences which led him to modify his
judgments about it so substantially. Some of the most stimulating historical
studies of his changing views have lacked balance,[66] and failed particularly
to register the degree to which he came to see it less as one of the key stakes in
English domestic politics, and more as the fulcrum of the fate of European
Christendom as a whole.[67] This distortion was principally occasioned by one
of the most protracted public wrangles of Locke's declining years, his

defense of the argument of the original *Epistola de Tolerantia* against the assault launched on William Popple's English translation by the Anglican clergyman Jonas Proast,[68] the final installment of which was still unpublished at Locke's death. Since no comparably sustained attacks were leveled at the initial Latin edition which emerged from Locke's continental exile, he never had occasion to try to defend this against the wider range of continental antagonists which its arguments certainly called for, and in particular never faced the intellectual challenge of vindicating what was at best an extreme Protestant view against the intellectual defenders of a still militarily dynamic Catholicism.

By 1667, as is well known, Locke had already come to deplore the use of coercion in the attempt to alter the religious convictions of others. Over the final two decades of his life, Locke in his *Letters on Toleration* sharpened and deepened this judgment, leaving, alongside the works of Pierre Bayle, a magisterial verdict on the wars of religion unleashed by the Reformation, and a classic repertoire of grounds for favoring toleration, to their Enlightenment successors.[69] Contemporary liberals have quarried these texts principally for components of a potentially decisive secular defense of freedom of speech, thought, and worship. The most distinguished liberal political philosopher of at least the last half century, John Rawls, has quite explicitly adopted this defense as model for how to ground a coherent conception of social justice on a full recognition of the equal right to see, value, and live differently of all adult human beings.[70] Three decades after the publication of *A Theory of Justice,* however, it is still unclear how far this conclusion can be stabilized rationally rather than rhetorically. Locke himself was not merely addressing rather obviously different issues (which in some sense may no longer be relevant); he also reached, in his own judgment, very different conclusions.

What those conclusions were can be seen best if we start out by considering the issues which he did wish to address. The central question for him, as it was likely to be for any Protestant thinker facing a militarily and ideologically (perhaps even in part a spiritually) renascent Catholicism, was whether human holders of political authority did or did not have a clear duty to try to impose their own best assessment of the requirements of Christianity on those whom they ruled. This issue had pressed on Christian thinkers ever since they inherited the coercive facilities of the Roman empire. To any Christian ruler who saw themselves as legitimate, and had already presumptively done their best to ascertain, with due sacerdotal assistance, what those requirements were, it was hard to explain how they could escape having a duty to act on this judgment: hard, indeed, to see how they could be fit to hold the authority in the first place if they shrank from exercising it on behalf of the most important and weighty of all their subjects' interests, the fate which awaited them at the Last Judgment. Contemporary liberals have parted company too decisively with this problem to be able still to see it as a problem. They see it instead as an index of archaic superstition. Accordingly, they are slow to recognize the value which Locke very reasonably placed on the special advantages of his arguments from his own point of view, and quick to resent the very limited provision which those arguments offered for their own quite distinct requirements. For Locke what was essential was to refute the view that persecution was a Christian duty. For contemporary liberals the most intellectually reassuring result (and for some the only acceptable conclusion) must be that any form of molestation of adult belief or thought is both an impertinence and an absurdity, and any encroachment on freedom of speech therefore a ground for acute suspicion, entertainable at all only where the speech in question collides immediately with some at least equally peremptory right on the part of those whom it threatens.

This is a very complicated subject matter, not to be compressed into a brisk formula. But for all its inherent complexity it is far from clear that any consistently pragmatic and skeptical assessment of it could possibly vindicate the conclusions which contemporary liberals favor. In practice, as the history of American public law endlessly attests, claims to freedom of expression regularly collide with the rights of others, through immediate threats to public order, direct incitements to violence, and perhaps, more ecologically and elusively, in the economic dynamics of entire industries (pornography, drugs). Adjudicating the collisions (and hence confining freedom of expression in practice) is a coherent and readily defensible legal and political exercise, which in itself does nothing to impugn the value of free expression. But what it does do is to make clear why freedom of expression cannot be a self-defining and self-subsistent political and social good, let alone a wholly untrammeled individual right, independently of the consequences of the ways in which it comes to be exercised. Modern liberal readers of Locke are quite right in seeing him as rejecting religious persecution as cruel, futile, and unjust. They see that the charge of cruelty, while cogent enough in itself, will hardly do the necessary work. (Prisons, for example, are scarcely a consistently successful orchestration of kindness to the greatest number.) They see that the charge of injustice, whilst more conclusive in their own eyes, is bound to seem question-begging in this context to anyone who seriously opposes them, and they have turned accordingly with particular gratitude to the charge of futility, as this figures in the thought of Locke (or, perhaps more encouragingly, in that of Bayle).[71] The attempt to coerce belief is inherently futile since coercion acts upon the will, and belief is not a voluntary matter. Very few human beings can change their beliefs simply by choosing to do so, and, it is reasonable to assume, none at all can do so instantaneously. It may be relatively easy to modify how others choose to express themselves through a judicious blend of menaces and bribes, but you cannot sensibly hope to make them believe what you want by even the most lurid extremes of intimidation. (There are few more compelling sites for this insight than the practice of child-rearing.)[72] The main insecurity in this argument lies in the timespan over which it is to be applied. What you can do at once to modify the belief of another by direct assault is pretty modest. But over far longer spans of time (for instance, over several generations), the room for rational hope is far wider, and the room for entrepreneurial fantasy all but limitless. Well over a millennium of interpreting the thorny Christian path to personal salvation had registered this distinctly less hectic tempo of credal manipulation quite deeply, and reasonably concluded that decisive proof of the long-term futility of determined, relentless, and lucky persecution was out of the question. To win his argument, accordingly, Locke needed to argue much more narrowly, and with much greater contextual care.

Read with due care within this context, his conclusions differ notably from those of contemporary liberals.[73] At the core of his argument were the distinctions between theoretical and practical beliefs and between civil and religious associations. The purpose of civil associations was to provide for the needs of living human beings within this world. The purpose of religious associations was, in the Christian case, to provide for the salvation of their souls, and, in all cases which Locke himself recognized as genuinely religious, for the requirements of their relation with a divine authority whose powers and concerns reached decisively beyond this life. What made religious persecution potentially mandatory for its exponents was the clear priority of the second schedule of interests. Locke fully accepted this priority, and assumed it without hesitation. What he disputed was that the priority itself could ever extend to the services provided by those who hold authority within a civil association. His arguments were always far from convincing, if seen from a religion like Islam.[74] Their force for a Christian audience depended on the clear duty of each individual Christian to do their best to save their own soul, and on their manifest interest in succeeding in that endeavor. To save their soul every individual Christian must live, as best they could, as God required, a task likely always to prove beyond them. More manageably, at least in the luckier cases, they must also worship Him as they believed He required them to do. Only the sincere expression of devotion through these forms could discharge the central responsibility of a Christian and close the alarming gap between God's requirements and their own relatively feeble capabilities. In that delicate and awesome relation the intrusion of human power was not merely certain to contaminate motivation and worsen the prospects of the individual believer. It was also categorically quite irrelevant — as impertinent as it was prospectively harmful. Locke's defense of toleration assumed a distinctively Protestant vision of the relation between human beings and their God. It refused, notoriously, to extend a comparable degree of immunity to Catholic members of his own society. More strikingly still, it showed no trace of tolerance toward those who rejected theism in its entirety.[75]

To see this combination of commitments as integrated and rational (and not as shamelessly and ludicrously incoherent), it is necessary to view it in its own terms. In his analysis the salvationary requirements of individual religions are matters in themselves of theoretical belief (indeed paradigm cases of theoretical belief). They depend upon how human beings conceive and imagine something which does not lie clearly or steadily within human view. It is only as theoretical beliefs, beliefs with no determinate implications for how their bearers have reason to behave in this world, and more specifically none which threaten the interests of their human fellows, that they are immune to civil coercion. As soon as, or insofar as, they merge with practical beliefs, beliefs which clearly do prompt or even require their bearers to act very differently, and act in ways which do threaten the vital interests of others, that immunity lapses. Any form of political allegiance is a practical belief, and Catholicism, as Locke construed it, was incipiently a form of political allegiance. The decision on whether or not to tolerate it was therefore a classic issue of political judgment, a matter of assessing the balance of threats and advantages, and acting for the net benefit of the subjects for whom a sovereign holds public responsibility. With atheists the issue for Locke was simpler and even more decisive. Since they disbelieved in either Gods or an afterlife, they could scarcely stand in need of religious toleration: the entitlement to worship as they believed themselves obliged to do. But on Locke's account, they also had no right to avow their disbelief in public (or, more bewilderingly, perhaps even to believe it), since that belief itself was in his eyes all too devastatingly practical: a menace to the entire structure of motivation which rendered human beings minimally fitted to live with one another. It was thus a paradigm case of a practical belief of the most threatening kind, and the duty to suppress it as thoroughly as they could fell clearly on every civil ruler (Christian or otherwise).

Three centuries later this assessment has come to look very odd (especially when set beside the judgments of Locke's contemporary Pierre Bayle).[76] But what is odd about it is not the judgment that some beliefs can and do carry practical menaces (or indeed practical blessings) for other human beings. To distinguish menacing from benign practical beliefs requires an extraordinarily delicate assessment of social, economic, and political causality. No government can hope to carry out such assessments with consistent success. But it is not easy to see how any government can hope to avoid the permanent duty to monitor with the utmost vigilance the balance of menace and promise within the practical beliefs held by its fellow citizens, and to intervene to limit the menace before it is too late. Murderous sects and hideous purposes are no prerogative of the late seventeenth century. It is intrinsic to human belief that the relations between the theoretical and the practical should always be intensely precarious. In many settings since Locke's day we have made impressive headway in the practice of toleration (religious and secular). But we have yet to think our way commandingly beyond his fragile synthesis. Atheism may seem to most Europeans and Americans today (not least the atheists amongst them) an unlikely source of practical hazard. But it has plenty of less implausible competitors.

Locke's Vision of the Place of Politics in Human Life

Many other aspects of Locke's political thinking have been analyzed illuminatingly in recent decades, not least the subtle and fascinating issue of his sensitivity or obtuseness to the normative bearing and practical presence of gender throughout the lives of human beings.[77] It would be reckless to predict which aspects, whether from these and older themes or wholly novel, will loom as large in the decades to come. What can be confidently expected to carry continuing force is the synoptic vision of the human political predicament offered by his work as a whole — its imaginative arc from the process of psychic individuation, and linguistic and cultural construction, across the theorization of value and the practical bonds between individual human beings in cooperation and conflict, to the legal and political structures of organized communities, and the emerging economic logic of what is now a globalized system of production and exchange. At the center of this vision are the precariousness and onerousness, but also the endless revitalization, of human judgment[78] — its incessant collisions and aberrations, but also its enduring capacity for creative recovery. This is overwhelmingly less brash or encouraging than the ideological materials which have made such remarkable global headway in the last half of the twentieth century.[79] But is also deeper and wiser. It is hard to see how it could ever simply cease to apply.

Chasing the Shadow

If we view it from today, the shadow which Locke casts has lengthened every day since the afternoon that he died.[80] It is natural to assume that it must also have grown ever fainter and more notional as time has gone by. By the same token, too, it is also natural to assume that we, in our turn, must have become ever worse placed to see quite what it was that could have cast a shadow of this intimidating length. In response to this combination of prominence and elusiveness, three centuries and more of division of intellectual labor have offered in exchange a variety of techniques of more or less disciplined inquiry, which volunteer to show us how to distinguish our questions ever more precisely, in order to answer them with ever greater security. You can see the relation between these two processes as a race, and wonder which of the two has been gaining on the other, and whether the gain, where gain there has been, has been steady and deeply grounded, or altogether more fitful, and based upon the most arbitrary of contingencies. I doubt myself whether the gain has ever been for any length of time at all steady or dependable, and doubt even more acutely whether the history of the human sciences as a whole has ever been one of reliable headway in specifying how to answer such questions with real security. Whether we see Locke as an incompetent modern,[81] a heroic Masterbuilder of Modernity,[82] or, still more recklessly, as someone marooned on the far side of an ever widening chasm,[83] we must take most of the weight of such judgments on our own shoulders. As we do so, the most prudent conclusion to draw from the last half century of Locke scholarship is that we should shoulder it as humbly as we can. The motive for making the judgment in this spirit might be epistemic or moral — a respect, however uneasy or reluctant, for distant greatness or alien power. Perhaps by now, though, to strike a more defiantly incorrect note, we might just recognize instead how ill-placed those whose puny shadows can barely hope to stretch across their own lifetimes will always be to take in fully the source of shadows cast from so very far away.

NOTES

1. Compare Locke's own analysis of the relation between human beings and the Law under which they find themselves: "A dependent intelligent being is under the power and direction and dominion of him on whom he depends and must be for the ends appointed him by that superior being. If man were independent he could have no law but his own will no end but himself. He would be a god to himself." Ethica B (Bodleian Ms. Locke C28, 141: John Dunn, *The Political Thought of John Locke* [Cambridge: Cambridge University Press, 1969]), Epigraph.

2. "Person is a Forensick Term, appropriating Actions and their Merit; and so belongs only to intelligent Agents capable of a Law, and Happiness and Misery."(John Locke, *An Essay Concerning Human Understanding,* ed. P. H. Nidditch [Oxford: Clarendon Press, 1975], Bk. II, xxvii, 26, ll 26–28; cf. John Dunn, *Rethinking Modern Political Theory* [Cambridge: Cambridge University Press, 1985], chapter 1, 13–33). And cf. Derek Parfit, *Reasons and Persons* (Oxford: Clarendon Press, 1984).

3. For a contemporary assessment see David Bostock, *Aristotle's Ethics* (Oxford: Oxford University Press, 2001), and Parfit, *Reasons and Persons.*

4. See, generally, John Dunn, *Political Obligation in Its Historical Context* (Cambridge: Cambridge University Press, 1980), chapter 4 . Mark Goldie, ed., *The Reception of Locke's Politics,* 6 volumes (London: Pickering & Chatto, 1999). For North America, D. S. Lutz, "The Relative Influence of European Writers on Late Eighteenth Century American Political Thought," *American Political Science Review,* 78 (1984), 189–97; Stephen Dworetz, *The Unvarnished Doctrine: Locke, Liberalism and the American Revolution* (Durham: Duke University Press, 1990); J. Huyler, *Locke in America: The Moral Philosophy of the Founding Fathers* (Lawrence: University of Kansas Press, 1995); Laura J. Scalia, "The Many Faces of Locke in America's Early Nineteenth Century Democratic Philosophy," *Political Research Quarterly,* 49 (1996), 807–35; J. F. Dienstag, "Between History and Nature: Social Contract Theory in Locke and the Founders," *Journal of Politics,* 58 (1997), 985–1009; T. H. Breen, "Subjecthood and Citizenship: The Context of James Otis's Radical Critique of John Locke," *New England Quarterly,* 71 (1998), 378–403. For France, see Ross Hutchison, *Locke in France 1688–1734 (Studies in Voltaire and the Eighteenth Century.* Oxford: Volatire Foundation, 1991); John W. Yolton, *Locke and French Materialism* (Oxford: Clarendon Press, 1991); Jorn Schosler, *John Locke et les philosophes français: La critique des idées en France au dix-*

huitième siècle (Studies in Voltaire and the Eighteenth Century. Oxford: Voltaire Foundation, 1997).

5. For a succession of assessments of the trade-offs along the way, see Dunn, *Political Obligation,* chapter 2; James Tully, ed., *Meaning and Context: Quentin Skinner and His Critics* (Cambridge: Polity, 1988); Richard Tuck, "The Contribution of History," Philip Pettit and Robert Goodin, eds., *A Companion to Contemporary Political Philosophy* (Oxford: Blackwell, 1993), pp. 72–89; John Dunn, *The History of Political Theory* (Cambridge: Cambridge University Press, 1996); Quentin Skinner, *Liberty before Liberalism* (Cambridge: Cambridge University Press, 1998); David Runciman, "History of Political Thought: The State of the Discipline," *British Journal of Politics and International Relations* 3 (2001), 84–104.

6. John Locke, *Essays on the Law of Nature,* W. Von Leyden, ed. (Oxford: Clarendon Press, 1954).

7. Merle Curti, "The Great Mr. Locke, America's Philosopher, 1783–1861," *Huntington Library Quarterly,* 107–51; and cf. Louis Hartz, *The Liberal Tradition in America* (New York: Harcourt Brace, 1955).

8. Michael Oakeshott, "John Locke: Born 28 August 1632," *Cambridge Review,* 54 (4/11/1932), 27 (reprinted in J. Dunn and Ian Harris, eds.), *Locke,* vol. 1, 26–27 (Cheltenham: Edward Elgar, 1997).

9. Cf. Dunn, *Political Thought of Locke.*

10. Dunn, *Political Obligation,* chapter 5.

11. Dunn, *History of Political Theory,* chapter 2.

12. "Propriety, the subject matter about which Laws are made. I have nowhere found more clearly explain'd than in a Book intitled *Two Treatises of Government.*"(E. S. de Beer [ed.], *The Correspondence of John Locke,* [Oxford: Clarendon Press, 1976–], letter 3328, 25 August 1703: VIII, 58.)

13. Locke, *Second Treatise of Government,* chapter 5.

14. James Tully, *A Discourse of Property* (Cambridge: Cambridge University Press, 1980); Jeremy Waldron, *The Right to Private Property* (Oxford: Clarendon Press, 1988); Ian Shapiro, *The Evolution of Rights in Liberal Theory* (Cambridge: Cambridge University Press, 1986); G. A. Cohen, "Marx and Locke on Land and Labour," *Proceedings of the British Academy,* LXXI, (1985), 357–88; M. H. Kramer, *John Locke and the Origins of Private Property* (Cambridge: Cambridge University Press, 1997); G. Sreenivasan, *The Limits of Lockean Rights in Property* (Oxford: Oxford University Press, 1995); Dunn, *History of Political Theory,* chapter 7.

15. Cohen, "Marx and Locke on Land and Labour"; Istvan Hont, "Free Trade and the Economic Limits to National Politics: Neo-Machiavellian Political Economy Reconsidered," John Dunn, ed., *The Economic Limits to*

Modern Politics (Cambridge: Cambridge University Press, 1990), 41–120; Dunn, "The Emergence into Politics of Global Environmental Change," Ted Munn, ed., *Encyclopedia of Global Environmental Change* (London: John Wiley, 2002), vol. 5, 124–36.

16. Locke, *Second Treatise*, §§37, 10–29.

17. James Tully, *An Approach to Political Philosophy: Locke in Contexts* (Cambridge: Cambridge University Press, 1993), chapter 5.

18. C. B. Macpherson, *The Political Theory of Possessive Individualism* (Oxford: Clarendon Press, 1962).

19. James Tully, A Discourse of Property and *An Approach to Political Philosophy: Locke in Contexts* (Cambridge: Cambridge University Press, 1993); Waldron, *The Right to Private Property*.

20. Michel Foucault, *Power* (Harmondsworth: Penguin, 2001).

21. Leo Strauss, *Natural Right and History* (Chicago: University of Chicago Press, 1953); Thomas L. Pangle, *The Spirit of Modern Republicanism: The Moral Vision of the American Founders and the Philosophy of Locke* (Chicago: University of Chicago Press, 1988); Michael Zuckert, *Natural Rights and the New Republicanism* (Princeton: Princeton University Press, 1994); S. Zinaich, "Locke's Moral Revolution: From Natural Law to Moral Relativism," *Locke Newsletter,* 31 (2000), 79–114.

22. John Marshall, *John Locke: Resistance, Religion and Responsibility* (Cambridge: Cambridge University Press, 1994), and "John Locke, Socinianism, 'Socinianism,' and Unitarianism," in M. A. Stewart, ed., *English Philosophy in the Age of Locke* (Oxford: Oxford University Press, 2000), 111–82; Ian Harris, *The Mind of John Locke* (Cambridge: Cambridge University Press, 1994), and "Locke on Justice," M. A. Stewart, ed., *English Philosophy in the Age of Locke,* 49–85.

23. Harris, *The Mind of John Locke*; Marshall, *John Locke: Resistance, Religion, and Responsibility,* and "John Locke, Socinianism, 'Socinianism,' and Unitarianism"; Victor Nuovo, "Locke's Theology 1694–1704," M. A. Stewart, ed., *English Philosophy in the Age of Locke,* 183–215; and the volumes of the *Clarendon Edition of the Works of John Locke* (Oxford: Clarendon Press, 1976–).

24. There is, of course, substantial variation between these writers in this respect. Ruth W. Grant, *John Locke's Liberalism* (Chicago: University of Chicago Press, 1987); Nathan Tarcov, *Locke's Education for Liberty* (Chicago: University of Chicago Press, 1984); Pangle, *The Spirit of Modern Republicanism;* Zuckert, *Natural Rights and the New Republicanism.*

25. J. G. A. Pocock, *The Machiavellian Moment* (Princeton: Princeton University Press, 1975).

26. Bernard Bailyn, ed., *Pamphlets of the American Revolution 1750–1776*, vol. 1 (Cambridge, Mass.:Harvard University Press, 1965).

27. Bernard Bailyn, *The Ideological Origins of the American Revolution* (Cambridge, Mass.: Harvard University Press, 1967).

28. Tarcov, *Locke's Education for Liberty.*

29. Grant, *John Locke's Liberalism.*

30. Cf., still, Dunn, *Political Obligation,* chapter 4; and compare Goldie, *The Reception of Locke's Politics.*

31. Except in the case of the grandest and most formal of public pronouncements (cf. Carl L. Becker, *The Declaration of Independence: A Study in the History of Political Ideas* [New York: Vintage, 1959]), where citing a partisan intellectual champion would hardly be appropriate and might well prove prejudicial, most evident American citations from Locke's own texts in this period were quite explicit, and the attempt to invoke his intellectual authority was clearly part of the point of citing them.

32. Becker, *Declaration of Independence.*

33. Dworetz, *The Unvarnished Doctrine*; Huyler, *Locke in America.*

34. Goldie, *Reception of Locke's Politics.*

35. Skinner, *Liberty before Liberalism;* Dunn, *History of Political Theory*; Runciman, "History of Political Thought: The State of the Discipline."

36. John Dunn, *The Cunning of Unreason: Making Sense of Politics* (London: HarperCollins and New York: Basic Books, 2000).

37. Dunn, *Cunning of Unreason,* and "The Contemporary Political Significance of John Locke's Conception of Civil Society," Sudipta Kaviraj and Sunil Khilnani eds., *Civil Society: History and Possibilities* (Cambridge: Cambridge University Press, 2001), 39–57.

38. A. John Simmons, *The Lockean Theory of Rights* (Princeton: Princeton University Press, 1992), and *On the Edge of Anarchy: Locke, Consent, and the Limits of Society* (Princeton: Princeton University Press, 1992).

39. Macpherson, *Political Theory of Possessive Individualism.*

40. Richard Ashcraft, *Revolutionary Politics and Locke's Two Treatises of Government* (Princeton: Princeton University Press, 1986); Shapiro, *Evolution of Rights in Liberal Theory;* Neal Wood, *The Politics of Locke's Philosophy* (Berkeley: University of California Press, 1983), and *John Locke and Agrarian Capitalism* (Berkeley: University of California Press, 1984).

41. Locke, *Essay Concerning Human Understanding,* IV, iii, 18: p. 549, ll. 28–29.

42. Compare Locke, *Second Treatise,* §§ 123, ll. 16–17, and Peter Laslett's gloss at p. 101.

43. Cf. Ian Harris, *The Mind of John Locke*, and "Locke on Justice"; and, more perfunctorily, John Dunn, "Justice and the Interpretation of Locke's Political Theory," *Political Studies*, 16 (1968), 68–87.

44. Tully, *A Discourse of Property* and *An Approach to Political Philosophy*, chapter 5; Cohen, "Marx and Locke on Land and Labour"; Wood, *John Locke and Agrarian Capitalism*.

45. Richard Rorty, *Philosophy and the Mirror of Nature* (Oxford: Blackwell, 1980); Foucault, *Power*.

46. Leo Strauss, *Natural Right and History*.

47. Charles Taylor, *Sources of the Self* (Cambridge, Mass.: Harvard University Press, 1989).

48. Alasdair MacIntyre, *After Virtue* (London: Duckworth, 1981).

49. Michael Ayers, *Locke: Epistemology and Ontology*, 2 vols. (London: Routledge, 1991); John W. Yolton, *John Locke and the Way of Ideas* (Oxford: Clarendon Press, 1956), etc.; Harris, *Mind of John Locke*; Marshall, *John Locke: Resistance, Religion, and Responsibility*, and the editors of the Clarendon edition of Locke's Works.

50. Dunn, *Political Thought of John Locke*, and *Locke: A Very Short Introduction* (Oxford: Oxford University Press, 2003), and "Bright Enough for All Our Purposes," "John Locke's Conception of a Civilised Society," *Notes and Records of the Royal Society*, 43 (1989), 133–53; cf. Harris, *Mind of John Locke*; Marshall, *John Locke: Resistance, Religion, and Responsibility;* and, more analytically, Ayers, *Locke: Epistemology*, and *Ontology*.

51. Tully, *A Discourse of Property;* Shapiro, *Evolution of Rights*; Harris, *Mind of John Locke*.

52. Simmons, *Lockean Theory of Rights*.

53. Or, for that matter, attribute the expanding power of the United States of America to it.

54. Compare Rorty, *Philosophy and the Mirror of Nature*.

55. John Dunn, *Interpreting Political Responsibility* (Cambridge: Polity, 1990), 44–60.

56. Compare Ronald Dworkin, *Taking Rights Seriously* (London: Duckworth, 1977).

57. Raymond Geuss, *History and Illusion in Politics* (Cambridge: Cambridge University Press, 2001).

58. Dunn, *Locke: A Very Short Introduction*, and "Bright Enough for All Our Purposes."

59. Dunn, "Bright Enough for All Our Purposes."

60. Tully, *A Discourse of Property*, and Dunn, *Political Thought of John Locke*.

61. John Dunn, ed., *Democracy: The Unfinished Journey* (Oxford: Oxford University Press, 1992), conclusion; and Francis Fukuyama, *The End of History and the Last Man* (London: Hamish Hamilton, 1992).

62. John Rawls, *A Theory of Justice* (Oxford: Clarendon Press, 1972); Ronald Dworkin, *Sovereign Virtue* (Cambridge, Mass.: Harvard University Press, 2000).

63. Dunn, *Cunning of Unreason.*

64. This is an extraordinarily rich topic, which has been explored with great interest since the 1980s and will clearly continue to hold its fascination for some time to come. In view of Ruth Grant's contribution to this volume I shall confine myself here to drawing attention to the judicious treatment of a central issue in Ruth Sample, "Locke on Political Authority and Conjugal Authority," Locke Newsletter, 31 (2000), 115–56.

65. Cf. Martyn P. Thompson, "Significant Silences in Locke's *Two Treatises of Government,*" *The Historical Journal,* 31 (1987), 275–94; Julian Franklin, *John Locke and the Theory of Sovereignty* (Cambridge: Cambridge University Press, 1978); Dunn, *Political Thought of John Locke.*

66. Cf. Ashcraft, *Revolutionary Politics and Locke's Two Treatises.*

67. For the English context see especially Ashcraft, *Revolutionary Politics*; Mark Goldie, "The Theory of Religious Intolerance in Restoration England," O. P. Grell, J. Israel, and N. Tyacke, eds., *From Persecution to Toleration* (Oxford: Clarendon Press, 1991), 331–68, and "Locke, Proast and Religious Toleration," J. Walsh, C. Haydon, and S. Taylor, eds., *The Church of England c1689–c1833: From Toleration to Tractarianism* (Cambridge: Cambridge University Press, 1993), 143–71; Richard Vernon, *The Career of Toleration: John Locke, Jonas Proast, and After* (Montreal: McGill-Queens University Press, 1997); and Marshall, *John Locke: Resistance, Religion, and Responsibility.* For broader treatments of the argument and its context see Richard Tuck, "Hobbes and Locke on Toleration," Mary Dietz, ed., *Thomas Hobbes and Political Theory* (Lawrence: University of Kansas Press, 1990), 153–71; Tully, *An Approach to Political Philosophy;* Jeremy Waldron, "Locke: Toleration and the Rationality of Persecution," Susan Mendus, ed., *Justifying Toleration: Conceptual and Historical Perspectives* (Cambridge: Cambridge University Press, 1988), 61–86; Harris, *The Mind of John Locke;* and for the significance of the wider European context see especially Dunn, *History of Political Theory,* chapter 6, and the forthcoming study by John Marshall. For an illuminating recent analytical placing see Alex Tuckness, "Rethinking the Intolerant Locke," *American Journal of Political Science,* 46 (2002), 288–98.

68. Goldie, "Locke, Proast and Religious Toleration"; and Vernon, *The Career of Toleration.*

69. Dunn, *History of Political Theory,* chapter 6.

70. Rawls, *A Theory of Justice* and *Political Liberalism* (New York: Columbia University Press, 1993).

71. Pierre Bayle, *Political Writings,* Sally L. Jenkinson, ed. (Cambridge: Cambridge University Press, 2000); S. L. Jenkinson, "Two Concepts of Tolerance: Why Bayle Is Not Locke," *Journal of Political Philosophy,* 4 (1996), 302–22; Dunn, *History of Political Theory,* chapter 6.

72. John Locke, *Some Thoughts Concerning Education,* John W. Yolton and Jean S. Yolton, eds. (Oxford: Clarendon Press, 1989); Tarcov, *Locke's Education for Liberty.*

73. Dunn, *History of Political Theory,* chapter 6.

74. Michael Cook, *Commanding Right and Forbidding Wrong in Islamic Thought* (Cambridge: Cambridge University Press, 2000), and *The Koran: A Very Short Introduction* (Oxford: Oxford University Press, 2000).

75. Dunn, *History of Political Theory,* chapter 6.

76. Ibid.

77. See the essay by Ruth Grant in the present volume.

78. Cf., a trifle ponderously, Kirstie M. McClure, *Judging Rights: Lockean Politics and the Limits of Consent* (Ithaca: Cornell University Press, 1996).

79. Dunn, *The Cunning of Unreason,* or, on very different premises, Michael Zuckert, "Big Government and Rights," Arthur M. Melzer, Jerry Weinberger, and M. Richard Zinman, eds., *Politics at the Turn of the Century* (Lanham: Rowman & Littlefield, 2001), 123–39.

80. Maurice Cranston, *John Locke: A Biography* (London: Longmans, 1957), 480.

81. Waldron, "Locke: Toleration and the Rationality of Persecution."

82. Pangle, *The Spirit of Modern Republicanism.*

83. Dunn, *Political Thought of John Locke,* and *Locke: A Very Short Introduction.*

John Locke on Women and the Family

RUTH W. GRANT

Was John Locke a feminist? Certainly not. But just as certainly, this cannot be the right question. For John Locke, the status of women in society was not a central concern. He paid far less attention to the matter than thinkers like Jean-Jacques Rousseau or John Stuart Mill, for example. Locke's central political concern was to challenge contemporary authoritarian doctrines of Divine Right and patriarchalism that legitimized subjection to absolute monarchical power. To be sure, in launching that challenge, he was led to distinguish between political authority and authority within the family. His reflections on authority within the family, on relations between husbands and wives as well as parents and children, are part of his broader argument about the justification of authority and obligation altogether. It is an argument meant to establish the limits of political subjection and to justify revolutionary resistance to government. What can we learn by revisiting his discussion, penned over three hundred years ago, about the issues that most concern us? I think we can learn a great deal, but only by beginning with the awareness that we are bringing our question to his texts.

What, then, is our question? Contemporary interest in Locke's writings on women and the family is driven by the question of the status of women and the place of the nuclear family in modern liberal societies. The problem looks like this: we find ourselves living in societies where the dominant liberal ideology teaches equality of rights and individual freedom, yet women continue to be subordinated, not least through the constraints imposed by the role they have been expected to play in family life. How are we to understand this disjunction between liberal theory and modern practice? One possibility is to credit liberalism with providing the principles with which to transform traditional oppressive practices. Struggles for women's suffrage, for example, appealed to accepted liberal conceptions of equality, consent and rights.[1] The very real gains of the recent past also can be understood as an extension of liberal ideals. From this point of view, if we are concerned to secure equality and freedom for women around the world, what we need is more liberalism, not less.

Alternatively, liberal theory itself can be criticized in a variety of ways. In the light of liberal theory, the family appears to be a miniature liberal polity: nothing more than a group of individuals held together by mutual benefits and contractual agreements. Individual family members believe that they can choose the extent of their ties with their kin, negotiating and renegotiating their obligations to one another, rather than viewing themselves as bound together as members of a transgenerational, natural whole which is bigger than the sum of its parts and within which certain obligations are simply given. With its emphasis on the priority of the individual and particularly of individual rights, liberalism seems unable to recognize the importance of such crucial dimensions of human life as affective ties of kinship and concomitant intergenerational responsibilities. Yet, the family remains a vital social institution as the locus of the cultivation of these very aspects of our humanity and of values like loyalty and sympathy that curb egotism and sustain public life. Paradoxically, liberal political theory seems unable to provide the theoretical justification for those social institutions, like the family, which it needs most for its own support.

Liberal theory has been criticized from a very different vantage point as well. The liberal propensity to conceptualize oppression solely in legal and political terms leaves us without the intellectual tools to understand crucial cultural and psychological aspects of gender inequality. Equality of rights under the law seems an insufficient instrument to reach the subtleties of sexual harassment or the processes of socialization that shape identities and conceptions of gender difference, for example. Lastly, liberalism is said to be blind to its own role in providing the conceptual ground for the subordination of women and for oppressive family structures. To take just one example, liberalism's sharp division of public and private spheres, which has been a crucial protection of individual rights, has contributed at the same time to serious deprivations of the rights it purports to protect. While the dictum that "a man's home is his castle" has provided protection from illegitimate government interference in citizens' private affairs, it often has left women and children vulnerable to abuses by husbands and fathers. Moreover, the public/private distinction leads us to depoliticize the domestic realm, which has been the primary locus of women's work, and thus to view women as unsuited for public life. From this perspective, emancipation requires nothing less than a radical critique of liberal principles.[2]

To begin to address these issues, some turn to the writings of John Locke as one of the most articulate progenitors of liberal ideas. But this inevitably involves adopting assumptions about the role of ideas in history and the relation of theory and practice — and a cautionary note is in order. There are a number of common, but fallacious, assumptions to be avoided. Among them is the notion that contemporary American liberalism is a continuation of, or further development from, its Lockean roots and that for all practical purposes, the two are indistinguishable. It is well to remember that the term, "liberal," did not even exist until long after Locke was dead, and that Lockeanism might represent a distinct alternative to contemporary liberalism in important respects rather than simply an early articulation of it.[3]

Moreover, errors can emerge both from taking ideas too seriously and from not taking them seriously enough. In the latter category is the presupposition that historical writings are simply circumscribed by the dominant practices of their time and place — Aristotle could not have criticized slavery[4]; Locke must be an apologist for the seventeenth century status quo with respect to gender relations, and so on — but there is no period without contested ideas and a range of available opinions, and there is no reason to assume that in earlier times people were less capable of social criticism than we are. On the other side of the balance lies the variety of ways in which ideas are assumed to be weightier than perhaps they actually are. To what extent is liberalism to be credited with advances in the status of women and to what extent ought other sorts of forces to be considered: changes in demographics, economics, and medicine for example?[5] And, alternatively, when injustices persist, to what extent can we conclude that it is liberal ideology that is at fault? Has there ever been an ideology, or a religious doctrine for that matter, that has not been perverted to rationalize injustice? There may well be permanent sources of human evils that getting the ideas "right" will never entirely remove. This is a sobering thought, and one not usually confronted by a people who take the liberal idea of progress for granted, but it is a serious possibility nonetheless. The bearing of the investigation of Locke's thought on our judgments of our contemporary situation will depend a great deal on the positions we adopt with respect to the impact of political thought more generally on our common life.

But the investigation of Locke's thought itself can be conducted independently of these issues, and that is my primary task here. We need to know what Locke said and its meaning in the context of his own concerns before determining what it means for us. Locke framed his political theory in the *Two Treatises of Government* as a reply to Sir Robert Filmer's *Patriarcha*. Filmer's basic position can be characterized as follows: all authority is paternal authority. Just as the Lord governs the world as the Heavenly Father of us all, the king governs his subjects, and the earthly father governs his household. Since all authority is paternal authority and women cannot be fathers, the status of women as subjects hardly requires argument. The authority of kings, who are not literally fathers of their subjects, does require some justification. In Filmer's account, God's grant of dominion to Adam, told in Genesis, is inherited through the eldest son of Adam's line to the monarchs of his own day.

Of course, Filmer's particular version of patriarchalism was not universally shared among Englishmen at the time, but patriarchalism in some form was common.[6] The official Prayer Book catechism included "to honour and obey the King" along with "to love, honour and succour my father, and mother" in the text of the fifth commandment.[7] The doctrine of the Divine Right of Kings meant, not only that the authority of the king had a divine source, but that the subject's obligation to obey regal authority was inseparable from his obligation to God. Moreover, in Filmer's view, it meant that the extent of sovereign authority was identical whether wielded by God, king or father. Sovereign power included the power of life and death; it was exercised at the will of the sovereign; it could not be limited by law. Sovereignty was absolute and the obligation of the subject was equally so. Locke, aiming to justify revolution, sets out to attack this position in the *First Treatise*.

And because Filmer's position rests on the notion that sovereignty is founded in paternity and that political authority relationships can be understood in the same terms as familial ones, Locke begins his constructive argument in the *Second Treatise* by declaring that he will distinguish between "the power of a *magistrate* over a subject . . . a father over his children, a master over his servant, a husband over his wife, and a lord over his slave."[8] Failing to make these distinctions, Filmer is unable to tell the difference between legitimate monarchy and tyranny, or between a "subject" and a "slave," which is the distinction of greatest importance to Locke. And since Filmer relies on scriptural argument to a large extent, scriptural interpretation is one of Locke's weapons as well.

In Locke's view, Scripture provides no evidence of a divine grant either for Adam's rule as the first father over the rest of mankind, or for the exclusive rule of fathers over their children, or for the rule of husbands over their wives. God granted mankind dominion over the nonhuman creatures, rather than granting Adam dominion over all other human beings, which is evidenced in part by the fact that Eve was included in the grant on Locke's reading of the biblical passage.[9] Further, Locke never tires of reminding the reader that the fifth commandment includes mothers as well as fathers and that properly we ought to speak of parental, rather than paternal, authority.[10]

And on Eve's subjection to Adam ("and he shall rule over thee," Genesis 3:16), Locke's scriptural reading is remarkable:

> [B]ut there is here no more law to oblige a woman to such subjection, if the circumstances either of her condition, or contract with her husband, should exempt her from it, than there is, that she should bring forth her children in sorrow and pain, if there could be found a remedy for it, which is also a part of the same curse upon her.

Locke emphatically denies any biblical support for the claim that husbands have the right to rule their wives. It cannot be a sin for a wife to disobey her husband because there is no divine command requiring obedience. According to Locke, the biblical text grants no authority, not even to Adam over Eve, much less to husbands in general over their wives. The passage only foretells what a woman's lot in life will be: she will bring forth children in pain and she will be subordinated to her husband by the customary practices of nations, both of which conditions could change.[11]

What, then, of the authority of custom or tradition? English political traditions pose a problem for the patriarchalist who would identify paternal and monarchical power, since English monarchs have traditionally been Queens as well as Kings, and this is an argument that Locke does not hesitate to employ.[12] But his deeper argument is that customs, traditions, and historically established practices simply are without authority. We can find examples of horrible cruelties, including infanticide and cannibalism, that became established practice and even sacred custom within a given society, but the fact that such practices exist has no bearing on their justification.[13] In one of his most radical statements, Locke remarks, "an argument from what has been, to what should of right be, has no great force."[14] Irrational and oppressive customs and rituals often survive because it serves the interests of the powerful, priests in particular, to maintain them.[15] That they have withstood the test of time is meaningless as a standard for moral judgment. Customary practices and established prejudices must be judged at the bar of reason.[16] This is a major thrust of all of Locke's work.[17]

Having eliminated both scripture and custom as the ground for the justification of political and paternal authority, only nature remains as a possibility. Locke's position with respect to political authority is clear; there is no natural political power. Rather, the natural condition of men is a condition

> of perfect freedom to order their actions and dispose of their possessions and persons, as they think fit, within the bounds of the law of nature; without asking leave, or depending upon the will of any other man.

A state also of equality, wherein all the power and jurisdiction is reciprocal, no one having more than another; there being nothing more evident than that creatures of the same species . . . should also be equal one amongst another without subordination or subjection.[18]

This is the fundamental premise from which the entire argument of the *Second Treatise* proceeds. In the absence of any indication that God has set one man above the rest, nobody can claim a natural superiority that would justify subordinating others to his will. Legitimate political rule can come about only by human artifice, when people with equal natural rights to self-government agree to establish a government amongst themselves.[19] There can be no doubt that women are included in the generic term "man" in this passage and that they enjoy the same natural rights as men as "creatures of the same species."[20]

Nonetheless, there is legitimate power within the family, and, while it cannot be understood to be political power, much less monarchical sovereignty as Filmer would have it, there are genuine obligations between parents and children, husbands and wives. What is their source and what is their extent? The power of parents over their children follows from their duty to care for them and to educate them until they are capable of caring for themselves. Not only are these powers and duties shared by fathers and mothers, they can be forfeited by negligent natural fathers and acquired by caring foster fathers. They are by no means tied exclusively to natural paternity. Moreover, a father's authority does not include powers governing the child's life, liberty or property, for these are political powers belonging only to the magistrate. And while the obligation of children to honor parents who cared for them is lifelong, parental authority ceases when it no longer serves the purpose which justifies it; that is, when children reach maturity.[21] This is a general principle in Locke's thought: the power of one person over another is legitimate only to the extent that it serves the purposes of their association.

Association between a man and a woman in marriage, which Locke calls "conjugal society," is formed by voluntary contract for the purpose of producing and rearing children.[22] Once that purpose is served, there is no reason that the association must continue; thus, divorce under certain circumstances is reasonable. And because the purposes of the association can be served by a variety of arrangements, the terms of marriage contracts might vary considerably.[23] But in every conjugal society, according to Locke, there must be a power to govern whatever has been designated as common to husband and wife. Since unanimity of judgment cannot always

292 Ruth W. Grant

be expected, the final determination must be lodged in one or the other of them in cases of conflict. This conjugal power is "naturally" lodged in the husband as "the abler and the stronger,"[24] and Locke remarks, "there is, I grant, a foundation in nature for it,"[25] though it is a customary or conventional arrangement.

There are striking parallels between Locke's argument for placing conjugal power in the husband and his argument later in the work for locating political authority initially in the majority of the community, though the comparison is not exact in every particular.[26] In both cases, the society itself is created by the unanimous, voluntary consent of equal individuals. For the society to be ongoing, whether civil or conjugal, there must be a dominant power within it. In the case of political society, Locke observes that it is "necessary for one body to move one way;"[27] in the case of marriage, it is "necessary that the last determination . . . should be placed somewhere."[28] Since there will be differences of opinion, unanimity is impracticable as the ruling principle in either case. In civil society, the dominant power is the majority; in conjugal society, it is the husband. It is by agreeing to the original contract to form a society that one agrees to obey the power within it. But in both cases, that power could be placed differently and still be legitimate. In conjugal society, it could be placed in the wife; the dominance of husbands within marriage is a matter of convention, as we have seen.[29] And in civil societies, the people can agree to place it in a number greater than the majority.[30] But it is worth noting that they cannot place it in a number less than a majority; "the majority have a right to act and conclude the rest" because "that which acts any community [is] only the consent of the individuals of it."[31] The argument justifying the authority of the majority is stronger than that justifying the authority of husbands. In the latter case, the justification follows from the greater likelihood of effective rule, rather than from the principled ground of the association.[32]

The customary dominance of husbands seems reasonable enough, according to Locke, as it recognizes the usual natural superiority of strength and ability in men, but this by no means implies a general inequality of rights between men and women.[33] The argument is not a defense of a natural right for husbands to rule their wives and does not even approach a claim of a right for men in general to rule women. Women are by nature "at their own disposal."[34] Only by voluntarily joining in marriage does a woman accept subordination to her husband's judgment, and then only with respect to their limited common concerns. Immediately after asserting that the final determination in a marriage rests with the husband, Locke writes: "But . . . this leaves the wife in the full and free possession of what by contract is her peculiar right, and gives the husband no more power over her life than she has over his."[35] Moreover, with respect to governing others in the family unit, including servants, the power may belong to the mistress as well as to the master.[36] And finally, within a political community, the civil magistrate is the ultimate arbiter: deciding "any controversy that may arise between man and wife" about their common concerns.[37]

The overall effect of Locke's argument with respect to husbands and fathers is to significantly circumscribe their authority, both in duration and extent. Moreover, what authority they have is not theirs to use as they will, but only so long as they use it for the ends for which it was given. This is a crucial component of Locke's argument: power can always be subjected to judgment in this way, and those who hold power do so only conditionally. When a father "quits his care" of his children, "he loses his power over them,"[38] and "The power of the husband being so far from that of an absolute monarch, that the wife has in many cases a liberty to separate from him."[39] As compared to Filmer's claims for the absolute and arbitrary rights of sovereignty in the fathers with respect to their wives as well as their children, Locke's understanding of authority within the family represents a vastly liberalizing alternative. Locke accepts and defends the dominance of husbands over wives in some form, but alters its status significantly by altering its justification. One crucial consequence of this approach is that the superiority of husbands over wives, whatever its extent, does not prejudice the rights of women in other relationships within the household or without. In Locke's view, subjection to conjugal authority, or to parental authority for that matter,[40] does not imply political subjection of any kind.

The purpose of Locke's discussions of paternal power and conjugal society is to demonstrate that a family unit, no matter how large and complex, is not a political society.[41] In very important respects, for Locke, the whole point is that a man's home is *not* his castle.[42] It is a grave error to believe that a father is king of his household and that the King is father of his subjects, an error with significant consequences. To offer just one example, in Locke's time, "high treason" was a crime committed against the political sovereign. But since the head of a household was considered lord and sovereign there, crimes against him were also a form of treason. "Petty treason" was the crime committed by a wife in killing her husband, or a servant his lord or master, or a clergyman his prelate. The penalties for petty treason were harsher than they were for ordinary murder (and the killing of a wife by her husband was only murder, since the wife could not be lord over her husband).[43] Against the patriarchalists, Locke argues that there is no sovereignty within the family. If patriarchalists, like Filmer, truly understood the very limited powers of fathers over their wives or their children, they would find fatherhood a slim reed indeed to support the claims of absolute sovereignty in the monarch. And if they truly understood political power, they would find that it too is grounded in the voluntary consent of naturally equal individuals and limited by the purposes it is meant to serve.

We turn now to consider the status of women with respect to political authority, and here the interpretive task becomes more difficult. Since Locke never directly addressed the question apart from his general discussion, we will have to proceed by inference on some points and remain satisfied with uncertainty as to others. According to Locke, the only source of political subjection is the voluntary agreement of each individual to become a member of the political community. This proposition follows directly from the premise of natural freedom and equality. If political authority is not natural, it must be artificially created through some sort of voluntary human action. All legitimate government is founded in consent of some kind. Let us suppose that a consent theorist, like Locke, wanted to justify the political subjection of women to men; he would have three alternative approaches available to him. First, he could argue that women consent to government, and thus become subject to the laws, through the consent of their husbands. Some political writers of the time took this approach, but Locke was not one of them.[44] Wives are not bound by the consent of their husbands any more than children can be bound by the consent of their fathers once they come of age. The political independence of each member of the family is made clear in Locke's discussion of conquest where the power a just conqueror acquires over defeated combatants yields no power over their wives or children.[45] For Locke, a political community is a group of individuals, not a group of families or households.

The second alternative is to argue that women as such, in contrast to men, cannot become members of the political community because they do not possess natural rights equally with men. (Note that it would be contradictory to embrace both this second alternative and the first one: if women are not naturally free, then they must be naturally subjects and there is no need to explain their consent, either through their husbands or otherwise.) That women are simply excluded from the political community seems an implausible interpretation of Locke's account on the face of it. According to Locke, people belong to the same political unit when they have a common law and established judge between them. And in Locke's account, controversies between husband and wife are judged by the civil magistrate;

women owe obedience to the laws; they can own property independently of men and make enforceable contracts; there is such a thing as an "English woman,"[46] and it would be odd indeed for a woman to rule as monarch over a political community of which she could not be a part.

But some have argued that women can be subjects of political authority without being consenting members of the body politic.[47] The argument turns on the notion that Locke did not consider women sufficiently rational to govern themselves according to the law of nature, which is the law of reason or the moral law. If women are not capable of self-government, their voluntary consent to be governed by others would not be required. But if this were so, Locke would have to argue also that women are incapable of obligation to God, who is the source of the law, or of moral obligation altogether. It would be as unreasonable to expect a woman to be a Christian or to consider her guilty of a crime as it would be to expect moral responsibility of a dog or a cat. Subjection to the law of nature is what distinguishes human beings from the other animals. Locke is explicit that the sort of rationality that is required for subjection to the law of nature is available to all mankind.[48]

Moreover, if women do not become members of the political community through their own consent, what *are* the grounds of their subjection to the laws of the polity? It would be incumbent upon Locke to explain this to the reader, but he does not say.[49] Locke does not argue anywhere for a different grounds for political authority over women than over men, yet he had ample opportunity to do so in the process of sorting through the various types of authority within the family and the polity, and it is unlikely that it would have been particularly controversial if he had. Instead, particularly in responding to Filmer, Locke undermines all claims for scriptural, natural, or traditional foundations of political authority. Again, Locke argues emphatically throughout the work that political authority can be grounded only in individual consent. That women can become political subjects and members of the political community in the same manner as men is tolerably clear.

The third possibility is to argue that, while women have fundamental natural rights and cannot be obliged to the laws without their own consent, they are not capable of effective participation in government, and, since such participation is a matter of convention rather than right, they can and ought to be excluded from it. Again, this is not a subject that Locke ever addresses explicitly, and it is even more difficult in this case to follow out the implications of his general argument because that argument is ambiguous on two important issues. First, it is not clear what membership in the political community implies about participation in the processes of governance for men or women, and, second, Locke makes apparently contradictory statements concerning the criteria for determining what sort of action counts as consent to membership and the process by which consent is given.

With respect to political participation, it appears at first blush that membership in the body politic implies nothing at all with respect to a role in its governance or a right to be represented in its councils. Once the community is formed, the majority can entrust the community's power in any manner it chooses. It can constitute a monarchy, oligarchy, democracy, or any form or combination of these.[50] By inference, it would be perfectly legitimate to constitute a representative government where women and a goodly portion of men were disenfranchised. Women might have the rights of conscience, of property, and even of revolution, but not the right to vote. So long as the subjects are protected in their fundamental rights to life, liberty, and property and have established the government on the basis of consent, the government is a legitimate one. Locke is a liberal, but not a democrat. But a problem arises because there are passages which do imply greater pressures toward democratic and representative forms of government in the *Second Treatise*. For example, Locke argues that there can be no taxation without representation;[51] that a conquered people can accept the government of a conqueror only by consenting to the laws either directly or through their representatives;[52] and that "well ordered commonwealths" have carefully structured legislatures as well as other institutional limitations on their powers.[53] It is difficult to determine with certainty what sorts of political rights, if any, follow necessarily from equality of natural rights in Locke's view.

It is equally difficult to determine the precise meaning of the requirement of consent to establish political authority. At one point, Locke states quite strongly that nothing can make a man a member of society except "positive engagement, and express promise and compact."[54] Yet elsewhere, Locke writes that tacit consent, often "little taken notice of," is sufficient to establish political obligation.[55] And of course historically, if women and men have consented to membership in political society at all, it has certainly been a tacit consent most everywhere and always. That consent is the only legitimate basis for a political community is clear; how that community is constituted on the basis of consent is quite obscure.

These two problems, of consent to membership and of participation in political society, represent major areas of tension in Locke's political thought, and I believe the difficulties flow from the same source. Locke is attempting to specify criteria of legitimacy that will justify a right of revolution in certain circumstances. But he must accomplish this without at the same time unsettling most governments in the world. In particular, he must be careful to ensure that his criteria support a distinction between abusive monarchies and monarchy per se. In fact, part of Locke's rhetorical strategy is to turn the tables on the usual claim and argue that his consent theory, which implies a right of revolution, is actually more likely to lead to peaceful politics than is Filmer's doctrine of absolute subjection to Divine Right monarchy.[56] It is important for Locke to be convincing on this point, given England's recent history of regicide and bloody civil war.

Locke proceeds by establishing minimal criteria for legitimacy; that is, consent and protection of natural rights. In the early ages of human history, even tacit consent to monarchical power in the father of a family could transform that family into a legitimate commonwealth by these criteria. Such consent would be reasonable since the father had the power to effectively execute his judgments and his judgment could be trusted.[57] But this "Golden Age" was temporary:

> when ambition and luxury, in future ages would retain and increase the power without doing the business, for which it was given, and, aided by flattery, taught princes to have distinct and separate interests from their people, men found it necessary to examine more carefully the original and rights of government; and to find out ways to restrain the exorbitances, and prevent the abuses of that power which they having intrusted in another's hands only for their own good, they found was made use of to hurt them.[58]

As historical conditions changed, more stringent requirements (such as the creation of a legislature, the limitation of executive prerogative by known and standing laws, and explicit oaths of allegiance indicating consent to membership) might have to be met in order to satisfy the same general criteria of legitimacy in practice. In a large and complex society with weaker ties amongst the people and greater conflicts of interest, it is a more difficult task to construct a government grounded in consent and devoted to the pursuit of the public good. Some institutional protections, unnecessary in simpler times, become essential to the task.[59] Moreover, Locke sometimes describes maximum standards for the best governments, rather than minimal requirements of legitimacy. Violations of the latter justify revolution; violations of the former do not. Locke needs to assure his readers that revolutions are justified only rarely and not in response to every government that falls short of perfect justice.

This rhetorical situation makes it difficult to discern Locke's final position on those questions which are peripheral to his main task, which was to establish the illegitimacy of absolute monarchy and the right to oppose the rule of any king who is likely to become a tyrant, James II in particular. Locke only took up the question of women and the family in order to counter Filmer's patriarchalism and further his own claims regarding the limitations of political obedience. He had no need to take up the question of the political and social inequality of women on its own terms (or the similar inequalities among men), and arguably, it would have been counterproductive to do so. Government by a select group of men could meet the minimal standards of legitimacy in principle. Locke does not argue against the political inequality of men or women; this issue is not a *casus belli*. But it should be noted that he doesn't argue for it either, though he certainly could have done so.[60] He undermines the standard arguments that were used to support the subordination of women politically — scriptural, traditional, and natural — and does nothing expressly to provide an alternative support. It is an open question what Locke's "maximalist" view on the matter might have been.

My best guess would be that Locke would approve of systems of government that acknowledge both equality of right and inequality of ability to rule.[61] Considerable social and political inequality could be justified in a system that protected rights and promoted the public good. Full social and political equality is not a necessary component of the public good in and of itself. In Locke's view, unequal social arrangements ought to be judged by their effects. In a particular historical situation, political equality would be required if the rights of community members proved insecure in its absence. Thus far, the argument applies to inequalities among men as well as to inequalities between men as a group and women as a group.

We do not have direct evidence to determine whether Locke would have argued that women as such are less politically capable than men. There is evidence that he did not share the prejudices of his day regarding women's weak spiritual and intellectual capabilities,[62] though, in all likelihood, he would be astonished at the contemporary experiment aimed at abolishing gender differences as the basis for the division of labor in society in every significant respect. What we can say with some certainty is that, in Locke's view, the justification for barring any group of people, male or female, from participation in politics requires a showing that that group, for whatever reason, is incapable of exercising sound political judgment.[63] If there is an implied argument for the social and political inferiority of women, it is an argument made on meritocratic, not patriarchal, grounds. And this means that it can be challenged on the basis of experiential evidence. After Locke, the terms of the argument over the status of women have to change.

With respect to women, Locke demolishes the idea, prevalent in his own time, that women are born subject to male authority in the form of paternal authority of one kind or another and are destined to remain so throughout their lives. He establishes instead the natural freedom and equality of each individual and makes the individual, not the family, the basic unit of political society. These are now propositions that are generally taken for granted. What Locke does not do is provide an explicit justification for the equal participation of women with men in politics. Locke's argument regarding women and the family is embedded in his general attack on Filmer's patriarchalism. In the process of challenging Filmer, Locke argues that paternal power is quite different from political power, and that paternal power is so limited in duration and extent that it cannot be the basis for claims of political authority.

Locke teaches his readers to think about power and obligation in a new way. Power comes in a variety of forms, each determined in extent by its origins and its ends.[64] Power of any kind must be justified by its purposes and, to the extent that we create our own obligations, the exercise of power can always be judged by those subject to it. The duty of obedience has its limits. Nobody owns his or her authority; rather, power must be "authorized" in order to be legitimate. Practically speaking, this is the real significance of the argument from consent; that it justifies a right of revolution or a right to alter government in response to abuses. And this is the crucial difference between Filmer's understanding of patriarchal monarchy and Locke's.[65] The ambiguities surrounding how consent is given are less important than the demonstration that it can be rightfully withdrawn. Locke changes the terms of the discussion: when considering power relations of any kind, the question becomes how to recognize where the limits of authority and obedience lie. Power always requires justification and is always subject to scrutiny. Again, these are propositions that we now take for granted entirely. And they are the propositions that emerge from Locke's consideration of the issues that most concerned him.

What, then, can we learn from reading Locke about issues of contemporary concern, particularly the concern for social and political equality for women? There is an indeterminacy in the implications of Locke's argument on this issue that set the stage for future controversies. On the one hand, his argument provides a large opening wedge for claims for increasing equality for women. Under modern conditions, equality of rights cannot coexist with political and social inequality since to ensure equality of rights necessarily requires full participation in public life. If women do not have both equal participation and equal fundamental rights, then they will have neither.[66] On the other hand, though Locke doesn't himself make the case, his argument also permits the claim that women ought to remain unequal in political participation on account of their inferior capabilities.[67] This claim is far more tenable on Lockean grounds in a world where most people, men as well as women, share second-class status and the rule of the few is justified on the grounds of their superior fitness for public service. It loses a good deal of its force once men are universally included in public life. Once it is established that the rights of men cannot be secured without direct equal participation in political life, and that even the least educated male is capable of such participation, it is much more difficult to maintain consistently any grounds for the exclusion of women as a group.

The indeterminacy of the Lockean position on the question of social and political equality for women is sufficient to make clear that Locke was not a liberal democrat in any contemporary sense, though this should come as no surprise. Nonetheless, within the terms of a Lockean sort of liberalism, contemporary liberals confront some of the same theoretical tensions that Locke confronted. At the outset, I portrayed the focus of contemporary concerns about the status of women as the disjunction between egalitarian principles of liberal theory and modern practices of subjection. But it now appears that one dimension of the problem is located within liberal theory itself. Liberal theory must confront the question: What is the relation between the basic liberal claim of equality of fundamental natural rights and the democratic requirements of equality of participation in governing arrangements? It seems incoherent to us for Locke to be a liberal and not a democrat, since we assume that liberalism entails a substantial degree of democracy in principle everywhere and always. We do not tend to view the relation between the two historically, as Locke did. But while we tend to speak of "liberal democracy" as if the two terms were synonymous and, while we certainly see the right to vote as essential, even we do not require complete equality in the distribution of political power. No one today recommends assigning political office randomly by lot, as the ancient Greeks did. Powerful courts with appointed judges serving life terms, undemocratic institutions to be sure, are construed as an important instrument for the protection of rights. There is always some combination of institutional provisions that recognize the principle of equality and other elements that attempt to ensure effectiveness in achieving the ends of government as liberalism defines them, namely preservation of rights and pursuit of the public good. To the extent that we see any particular system of government, not as one among a variety of means to achieve these ends, but as essential to these goals, we will find that we have condemned all other possibilities.

And this is the locus of the second area of tension shared by Locke and contemporary liberals. In today's world, we concern ourselves a great deal with the problem of how to uphold a universal standard of human rights without imposing the views of one culture on all others. This is a central area of concern in the international community with respect to the status of women globally. The shared dilemma is this: either we specify the one essential way of achieving a regime that recognizes fundamental natural equality (the maximum requirements), in which case we find ourselves in the uncomfortable position of advocating one uniform standard to impose everywhere, or we specify minimum conditions that allow room for variety, in which case we are forced to accept practices that do not meet ideal standards of justice.[68]

Locke takes the second approach but in a way that offers an alternative to contemporary perspectives. Locke's liberalism differs from many forms of contemporary liberalism in important respects. One of these has been mentioned already, his view that what is essential for legitimate rule varies as historical conditions change. Another is that Locke's liberalism has nothing to do with cultural relativism, which is the view that cultural practices can be judged in relation only to the standards of the particular culture in which they are found and not by the light of a universal standard. Locke is crystal clear that custom itself provides no justification. Nonetheless, a variety of practices can be respected, not because culture as such is respectable, but because there are a variety of ways that societies can achieve legitimate human purposes. Locke mentions the form of polygamy in which a woman takes more than one husband and arrangements in which marriage is quite temporary, for example, as practices adequate for rearing children (rather than denouncing either as a heathen practice).[69] This is the minimal requirement, and many sorts of marital institutions can accomplish that goal.

[C]ommunity of goods, and the power over them, mutual assistance, and maintenance, and other things belonging to conjugal society, might be varied and regulated by that contract which unites man and wife in that society, as far as may consist with procreation and the bringing up of children till they could shift for themselves; nothing being necessary to any society, that is not necessary for the ends for which it is made.[70]

At the same time, those minimal requirements are firm and universal standards for judgment, and, just as Locke clearly condemned cannibalism and infanticide, he would surely condemn practices such as killing women upon the death of their husbands. Some rights are inviolable; Locke would say inalienable — the right to life, the right to own what you earn, the right to be a party to a marriage contract, the right to choose your own religion, the right to remain free from subjection to the arbitrary will of another. These rights provide a standard which applies to every human society. But they do not dictate a monolithic approach to political and social arrangements. In other words, Lockean liberalism allows both moral and political judgment and acceptance of diversity by focusing on defining minimal criteria for legitimacy rather than articulating a model of the ideal form of political society.

The tensions we have been discussing, between liberalism and democracy and between universalism and particularism, are tensions that arise from within the terms of "Lockean liberalism," and while these are the dominant terms of discourse in the West today, they are certainly not the only possible terms. There may be important problems for which they simply are inadequate as tools for understanding. To take just one illustration, Locke's perspective allows him to demonstrate the limits on any one person's power to stand in the way of what another person wants to do. But reading Locke will not help if the question is why some groups of people tend to want certain things. To understand the subtle psychological forces of subordination and identity formation involved in a question such as this, you have to look elsewhere. Locke has little to say about the political psychology of inequality, though this should not surprise us particularly either.[71]

In every place and time, new questions will come to prominence, or old questions will arise in a new way. For this reason, we should not expect to be able to return to texts from an earlier time for answers to our questions. We cannot ask authors for the answers to questions that they never asked. The conceptual fabric of historical discourses was woven within a context of argumentation that we do not share, and it is unlikely simply to suit contemporary circumstances. But by knowing the historical antecedents and the historical alternatives to our own efforts to comprehend our situation, we can gain clarity on our conceptual vocabulary and perspective on the dilemmas associated with it. Without that knowledge, we will be blind to the dangers of weakening the principles we now take for granted and blind also to the dangers of forgetting their limits.

NOTES

I would like to thank Susan Liebell for her helpful comments on an earlier version of this essay.

1. See "The Declaration of Sentiments," Seneca Falls Conference, 1848, reprinted in Elizabeth Cady Stanton, *A History of Woman Suffrage,* vol. 1 (Rochester, N.Y.: Fowler and Wells, 1889), pp. 70–71.

2. For a discussion that incorporates the range of criticisms mentioned here see Jean Bethke Elshtain, *Public Man, Private Woman: Women in Social and Political Thought* (Princeton, Princeton University Press, 1981), chapter 3.

3. "Liberal" as a political designation came into the language in Britain in the early nineteenth century. *Oxford English Dictionary.*

4. Aristotle actually mentions contemporary critiques of slavery. *Politics* I.6, 1255a.

5. Such forces sometimes bring advancements and sometimes not. On the greater economic independence of women in the seventeenth than in the eighteenth century see Teresa Brennan and Carole Pateman, " 'Mere Auxiliaries to the Commonwealth': Women and the Origins of Liberalism," *Political Studies,* vol. XXVII, no. 2, 1979 (183–200), pp. 186, 196.

6. See Gordon J. Schochet, *Patriarchalism in Political Thought: The Authoritarian Family and Political Speculation and Attitudes, Especially in Seventeenth Century England* (Oxford: Oxford University Press, 1975) and Nathan Tarcov, *Locke's Education for Liberty* (Chicago: University of Chicago Press, 1984), chapter 1.

7. Filmer excluded mothers from his version of the fifth commandment. Locke, *First Treatise,* §60. See Ian Green, *The Christian's ABC: Catechisms and Catechizing in England, c. 1530–1740* (Oxford: Clarendon Press, 1996), pp. 452–60, esp. p. 455.

8. Locke, *Second Treatise,* §2.

9. Locke, *First Treatise,* §§29–30.

10. See e.g., Locke, *First Treatise,* §6, 11–12, 60–61, *Second Treatise,* §§52–53.

11. Locke, *First Treatise,* §47. See the discussion of this passage in Tarcov, *Locke's Education for Liberty,* pp. 64–65. Locke rejects here as elsewhere the notion that the customary practices of nations, or the "common consent" of mankind, is any indication of a divine providence that would make those practices authoritative.

12. Locke, *First Treatise,* §§11, 47.

13. Locke, *First Treatise*, §§57–59. See also John Locke, *An Essay Concerning Human Understanding* (Oxford: Oxford University Press, 1975), I.3.9–12. Hereafter cited as *Essay*.

14. Locke, *Second Treatise*, §103.

15. See, for example, Locke, *Second Treatise*, §§92, 94, line 20, and John Locke, *On the Reasonableness of Christianity* (Stanford University Press, 1958), §238. Hereafter cited as *Reasonableness*.

16. Locke did not thematically challenge the prejudices of his day with regard to the status of women in his public writings. There is evidence, however, that he did not share those prejudices. After listening to a female preacher, Locke wrote her a letter of encouragement indicating that he saw no reason to exclude women from the ministry. Quoted in Melissa A. Butler, "Early Liberal Roots of Feminism: John Locke and the Attack on Patriarchy," *American Political Science Review*, vol. 72, no. 1, 1978 (135–50), p.150. Believing the author of a tract he admired to be a woman, Locke wrote "I am of the opinion she deserves one of the best places in the university." Quoted in David Wootton, ed. *Political Writings of John Locke* (New York: Penguin Books, 1993), p. 126. Wootton comments, "It would be difficult to find a more straightforwardly feminist sentiment written by a seventeenth-century male." In a letter to Mrs. Clarke concerning the education of her daughters dated January 7, 1684, Locke wrote that, since he saw "no difference of sex in your mind relating to truth, virtue and obedience," his educational advice concerning her son could be applied to her daughters as well. Quoted in Nathan Tarcov and Ruth W. Grant, eds., *John Locke, Some Thoughts Concerning Education and Of the Conduct of the Understanding* (Indianapolis: Hackett, 1996), p. xi. Locke certainly took seriously the intellectual capabilities of the only woman who was important in his life, Damaris Cudworth (Lady Masham), the daughter of a Cambridge philosopher and an extremely intelligent and philosophically sophisticated person.

17. For just a few examples see John Locke, *Of the Conduct of the Understanding*, §§10–12; *Essay* II.33.18; IV.20.17–18; for a discussion of the issue see Ruth W. Grant, "Locke's Political Anthropology and Lockean Individualism," *The Journal of Politics*, vol. 50, 1988 (42–63), section III.

18. Locke, *Second Treatise*, §4.

19. The "state of nature" is simply the phrase referring to the condition between any two or more people who have not entered such an agreement. The concept of the state of nature is inseparable from the premise of natural equality. Since there is no natural political power, such power must be

created by human beings, and unless and until it is, they remain in the state of nature (i.e., their natural condition) with respect to one another.

20. To deny this would lead to endless absurdities, including that Locke would have excluded from the "species" half of those necessary for reproduction; denied that women could be held morally responsible for their actions; and essentially read women out of God's creation of mankind. See also *Second Treatise*, §6. The generic understanding of the terms "man" and "mankind" was even stronger in Locke's day than in ours. See *The Oxford English Dictionary* entry for "man," which includes the following examples: "The Lord had but one pair of men in Paradise. (1597)" and "There is in all men, both male and female, a desire and power of generation. (1752)." We return to this subject below; see n. 48 and accompanying text.

21. Locke, *Second Treatise*, §§58, 65–67. See Ruth W. Grant, *John Locke's Liberalism* (Chicago: University of Chicago Press, 1987), pp. 59–64, for a fuller treatment of these subjects including Locke's critique of Filmer's argument that paternal power can be inherited and Locke's defense of the rights of children, regardless of birth order or gender, to inherit their parents' estate.

22. The legitimacy of arranged marriages would seem to be ruled out by the combination of the limitation of parental authority and the requirement that the marriage contract be voluntary.

23. Locke, *Second Treatise*, §§78–83.

24. Locke, *Second Treatise*, §82.

25. Locke, *First Treatise*, §47.

26. Locke, *Second Treatise*, §§95–99.

27. Locke, *Second Treatise*, §96.

28. Locke, *Second Treatise*, §82.

29. Locke, *First Treatise*, §47; *Second Treatise*, §83.

30. Locke, *Second Treatise*, §99.

31. Locke, *Second Treatise*, §§95–96.

32. For a discussion of the status of majority rule in Locke's account see Grant, *John Locke's Liberalism*, pp. 115–19.

33. See Locke, *Second Treatise*, §54.

34. John Locke, "Virtus" (1681; from the 1661 Commonplace Book), reprinted in Wootton, *Political Writings*, p. 241.

35. Locke, *Second Treatise*, §82.

36. Locke, *Second Treatise*, §§77, 86.

37. Locke, *Second Treatise*, §83.

38. Locke, *Second Treatise,* §65.

39. Locke, *Second Treatise,* §82.

40. See Locke, *Second Treatise,* §§116–118. Locke makes clear that adult children are not bound to any political society by their parents' consent. Each person must consent individually to membership in political society.

41. Locke, *Second Treatise,* §77; *First Treatise,* §§130–131.

42. Locke was the first to effectively challenge the analogy between the family and the state. This was a critical move in undermining the claims for permanent, extensive, and hierarchical authority in husbands over wives. The analogy had structured debates between Royalists and Parliamentarians over the right of the subjects to challenge the King's authority for quite some time. Mary Lyndon Shanley, "Marriage Contract and Social Contract in Seventeenth Century English Political Thought," *Western Political Quarterly,* vol. 32, 1979 (79–91).

43. Bryan A. Garner, ed. *Black's Law Dictionary,* 7th edition (St. Paul, Minn.: West Group, 1999), p.1506.

44. See the discussion of the different ways in which Edward Gee, James Tyrrell, and Algernon Sidney combine patriarchal notions with consent theory in Butler, "Early Liberal Roots of Feminism," pp. 139–42. On Tyrrell, see also Shanley, "Marriage Contract and Social Contract," pp. 85–86.

45. Locke, *Second Treatise,* chapter 16.

46. Locke, *Second Treatise,* §118.

47. See Brennan and Pateman, " 'Mere Auxiliaries to the Commonwealth,' " for one example.

48. Lunatics, idiots, and madmen alone are excepted as "defects" . . . "out of the ordinary course of nature" (Locke, *Second Treatise,* §60). Members of the species are characterized by "the use of the same faculties;" "every one" is "furnished with like Faculties" (Locke, *Second Treatise,* §§4, 6). For the connection between the natural law, reason, and the human species in contrast to animals see, for example, *Second Treatise,* §§8–11, 62. See also n. 20, and *Essay* III.11.16.

49. Locke does explain that foreigners must obey the laws of the country in which they reside and are thus subjects without being members. But even this he explains as an example of tacit consent, the necessity of which presumes a natural equality of rights. Moreover, I see no reason to assume that Locke treats English women as if they were temporary foreign residents.

50. Locke, *Second Treatise,* chapter 10.

51. Locke, *Second Treatise*, §§138, 142.

52. Locke, *Second Treatise*, §192.

53. Locke, *Second Treatise*, §143, and chapters 12–14.

54. Locke, *Second Treatise*, §122.

55. Locke, *Second Treatise*, §§74, 76, 117, 175.

56. Locke, *First Treatise*, §106; *Second Treatise*, §§1, 224–239.

57. Locke, *Second Treatise*, §§105, 107.

58. Locke, *Second Treatise*, §111.

59. See Grant, "Locke's Political Anthropology," sections I and II.

60. As some of his contemporaries did. See note 44.

61. Locke, *Second Treatise*, §54.

62. See note 16. Outside of the *Two Treatises*, I have found only one disparaging remark about women, or perhaps about women of the laboring classes. Locke comments that laboring men "(to say nothing of the other sex)" need to have access to religious truths in simple form because they have neither the leisure nor the capacity to follow lengthy theological arguments. *Reasonableness*, §252.

63. In America, excluding women and propertyless men from the franchise often was defended on the grounds that their economic dependence would compromise the independence of their political judgment, particularly before the institution of the secret ballot. This claim is unrelated to the claim of natural incapacity.

64. The full title of the work is *The Second Treatise of Government: An Essay Concerning the True Original, Extent and End of Civil Government.*

65. Locke acknowledges that, historically, governments often began when families were transformed into small polities ruled by a single man, usually the father. But he is at pains to argue that even these were governments based on consent, and for that reason, the people were always free to establish and reestablish political authority to protect themselves from abuses and to best serve their common purposes. *Second Treatise*, §§105–112.

66. A strict Lockean might make this claim, not as a timeless principle, but as necessarily true under modern conditions. Locke took the position that the necessary requirements for legitimate rule may vary as conditions change over time and as people progress in their understanding of political power. Locke, *Second Treatise*, §§94, 107, 110–111.

67. Again, a strict Lockean could only make this claim conditionally. Political subordination could only be sustained on Lockean grounds so long as women themselves could consent to that position reasonably. It would have to be demonstrably clear that they benefitted from the arrangement,

since people never can be thought to voluntarily change their position for the worse. Locke, *Second Treatise,* §131.

68. This is the dilemma that arises over whether to classify "new rights" as basic human rights, e.g., a right to health care.

69. Locke, *Second Treatise,* §65. In unpublished notes, Locke also wrote that a man may have two wives simultaneously. Cited in John Locke, *Two Treatises of Government,* ed. by Peter Laslett (Cambridge: Cambridge University Press, 1960, 1988), p. 321n.

70. Locke, *Second Treatise,* §83.

71. Though he is not entirely silent on the subject. See *Some Thoughts Concerning Education,* §§31–62, and Tarcov, *Locke's Education for Liberty,* chapter 2.

John Locke's Democratic Theory

IAN SHAPIRO

The democratic tradition has ancient origins, but contemporary formulations are generally traced to Jean-Jacques Rousseau's discussion of the general will in *The Social Contract,* published in 1762. Joseph Schumpeter went so far as to characterize Rousseau's account as the "classical" theory of democracy, even though his was really a neoclassical view — an eighteenth century adaptation of the ancient Greek theory in which democracy had meant ruling and being ruled in turn.[1] Many commentators have followed Schumpeter's lead in treating Rousseau as the father of modern democratic theory, yet it is my contention that John Locke merits the distinction. He developed the elements of an account of democracy that is more realistic, far-reaching, and appealing than is Rousseau's, and it has greater continuing relevance than does Rousseau's to contemporary democratic thinking. Locke conceived of the relationship between people and ruler as one of authorship at a more fundamental level than did Rousseau, placing the authorizing people, acting collectively, at the center of his account of political legitimacy. Yet, unlike Rousseau, he did not reify collective action or the general will in ways that have since been debunked by social choice theorists. Moreover, Locke's democratic theory had other dimensions as well, ranging over accounts of the moral equality of persons, what we might today describe as a political rather than a metaphysical approach to moral and political disagreement, and a strong defense of majority rule as the wellspring of institutional legitimacy.

Some will find my suggestion jarring not so much for the invidious comparison with Rousseau as for the fact that Locke is typically portrayed as a theorist of individual rights rather than of democracy. In the debate over the ideological origins of the American Revolution, for instance, the Lockean view is contrasted, as a rights-centric one, with a civic republican interpretation of the Founders' self-understandings. There is no suggestion in this debate that Locke's view was democratic.[2] Add to this the fact that Locke spent almost no time discussing political participation, and the case for him as a democratic theorist would seem to be rather bleak. It is my contention, however, that the deep structure of Locke's account of politics is profoundly democratic. His understanding of the moral equality of persons lends itself better to democratic than to liberal thinking, even if his is not the "strong democracy" characteristic of the participatory and deliberative democratic traditions.[3] Moreover, as an institutional matter his defense of individual rights is nested in and subordinate to majority rule — casting his historical role as a proto-liberal rights theorist in a questionable light. This last contention is not new. As long ago as 1940 Willmoore Kendall noted that Locke's partiality to majority rule lived in tension with his account of individual rights.[4] Kendall saw this as a deficiency of Locke's theory, whereas on my account his defense of majority rule is part of a more sophisticated view of institutional legitimacy than Kendall was able to grasp. Another way to put this is to say that although Locke was no theorist of democratic participation, he was an innovative theorist of democratic legitimacy.

Does this mean the historical Locke was a democrat? Up to a point, albeit a debated one.[5] The gravamen of my claim here has more to do with the logic of his argument than with his intentions, but I mean to show that even they exhibited a democratic hue that has not been fully appreciated. As a matter of personal biography we know that Locke evolved over the course of his life from being a fairly conservative, or, at any rate, apolitical person in his early adult years, who gave unreflective endorsement to authoritarian political arrangements, into a political insurrectionist in Shaftesbury's circle in the 1670s and after. His political outlook expressed itself mainly in terms of the great issue of the day: is there a legitimate right to resist an illegitimate monarch to the point of removing him by force? Locke famously concluded that there is indeed such a right. This argument might be thought to have little consequence for democratic politics, dealing, as it does, with the legitimacy of revolution. Moreover, it seems clear that in some respects even the Locke of the 1680s and after distanced himself from the most radical political movements of his day. Without delving deeply into these historical controversies, I will argue that Locke's account of the conditions under which revolution is legitimate is nonetheless decidedly democratic in its assumptions, and that the ever-present possibility of legitimate revolution has significant democratic consequences for thinking about day-to-day politics.

I begin with an exploration of Locke's account of the dimensions of human moral equality, showing that his view of all human beings as equally God's property, as intrinsically rational, and as the "authors" of the state, revealed a fundamentally democratic egalitarian outlook. This is followed by a discussion of Locke's views on toleration and dissent, where I show that, in addition to embracing a comparatively capacious view of toleration for his own day, Locke's justification for the limits on toleration that he advocated was in some respects akin to the mature John Rawls in his "political, not metaphysical" mode, though Locke's political, not metaphysical stance turns out on close inspection to be more thoroughly political and less problematic than does Rawls's. This leads to a discussion of Locke's account of the relations between majority rule and institutional legitimacy, where I argue that Locke's embrace of majority rule was less starry-eyed than that of subsequent democratic theorists, but that it was by the same token more attractive given the realities of politics in diverse societies.

Human Moral Equality

The first and most basic sense in which we are equal, for Locke, is as God's property. Here we need to elucidate both the senses in which we are equal and those in which we are God's property, since both turn out to be relevant to subsequent democratic understandings. Starting with the account of property, Locke's view of humans as God's property is a special case of his workmanship theory by reference to which authority, ownership, and even authentic knowledge are all rooted in acts of creative making. This theory was developed as a consequence of Locke's position on the nature and meaning of natural law. If one took the view, common among natural law theorists of his day, that natural law is eternal and unchanging, this threatened another notion many thought compelling: that God is omnipotent. By definition, an all-powerful God could not be bound by natural law. Yet if God is conceded to have the capacity to change natural law, then we cannot declare it to be timeless. Locke wrestled with this tension without ever resolving it to his own satisfaction, but in his moral and political writings he came down decisively in the voluntarist, or will-centered, camp.[6] He could not relinquish the proposition that for something to have the status of a law, it must be the product of a will. By adopting this voluntarist view, Locke aligned himself with other will-centered theorists of the early Enlightenment, notably the German philosopher and natural law theorist Samuel von Pufendorf.[7]

We find similar reasoning in Locke's *Essays on the Law of Nature,* delivered as lectures at Christ Church in 1663–1664. Here, Locke's treatment of human capacities was linked to his theology in a different way; it rested on his categorial distinction between natural right and natural law, which explained human autonomy. Rejecting the traditional Christian correlativities between right and law, Locke insisted instead that natural law "ought to be distinguished from natural right: for right is grounded in the fact that we have the free use of a thing, whereas law is what enjoins or forbids the doing of a thing."[8] What humans perceive as natural law is in fact God's natural right; an expression of His will. In this sense right is prior to law in Locke's analytical scheme.[9] Locke's theory of ownership flows naturally out of this scheme, transforming the workmanship model of knowledge into a normative theory of right. It is through acts of autonomous making that rights over what is created come into being: making entails ownership so that natural law is at bottom God's natural right over his creation.[10] Locke's frequent appeals to metaphors of workmanship and watch making in the *Two Treatises* and elsewhere make it fundamental that men are obliged to God because of his purposes in making them. Men are "the Workmanship of one Omnipotent, and infinitely wise Maker. . . . they are his property, whose workmanship they are, made to last during his, not another's pleasure."[11]

Why does this account of natural law and God's workmanship matter for the moral equality of persons? Two reasons. First, because we are all God's creatures, on Locke's account, we were all protected from being owned by one another. It might ring strange to the contemporary ear that Locke felt the need to deny that people can be one another's property, but his central preoccupation in the *First Treatise* was to refute defenses of absolutism that appealed to Adam's "right of dominion over his children."[12] Conventional defenders of absolutism, notoriously Sir Robert Filmer, had contended "that fathers, by begetting them, come by an absolute power over their children."[13] Locke insisted, by contrast, that God makes children and uses their parents for that purpose. Parents are "but occasions of [children's] being, and, when they design and wish to beget them, do little more towards their making, than Ducalion and his wife in the fable did towards the making of mankind, by throwing pebbles over their heads."[14] Were parents givers of life, Locke conceded, they might have some sort of quasi-ownership claim, but they are not. Even in this hypothetical eventuality, Locke resists the absolutist case by arguing that "every one who gives another any thing, has not always thereby a right to take it away again,"[15] and he insists that because the woman "hath an equal share, if not greater" in nourishing a child, the creationist theory in any case does not justify paternal absolutism. It is "so hard to imagine the rational soul should presently inhabit the yet unformed embryo, as soon as the father has done his part in the act of generation, that if it must be supposed to derive any thing from the parents, it must certainly owe most to the mother."[16]

In short, to give life "is to frame and make a living creature, fashion the parts, and mold and suit them to their uses; and having proportioned and fitted them together, to put into them a living soul."[17] Parents do not fashion the child and most commonly, do not even intend to create it; they do so as a byproduct of the instinctive desires God has placed in them. In response to Filmer's claims, Locke states, "They who say the father gives life to children, are so dazzled with the thoughts of monarchy, that they do not, as they ought, remember God, who is 'the Author and Giver of Life.' "[18] Parents have fiduciary responsibility for their children on Locke's account, but it expires upon their maturity. Parents are obliged to provide for their children "not as their own workmanship, but the workmanship of their own maker."[19]

This is why Locke insists that although children are not born in a "state of equality, though they are born to it." Adults have "a sort of rule and jurisdiction over them when they come into the world, and for some time after; but it is a temporary one." The bonds of children's subjection "are like the Swadling Cloths they are wrapt up in, and supported by, in the weakness of their Infancy." Developing age and reason loosen these bonds, "till at length they drop quite off, and leave a man at his own free disposal."[20] The power to command "ends with nonage." Thereafter, although "honour and respect, support and defense, and whatsoever gratitude can oblige a man to, for the highest benefits he is naturally capable of, be always due from a son to his parents; yet all this puts no sceptre into the father's hand, no sovereign power of commanding."[21] The only legitimate sanction at the parent's disposal is the power to withhold inheritance, or "to bestow it with a more sparing or liberal hand, according as the behaviour of this or that child hath comported with his will and humor."[22] Parents are to "inform the mind, and govern the actions of their yet ignorant nonage, till reason shall take its place, and ease them of that trouble."[23] This treatment of children reflects an inclusive view of the right to make decisions for oneself: the only justifiable basis for paternalism is incapacity.

One reason that Locke's view of moral equality has had staying power since he wrote is that the obvious secular analogue of his claim that we are all God's property is that we are nobody's property. The workmanship model persisted in the western intellectual consciousness long after it was cut loose from its Lockean theological moorings. If we abandon the theology yet still embrace the workmanship ideal as most in the Enlightenment tradition since Locke — be they conservatives, liberals, or radicals — have done, the logic of his argument against Filmer continues to hold. Indeed, it can be extended: parents cannot own children because they do not make them, but by the same token nor can anyone else own them. In this way the egalitarian logic of his argument against Filmer extends beyond their theological disagreements.[24]

A comparably inclusive view is reflected in Locke's discussion of women. Feminist commentators on the history of political theory note correctly that there were limits to Locke's embrace of gender equality.[25] In the *First Treatise* he describes women as the "weaker sex," and, although he insists there is no biblical authority for men's dominion over women, that it is a matter of human law, he says "there is, I grant, a foundation in nature for it."[26] Moreover, in the *Second Treatise,* he says that it "being necessary that the last determination, *i.e.* the rule, should be placed somewhere; it naturally falls to the man's share, as the abler and the stronger."[27] Yet, taken in context, in both cases these statements were concessions to considerably more paternalistic views that Locke was challenging, and it should be noted that the bulk of his discussion is concerned with hemming in what Locke took to be the husband's inevitable power. We have already seen that Locke resisted patriarchalism with respect to children partly on the ground that if children were seen as human creations women's ownership claim would outweigh that of men. Beyond this, Filmer had contended that "God at the Creation gave the Sovereignty to the Man over the Woman, as being the Nobler and Principal Agent in Generation,"[28] a belief that Locke maintained is utterly inconsistent with a biblical teaching, "for God in the Scripture says, 'his father and his mother that begot him.' "[29] Locke is equally dismissive of Filmer's claim that " 'monarchical power of government [is] settled and fixed by the commandment, honour thy father and thy mother,' " since as Locke observes, "nobody will say a child may withhold honour from his mother, or, as the Scripture terms it, 'set light by her,' though his father should command him to do so; no more than the mother could dispense with him, for neglecting to *honour* his father: whereby it is plain, that this command of God, gives the father no sovereignty, no supremacy."[30]

Perhaps more remarkably, Locke treated marriage as an egalitarian contract, grounded in the idea of mutual consent: "conjugal society is made by a voluntary compact between man and woman; and though it consist chiefly in such a communion and right in one another's bodies as is necessary to its chief end, procreation; yet it draws with it mutual support and assistance, and a communion of interests too."[31] The husband prevails in situations of unavoidable conflict, but this nonetheless "leaves the wife in the full and free possession of what by contract is her peculiar right, and gives the husband no more power over her life, than she has over his." Indeed, the power of the husband "being so far from that of an absolute monarch, that the wife has in many cases a liberty to separate from him, where natural right or their contract allows it; whether that contract be made by themselves in the state of nature, or by the customs or laws of the country they live in; and the children, upon such Separation fall to the father's or mother's lot, as such contract does determine."[32] In short, Locke was remarkably ahead of his time with respect to women's equality, and, as Carole Pateman and Rogers Smith have noted, the egalitarian logic of his argument is subversive of all authority relations, including those arising in marriage.[33]

Likewise in his discussion of slavery in the *Second Treatise,* Locke insists that "The natural liberty of man is to be free from any superior power on earth, and not to be under the will or legislative authority of man, but to have only the law of nature for his rule."[34] Human beings may not sell themselves into slavery because they are God's property. "Nobody can give more power than he has himself; and he cannot take away his own life, cannot give another power over it."[35] Slaves may be taken as a result of legitimate victory in war on Locke's account, but only because the defeated enemy has forfeited his right to life "by some act that deserves death," and the victor "to whom he has forfeited it, may (when he has him in his power) delay to take it, and make use of him to his own service, and he does him no injury by it."[36] Legitimate slavery is, in effect, nothing more than the continuation of a state of war between the lawful victor and the captive, who never, strictly, becomes his master's property.[37] There can be no slave relationship among members of a legitimate political association, which has to be based on consent. We are all equally immune from being owned by other humans, and by the same token bound to recognize that we cannot own others.[38]

In addition to our all being equally God's property, Locke argued that " 'all men by nature are equal' "[39] due to God's decision. On Filmer's account, God had given the world to Adam and his heirs. Existing property rights and the system of political authority had allegedly passed to current owners and European monarchs in this way through primogeniture. Locke insisted, by contrast, that God gave the world to mankind in common — subject to the provisos that it not be wasted, and that "enough, and as good" remain available to others to use in common.[40] Locke added two dubious empirical claims to his theory of inclusive use-rights to the common. The result was something like the view of property that contemporary libertarians embrace. First was that with the introduction of money the injunction against waste, although not in principle transcended, for practical purposes became obsolete.[41] Second, Locke was convinced that the productivity effects of enclosing common land would be so great that the "enough, and as good" proviso could in practice also be dispensed with, thereby legitimating private ownership. For "he who appropriates land to himself by his labour, does not lessen, but increase the common stock of mankind."[42]

Although Locke's theory permitted substantial inequalities to develop, it nonetheless provided the basis for an egalitarian collective constraint on them: if either of his empirical beliefs turns out not to be true, the provisos kick in with all the force of natural law behind them. In short, Locke was not a believer in equality of result, nor was he a mere proponent of equality of opportunity or what Ronald Dworkin has described as starting-gate equality.[43] Use-rights to the common are universal and inextinguishable on Locke's account. Although he does not say this, it would thus be reasonable to infer that anyone who is deprived of access to the common due to private ownership thus has a legitimate claim to at least what he would have been able to earn from unenclosed land. If this does not "trickle down" as a byproduct of the productivity effects of enclosure, then the natural law guarantee is activated.[44]

God's decision to treat humans as one another's peers extends beyond these natural law protections; for Locke, it is built into the nature of human agency. We are all miniature gods on his account in that, provided we do not violate natural law, we stand in the same relation to the objects we create as God stands to us. We own them just as he owns us.[45] Natural law, or God's natural right, sets the outer boundaries to a field within which humans have divine authorization to act as little gods, creating rights and obligations of their own. And although he denies that parents create children for reasons already discussed, Locke insists that God has endowed humans with great creative power. He minimizes the independent contribution of common resources to the value of what people produce by arguing that the world which has been given us in common is God's "waste," and insisting that "labour makes the far greater part," of its value.[46] This is why Locke was so confident of the productivity effects of enclosure. The goods produced on an acre of enclosed land are at least ten — more like a hundred — times more than those "yielded by an acre of land, of an equal richness, lying waste in common." As a result, someone who encloses ten acres "may truly be said to give ninety acres to mankind," at least.[47]

Locke applied his workmanship model to political arrangements no less than to property. Whereas for Filmer political rulers received their authority from God, on Locke's account political institutions are the property of the human beings who create them through a social contract. Indeed, in what might seem quaint by today's criteria for knowledge, Locke held that the study of ethics and politics is superior to that of the physical world because it concerns products of the human will to which every individual has privileged access through introspection. He distinguished "ectype" from "archetype" ideas, ectypes being general ideas of substances, archetypes are constructed by man. This generated a radical disjunction between natural and conventional knowledge, underpinned by a further distinction between "nominal" and "real" essences. In substances that depend on the external world for their existence (such as trees or animals), only nominal essences can be known to man. The real essence is available only to the maker of the substance, God. In the case of archetypes, however, nominal and real essences are synonymous so that real essences can by definition be known by man. Because the social world is a function of archetype ideas, it follows that real social essences can be known by man. We know what we make. Man can thus have incontrovertible knowledge of his creations — most importantly, for our purposes, of his political arrangements and institutions.[48]

We know what we make just as we own what we make, be it property created through individual work or a commonwealth created by collective agreement. God makes man, we are told in the *First Treatise,* " 'in his own image, after his own likeness; makes him an intellectual creature and so capable of dominion.' "[49] Human beings are equal to one another in these endeavors because their capacity for creativity, their status as miniature gods, is both universal and God-given. It may not legitimately be given, taken away, or otherwise compromised by other human beings. Indeed, natural law requires that each person preserve himself and that "when his own preservation comes not in competition," that each person ought "as much as he can, to preserve the rest of mankind, and may not, unless it be to do justice on an offender, take away or impair the life, or what tends to the preservation of life, the liberty, health, limb or goods of another."[50] Locke was adamant that "the state of nature has a law of nature to govern it, which obliges every one: and reason, which is that law, teaches all mankind, who will but consult it, that being all equal and independent, no one ought to harm another in his life, health, liberty, or possessions."[51]

Reason, then, is equally available to all. Locke was quick to defuse arguments from authority by appealing to man's natural and unencumbered reasoning capacities, a view that infuses his discussion in the *Essay Concerning Human Understanding* as well as *A Letter Concerning Toleration.* So he insists in the *Essay* that it is not only those who are trained in logic that are capable of reason. "He that will look into many parts of Asia and America, will find men reason there perhaps as acutely as himself, yet who never heard of a syllogism, nor can reduce any one argument to those forms."[52] God, Locke insists,

> has not been so sparing to men to make them barely two-legged creatures, leaving it to Aristotle to make them rational. . . . He has given them a mind that can reason, without being instructed in methods of syllogizing: the understanding is not taught to reason by these rules; it has a native faculty to perceive the coherence or incoherence of its ideas, and can range them right, without any such perplexing repetitions.[53]

Rank does not give privileged access to reason any more than education does. Locke insists in the *Letter Concerning Toleration* that although princes are born superior to other men in power, "in nature" they are equal. "Neither the right, nor the art of ruling, does necessarily carry along with it the certain knowledge of other things."[54] And we have seen that in the *Second Treatise,* Locke avers that the laws of nature are more easily intelligible than positive laws, and in his discussion of parental authority the whole basis of his attack on Filmer is that this is limited to their children's "ignorant nonage." For Locke, adults are all assumed to be equally capable of rational behavior. He thus thought human moral equality was manifest in the Scriptures, but that it can also be seen in our rational capacities and by observing our place in nature.[55]

Toleration and Dissent

Human beings have liberty to act as miniature gods within the constraints of natural law, but they do not have license to violate the constraints themselves. This status inevitably raises the question: What happens when people disagree about their obligations to one another, about what respecting one another's autonomy as God's creatures requires, or about whether natural law is otherwise being compromised by actions people are taking or contemplating? That which humans comprehend as reason is part God's law, as I have just noted, but Locke realized that he had to confront the possibility that people might disagree about the meaning of the Scriptures or what reason otherwise requires. One way in which he responded was by embracing a capacious doctrine of toleration.

Locke went out of his way to make toleration in general not contingent on the truth or falsity of the belief to be tolerated. We are all subject to "the duties of peace and goodwill . . . as well towards the erroneous as the orthodox."[56] In *A Letter Concerning Toleration,* he insisted that the state

may not force religious conformity on anyone, for "every church is orthodox to itself; [and] to others, erroneous or heretical." A church must therefore be a voluntary association of individuals in which the magistrate both
safeguards and limits, but may not regulate internally. "[T]he care of souls
is not committed to the civil magistrate." His power consists in "outward
force," but "true and saving religion consists in the inward persuasion of
the mind."[57]

Locke was well aware that an unqualified principle of toleration can
generate paradoxes, conflicting injunctions, and self-defeating conclusions.
He therefore imposed three kinds of limits on toleration. The first concerns
toleration of practices inimical to the principle of toleration itself; that is,
actions which, if tolerated, result in people being forced to do things they
would not otherwise do. "For all force, as has often been said, belongs only
to the magistrate, nor ought any private persons at any time use force unless
it is in self-defense against unjust violence."[58] "Unjust violence" seems to
mean direct violation of another's will, a refusal to tolerate another's private
actions. Toleration requires intolerance of anti-tolerant acts: "[F]or who
could be free, when every other man's humour might domineer over
him?"[59]

Next, Locke is unequivocal in the *First Treatise* that because all people
are bound by the laws of nature, they have liberty to act freely but not
license to do as they please. Thus children are under the authority of parents
until they are old enough to understand that law, and thus practices like
cannibalism, sale of children, adultery, incest, and sodomy, all of which
"cross the main intention of nature,"[60] cannot be tolerated. Leaving aside,
for now, how Locke expects us to know what is and is not against the main
intention of nature, he clearly expects that the civil law will uphold this law
and will not tolerate transgressions against it.

Finally, actions should not be tolerated if they are prejudicial to the
existence of the political order. Thus atheists ought to be suppressed not
because Locke disagrees with their beliefs (though he does), but because
those beliefs threaten the commonwealth. "Promises, covenants, and oaths,
which are the bonds of human society, can have no hold upon an atheist."[61]
Analogous considerations lead Locke to the conclusion that Papists and
"Mahometans" ought not to be tolerated because they owe allegiance to
alien civil powers. "That church can have no right to be tolerated by the
magistrate, which is constituted upon such a bottom, that all those who
enter into it, do thereby, *ipso facto*, deliver themselves up to the protection
and service of another prince."[62]

It is difficult to know to what extent such beliefs were sincerely held by any writer in the political climate of Restoration and revolutionary England. On the subject of atheism, Locke regarded questions about the existence of God as separate from questions about alternative religions. It is clear from the *Essay* that he was convinced by versions of the cosmological proof and the argument from design.[63] In *A Letter Concerning Toleration,* he seems to follow Hooker in invoking a version of the argument from common consent.[64] For whatever reason, Locke regarded the existence of God as self-evident. But his decisive *political* reason for denying toleration to atheists, Catholics, and Muslims rested on his worry about their incentives for fidelity to the commonwealth. In this he was an early proponent of a view akin to John Rawls's "political, not metaphysical" outlook concerning political legitimacy. True and saving religion might consist of inward persuasion of the mind, but if the mind of an Englishman becomes persuaded of the veracity of Catholicism or Islam, or, indeed, unpersuaded of God's existence, then he is out of luck. In short, the acceptability of a belief turns on its compatibility with the legitimate political order, not on whether its veracity is demonstrable by Locke's criteria.[65]

These constraints notwithstanding, Locke's view of toleration was a variant of the conventional Whig one in the 1680s. Since the Restoration, Charles and James had been attempting to expand toleration of Catholics and nonconformists to undermine the religious and political power of the Anglican clergy. Charles's embrace of toleration in 1662 and his declaration for indulgence a decade later met with insurmountable political opposition, but James had considerably more success with his similar declaration in 1687. James's uneasy alliance with both Catholic and Protestant nonconformists was broken at the Revolution as a result of Anglican promises to tolerate nonconformists in the general interests of Protestantism. A more liberal regime was realized to some extent in the Toleration Act of 1689, although it did little more than exempt some narrowly defined groups of dissenters from some specific penalties. The Act achieved its purposes, however. It split Protestant from Catholic dissenters, the latter being excluded from toleration legislation. Henceforth, Catholicism could be regarded as treasonable as it was in the Act Against Popery of 1700, aimed at "preventing the further growth of popery and of such treasonable, and execrable designs and conspiracies against his Majesty's person and government."[66] Locke's view was thus in the mainstream of Whig thinking on toleration that triumphed at the Revolution, even if he advocated tolerating a wider array of dissenting groups than would most.

Locke's account of toleration was buttressed by an anti-authoritarian theory of biblical hermeneutics. Underlying his rejection of Filmer's patriarchalism was a challenge to Filmer's reading of the Scriptures, and particularly to the inherently hierarchical world view that emanates from Filmer's contention that God gave the world to Adam and his heirs. Underlying *that* rejection, as Richard Ashcraft has noted, was Locke's radical claim that where the Scriptures admit of more than one interpretation no earthly authority may declare one reading to be authoritative.[67] Our prejudices and opinions "cannot authorize us to understand the Scripture contrary to the direct and plain meaning of the words," but where there is silence or ambiguity the reader must judge how "they may best be understood."[68] In the course of rejecting Filmer's claim that scriptural warrant for Adam's sovereignty over Eve can generate a justification for absolute monarchical authority, Locke insists that the burden lies with whoever is advancing an interpretation to give reasons that the reader will find plausible.[69]

Locke insisted that each reader is sovereign over what counts for him as a convincing interpretation of a text. As Locke argued in the *Letter on Toleration,* those things "that every man ought sincerely to inquire into himself, and by meditation, study, search, and his own endeavours, attain the knowledge of, cannot be looked upon as the peculiar profession of any one sort of men."[70] When people disagree over the meaning of the Scriptures, they have to weigh the evidence for themselves. God speaks directly to every individual through the text, so that no human authority is entitled to declare one interpretation authoritative in the face of a conflicting one.[71] This freedom to comprehend natural law by one's own lights supplied the basis for Locke's right to resist that could be invoked against the sovereign, and to which he himself appealed in opposing the English crown during the 1680s. Ashcraft captures Locke's interpretive radicalism well when he notes that it was "designed to undermine the authoritative weight of an interpretation of the Bible advanced by any individual or group of individuals as an interpretative guide to the meaning of that work."[72]

This is not to say that Locke believed every interpretation of the Scriptures equally valid. On the contrary, he thought that there is a correct interpretation on which reasonable people will usually agree, and he seemed confident that he could convince people that his reading of the Scriptures was consistent with their commonsense interpretations. Although God speaks with more truth and certainty than men, "when he vouchsafes to speak to men [through the Scriptures], I do not think he speaks differently from them, in crossing the rules of language in use amongst them: this would not be to condescend to their capacities, when he humbles himself to speak to them, but to lose his design in speaking what, thus spoken, they could not understand."[73] Commonsense readings of the Scriptures must, therefore, reveal their true meaning. We have to countenance the possibility that people will continue to disagree, and protect their right to do so, but Locke did not doubt that most of the time people could be brought to agree.

I will have more to say about Locke's treatment of political disagreement anon. For now it is worth noting that there is a certain circularity to his view, parallel to that which attends Rawls in his "political, not metaphysical" mode. Rawls seeks a "political" conception of justice that "can gain the support of an overlapping consensus of reasonable religious, philosophical, and moral doctrines in a society regulated by it." He regards this as essential for people who disagree profoundly on religious, philosophical, and moral matters to "maintain a just and stable democratic society."[74] It is not entirely clear on Rawls's account whether, in order for a religious, philosophical, or moral doctrine to be judged reasonable it must meet independently derived criteria as he sometimes claims, or whether it must be compatible with political arrangements that can be endorsed by adherents to any of the other doctrines that happen to prevail in the society — whether overlapping consensus is derived from reasonableness or the reverse.[75]

To be sure, expansive as it was for his day, Locke's view of toleration is more restrictive than Rawls's. Yet it seems to exhibit an analogous ambiguity in that it is difficult to pin down whether he ultimately thinks commonsense interpretations of the Scriptures should be thought commonsensical because they are compatible with political arrangements that those with different readings can endorse, or rather for some independent reason. And, as with Rawls, difficulties attend both views. If there is to be an independent criterion, the question arises as to where it comes from and what is to be said to those who are unpersuaded of its basis in reason or common sense. If, on the other hand, we adopt the contingent view, there is the danger that there might not be an overlapping consensus. There might not be enough common ground between competing interpretations — say Locke's and Filmer's — to sustain any political order. After all, considerations of this kind were presumably partly what was at issue for Locke in the 1680s. In some moods at least Rawls seems to want to square the relevant circle by claiming that his proposed principles are compatible with the most diverse possible array of doctrines while still being able to sustain a stable political order. The reasons Locke gives for limiting toleration as he does suggest that analogous considerations played into his thinking, but we will see that when push comes to shove, he moves in a more decidedly democratic direction.

Democratic Foundations

At this point it might reasonably be asked whether Locke's view is not more liberal than democratic. After all, we have seen that it is the traditional liberal value of toleration, buttressed by a strongly individualist view of scriptural interpretation, that lies at the core of his political doctrine — a far cry from the conventional democratic commitment to participation. This is true; indeed as Kendall notes, given his doctrine, Locke is surprisingly thin on mechanisms of popular consultation.[76] Moreover, as Ruth Grant argues convincingly in this volume, Locke did not think of day-to-day participation as a basic category of political legitimation. Closer examination reveals, however, that his underlying conception of legitimacy is democratic more than liberal, particularly once we focus on his discussion of the practical implications of disagreement over the meaning of natural law and the right to resist.

Locke's assumption that people can always be brought to agree on fundamental moral and political questions was obviously at variance with his own political experience. He acknowledged this in the most Hobbesian of terms: "For though the Law of Nature be plain and intelligible to all rational Creatures," he tells us in his discussion of the aims of political society in the *Second Treatise,* "yet men being biased by their interest, as well as ignorant for want of studying it, are not apt to allow of it as a law binding to them . . . men being partial to themselves, passion and revenge is very apt to carry them too far, and with too much heat, in their own cases."[77] For Hobbes, this view could generate a command theory of law to force men to be rational; for Rousseau, it would generate a Lawgiver to manipulate men to be "genuinely" free. Locke, however, takes the idea of consent of the governed too seriously to make an analogous move. Like the young Rawls of *A Theory of Justice,* he seems to want to reason about the legitimacy of political institutions in a way that pays homage to considerable diversity of belief yet shields it from self-interest. As is well known, Rawls deploys a "veil of ignorance" to get at this: people are assumed to be choosing institutions knowing that there is a plurality of world views and conceptions of the good but not what their particular one is.[78] Locke, who conceived of the social contract as an actual agreement, would not have been much interested in hypothetical speculation of this kind. For him, reconciling disagreement with the view that political legitimacy is based on consent is an inescapable political problem. Whereas Rawls's "political, not metaphysical" move retains a rationalist component, Locke's is political all the way down. This is because Rawls restricts the range of acceptable views based on where they come from, whereas for Locke the decisive criterion is what they should be expected to lead to.

For Rawls, acceptable political arguments appeal only to public reason rooted in the overlapping consensus among the different views in society, not to the comprehensive religious and metaphysical doctrines to which people may be committed. This creates difficulties for him in thinking about the legitimacy of movements for political reform such as the civil rights movement. Such movements were often avowedly religious in inspiration, manifestly rooted in the comprehensive doctrines of their adherents. Of their leaders he says that "they did not go against the ideal of public reason; or rather, they did not provided they thought, or on reflection would have thought (as they certainly could have thought), that the comprehensive reasons they appealed to were required to give sufficient strength to the political conception to be subsequently realized."[79] The obvious question to ask Rawls is what would he say to the pro-segregationist who believes his views, though right because dictated by God, were compatible with what public reason should endorse. Because Locke focused exclusively on the political effects of beliefs in determining what should be tolerated, he did not need to indulge in such conceptual gymnastics to adjudicate among comprehensive doctrines while trying to appear not to be so doing. This consequentialist understanding of "political, not metaphysical" places him closer to Habermas than to Rawls in the contemporary debate.[80]

The right of resistance defended in the *Second Treatise* was intensely charged politically. Locke placed himself at odds with the Whig establishment in 1689 by embracing the Lawsonian view that when James had been compelled to leave the throne an entire dissolution of government had resulted. In violating the terms of the social contract James had, in Locke's view, gone into a direct state of war with the people. Accordingly, they had the right to resist him and to remove him as king.[81] Locke's view entailed not only that the king had been removed from office justly but also that the rule of law and the legal authority of Parliament had ended, necessitating a return of power to the general community. As a general matter, this means that, once the right to resist potentially comes into play, the political stakes cannot be higher. It also makes the issue of what to do in the face of disagreement concerning how and by whom resistance is to be deemed legitimate all the more consequential.

In the course of arguing against both mixed and limited monarchy, Filmer had noted that in either case there is no final and authoritative judge within the constitution. Neither Parliament nor any court could resolve a charge of tyranny against the king. Locke tacitly accepted this position, as Franklin notes,[82] yet he never answered Filmer's charge that this would be an open invitation for continual resistance and even attempted revolution by anarchic individuals and groups disaffected by the actions of the king or Parliament. It was exactly this type of conflict that the Whigs wanted to avoid. Locke tried to downplay these radical implications of his view by holding that not every illegal act by the king justified revolution, "[I]t being safer for the Body, that some few private Men should be sometimes in danger to suffer, than that the head of the Republick should be easily, and upon slight occasions exposed." Unless a ruler actively places himself "into a state of war with his people, dissolve the government, and leave them to that defense which belongs to everyone in the state of nature," he may not legitimately be resisted.[83] Indeed, in the chapter on prerogative power, Locke went so far as to maintain that the independence of the ruler is such that there may be circumstances in which he may act where there is no law, and even in some cases "against the direct letter of the law"[84] provided this is for the public good. Wise and good princes will use this power well; others will misuse it.

This is only to push the matter back an additional step, however. Even in extreme cases — arguably especially in such cases — disagreement over whether the ruler has placed himself at war with his people has to be anticipated. Locke's instructive answer is that the "people have no other remedy in this, as in all other cases when they have no judge on earth, but to appeal to heaven."[85] This appeal to heaven implies a resort to force. It might seem to bring Locke uncomfortably close to the Hobbesian position that although a person cannot be blamed in certain circumstances for resisting legitimate authority, such resistance is not itself legitimate — all he can do is hope that it will be recognized as valid in the life to come.[86]

Majority Rule

But Locke's view differs from Hobbes's. Locke clearly supposes that genuine cases of a government's violation of its trust will be obvious, because he expects those who are not biased by interest, who he assumes — perhaps heroically — will be most people, to converge on commonsense conclusions. The operational test of this conclusion is majoritarian for him: the right to resist does not lay "a perpetual foundation for disorder" because it "operates not, till inconvenience is so great, that the majority feel it, and are weary of it, and find a necessity to have it amended."[87] There is no protection for minority perceptions of violations of the social contract or natural law in this scheme, or any provision to protect minorities from majority perceptions that the social contract or natural law have been violated. Given the importance Locke famously attaches to personal consent as the final legitimating mark of all political action and institutions, it might seem remarkable that at the end of the day majority rule is its only guarantor.[88] Locke *predicts* that people will be slow to resist in fact, that the right to resist, even in circumstances of manifestly tyrannous acts, will frequently not be exercised.

> [F]or if it reach no farther than some private men's cases, though they have a right to defend themselves, and to recover by force what by unlawful force is taken from them; yet the right to do so will not easily engage them in a contest, wherein they are sure to perish; it being as impossible for one or a few oppressed men to disturb the government, where the body of the people do not think themselves concerned in it, as for a raving madman, or heady malecontent, to overturn a well-settled state; the people being as little apt to follow the one as the other.[89]

In short, unless and until "a long train of abuses, prevarications, and artifices, all tending the same way," trigger the right to revolution, people must accept the decisions emanating from the prevailing political order.[90] Until that threshold is crossed for a great many, even perceived violations of natural law must for all practical purposes be endured. The individual right to self-enforcement is given up on entering civil society and people can reassert it only at the risk of being executed for treason. On the other hand, if a long train of abuses, and so on, *does* convince the great majority to revolt, there is no legitimate earthly power to stop them. In these respects, Locke's account recognizes the priority of politics to disagreements about rights and laws, so that Kendall is right to insist that those who appeal to Locke as a conventional defender of rights-based liberalism are misguided.[91]

If this were all Locke had to say on the subject of majority rule, the case for him as an early theorist of democracy would be flimsy indeed. In fact, however, he is quite explicit about the majoritarian foundations of political legitimacy. In the state of nature, " 'every one has the executive power' of the law of nature," but this right is given up at the formation of civil society.[92] Thereafter, "it being necessary to that which is one body to move one way; it is necessary the body should move that way wither the greatest force carries it, which is the consent of the majority: or else it is impossible it should act or continue one body, one community, which the consent of every individual that united into it, agreed that it should; and so every one is bound by that to be concluded by the majority."[93] This leads Locke to defend a default presumption in favor of majority rule "in assemblies, empowered to act by positive laws, where no number is set by that positive law which empowers them." Majority rule thus has "by the law of nature and reason, the power of the whole."[94]

Locke recognizes that the public assembly will be characterized by a "variety of opinions, and contrariety of interests, which unavoidably happen in all collections of men," and therefore, unanimity is unlikely.[95] For Rousseau, this reality would necessitate a Lawgiver to guide and enlighten the public as to the general will. But for Locke, the determination of the majority is sufficient "for where the majority cannot conclude the rest, there they cannot act as one body, and consequently will be immediately dissolved again."[96] It is "the consent of any number of Freemen capable of a majority to unite and incorporate into such a society" that provides the "beginning to any lawful government in the world."[97] It may be true, as Ellen Wood has emphasized, that Locke never advocated expansion of the franchise (which was unusually wide in seventeenth century England).[98] But the more salient point for the longer term is that his argument provides no basis for limiting the franchise. His egalitarian commitments discussed in the first half of this chapter press inexorably in the direction of universal inclusion — the only legitimate grounds for excluding people from decision-making that affects them being incapacity.

For Locke, it is majoritarian rather than individual consent that authorizes institutional arrangements. The majority may choose to retain all powers of government, thereby creating a "perfect" democracy. Alternatively, it may delegate some or all of its powers, creating various "forms of commonwealth," such as oligarchies or elective or hereditary monarchies. As Ashcraft notes, "formally, Locke is committed to the view that the majority of the community may dispose of their political power as they see fit, and this includes, of course, their power to constitute a democracy," which is the "form of government that remains closest to the institution of the political community itself."[99] Whatever form of government is chosen, it rests ultimately on conditional delegation from the majority. The majority never relinquishes its "supreme power," which comes into play when delegated power either expires or is abused.[100] Unless a substantial majority comes to agree that abuse has occurred, the opposition of the individual will have no practical effect.[101] Opposition may otherwise be legitimate, but even when it is to an action that is life threatening, an individual or minority might have to wait for vindication until the next life as we have seen.[102] In practice, in this world, natural law constrains the actions of governments only to the extent that a majority discerns it and acts on it.

But why *majority* rule? Liberal writers for whom consent supplies the basis of political legitimacy typically appeal to unanimity, not majority rule, particularly on significant questions — effectively giving everyone who might wish to withhold their consent a veto. For instance, James Buchanan and Gordon Tullock argue in *The Calculus of Consent* that people would insist on unanimity rule before collective action could be taken concerning the issues they regard as most important. Only on less consequential matters would they see the sense of accepting majority rule, or perhaps even delegation to an administrator, when they trade off the costs of participating in decision-making against the likelihood that an adverse decision will be made.[103] Buchanan and Tullock do not supply us with criteria for distinguishing more from less consequential decisions, but it seems safe to assume that Locke's right to resist would be at or close to the top of the list. Yet, as we have seen, he protects it with majority rule only. Why?

The answer is that Locke had a more realistic view of politics than the hypothetical contract theorists of the second half of the twentieth century. As Patrick Riley has noted, "the social contract, for Locke, is necessitated by natural law's inability to be literally 'sovereign' on earth, by its incapacity to produce 'one society.' "[104] Theorists like Buchanan and Tullock, Rawls, and Robert Nozick are often criticized for writing as if the institutions of civil association — private property, contracts, rules of inheritance — can exist independently of collective action.[105] Locke made no such assumption and he would surely have recognized its infeasibility — after all, in his lifetime every enclosure of land required an Act of Parliament. Once we recognize that collective action is ubiquitous to civil association, then it makes little sense to assume that regimes in which change is difficult are those in which important individual freedoms will be best protected. As Locke was acutely aware, the status quo can be the source of political oppression. When this is so, obstacles to collective action will sustain that oppression. In the real world of ongoing politics, Brian Barry and Douglas Rae have shown that majority rule or something close to it is the logical rule to prefer if one assumes that one is as likely to oppose a given outcome as to support it regardless of whether it is the status quo.[106] From this perspective the libertarian constitutional scheme is a collective action regime maintained by the state, and disproportionately financed by implicit taxes on those who would prefer an alternative regime. Locke recognized, as Laslett put it, that "it is the power that men have over others, not the power that they have over themselves, which gives rise to political authority."[107]

In short, Locke's institutional theory differs from that of modern libertarians because he operates with a different underlying theory of power — as ubiquitous to human interaction rather than as a byproduct of collective action. As a result, unequivocal as he was that consent is the wellspring of political legitimacy, he saw majority rule as its best available institutional guarantor. Hence his concluding insistence that the "power that every individual gave the society, when he entered into it, can never revert to the individuals again, as long as the society lasts, but will always remain in the community; because without this there can be no community."[108] And the judgment whether or not the government is at war with the community must reside with the people: "If a controversy arise betwixt a prince and some of the people, in a matter where the law is silent or doubtful, and the thing be of great consequence, I should think the proper umpire, in such a case, should be the body of the people."[109] Common misconceptions to the contrary notwithstanding, the relation between the people and the government is not a contract. Rather, it is one of trust. Should a question arise as to whether that trust has been violated by a prince or legislature, " 'The people shall be judge;' for who shall be judge whether his trustee or deputy acts well, and according to the trust reposed in him, but he who deputes him, and must, by having deputed him, have still a power to discard him, when he fails in his trust."[110] And the people act by majority rule.

Locke understood that the fundamental political question for human beings is not: collective action or not? Rather, it is: what sort of collective action? His presumption in favor of the supremacy of legislative authority reflects this. Legislatures are legitimate just because they embody majority rule which, in the end, is the best available guarantor of the freedoms people seek to protect through the creation of government. Although Locke perceived advantages to a separation of powers involving an independent executive and "federative" (geared to foreign affairs and to relations with those in the state of nature), he was unequivocal that these institutions are subordinate to the legislative power because it alone embodies the consent of the governed through majority rule.[111] Even in the case of a dissolution of government there need not be a return to a state of nature. Rather, power can devolve to the people who "may constitute to themselves a new legislative, as they think best, being in full liberty to resist the force of those, who without authority would impose any thing on them."[112] The people, acting as a body by majority rule, have greater legitimacy than the alternative: individuals or arbitrary powers acting unilaterally.[113]

Locke's recognition that power is inevitably exercised in collective life perhaps also accounts for why his discussion of tacit consent seems so cavalier, at least in comparison to a theorist like Nozick (who engages in a tortured, and ultimately unsuccessful, argument for forcibly incorporating "independents" who refuse to join the society in a manner that can be said not to undermine their consent).[114] Locke insists that "every man, that hath any possessions, or enjoyment of any part of the dominions of any government, doth thereby give his tacit consent, and is as far forth obliged to obedience to the laws of that government, during such enjoyment, as any one under it."[115] His claim that their tacit consent is reasonably taken for granted because they are free to leave is obviously belied by most people's circumstances.[116] Yet if one takes the view that even those who have given express consent must inevitably expect often to be at odds with actions of the government then this seems less troubling. Only from the unrealistic perspective of someone who thinks it possible to live in a form of political association with others in which one's consent is never violated does it seem troubling that one's only protection is majority rule. No other decision rule provides better protection.[117]

It is sometimes said this is why constitutional courts and bills of rights are needed to protect individuals and minorities from the vicissitudes of democratic politics. At least since Mill's and Tocqueville's time, it has been characteristic for liberal constitutionalists to worry about majority tyranny, but as Robert Dahl has recently reminded us, history has revealed these worries to be misplaced.[118] Since the advent of the universal franchise, political freedoms have turned out to be safer in democracies than in nondemocracies by a considerable margin. In 1956 Dahl had registered skepticism that, even within democracies, constitutional courts and judicial review could be shown to have a positive effect on the degree to which individual freedoms are respected.[119] Subsequent scholarship has shown skepticism to be well founded.[120] It seems that Locke's underlying institutional commitment to majority rule was more indeed far-sighted than critics such as Kendall appreciated. Indeed, there are reasons to think that the popularity of independent courts in the contemporary world may have more in common with the popularity of independent banks than with the protection of individual freedoms. They operate as devices to signal foreign investors and international creditors that the capacity of elected officials to engage in redistributive policies or interfere with property rights will be limited. That is, they may be devices for limiting domestic political opposition to unpopular policies by taking them off the table.[121]

That said, it might nonetheless be objected that Locke's insistence that majority rule is the ultimate guarantor of the entitlements human beings create for themselves, the agreements human beings make with one another, and the natural law constraints on all their actions, has few — if any — implications for day-to-day politics. This is partly what Kendall has in mind when complaining that Locke's commitment to majoritarianism is not buttressed by any mechanism of popular consultation. There is truth to this, but two points should be noted in mitigation. First, Locke's account looks a good deal more plausible if we think of the reality of democratic systems rather than participatory democratic ideals. Actual democratic systems involve a mix of decision-making mechanisms, considerable delegation to administrative agencies, and many empower courts to conduct judicial review. But these different mechanisms are all subservient to majoritarian political decision-making in various ways, whether through systems of appointment, control of funding and jurisdiction, oversight, or some combination of these. Constitutional systems sometimes limit democracy's range, to be sure, particularly in separation-of-powers systems such as those of the United States. But constitutions generally contain entrenched guarantees of democratic government as well. Moreover, they are themselves revisable at constitutional conventions or via amendment procedures whose legitimacy is popularly authorized. Even liberal constitutionalists like Bruce Ackerman agree that critical moments of constitutional founding and change require popular democratic validation if they are to be seen as legitimate over time.[122] In short the practice in modern democracies is consistent with Locke's picture of various institutional arrangements — some more participatory than others — existing against a backdrop of popular sovereignty.

There is a second and more specific sense in which Locke might be seen as being more prescient about democracy than Kendall gives him credit for having been, linked to the reality that mechanisms of popular consultation turn out to be fraught with difficulty. Modern social choice theory has taught us that it is doubtful that there can be any such thing as a Rousseauian general will in even minimally diverse societies. As a result, we should think of democracy as a way of ensuring that, however inclusive decision-making can be made to be, the possibility of opposition from those whose interests may be harmed by the exercise of power is an important discipline. Majority rule is less a system of representation from this point of view as "flexing muscles," as Adam Przeworski puts it, "a reading of the chances in the eventual war."[123] Though he did not intend it thus, it would be difficult to conjure up a more apposite expression of the sentiment behind the discussion of majority rule in chapter XIX of the *Second Treatise*. That Locke

fails to provide for mechanisms of popular consultation looks less worri-
some, from this perspective, as does the objection that his right to resist
issues in a theory of revolution more than one of government. All governments live in the shadow of possible revolution. The way for them to avoid
it is to be responsive to the interests of the majority, who might otherwise
conclude that their trust has been violated.[124] This may be a more sober
view of democratic politics than those that have enthralled many theorists
since Locke's time. At the same time, however, Locke's view has done
better over the long run — and with good reason.

NOTES

1. See Joseph Schumpeter, *Capitalism, Socialism, and Democracy*
(New York: Harper, 1942), pp. 250–68.

2. For a discussion of this debate, see my "J. G. A. Pocock's Republicanism and Political Theory: A Critique and Reinterpretation," *Critical
Review*, vol. 4, no. 3 (Spring 1990), pp. 433–71.

3. Benjamin Barber, *Strong Democracy* (Berkeley: University of Cal-
ifornia Press, 1984), James Fishkin, *Democracy and Deliberation: New
Directions for Democratic Reform* (Yale University Press, 1993), and Amy
Gutmann and Dennis Thompson, *Democracy and Disagreement* (Harvard
University Press, 1998).

4. Willmoore Kendall, *John Locke and the Doctrine of Majority Rule*
(Urbana: University of Illinois Press, 1965 [1940]).

5. See Richard Ashcraft, *Revolutionary Politics and Locke's Two Trea-
tises of Government* (Princeton University Press, 1986), Mark Goldie,
"John Locke's Circle and James II," *The Historical Journal*, vol. 35, no. 3
(1992), pp. 557–86, Ellen Wood, "Locke against Democracy: Consent, and
Suffrage in the *Two Treatises*," *History of Political Thought*, vol. XIII, no. 4
(Winter 1992), pp. 657–89, Ashcraft, "The Radical Dimensions of Locke's
Political Thought: A Dialogic Essay on Some Problems of Interpretation,"
History of Political Thought, vol. XIII, no. 4 (Winter 1992), pp. 703–71,
and Wood, "Radicalism, capitalism, and historical contexts: Not only a
reply to Richard Ashcraft on John Locke," *History of Political Thought*,
vol. XV, no. 3 (Autumn 1994), pp. 324–72.

6. John Locke, *Second Treatise of Government*, §§58, 136. All italics in
subsequent quotations from Locke appear in the original work. For further
discussion see Patrick Riley, *Will and Political Legitimacy* (Cambridge,
Mass.: Harvard University Press), pp. 61–97. See also Ian Shapiro, *The*

Evolution of Rights in Liberal Theory (New York: Cambridge University Press, 1986), pp. 100–118.

7. See T. J. Hochstrasser, *Natural Law Theories in the Early Enlightenment* (Cambridge University Press, 2001), Ian Hunter, *Rival Enlightenments: Civil and Metaphysical Philosophy in Early Modern Germany* (Cambridge University Press, 2001) and James Tully, *A Discourse on Property: John Locke and His Adversaries* (New York: Cambridge University Press, 1980).

8. John Locke, *Essays on the Law of Nature*, ed. W. Von Leiden (Oxford: Clarendon Press, 1958 [1663–64]), p. 111.

9. By following Thomas Hobbes and Samuel von Pufendorf in this formulation of the distinction, Locke was embracing an important departure from the Thomist tradition, rooted in Grotius's revival of the Roman law conception of a right as one's *suum,* a kind of moral power or *facultas* which every man has, and which has its conceptual roots, as Quentin Skinner has established, in the writings of Francisco Suarez and ultimately Jean de Gerson and the conciliarist tradition. *The Foundations of Modern Political Thought* (Cambridge University Press, 1978), vol. II, pp. 117, 176–78. See also Richard Tuck, *Natural Rights Theories* (Cambridge University Press, 1979) and John Finnis, *Natural Law and Natural Right* (Clarendon Press, 1980), pp. 207–8.

10. Locke, *Essays on the Law of Nature,* pp. 111, 187.

11. Locke, Second *Treatise,* §6. For further discussion see Tully, *A Discourse on Property,* pp. 35–8, and John Dunn, *The Political Thought of John Locke* (Cambridge University Press, 1969), p. 95.

12. Locke, *First Treatise,* §50.

13. Ibid., §52.

14. Ibid., §54.

15. Ibid., §52.

16. Ibid., §55. See also *Second Treatise,* §§52–53.

17. Ibid., §53.

18. Ibid., §52.

19. Locke, *Second Treatise,* §56.

20. Ibid., §55.

21. Ibid., §69.

22. Ibid., §72.

23. Ibid., §§52–58.

24. For discussion of the evolution of secular variants of the workmanship ideal since the seventeenth century, see my *Democracy's Place* (Ithaca: Cornell University Press, 1996), chapter 3.

25. Carole Pateman, *The Sexual Contract* (Stanford: Stanford University Press, 1988), pp. 38, 41, 54, 94. Susan Moller Okin, *Women in Western Political Thought* (Princeton: Princeton University Press, 1979), p. 199.

26. Locke, *First Treatise,* §47.

27. Locke, *Second Treatise,* §82.

28. Sir Robert Filmer, *Patriarcha and Other Political Writings of Sir Robert Filmer, edited from the Original Sources.* Peter Laslett, ed. (Oxford: Blackwell's Political Texts, 1949), p. 245.

29. Locke, *First Treatise* §55.

30. Ibid., §62.

31. Locke, *Second Treatise,* §78.

32. Ibid., §82.

33. Rogers Smith, "Beyond Tocqueville, Myrdal, and Hartz: The Multiple Traditions in America," *American Political Science Review,* vol. 87, no. 3 (September 1993), p. 556; Carole Pateman, *The Sexual Contract,* pp. 38, 41, 54, 94.

34. Locke, *Second Treatise,* §22.

35. Ibid., §23.

36. Ibid.

37. As a result, if the slave concludes that "the hardship of his Slavery out-weigh the value of his Life, 'tis in his Power, by resisting the Will of his Master, to draw on himself the Death he desires." Locke, *Second Treatise,* §23.

38. Numerous Locke scholars have puzzled over how, if at all, Locke's views about slavery can be reconciled with the fact that he supported and even profited from the African slave trade and slavery in America — not least because African slaves were not captured in war and women and children were enslaved which was expressly prohibited on the just war theory. The most comprehensive treatment of this subject is James Farr's " 'So vile and miserable an estate': The problem of slavery in Locke's political thought," *Political Theory,* vol. 14, no. 2 (May 1986), pp. 263–89. Farr makes a convincing case that the two really cannot be reconciled, and that Locke simply avoided the contradiction. This is in line with Dunn's earlier conclusion that "what we confront here is not an example of bland but deliberate moral rationalization on Locke's part but merely one of immoral evasion." John Dunn, *The Political Thought of John Locke* (London: Cambridge University Press, 1969), p. 175n. Of course the fact that Locke never publicly embraced authorship of the *Two Treatises* in his lifetime meant that he was not forced to account for the contradiction publicly

or confront the charges of hypocrisy that his enemies might otherwise have leveled at him.

39. Locke, *Second Treatise,* §54.

40. Ibid., §27.

41. Locke believed that as well as itself not being subject to physical decay, money made possible the comparatively more productive of natural resources through trade and productive work. See Richard Ashcraft, *Locke's Two Treatises of Government* (London: Allen and Unwin, 1987), pp. 123–50, and *Revolutionary Politics and Locke's Two Treatises of Government* (Princeton: Princeton University Press, 1986), pp. 270–85 and, for the view (which Ashcraft criticizes) that Locke thought the proviso transcended with the introduction of money, C. B. Macpherson, *The Political Theory of Possessive Individualism* (Oxford University Press, 1962), pp. 203–21.

42. Locke, *Second Treatise* §37.

43. Ronald Dworkin, "What is equality? Part I: Equality of welfare," *Philosophy and Public Affairs,* vol. 10, no.3, (Summer 1981), pp. 185–246, and "What Is Equality? Part II: Equality of Resources," *Philosophy and Public Affairs,* vol. 10, no. 4 (Fall 1981), pp. 283–345.

44. For additional discussion of this point, see Shapiro, *The Evolution of Rights in Liberal Theory,* pp. 89–100.

45. See John Locke, *An Essay Concerning Human Understanding,* Book II, chapter 27 and Book I, chapter 30. See also Tully, *A Discourse on Property,* pp. 108–10, 121.

46. Locke, *Second Treatise,* §§25–51.

47. Ibid., §37.

48. See John Locke, *An Essay Concerning Human Understanding,* ed. Peter Nidditch (Oxford: Clarendon Press, 1975 [1690]), Book II, chapters 31–32, Book III, chapter 3, 6. In this he was following Hobbes, who had distinguished knowledge that depends on the human will from knowledge that is independent of it. As Hobbes put it, the pure or "mathematical" sciences can be known a priori, but the "mixed mathematics" such as physics depend on "the causes of natural things [which are] not in our power." Hobbes, *De Homine* (New York: Anchor, 1972 [1658]), p. 42. So he likened study of politics to that of mathematics on the grounds that "civil philosophy is demonstrable, because we make the commonwealth ourselves." As far as the natural world is concerned, we can only speculate, because we "know not the construction, but seek it from effects." See his Epistle Dedicatory to his *Six Lessons to the Professors of Mathematics* in

The English Works of Thomas Hobbes (London: John Bohn, 1966), VII, pp. 183–84. For further discussion of this issue, see James Tully, *A Discourse on Property,* pp. 9–27, and Shapiro, *The Evolution of Rights in Liberal Theory,* pp. 109–10.

49. Locke, *First Treatise,* §30.

50. Locke, *Second Treatise,* §6.

51. Ibid.

52. Locke, *An Essay Concerning Human Understanding* (New York: Dover, 1959), vol. II, Book IV, p. 389.

53. Ibid., p. 391.

54. Locke, *A Letter Concerning Toleration,* p. 230.

55. Locke's characteristic mode of argument is to insist that nature, reason, and scripture all converge on the proposition he seeks to defend. For further discussion see Shapiro, *The Evolution of Rights in Liberal Theory,* pp. 80–149.

56. Ibid., p. 184. This exceptionally broad theory of religious toleration, and Locke's view that the ends of civil society are purely secular, are further reasons for questioning the interpretation of Locke as a conservative Thomist. For further discussion of Locke's religious radicalism in his later writings, see Ashcraft, *Locke's Two Treatises of Government,* chapters 1 and 2.

57. Locke, *A Letter Concerning Toleration,* pp. 225, 218–19.

58. Ibid., p. 223.

59. Locke, *Second Treatise,* §57.

60. Locke, *First Treatise,* §59.

61. Locke, *A Letter Concerning Toleration,* p. 246. For an extended account of Locke's views on promising and trust, and their political applications, see Dunn, "The Concept of 'Trust' in the Politics of John Locke," R. Rorty, J. B. Schneewind, and Q. Skinner, eds. *Philosophy in History: Essays on the Historiography of Philosophy* (Cambridge: Cambridge University Press, 1984), pp. 279–301.

62. Locke, *A Letter Concerning Toleration,* p. 245.

63. See Locke, *An Essay Concerning Human Understanding,* II, pp. 306–24. For commentary, see Tully, *A Discourse On Property,* pp. 38–43.

64. "All men know and acknowledge that God ought to be publicly worshipped. Why otherwise do they compel one another unto the public assemblies? Men, therefore, constituted in this liberty are to enter into some religious society." Locke, *A Letter Concerning Toleration,* p. 232.

65. Rawls defines his "political, not metaphysical" approach by refer-

ence to an "overlapping consensus" on principles that are likely to "persist over generations and to gain a sizable body of adherents in a more or less just constitutional regime, a regime in which the criterion of justice is that political conception itself." Rawls, *Political Liberalism* (New York: Columbia University Press, 1993), p. 15.

66. The acts referred to in this paragraph are reprinted in A. Browning, ed. *English Historical Documents 1660–1714* vol. 8 (London: Eyre & Spottiswoode, 1953), pp. 359–410.

67. Richard Ashcraft, *Locke's Two Treatises of Government* (London: Allen & Unwin, 1987) pp. 65–68.

68. Locke, *First Treatise* , §36.

69. Ibid., §49.

70. Locke, *A Letter Concerning Toleration,* pp. 229.

71. Locke, *First Treatise,* §46. For an extended discussion of Locke's hermeneutical and methodological critique of Filmer's reading of the Scriptures, see Ashcraft, *Locke's Two Treatises of Government,* chapter 3.

72. Ashcraft, *Locke's Two Treatises of Government,* p. 67.

73. Locke, *First Treatise,* §46.

74. John Rawls, *Political Liberalism* (New York: Columbia University Press, 1993), p. 10.

75. For further discussion see Ian Shapiro, *The Moral Foundations of Politics* (Yale University Press, 2003), chapter 5.

76. Kendall, *John Locke and the Doctrine of Majority Rule,* p. 34.

77. Locke, *Second Treatise,* §124–251.

78. See John Rawls, *A Theory of Justice,* Second Edition (Cambridge, Mass.: Harvard University Press, 1999), pp. 11–24.

79. Rawls, *Political Liberalism,* p. 251.

80. See Jürgen Habermas, "Reconciliation through the Public Use of Reason: Remarks on John Rawls's *Political Liberalism,*" *The Journal of Philosophy,* vol. 92 (March 1995), pp. 109–31.

81. For an excellent discussion of Tory and Whig attitudes toward resistance, and how they differed from Locke's view, see J. H. Franklin, *John Locke and the Theory of Sovereignty* (Cambridge: Cambridge University Press, 1978), pp. 98–123. See also Ashcraft, *Locke's Two Treatises of Government,* chapter 3.

82. Franklin, *John Locke and the Theory of Sovereignty,* pp. 94–95.

83. Locke, *Second Treatise,* §205. See also Franklin, *John Locke and the Theory of Sovereignty,* p. 95.

84. Locke, *Second Treatise,* §164.

85. Ibid., §168.

86. Thomas Hobbes, *Leviathan* (London: Pelican Books, 1968 [1651]), pp. 268–70.

87. Locke, *Second Treatise* §168.

88. For a useful discussion of the weaknesses in Locke's account of majority rule as a mechanism for representing personal consent, see Riley, *Will and Political Legitimacy*, pp. 93–97.

89. Locke, *Second Treatise*, §208.

90. Locke, *Second Treatise*, §225. See also §§226–33.

91. Kendall, *John Locke and the Doctrine of Majority Rule*, pp. 63–74.

92. Locke, *Second Treatise*, §13.

93. Ibid., §96.

94. Ibid.

95. Ibid., §98.

96. Ibid.

97. Ibid., §99.

98. Wood, "Locke against Democracy," pp. 660–63.

99. Ashcraft, *Locke's Two Treatises of Government*, p. 183. Ashcraft is quick to point out, however, that this does not necessarily mean that Locke is advocating democracy as the most desirable form of day-to-day government.

100. Locke, *Second Treatise*, §132.

101. Ibid., §§208–9.

102. Ibid., §§202–10.

103. James Buchanan and Gordon Tullock, *The Calculus of Consent: Logical Foundations of Constitutional Democracy* (Ann Arbor: University of Michigan Press, 1962), pp. 172–262.

104. Riley, *Will and Political Legitimacy*, p. 64.

105. See Ian Shapiro, *Democracy's Place* (Ithaca: Cornell University Press, 1996), chapter 2 and Stephen Holmes and Cass Sunstein, *The Costs of Rights* (New York: W. W. Norton, 1999).

106. Brian Barry, *Political Argument*, second edition (Herefordshire: Harvester Wheatsheaf, 1990 [1965]); Douglas Rae, "The Limits of Consensual Decision," *American Political Science Review*, vol. 69 (1975), pp. 1270–94.

107. Peter Laslett, "Introduction," John Locke, *Two Treatises*, p. 111.

108. Locke, *Second Treatise*, §243.

109. Ibid., §242.

110. Ibid., §240.

111. Ibid., §§149–158.

112. Ibid., §212.

113. Radical as this indissoluble link between consent and majority rule might seem, John Marshall makes a compelling case that part of Locke's motive was conservative: he was attempting to convince the gentry, yeomanry, and merchants that a rare and limited right of resistance to the monarch could be endorsed "which would not threaten the social hierarchy and lay the foundations for anarchy or for frequent challenge of the political establishment and which was perfectly compatible with the re-establishment of a mixed monarchy with different personnel." John Marshall, *John Locke: Resistance, Religion and Responsibility* (Cambridge: Cambridge University Press, 1994), pp. xvi–xvii, 205–91.

114. For discussion of the difficulties attending Nozick's discussion of compensating independents who are forced to become members, see Shapiro, *The Evolution of Rights in Liberal Theory,* pp. 169–78.

115. Locke, *Second Treatise,* §119.

116. Ibid., §121. Taken in context it was a more radical claim than it might seem to us, since the king's subjects were not generally free to renounce that status — regardless of whether they had given express consent. Even in our own time the examples of the USSR and Iraq should remind us that even a right not to have exit legally proscribed is by no means without value. A useful discussion of Locke on tacit consent is Paul Russell, "Locke on Express and Tacit Consent: Misinterpretations and Inconsistencies," *Political Theory,* vol. 14, no. 2 (May 1986), pp. 291–306.

117. Indeed, from this perspective Locke's remark that in a marriage the husband prevails in situations of unavoidable conflict could be interpreted as a claim about what Locke expected would happen as an empirical matter rather than something he would choose to defend. The man prevails because someone must and the bulk of the force is on his side, but not because it is otherwise desirable that he should. And as I noted, he seeks to limit this power to their common endeavors and to preserve the wife's right of exit. For extended discussion of what democracy requires concerning the structure of domestic decision-making, see my *Democratic Justice* (New Haven: Yale University Press, 1999), chapter 5.

118. Robert Dahl, *How Democratic Is the American Constitution?* (New Haven: Yale University Press, 2002), pp. 132–39.

119. Robert Dahl, *A Preface to Democratic Theory* (Chicago: University of Chicago Press, 1956), pp. 105–112.

120. Robert Dahl, "Decision-making in a Democracy: The Supreme Court as a National Policy-maker," *Journal of Public Law,* vol. 6, no. 2, pp. 279–95; *Democracy and Its Critics* (Yale University Press, 1989), pp. 188–

92; Mark Tushnet, *Taking the Constitution Away from the Courts* (Princeton: Princeton University Press, 1999); Ran Hirschl, "Towards Juristocracy: A Comparative Inquiry into the Origins and Consequences of the New Constitutionalism," Unpublished Yale PhD thesis (1999).

121. Ran Hirschl, "The Political Origins of Judicial Empowerment through Constitutionalization: Lessons from Four Constitutional Revolutions," *Law and Social Inquiry,* vol. 25, no. 1 (2000), pp. 91–147.

122. Bruce Ackerman, *We The People: Foundations* (Cambridge, Mass.: Harvard University Press, 1993).

123. Adam Przeworski, "Minimalist Conception of Democracy: A Defense," in Ian Shapiro and Casiano Hacker-Cordón, *Democracy's Value* (Cambridge: Cambridge University Press, 1999), p. 48.

124. For reasons that would take me too far afield to explore here, I note that there are interesting parallels between this reading of Locke and John McCormick's reading of Machiavelli in "Machiavellian Democracy: Controlling Elites with Ferocious Populism," *American Political Science Review,* vol. 95, no. 2 (June 2001), pp. 297–313.

Index

Suffrage. *See* Women's suffrage

Swiss, 106

Sydenham, Thomas, xii

Tamerlain, 85

Tarcov, Nathan, 264

Taxation, 163, 264, 296

Taylor, Charles, 267

Thamar, 79

Theology, 271

Theorization of rights, 266–72

Theory of Justice (Rawls), 323–24

Thiefs, 107–8, 182

Timothy, Epistles of, 113, 215

Tocqueville, Alexis de, 330

Toleration: and Edict of Nantes in
France, xiii; Mill on, xiii–xiv;
overview of Locke on, xiii–xiv;
for Protestant nonconformists,
xiii; and nature of Christianity,
215–17; persecution versus,
216–19, 222–23, 227, 275; civil
power versus salvation of souls,
218–20, 318–19; church as free
and voluntary society, 220–21,
319; definition of church, 220,
232; power and laws of church,
221–23; and marks of true
church, 222; purpose of church,
222–23; and excommunication,
223–24, 245; extent of duty of
and requirements concerning,
223–32, 319; force of ecclesiastical authority, 223; prohibition
against private persons and
churches invading civil rights of
others, 224–26; clergy's duty for,
226–28; magistrate's duty for,
228–32; and outward worship,
233–40, 249, 336n64; and idola-

try, 237–40; and articles of faith,
240–46; and heresy, 245, 251–
53; and overthrow of government, 245–46; and atheism, 246,
276–77, 319–20; of ecclesiastical assemblies and meetings,
246–51; and schism, 253–54;
summary of Locke's argument
on, 273–77, 318–22

Toleration Act of *1689*, 320

Tories, 83, 259

Treason, 293

Troy, 91, 93

Trust, 197–208

Tullock, Gordon, 328

Turks, 224–25, 251, 252

Two Treatises (Locke): dating of, x;
Locke's acknowledgment of authorship of, xii, 334–35n38;
Locke's preface to, 3–4; as reply
to Filmer's *Patriarcha,* 3–4, 7–9,
288–90, 312–14; text of first
treatise, 3–99; text of second
treatise, 100–209; Locke's assessment of, 261, 280n12; summary of second treatise, 289–94

Tyranny, 48, 187, 188–93, 201, 203–
4, 325

Tyrrell, James, 258, 306n44

Ulysses, 201

Unanimity rule, 328

United States. *See* America

USSR, 339n116

Usurpation, 47, 48, 53, 75, 81, 187–
88

Utopia, 89

Vega, Garcilasso de la. *See* Garcilasso de la Vega

Venice, 144
Violence. *See* Conquest and con-
quorers; Force; Rebellion; War
and peace
Von Leyden, Wolfgang, 259–60,
267, 268

Wampompeke, 183
War and peace: federative power of,
65; and Israelites, 80–83, 90,
109, 147; as marks of sovereignty, 80–83; political power
and war, 107–9; state of nature
versus state of war, 107–8;
avoidance of war, 109; and
American Indians, 147; captives
of war, 177; and conquest, 178–
87, 193, 294; Christ as Prince of
Peace, 217, 227; religious intolerance and war, 226, 250–51,
273
West Indies, 80, 93
Whigs, 259, 320, 324, 325

William III, King, x, xi, 3
Winzerus, Ninian, 206
Wives. *See* Family; Marriage;
Mothers and maternal authority
Women's status, 286, 294–302,
304n16, 307n62, 314–15. *See
also* Family; Marriage; Mothers
and maternal authority
Women's suffrage, 286, 296, 307n63
Wood, Ellen, 327
Wootton, David, 304n16
Workmanship model, 102, 311, 312,
313–14, 316–17
World. *See* Earth
Worship, 233–40, 249, 336n64. *See
also* Religion

Xerxes, 143

Younger and elder. *See* Brothers; Elder and younger

Zechariah, book of, 41

Rethinking the Western Tradition

Also available in the series: